Dialogue Sustained

Dialogue Sustained

The Multilevel Peace Process
and the Dartmouth Conference

James Voorhees

UNITED STATES INSTITUTE OF PEACE PRESS
Washington, D.C.

CHARLES F. KETTERING FOUNDATION
Washington, D.C.   Dayton, Ohio   New York, N.Y.

United States Institute of Peace
1200 17th Street NW
Washington, DC 20036

Charles F. Kettering Foundation
444 North Capitol Street NW
Washington, DC 20001

© 2002 by the Endowment of the United States Institute of Peace

First published 2002

Printed in the United States of America

The paper used in this publication meets the minimum requirements of American National Standards for Information Science—Permanence of Paper for Printed Library Materials, ANSI Z39.48-1984.

Library of Congress Cataloging-in-Publication Data
Voorhees, James, 1952-
    Dialogue sustained : the multilevel peace process and the Dartmouth
Conference / James Voorhees.
        p. cm.
    Includes bibliographical references and index.
    ISBN 1-929223-30-7
    1. United States—Relations—Soviet Union. 2. Soviet Union—Relations—
United States. 3. Dartmouth Conference. 4. United States—Foreign relations—
1945–1989. 5. United States—Foreign relations—1989– I. Title.

E183.8.S65 V66 2002
303.48'273047—dc21

                                                                    2002017293

Contents

Foreword

WARS ARE OFTEN SAID to be seedbeds of invention, germinating all kinds of new ideas and technologies. Certainly, the Cold War saw its share of innovations, some of them good (satellites and microelectronics, for example), some of them bad (biowarfare agents, for instance). Many of these have not outlived the Cold War, passing like public fall-out shelters into the pages of history. Other innovations, however, have demonstrated their intrinsic worth by surviving, and even thriving, in the very different world that has emerged since the Soviet Union was disbanded. The Dartmouth Conference is one of these useful byproducts.

Launched in 1960 in the frigid atmosphere of the Cold War, the meetings of the Dartmouth Conference sought to counter the profound lack of contact and understanding between eminent citizens of the United States and Soviet Union. Leading Americans and Soviets from the arts, sciences, and politics—none of them in government at the time— were invited to sit down together at Dartmouth College in New Hampshire and talk. There was an agenda, but the topics of conversation were less important than the conversation itself. Over the next forty years, in a succession of plenary conferences and smaller meetings, the conversation deepened and widened. As James Voorhees explains in this fascinating account of a unique enterprise we would now characterize as "sustained dialogue," the participants began to talk *with*, rather than *at*, one another; propagandistic speeches gave way to genuine discussion unencumbered by the rituals of official diplomacy; mutual understanding grew. This sustained dialogue permitted participants to forge personal relationships and to exchange often surprising ideas and information, creating a new level of insight that filtered into policymaking circles both directly, as some participants entered government, and indirectly, through the media and in conversations with high-ranking officials.

With the end of the Cold War, it might have been expected that the Dartmouth Conference would end too. But instead "Dartmouth" (the shorthand term for a long list of activities, approaches, and techniques that had evolved in the context of the Dartmouth conferences and task forces) demonstrated continuing relevance by taking new directions and forms. Notably, it inspired the Inter-Tajik Dialogue, a series of meetings in which opposition groups helped to lay the foundation for a more peaceful and democratic Tajikistan. As the new century turned, Americans and Russians familiar with the spirit of Dartmouth sought to rekindle interest in the future of the Russian-U.S. relationship, with no fewer than one hundred public forums being held by citizens in both countries in the year 2001 alone.

What is it about Dartmouth that accounts for its enduring appeal and utility? What qualities set it apart from other approaches to conflict resolution and conflict management? What has it taught us about the limitations of traditional diplomacy and the role that citizens outside of government can play in shaping a peace process? Five lessons stand out from the forty-plus years of the Dartmouth Conference.

First, citizens outside government promoting sustained dialogue can become significant actors in helping to transform the most intractable relationships from enmity to mutual understanding. The essential role of government in managing foreign relations need not be diminished by their work. Indeed, their work can productively complement what governments do by addressing tasks that governments do not do well—such as changing conflictual relationships when conflict has deep human roots. As readers will discover in the following chapters, the idea that dialogue among citizens outside government could transform adversarial relationships between states was a bold and controversial one in 1960, when the first Dartmouth conference was held. Until that time, efforts to ameliorate conflict had traditionally focused on formal mediation, intergovernmental negotiation, and diplomacy. At its outset, Dartmouth enlarged the field of conflict resolution; over the succeeding years, it also enlarged the level of understanding among the makers and shapers of policy on both sides of the superpower divide.

The second lesson that Dartmouth teaches us is that networks— "transnational communities," to use James Voorhees' phrase—are as great a resource as dollars. They generate political will, which can't be bought. Dartmouth wasn't a series of events; it was—and is—a company of people. Dartmouth veterans attending the fortieth-anniversary reunion in the fall of 2000 referred to their extended dialogue as the "Dartmouth movement."

Third, as we learned in Tajikistan, ending violence alone does not ensure peace; the role of civil society is critical in building an enduring basis for the nonviolent resolution of conflicts. A comprehensive peace process requires opening spaces where citizens can resolve their differences peacefully through deliberative dialogue. As citizens work to create those spaces, they build elements of civil society around a multilevel peace process. They perfect the practices that permit citizens to work together across natural and social divisions and establish institutions to perpetuate them. As described in chapter 6, the Inter-Tajik Dialogue's Public Committee for Democratic Processes embodies this point. The committee also connects the development of civil society with economic development by building "social capital"—the long-missing ingredient now recognized as essential to economic development.

A fourth, related lesson is that the idea of a "multilevel peace process"— articulated by participants in the Inter-Tajik Dialogue—places the work of interactive conflict resolution within the whole body politic to embrace many actors, including government. While not incompatible with the thinking behind "multitrack diplomacy," the emphasis in the multilevel peace process differs in that the focus is on the process of interaction among individuals as individuals, not as formalized representatives of governmental organizations, professions, or institutions.

Fifth, and potentially most important, the process of sustained dialogue can be adapted for use in other conflicts. Much of the credit for making the process transferable must go to Harold Saunders, director of international affairs at the Kettering Foundation and coauthor of two chapters in this volume. Drawing on the experience of thirty-five meetings of the Dartmouth Conference Regional Conflicts Task Force, which was begun in 1982, and on thirty-two meetings of the Inter-Tajik Dialogue since 1993, Saunders has conceptualized the process of sustained dialogue into a five-stage process that can be applied in other conflict settings. Indeed, that process has already inspired a wide variety of efforts, including reconciliation projects in several American cities burdened with various types of internal tensions.

When the Dartmouth Conference began, few would have guessed that it would yield such a rich legacy. The project was heavily criticized in the Cold War environment. Experts advised against it. Editors criticized the "naiveté" of Americans who spoke honestly to Soviets while hearing only a Soviet party line in return. Initially, there were few visible indications of success, and tangible products were nonexistent. In such circumstances, the pioneers of Dartmouth had to demonstrate remarkable fortitude, commitment, and self-belief—and they deserve recognition and credit for doing so. On the U.S. side, Norman Cousins and David Rockefeller have been recognized among many contributors as the builders of Dartmouth's foundation. On the Soviet/Russian side, special leadership was exercised by Yuri Zhukov, Georgi Arbatov, Alexander Korneichuk, Vitali Zhurkin, and Evgeni Primakov.

As copublisher of this book, the Kettering Foundation is proud to have played a part in advancing the Dartmouth process. It is an example of the action-based research the foundation does. As an inventor, Charles F. Kettering always encouraged the foundation he created to take on the big problems, or what he called "the problems behind the problems." Knowing that such problems demanded time and patience, trustees such as Richard Lombard let change evolve. They weren't consumed with being successful in the sense of producing quick results. Their successors on Kettering's board have kept this tradition alive. It is an outlook that helps explains why, in 1969, Robert Chollar, then president of the foundation, and his fellow trustees turned to the Dartmouth Conference as a source for foundation research to develop a new form of nongovernmental dialogue. Now sustained dialogues are recognized as a useful means of addressing conflicts when differences can't be mediated by a third party or when differences are not ready for formal mediation or negotiation.

This support has been more than repaid, for Dartmouth has had a profound influence on the Kettering Foundation. The organizations in Russia that collaborated with Kettering in organizing the Dartmouth meetings have grown to more than two hundred in fifty-five countries in every part of the world, and their ties to the foundation ensure that it always looks at problems from the perspective of more than one country.

The other publisher of *Dialogue Sustained,* the United States Institute of Peace, also has a well-established record of supporting work on nongovernmental dialogue and Russian-U.S. relations. Mandated by the

U.S. Congress to promote research into, and awareness of, measures by which international conflict can be peacefully managed or resolved, the Institute is pleased to disseminate the important lessons learned from the Dartmouth Conference experience. Dartmouth is of particular interest to the Institute not least because it has lessons for the policymaking, NGO, and academic communities. In practical terms, Dartmouth seems to have made a significant difference in transforming Soviet-U.S. relations during the latter years of the Cold War, its influence extending on occasion to the topmost ranks of the policymaking elites in both countries. Unquestionably, the Inter-Tajik Dialogue has had a concrete and positive impact on the political situation within Tajikistan. In theoretical and analytical terms, Dartmouth has been no less productive, yielding important insights into the dynamics of communication and influence in situations of conflict, and inspiring such useful concepts as sustained dialogue and the multilevel peace process.

The degree to which the objectives of Dartmouth and the interests of the Institute coincide can be gauged from just a few of the books published by the Institute in recent years. For instance, *Herding Cats: Multiparty Mediation in a Complex World*, edited by Chester Crocker, Fen Hampson, and Pamela Aall, offers a series of firsthand accounts of mediation in action and features an article by Dartmouth participant Harold Saunders on the multilevel peace process. Another volume edited by Crocker, Hampson, and Aall, *Turbulent Peace: The Challenges of Managing International Conflict*, explores the sources of contemporary conflict and the array of possible responses to it by both governments and nongovernmental actors. The subject of reconciliation between deeply entrenched adversaries is addressed by John Paul Lederach in *Building Peace: Sustainable Reconciliation in Divided Societies*. The challenges confronting contemporary Russia are highlighted in *The Tragedy of Russia's Reforms: Market Bolshevism against Democracy* by Peter Reddaway and Dmitri Glinksi; in *Russia and Its New Diasporas* by Igor Zevelev; and in *Ukraine and Russia: A Fraternal Rivalry* by Anatol Lieven. And the future of relations between Russia and the West is taken up by James Goodby, Petrus Buwalda, and Dmitri Trenin in *A Strategy for Stable Peace: Toward a Euroatlantic Security Community.*

Together, then, the United States Institute of Peace and the Kettering Foundation applaud the goals that inspired the creators of the Dartmouth Conference and commend this thoughtful study of the fruits of their labors. *Dialogue Sustained* chronicles the development of a unique invention of the Cold War, one that by virtue of its intrinsic conceptual worth and of its ability to evolve not only influenced the management of Soviet-U.S. relations during that war but has since proved a powerful tool in promoting reconciliation in very different conflict situations in diverse places.

DAVID MATHEWS, PRESIDENT AND TRUSTEE
CHARLES F. KETTERING FOUNDATION

RICHARD H. SOLOMON, PRESIDENT
UNITED STATES INSTITUTE OF PEACE

Preface

SOMETIME IN THE SPRING OR EARLY SUMMER OF 1961, Norman Cousins, the editor of the prestigious *Saturday Review of Literature,* a man I had known and admired for many years, came to see me in my office at the Chase Manhattan Bank in Lower Manhattan. Norman invited me to attend, according to my notes at the time, a "US-USSR conference" in January of 1962 at Airlie House near Washington, D.C., as part of the American delegation. Norman said that this would be the third meeting of the group—the first of which had been held on the Dartmouth College campus in Hanover, New Hampshire, in the autumn of 1960— and that the conference had the support of senior officials in the Kremlin, as well as in the U.S. government. When I asked the purpose of the conference, Norman said it might improve relations between the two countries because the Soviets seemed eager to put the Stalinist era behind them and find ways to engage the West in "useful dialogue."

Norman loved the word "dialogue" and placed great stock in face-to-face meetings as a means of changing attitudes and solving problems. I was much less optimistic than he that conversations would somehow diminish the ideological, political, and military threat that the Soviet Union posed to the United States. But Norman was a tremendously persuasive man. In the end, he convinced me that there was merit to his idea.

After consulting with my advisors and checking my schedule, I agreed to join the delegation and attend the January meeting. As luck would have it, the meeting was postponed and the location changed to October of 1962 in Andover, Massachusetts, on the campus of Phillips Academy. Meanwhile, my own schedule (I was president and co-chief executive officer of the Chase at the time) prevented me from participating in all but the initial stages of the conference, which, in retrospect, was probably the most memorable of all Dartmouth conferences. The Soviet and American delegates met and continued their "dialogue" against the chilling backdrop of the Cuban missile crisis—certainly the darkest and potentially deadliest moment in the entire Cold War.

I attended most of the Dartmouth meetings over the following thirty years and found them incredibly useful in exactly the way that Norman Cousins had claimed they would be. Both the Americans and the Russians who were privileged to attend these annual gatherings learned a great deal about each other. It was as if we were holding up gigantic mirrors in which we could see exactly how others saw us. And, while I cannot claim that our meetings hold the key to understanding the end of the Cold War or explain why neither side resorted to the use of nuclear weapons—Norman Cousins' deepest concern—it is nevertheless my belief that Dartmouth made a profound difference in the relationship between the two superpowers.

That is why this book is so valuable. It places these meetings in the context of the times and carefully documents how that context changed from confrontation to détente to renewed confrontation in the late 1970s and 1980s. It is ably written and carefully researched. I found the meetings coming to life vividly—I could almost taste the caviar and savor the vodka we were served. It also reminded me of many old friends who are now departed—most especially Norman Cousins. This book is a tribute to his steadfast courage and indomitable belief that "dialogue" between people of good faith can indeed make a difference. We shall have to put that lesson to use again and again in the years to come.

DAVID ROCKEFELLER
NEW YORK CITY, DECEMBER 2001

Acknowledgments

THE DARTMOUTH CONFERENCE was a nebulous thing for many of us who studied the Soviet Union through the 1970s and 1980s. We sensed that some meetings were being held and that they were important, whatever they were about. But we knew little about them. Even today, scholars working on the history of the Cold War find it difficult to learn much about the conferences.

I had the good fortune to be drawn into the circle of those associated with Dartmouth while a graduate student. I took a course on conflict resolution that Hal Saunders co-taught with William Zartman. I came to the course as a dedicated skeptic and self-described hardheaded realist about international politics. Hal, ever patient, gave me the benefit of his experience, gained in the Dartmouth conferences and elsewhere. He opened my eyes to the potential that properly conceived and prepared dialogue held for managing, and perhaps even resolving, conflict.

Hal later asked me to work with him on a project that was run by Phil Stewart at the Mershon Center. Later still, he had the courage to ask me to work for him at the Kettering Foundation. These opportunities were blessings. Not only did I learn about Dartmouth; I met many of the people involved in Dartmouth—David Mathews, Vitali Zhurkin, Georgi Arbatov, the inestimable pair of interpreters George Sherry and George Klebnikov, and many others. I was even able to attend a meeting of the Regional Conflicts Task Force.

I came to my classes with Hal convinced that it was unrealistic to view dialogue as useful in mitigating or resolving conflict. The picture I had was of well-meaning gentlemen dispassionately exchanging views about the abstractions that divided them. But dialogue is not just for gentlemen. And it is about passions more than abstractions. Indeed, a dialogue in which the passions that underlie a conflict are not aired is useless. People have to get mad, and the course of dialogue cannot run smooth. The Dartmouth dialogues have not run smooth, as the pages that follow will show. It was this very roughness that made the achievements of Dartmouth possible.

As I came to understand the Dartmouth process, I became convinced of its value. At this writing, the murderous terrorist actions committed on September 11, 2001, have produced a call to arms against terrorism that promises to commit the United States and other countries to a battle that will be waged across the world for years or even decades to come. But it is against a nebulous foe. We know not his number, his face, or his country. We may, indeed, find ourselves fighting against foes that seem to multiply the more we try to destroy them, like the broomsticks empowered by the sorcerer's apprentice. But we can know that conflict engenders terrorists. Our efforts to hunt down those responsible for the killing in September will not end the terrorist threat. Too often, terror is a tool used by the weaker side in conflict. Israel itself, now terror's victim, was made possible, in part, by it.

To end terror, we must facilitate other means of struggle. The Dartmouth process is one of these. The process emphasizes talk, and so might be dismissed as "mere talk" by those inclined solely to "action." But action alone, particularly military action, has often proved itself ineffective or, worse, counterproductive. It is true that talk can be used for many purposes. It can be glib and facile. It can be deceptive. It can be divorced from the reality that lies behind the spoken word.

Talk in Dartmouth is not easy, however. Dartmouth provides a forum where people can struggle to end conflict. This is not a struggle where people suffer and die—it is precisely the desire to end struggles of that kind that leads people to Dartmouth. It is the difficult struggle to make one's enemies understand one's side and to try to understand the reasons behind the actions of one's enemy. This is not a struggle that can be fashioned into a best-selling novel. And it is best kept out of the newspapers. But it is vital that we conduct it now, with our new goals found in the rubble of the World Trade Center and the Pentagon, if we wish to meet those goals, keep terrorists finite, and prevent the horror from recurring.

There are many people to thank for making this project possible. First and foremost, it would not have been possible without the inspiration and encouragement of Hal Saunders. Nor could it have been done without the support and advice of David Mathews, the president of the Kettering Foundation. Pat Coggins was also essential, to me as to Dartmouth, in numerous ways. I owe Vitali Zhurkin thanks for his support and for coordinating suggestions from Russian veterans of Dartmouth. My work here follows earlier work by Alla Bobrysheva, who has been helpful in numerous ways. Not the least of these is her compelling enthusiasm for Dartmouth and its people. Philip Stewart and Yale Richmond were generous in the time they gave to reading and commenting on the manuscript. Many of the people associated with Dartmouth also commented on at least part of the manuscript. They include David Mathews, Brent Scowcroft, Paul Doty, Antonia Chayes, Arnold Horelick, Thomas Gouttierre, Randa Slim, Robert Kaiser, Allen Lynch, Evgeni Primakov, Aleksei Arbatov, Gennadi Chufrin, Apollon Davidson, Aleksandr Kislov, Andrei Kortunov, Viktor Kremenyuk, Stanislav Kondrashov, Vladimir Lukin, Vitali Naumkin, Sergei Rogov, Nikolai Shmelev, Yuli Vorontsov, and Irina Zviagelskaya. Their comments helped to fill important gaps and saved me from significant errors. It hardly need be said that those that remain are my own. Two anonymous reviewers gave helpful criticism that has made this a significantly better book. Nigel Quinney of the United States Institute of Peace provided sage advice, invaluable assistance, necessary prodding, and a welcome dose of optimism.

The author was generously given access to the files on Dartmouth at the Kettering Foundation. The foundation also provided financial support and the help of Katharine Wheatley and Philip Lurie in the Washington office. Many thanks for their help in preparing the manuscript. A trip to the University of Illinois at Urbana-Champaign made it possible to go through Philip Mosely's files, which are held in the archives there. The account of the early conferences would be but a sketch without them. I am grateful to Robert T. Chapel for making them available. The project might not have happened at all had David Rockefeller not sent David Mathews copies of the documents about Dartmouth that he had saved in his files.

Lastly, the debt I owe my wife, Jenni, and my children, Gus, Rose, and Simon, is immeasurable. Norman Cousins conceived of Dartmouth as a means for preserving life in a dangerous age; they are constant reminders of why life is worthwhile.

Dialogue Sustained

1 | Sustained Dialogue in Perspective

IN 1960 THE SOVIET UNION AND THE UNITED STATES were much more distant from each other than Russia and the United States are today. This was true in an almost literal sense. There were no regular direct flights between the countries; the first direct commercial flight did not take place until 1969. Communications were so poor that during the Cuban missile crisis it took, on average, four hours to transmit a message between Kennedy and Khrushchev. It was easier to send urgent messages over the public airwaves, despite the loss of confidentiality that one would expect to be essential.[1] Few people traveled between the two countries. In fact, one official was told that Brezhnev met his first noncommunist American in 1962, after he had been in the highest circles of the Soviet leadership for a decade.[2] That meeting took place in Moscow. More than a decade would pass before Brezhnev himself came to the United States.

Americans saw the Soviet Union as through a glass, darkly. They saw Soviet leaders as implacably hostile, threatening to bury us, using language that Orwell had made Orwellian, expressing ideas that were antithetical to what Americans held most dear. The tanks that faced our troops across German borders and the bombers and missiles issuing forth, it seemed, in massive quantities from Soviet factories made those threats real. The people appeared to be ciphers, their minds chained by ideology, their bodies captured behind an iron curtain of gun posts, barbed wire, and secret police.

The Soviet view of the United States was no clearer or brighter. American leaders, too, were implacably hostile. The ideology of the United States and its system were corrupt and unfeeling, allowing a few to live in wealth while most suffered in poverty. American weapons also faced theirs across a future battlefield, and its bombs and missiles, gleaming symbols of the nuclear age, were aimed at their homes.

In the thirty years after 1960, the Dartmouth Conference continued its efforts to reduce the tensions of the Cold War. In the time since it has tried to reduce tensions in other conflicts. The format and the very concept of the conference have evolved. As time passed, hundreds of people came to take part in the conferences. Many left owing to changing personal commitments, the changing needs of the conferences, or simply old age and death. But the essence of Dartmouth remained unchanged—the belief in the importance of communication between peoples in conflict, the belief that a dialogue among people outside government can be useful.

The Dartmouth Conference outlasted the Cold War. The lessons learned by those who took part were used to extend the mission of the conference from fostering dialogue between enemies to creating partners able to work together toward peace. In the decade since the Soviet Union collapsed, the processes developed by the Dartmouth Conference have been used by people seeking peace in Louisiana, Moscow, and Dushanbe.

Much of this happened in what now seems a bygone era. So, why tell the story of Dartmouth? There are three reasons why that story remains of interest.

First, the Dartmouth Conference influenced the course of the Cold War, but scholars have known less about Dartmouth than about the Pugwash Conferences and other U.S.-Soviet dialogues. The influence of the Dartmouth Conference during the Cold War was significant. It was a channel that Washington and Moscow used to transmit information and clarify perspectives when official channels seemed insufficient. It influenced the thinking of participants who in their turn influenced both the course of the Cold War and relations between Russia and the United States since. These people included Zbigniew Brzezinski, Georgi Arbatov, Helmut Sonnenfeldt, Evgeni Primakov,

David Rockefeller, Andrei Kozyrev, John Kenneth Galbraith, and Buckminster Fuller. While Dartmouth was never a secret, the traditions of the conference have kept its achievements out of the limelight.

A second reason is that developments in international relations make the accomplishments of the Dartmouth Conference during the Cold War and since relevant to the concerns of theorists and practitioners. The notion that discussions such as those that took place at the Dartmouth conferences could influence the course of international relations runs counter to the traditional, realist paradigm of how states conduct their business with each other. This paradigm is a model that has guided statesmen and scholars for centuries.

Those who view the world through this realist prism see an international system made up of states—other actors have only supporting roles. In their relations with each other, these states are concerned mostly with their power relative to each other.[3] Power usually refers to a distribution of capabilities.[4] This distribution is physical; it can be measured, at least in theory, and exists apart from perceptions.[5] The motivations for a state's actions stem from rationally determined interests. The world is anarchic, a Hobbesian struggle of all against all. Cooperation, where it happens, stems from considerations of power. It is tactical in origin and exists only as long as it does not leave a cooperating state open to coercion by another.

This sketch of the realist paradigm is a simplification. The scholarship of Hans Morgenthau, Kenneth Waltz, and other realists is more sophisticated and complex. But it does in large measure describe how many people—scholars, policymakers, and the public—perceived U.S.-Soviet relations. They saw two states locked in battle across the globe, like two spiders in a bottle or two fighters in a ring: taking each other's measure, countering each other's moves, defending against the knockout blow, preparing to use the opening that would allow it.

Not everyone saw international politics that way. Certainly Norman Cousins, in founding the Dartmouth Conference, had a different vision. Since 1960, an increasing number of people have found the state-centered world of realism to be inadequate. Scientists, scholars, bankers, businesspeople legitimate and shady, activists dedicated to a variety of causes, and many other people have found opportunities for activity outside boundaries set by the state. This is not a new phenomenon, but the number of people and groups outside government involved in transnational activities has grown exponentially in the past twenty or thirty years. For example, the number of international nongovernmental organizations (NGOs) grew from 832 in 1951 to 4,518 in 1988.[6] The number of NGOs with a transnational orientation is now greater than 15,000.[7] In addition, the revolution in telecommunications that has brought us the Internet has made state borders porous as they have never been before.[8]

A growing number of scholars have seen these phenomena as growing challenges to the state and the state-centric realist paradigm. Rather than trying to replace the paradigm, most of these scholars are trying to amend it, to explain what realism in this purer form cannot.[9] Where realists focus on the state, these scholars focus on actors whose activities cross national boundaries. They are not concerned solely with governments, but with how whole bodies politic—governments and other significant elements of society—interact. Where realists see a virtually complete absence of lasting cooperation, these scholars see the growth of community. Where realists focus on the relative power of states as the engine that drives international politics, these scholars examine other forces, such as ideas, personal relationships, and domestic political structures.

This realist paradigm in its pure form allows little or no room for the influence of a forum like Dartmouth. The Dartmouth Conference began at the height of the Cold War as an unofficial dialogue between Soviet and American citizens. Its chief founder, Norman Cousins, intended Dartmouth to be an effort to forestall nuclear catastrophe stemming from a confrontation between the superpowers. Participants in the Dartmouth conferences came to form a loosely knit transnational community, joined by their experience at the conferences, though not by unity of views of policy by a set of principled or causal beliefs.[10] They hoped to have some influence on the policies of their governments. This influence might be direct or it might come by way of a change in how a problem was framed or how the intentions of the other side were perceived. This book will be, in effect, a case study of transnationalism. It will examine the kind of community Dartmouth formed, whether it had influence, and the nature of that influence.

A third reason for telling the story of Dartmouth is that it can suggest paths that can be followed by those trying to ameliorate or even resolve long-standing, bitter conflicts. Another strain of recent scholarship, adopted by a number of practitioners, has been interactive conflict resolution and multitrack diplomacy, which involves "unofficial, informal interaction among members of adversarial groups or nations" with the goal of trying to ameliorate or resolve a conflict.[11] A variation on this strain is the concept of a multilevel peace process, which grew out of the interactions in the Dartmouth Conference itself in the mid-1990s.[12]

Multitrack diplomacy and a multilevel peace process are similar. In fact, they complement each other. Both look on the interconnections between efforts to reach peace, between efforts made by officials and those made by citizens of various kinds. They both have, as Louise Diamond and John McDonald say, "a systems approach to peace" that operates "on a web of personal relationships that extend across time and space, across age, gender, and national boundaries."[13] They also share an approach to making peace that includes both official diplomacy and the efforts of many groups of people elsewhere in society.

The multilevel peace process is distinguished by its focus on process, on how participants in the process interact. It begins, as Dartmouth did, with a decision by people from different societies—or different parts of one society—in conflict to meet, come to a table, and talk. Those who come to the table interact. If the process—the dialogue—is sustained, they come to form relationships. The relationships can make it possible for those who have talked to consider acting and then to act. In acting, they can foster an end to conflict and a solid basis for peace. Their actions, should they take them, can take place on any of several levels; one might think of them as arenas—the official level, where the formal negotiations take place; the quasi-official level, such as was used at the Oslo talks on a settlement in the Middle East;[14] the public level, where sustained dialogue among nonofficial groups can occur; or in civil society. The concept of a multilevel peace process assumes that those who take part in sustained dialogue will be able to apply what they have learned in the dialogue to activity at one of the other levels, though that might not be possible until sometime after they have left the dialogue.

The Dartmouth conferences began in an effort to bridge the gap between two irreconcilable powers. It began with a group of people talking around a table. After the Cold War ended, it continued with an attempt to bring more than thirty years of experience to bear in an effort to help end a civil war. As chapter 6 explains, the multilevel peace process has been used in the former Soviet republic of Tajikistan since 1993.[15] The same process is also proving valuable in the United States. Indeed, with the Cold War ended and the Soviet Union gone, this process may be Dartmouth's most important contribution to conflict management and resolution.

INTERACTING WITH STATES

The work of scholars on transnational relations suggests an approach that can help put Dartmouth in its proper place in relation to global growth of transnational activity; it can be used to develop a framework for examining the significance of the Dartmouth dialogues. These scholars approach their work with a variety of concerns. But a common thread that runs through them is a concern with the relationship between the state and the actor that they focus on. Indeed, as Thomas Risse-Kappen notes, the truly interesting question is how transnational entities interact with states.[16]

A central concept that lies behind this question is power. Most of the entities analyzed by Risse-Kappen, Margaret Keck and Kathryn Sikkink, and their colleagues do not appear to have it, yet these entities have been able to effect changes in the behavior of states nonetheless. If states have close to a monopoly in the coercive means of power, how can nonstate actors effect such changes? Transnational firms have economic power. But international NGOs, advocacy networks, and dialogues such as Dartmouth have no apparent power of any kind, if power is defined by the resources available to an actor. Given the absence of these resources, a relational definition of power, that is, one based on outcomes rather than capabilities, is more useful to the study of transnational relations. Such a definition—one might be the ability of one actor to coerce another to do one's will—can suggest whether an actor has power even in the absence of a measurable set of capabilities.[17] Scholars who look at transnational relations tend to look at resources available to actors that are difficult to measure and are not included in the usual set of power resources.

They also look at politics in a broad, relational sense. It is not an arena for governments and politicians alone. Robert Dahl defines a political system broadly as "any persistent pattern of human relationships that involves, to a significant extent, control, influence, power, or authority." He goes on to say that under this definition many associations not always regarded as political—labor unions, clubs, clans, and civic groups—have political aspects.[18] Scholars of transnational relations examine such associations in the arena of world politics—in the world political system.

In addition, scholars of transnational relations recognize that change has many causes and that these are often not measurable. In a complex political context, many inputs are at work, and it might be that no one can know which was decisive in producing change. For instance, Risse-Kappen argues that the domestic political structure of a country affects whether transnational actors can effect change in the behavior of states. The factors that Keck and Sikkink examine in their study of networks of activists include the nature of the issues their networks address and how they are framed, the density of the networks themselves, and the vulnerability of their targets to moral suasion.[19]

The question for Dartmouth in this context is: Can a series of meetings between members of two hostile countries produce change in the policies of their governments? Dartmouth was but one of a small number of dialogues between Americans and Soviets that took place during the Cold War.[20] The Pugwash movement is the best known. Others included the Soviet-American Disarmament Study Group (SADS), begun in 1964; International Physicians for the Prevention of Nuclear War (IPPNW), organized in 1980; the Forum for U.S.-Soviet Dialogue, started in the early 1970s; and a series of conferences sponsored by the United Nations Association of the United States. Dartmouth was distinguished from the rest by having only participants from the two superpowers, by its concern with all issues in the U.S.-Soviet relationship, and by its longevity. Some groups, such as Pugwash, were multilateral. Most were concerned primarily with disarmament. Some—Pugwash again comes to mind—were formed as parts of advocacy networks animated by principled beliefs.[21] Individuals were sometimes attracted to Dartmouth because they held such beliefs, but Dartmouth as an institution did not have them. In fact, the American side, at least, went out of its way to attract people with a variety of views about issues in the U.S.-Soviet relationship.

Dartmouth was also distinguished by the proximity of its participants to government. Keck and Sikkink describe advocacy networks that, for the most part, act in opposition to governments, if not their own, then governments elsewhere. But Dartmouth was founded by people who walked the corridors of power, sought government approval of what they did, and made a point of transmitting to government whatever they learned.

THE CONCEPT OF INFLUENCE

The significance of Dartmouth is best comprehended with a precise conception of what influence is. "Influence" is one of a number of terms that are related to power defined in relational terms. Dahl includes it with "control" and "authority." Of these terms, "influence" is the most pertinent to Dartmouth, although all four—"influence," "power," "control," and "authority"—can be of interest in the study of transnational relations. Power, in this definition, involves coercion. Dartmouth had neither the means nor the will to exercise that. The same is true of control. Whether Dartmouth was ever able to acquire authority is a more interesting question. If, however, following Dahl again, we associate authority with the right to make binding rules, then authority is left to actors such as states, the pope, and, arguably, transnational actors such as Amnesty International. That leaves influence.

As Dahl explained in *Modern Political Analysis,* this term is not easily defined. It is related closely to power, but it remains something different. Power, as defined above, is wielded through coercion: an actor wants another to do something and is able to force the other to do it.[22] As will become clear, however, the participants in Dartmouth as a whole had no desire to coerce their governments even if they had had the resources.

As this suggests, this conception of power includes, implicitly, an assumption of intentionality: the powerful entity is able to exert its will on its target; the target does as the stronger entity intends. This is the classic scenario, desired by parents and coaches. On the other hand, if the target responds, but in a way the powerful entity did not intend, no power has been shown. For example, when Khrushchev came away from his talks with Kennedy in Vienna emboldened to take action against the United States, it can hardly be said that Kennedy was in any way powerful. Quantum physics offers us the Heisenberg principle to illustrate this point about intentionality. Presumably, the scientist would prefer to have no influence at all, yet she changes the thing she observes. A neutral outcome, devoutly to be wished, cannot be had. With power, then, those who have it get the outcome they seek.

Influence, on the other hand, is not necessarily concerned with the outcomes intended by the influencing actor. It need be concerned only with whether an outcome—a policy—is affected. In this book, influence will be defined, simply, as the ability to affect outcomes.[23] Kennedy, then, was influential in regard to Krushchev, though hardly in the way he sought. Other examples of influence abound, of course. Émile Zola was highly influential when he wrote "J'accuse" and changed the debate about the Dreyfus case. Indeed, the dream of many scholars and journalists who write on public policy is to affect the course of policymaking.

There are two reasons for adopting such a definition of influence. First, this analysis must be sensitive to the possibility that whatever influence participants in Dartmouth hoped to have, they in fact achieved the contrary. Second, this definition reflects the view of politics contained in Dahl's definition of a political system given above and implied in much of the work on transnational relations. Saunders' formulation, derived from his experience at Dartmouth and elsewhere, is that "political life is a process of continuous interaction among significant elements in a body politic."[24] Which elements count as significant varies, depending on the political structure of a country and the issue at stake. What matters to us, then, is merely whether an actor, or, rather, the actor we focus on here, is able to affect policy.

Influence over policy can be gained by means other than transmitting ideas. The mere transmission of information can be a source of influence.[25] Indeed, an important function of the Dartmouth Conference was to be a conduit for information from one state to the other. Policymakers need information about the intentions and capabilities of the actors with whom they deal; the policy they choose will depend on knowing whether the other actor is hostile or not, aggressive or passive, strong or weak. They get some of this information from intelligence sources, some from the media, some from diplomatic reporting, a little from scholarship, and the rest from a variety of other sources. They seek this information in order to perfect how they strive to achieve their objectives. Changes in values tend to be forced by changes in circumstances that a policymaker believes make it necessary to reexamine values.

Philip Mosely gave a description of the early conferences that suggested a useful distinction that can be made between direct and indirect influence. An actor has direct influence over another when the two communicate directly with each other, orally or in writing. Many of the Dartmouth conferees transmitted the results of the conferences directly to policymakers through written summaries, letters, and other documents and by meeting with them formally and informally.

Indirect influence, on the other hand, comes about when ideas or other pieces of information enter the general discourse on an issue. This has happened often with transnational communities, which often seek to obtain influence by publicizing the issues that they are concerned with. The demonstrations held in Seattle, Washington, and elsewhere by those protesting the effects of globalization are a recent example of this. Many efforts at obtaining indirect influence are less obvious. The Heritage Foundation, for example, encourages staff members to write op-ed pieces for newspapers and has programs set up in-house to facilitate them. Heritage, like other think tanks, understands that the ideas and information offered by those seeking indirect influence become a part of the climate of opinion and help form the parameters within which arguments about the issue are made. People concerned with an issue read about it, talk about it, and formulate their ideas about how to act on it. Policymakers develop and carry out policy on the basis of that information without being able to attribute it to any specific source or sources. There can be little doubt, for example, that U.S. policy in Bosnia was influenced by perceptions stemming from a figure for the number of people killed in the war that came to be accepted by the public and policymakers without knowing where the number came from or whether it was accurate.[26]

The concept of indirect influence naturally raises the question of evidence. How can one know whether one group or another has had influence on an issue? Particularly when, as with Dartmouth, the ideas generated by the conferees might be attributed to several sources: Pugwash, other meetings of Soviets and Americans, and a variety of official sources. The short answer is that one cannot. An analyst can say, however, that there is some probability that indirect influence over policy has been exercised when the ideas communicated by a group have become available in some form to a policymaker.

This access to a policymaker is merely the first step in gaining influence over policy. The policymaker must then incorporate whatever he or she has learned into policy. The information acquired can merely add detail to pictures of the other side already acquired and either confirm a course of action already chosen or foster a minor shift in tactics. That can happen at any time in the policy process. But a significant shift in policy can happen only when the policymakers themselves change or the previous policy proves inadequate. These circumstances create "policy windows" that allow the entry of new ideas either pushed by "policy entrepreneurs" or grasped from the set of ideas that are in the air, available to the policymaker.[27]

The first step—gaining access—is the easier of the two to determine. It is often easy to discover how a policymaker was exposed to certain ideas. In the case of the Dartmouth Conference, there are documents that show, for example, that Norman Cousins met with President Kennedy and Premier Khrushchev and that David Rockefeller spoke to Premier Kosygin and President Johnson. There is often evidence that shows that a policymaker held conversations with proponents, that certain memoranda and reports crossed his or her desk, or that certain ideas or pieces of information were "in the air" around the policymaker; that is, they were discussed among people with whom he or she had contact or were spread through the media available to the policymaker. The tools available to us do not, however, make it possible to understand clearly and precisely how the policymaker thinks. We cannot know enough about his or her cognitive processes to divine whether and how the policymaker incorporated these ideas or that information into policy. To determine whether the ideas came from one particular source—such as the Dartmouth Conference— is often impossible.

The second step in gaining influence, which links ideas and action, returns us to the realm of what can be observed. The task of determining how a policy was influenced is made difficult by a number of factors. First, the implications of ideas or information for policy may not always be clear. The ideas that lie behind any policy may be ambiguous. For example, the deployment of the Safeguard antiballistic missile (ABM) system by the United States may have been driven by the belief that an

ABM treaty was desirable and that such a "bargaining chip" made it easier to achieve. But at least some of those who favored deployment probably believed simply that an ABM defense was preferable to a treaty. In
addition, the processes through which policy is made often involve discussions and compromises among a number of people and bureaucratic
institutions. The deployment of Safeguard was, in fact, driven by both
motivations, as those who advocated Safeguard as a bargaining chip and
those who saw deployment as preferable to a treaty found common
ground. The way in which policy is made often also requires that a public face be put on private thinking, which can make statements about the
sources of influence misleading or incomplete.

Efforts to determine the influence of an actor on policy, therefore,
must often satisfy themselves with conclusions that are probabilistic.
There can rarely be certainty in such analyses. Our efforts to determine
the influence of the Dartmouth Conference, therefore, will focus first
on the more easily proven question of access. That ideas and information that originated within a transnational community such as Dartmouth were circulated among policymakers is itself significant. Our
efforts to determine whether those ideas found their way into policy
must remain more tentative. Yet the incorporation of ideas and information into policy is the most certain test of influence.

PATHS OF INFLUENCE

The definition of influence given here is a passive one, and purposely
so. It leaves open the paths through which influence is exercised. By
definition, transnational communities stand between states. In the case
of the Dartmouth Conference, which was bilateral in nature, the community stood between the United States and the Soviet Union. The
participants could have exerted influence in either country. Their influence could have been exerted either directly or through their colleagues
in the other delegation. The Soviet delegation, therefore, could seek
influence in the United States by meeting or speaking with policymakers themselves or by transmitting ideas and information to American
policymakers through their American colleagues. A similar statement
could be made about the American participants.

But when we seek to detect influence it can be useful to distinguish between decision makers and bureaucrats. They are both officials, but the path to influence through them is different. Decision makers decide what policy should be, which makes the path to influence that runs through them direct. In the American political system, decision makers include preeminently the president and Congress taken as a whole, but also, depending on the latitude they are given by the president, cabinet officers and the national security advisor. In the Soviet system, decision makers were generally understood to include members of the Politburo. As in the American system, however, cabinet members and others sometimes made policy when the issue and relationship between an official and the Politburo allowed it.[28]

Bureaucrats provide information and alternatives needed to make decisions and carry the decisions out after they are made. This unloved category is used here to include a number of people who do not think of themselves as bureaucrats: diplomats, soldiers, and analysts, for example. They are united by their function as people who support decision makers after policy has been made and, often, before. They are usually more accessible than decision makers. There are also more of them. Because they do not make policy themselves, they provide a less certain road to influence.

Like many such distinctions, this one is less clear-cut in reality than these descriptions suggest. As noted, bureaucrats can sometimes make policy. Compelled to interpret the sometimes ambiguous or simply confusing dictates of policymakers, bureaucrats can, in effect, make policy themselves. Members of Congress, decision makers according to the Constitution, are well known for providing their own extensive analyses of policy. Nor was the distinction between bureaucrat and decision maker always clear in the Soviet system.[29]

Both groups of officials share constraints that participants in an unofficial dialogue such as Dartmouth do not.[30] This can leave room for a transnational dialogue to provide officials with something of value. The primary limitation is that in the international arena, decision makers and bureaucrats alike represent not themselves but their country and the particular government of which they are a part. They work to further the positions their government has adopted officially. Informal conversation can be important, but it is used to explore the limits set by official positions.[31] A Dartmouth-style dialogue, however, can step outside those limits to explore them. As one delegate said, Dartmouth "can consider questions that are unnatural for diplomats to consider."[32] Such a dialogue strives to understand the perceptions and attitudes that lie behind the official positions of two countries, operating from the assumption that the official positions reflect a relationship between countries that can be improved. By virtue of their position, officials must speak carefully and exercise caution before entering dialogues and relationships that take them outside the strict requirements of their positions.

Another limitation is that officials tend to work in the short term. Day-to-day responsibilities and deadlines set by the press of events make it difficult to focus on (or allow time for) a long-term process such as Dartmouth or the long-term changes that the process is about. The limitation here is inherently more physical than intellectual; it is simply a matter of time and the priorities that the official must set. An official usually has too much to do to empty his or her in-box to spend much time contemplating the broader implications or more profound aspects of current issues.

SOVIET POLICYMAKING

Whatever influence Dartmouth had, it was exerted within the limits set by the Soviet system, and the Soviet system put severe constraints on efforts to influence it. Secrecy ensured that not all of these constraints were well understood during the Cold War by those who took part in Dartmouth or, for that matter, by anyone else in the West. It was clear to everyone that the system was highly centralized with the locus of control at the top, in the Politburo. But the precise ways in which information flowed and decisions were made were somewhat hidden.

The number of decision makers on foreign policy in the Soviet system as it existed was decidedly small, a function of its centralized state structure. Western scholars believed that it was limited to the members of the Politburo. There is some indication that on many issues it was effectively much smaller than that. In his memoirs, Anatoli Dobrynin, the longtime Soviet ambassador to the United States, indicates that, owing to the disinterest of most Politburo members, often only General Secretary Leonid Brezhnev and Foreign Minister Andrei Gromyko made the decisions.[33] On larger issues the Politburo would have had to express its approval, but while the number of bureaucrats was legion, on many issues the number of decision makers did not extend beyond its membership. During the Gorbachev era, major foreign policy decisions appear to have been made by Gorbachev, Eduard Shevardnadze, and Aleksandr Yakovlev.[34] Recent research has shown that merely four men, Brezhnev, Yuri Andropov, Gromyko, and Dmitri F. Ustinov, the defense minister, made the decision to invade Afghanistan.[35] Decisions about arms control were handled somewhat differently. They were effectively made by a small committee of the heads of the agencies concerned— "the Big Five"—with recommendations from another small committee of specialists—"the Five."[36] The Politburo gave its approval. That approval was routine but still necessary.

Another characteristic of the Soviet decision-making system was that it limited the flow of information, not only the amount that was made available, but also the channels through which it could move. The prime example of this was the oft-cited plaint of General Nikolai V. Ogarkov to an American delegate at the Strategic Arms Limitation Talks (SALT) talks that his civilian colleagues need not know the specifics of Soviet military hardware.[37] Arkadi Shevchenko, a Soviet official with the United Nations who defected to the United States in the 1970s, provides another example:

> The American delegation could contact their ambassadors to African, Asian, or Latin American countries directly and ask them to do business at the highest levels of the host governments. We, however, had no right to communicate with Soviet embassies abroad. We had to ask Moscow to issue instructions to our ambassadors to hold such discussions.[38]

Anatoli Adamishin, who was deputy foreign minister in charge of sub-Saharan Africa under Shevardnadze, gives this example: "[O]ur ambassador in Luanda had no protected telephone link with Moscow and was obliged to drive to the staff of the Soviet military mission advisers whenever he had to put an urgent call through to the Foreign Ministry."[39]

This suggests that it cannot be assumed that ideas and information acquired by the Soviet participants would have been able to influence policy even if they had been passed through to relevant sections of the bureaucracy. Whereas in the U.S. government information often spreads more or less freely from agency to agency, it was more likely to remain bottled up in the Soviet system. This is not to mention the wealth of information available from public media and organizations in the United States and the dearth of the same in the Soviet Union, a reflection of the differences in the domestic structures of the two countries.

Two more points need to be made about the Soviet approach to ideas and information from sources such as Dartmouth. First, as Mosely, George Kennan, and others among the first participants knew, the Soviets were accustomed to transnational dialogue and had long tried to use it to their benefit. Indeed, Soviet foreign policy had had a transnational element from the beginning in the form of like-minded parties and people across the world. The Comintern and, briefly, the Cominform formalized the link between these parties and the Soviet Communist Party. The International Department of the Central Committee maintained these links into the Gorbachev era. By 1960 the importance of these parties and people to the interests of the Soviet Union in its relations with the United States had diminished relative to Soviet relations elsewhere. But this history assuredly colored how Soviet officialdom saw Dartmouth. In the zero-sum game that the governments of the United States and the Soviet Union played in 1960, Dartmouth could not have happened without this perspective taken from Soviet history. But Mosely and others on the American side believed that despite this history the dialogue could become something more than a tool of the Soviet propaganda machine.

Second, some of those who began the Dartmouth dialogue in 1960 assumed that the Soviet citizens who took part in Dartmouth could speak from the heart without merely echoing the trite phrases of the party line and Soviet ideology. Those who assumed this were undoubtedly naive. It must be remembered that the Soviet citizens allowed to participate in dialogue with foreigners were chosen from those regarded by Soviet officialdom as "safe" and that the controls placed on them were formidable.[40] All the same, people such as Mosely and Kennan, who knew the Soviets intimately, found the dialogue useful.

THE DARTMOUTH PROCESS

This book tells the story of the development of what the people who took part in the Dartmouth conferences have come to call the "Dartmouth process." This process was not born whole, and the reader will find that what was done at Hanover, New Hampshire, more than forty years ago differed in many ways from what is now being adapted and used in conflicts in the former Soviet Union, the United States, and elsewhere. The conference can be seen, in fact, as a search for a process that would make it possible for two enemies to reduce their hostility.

2 | The Early Years, 1960–64

DARTMOUTH I: Hanover, New Hampshire; October 29–November 4, 1960

DARTMOUTH II: Nizhnaya Oreanda, Crimea; May 21–28, 1961

DARTMOUTH III: Andover, Massachusetts; October 21–27, 1962

DARTMOUTH IV: Leningrad; July 25–31, 1964

THE STORY OF THE DARTMOUTH CONFERENCE MUST BEGIN with Norman Cousins. By 1960 he had been editor of the *Saturday Review of Literature* for twenty years, building it into an institution with a circulation greater than the *New Yorker's*. He was a man of strong convictions and many interests. His convictions impelled him to act rather than simply to write. By his own account, a bout of tuberculosis and six months spent in a sanatorium as a child left him imbued with a strong sense of duty. As he was able to leave the sanatorium—many of his fellow patients could not—he felt he had been reprieved. As he put it:

> [F]rom the moment I walked out of the sanatorium and looked back at my Sunday perch on the old wall near the entrance, I knew that my life would be unbearable unless I could find some way of making good a debt I couldn't quite define but that I knew would be with me as long as I lived.[1]

The Dartmouth Conference was one result, one way of making good that debt, but he found many others. He helped the Hiroshima maidens (survivors of the first nuclear bombing), victims of Nazi medical experiments, and the hungry in Biafra. A founder of the Committee for a Sane Nuclear Policy (SANE), he was committed to finding a way for the superpowers to avoid nuclear destruction.[2] His interests found expression in his editorials and in more than a dozen books, which he wrote on topics as diverse as nuclear war and his own illness. His examination of the power of laughter and the mind in medical treatment—originally published in the *New England Journal of Medicine* and later as a book[3]—won him an appointment as an adjunct professor of medical humanities at the School of Medicine at the University of California at Los Angeles. His writings, many of which draw directly on his own experiences, and the recollections of others reveal an eminently humane man, able to connect with almost anyone, from General Douglas MacArthur to Albert Schweitzer, and a marvelous raconteur. He was the heart of the Dartmouth Conference. The dialogue was a result of his vision and efforts, and he took part in it until shortly before his death.

Cousins was drawn to the need for a conversation with the Soviets out of his conviction that the atomic bomb threatened the survival of humankind. He was less impressed with the danger posed by Soviet expansionism or ideology than some of his contemporaries, but he was convinced that humankind had to act to avoid nuclear holocaust. The action he believed was needed was the formation of a world government. This belief seems somewhat quixotic now, but it was central to his thinking and not as uncommon then. The establishment of such a government had to be a "plural enterprise" that included both the Soviet Union and the United States. "Therefore," he told the Soviets in 1959, "we have to find some way for getting through to each other, some way of drawing up the ground rules for our discourse."[4]

HARD ATTITUDES

In 1959 both sides were locked into the hardest of Cold War attitudes, which the crises of the time seemed to justify—tensions over Berlin, the U-2 spy-plane affair, the Hungarian Revolution of just a few years before, the space race opened by *Sputnik,* and the arms race, with its frightening "bomber gap" and "missile gap." The Soviet Union was emerging from the Stalin era; its image of the United States as a doomed, implacably hostile adversary was changing, but gradually. In the United States, Senator McCarthy had just recently been disgraced, though his paranoid vision of Soviet communism was still common among Americans. Even officials who had opposed McCarthy continued to see the Soviets as hostile and Machiavellian. This was the dominant view both in policymaking circles and among citizens at large.

No matter how accurate these images were, in 1959 there were few opportunities for the two countries to "get through to each other" as Cousins wished to do. The U.S.-USSR exchange agreement that made cultural and academic exchanges possible had been signed only the previous year. Until then, contact between citizens of the two countries had been sporadic at best.

For the Soviets, ideology reinforced suspicion of the West. So did the power of the state to make information about the United States conform to the images—mostly negative—approved by the state and party. Controls were stringent enough that there was even little contact between officials. A junior Soviet diplomat attending the 1958 session of the UN General Assembly could meet with his foreign colleagues, even those from other Soviet bloc countries, only with the permission of his superiors.[5] Fear of contamination by foreign ideas meant that access to information of any kind about the United States was limited, even for officials and specialists working on U.S.-Soviet relations. The exchange agreement did contain provisions that threatened to broaden the opportunity for contamination by Western ideas. These included large national exhibitions, illustrated monthly magazines to be distributed in the other country, and exchanges of performing artists.[6] However, the cultural and academic exchanges initiated in 1958, once they began, were used mainly to learn about American science and technology rather than to broaden understanding of the United States.

Information about the Soviet Union was somewhat more easily available in the United States. Would-be specialists could study the Soviet Union at institutions created for that purpose at Columbia University, Harvard University, and elsewhere beginning in the 1940s. These institutions had no Soviet counterparts until the 1960s. The exchanges that began in 1958 sent historians, linguists, sociologists, economists, and political scientists to the Soviet Union, where they could learn firsthand about the country.

Nonetheless, suspicion by American officials of the Soviets combined with the Soviet desire for secrecy to keep contacts to a minimum. An offer by Premier Nikolai Bulganin—formally the head of the Soviet government—in 1956 to hold lengthy, informal talks with the American ambassador was turned down. Congressmen visiting Moscow were denied the opportunity to meet with Soviet officials as a matter of policy.[7] Contacts between American diplomats and ordinary Soviet citizens were discouraged by the Soviet authorities and effectively limited.

PRECURSORS TO DARTMOUTH

The strong concern of governments and scientists about the potential for a nuclear Armageddon led to meetings in the 1950s that might be considered precursors of Dartmouth. Efforts to hold such meetings had been proposed shortly after World War II, but it took the thaw that followed the death of Stalin to make them possible.[8]

The first Pugwash conference was held in 1957. These meetings, which continue, are between scientists of many countries and focus on issues stemming from the threat posed by thermonuclear weapons. Unlike with Dartmouth, the Pugwash meetings are multilateral, most participants are scholars (in the beginning almost all were physicists), and the discussions focus on arms control issues. Nonetheless, the purpose of Pugwash was similar enough to the purpose of Dartmouth that a number of people took part in both conferences. These included Paul Doty, Jerome Weisner, Richard Leghorn, Herbert York, and Georgi Arbatov.

In 1958, following a proposal made by President Eisenhower, scientists and officials from the United States, the Soviet Union, and other countries met in Geneva for two conferences. One explored the possibilities for agreement on measures for preventing a surprise attack. The other examined potential limitations on nuclear testing. Many of the people appointed to take part were not government officials, though a few years later officials from the Arms Control and Disarmament Agency (ACDA) and other agencies would take their places at similar tables. The dialogue spawned in Geneva grew into the discussions of arms control continued by the Pugwash and Dartmouth conferences and other groups.[9] Indeed, some of the people involved in these conferences, including Jerome Weisner and Richard Leghorn on the American side and Evgeni Fedorov on the Soviet side, later became participants in the Dartmouth Conference.

NORMAN AND IKE

It was against this background that President Eisenhower and Norman Cousins held the conversations that led to the beginning of the Dartmouth Conference. They had come to know each other in 1951 after General Eisenhower, then head of NATO, wrote a brief note to Cousins praising an article that appeared in the *International Herald Tribune.*[10] This began a personal relationship that continued after the general became president and even after his retirement.[11] They shared a number of concerns about nuclear war, the Cold War, and the arms race. Their views on how to approach these problems differed greatly, but their respect for each other was clear. Arthur Larson, an aide to Eisenhower (and later a participant in Dartmouth), wrote that in August 1956 he asked the president whether he read the *Saturday Review.* In response, Eisenhower pulled out a copy of a recent editorial Cousins had written on the hydrogen bomb, which, Larson concluded, "had made a deep impression on him."[12] Cousins suggested that Eisenhower make a farewell address at the end of his presidency, much as George Washington had. The suggestion was taken and helped inspire the speech now remembered primarily for the use of the phrase "military-industrial complex."[13]

It is not clear when or how Eisenhower made the suggestion that led Cousins to propose a conference with the Soviets on his trip to Moscow in 1959. It was probably in a personal conversation in 1958 or 1959 that has been left off the public record. They did meet face-to-face more than once, including on Cousins' return from Moscow in 1959.[14] In Cousins' accounts, Eisenhower's basic idea was that private citizens who had the confidence of their government could serve as an advanced guard for diplomats. They could prepare the ground and scout for openings without committing their governments. Diplomats could then begin the search for formal agreement.

AN ICEBREAKER IN MOSCOW

Cousins was invited to go to the Soviet Union in 1958, following the signing of the Cultural Exchange Agreement. This was at least his second trip to the Soviet Union. As he described it later, on this trip he was to serve "as an icebreaker in the cultural exchange program."[15] The Soviet Union at the time insisted that each visitor have an official organization as a sponsor. For Cousins, this was the Union of Soviet Societies for Friendly and Cultural Relations with Foreign Countries, an organization that embodied the historical Soviet approach to transnational relations. He was to lecture to several audiences about American literature and world affairs and meet with people sharing his interests around the Soviet Union. Aware that many of his audiences had not been addressed by an American before and that what he wanted to say might be controversial, he felt it "only fair" to inform the Soviets about the nature of his lectures. They did not object. He arrived in Moscow in June 1959. His first talk, arranged by the Union of Soviet Societies, was to the Presidium of the Soviet Peace Committee on June 25, a little more than a week after he arrived.

The speech shocked the Soviet audience, particularly when he criticized the American Communist Party and Soviet policy in Eastern Europe.[16] No doubt his other audiences in the Soviet Union reacted similarly. It was late in the session when he suggested what would become the Dartmouth conferences, apparently in response to a question from Mikhail Kotov, executive secretary of the Soviet Peace Committee, about ways in which citizens in the United States and the Soviet Union could work together for peace. The account of his answer published in the *Saturday Review* contains nothing that resembles what Dartmouth became, except his suggestion for "a conference of scientists and experts to consider some of the obstacles that had come up at the nuclear talks in Geneva."[17] But he wrote later that while in Moscow he suggested to Soviet writers, academicians, and scientists that "the exchange program . . . would be substantially advanced by roundtable discussions between non-government leaders in both countries."[18] Indeed, he emphasized "the importance of a participative public opinion on the formation of important foreign policy."[19] The Soviet response, according to Cousins' notes, was "that the Soviet Prime Minister reflected the views of the

Soviet people and it was therefore unnecessary to hold such a conference. It was admitted, however[,] in response to further questioning by Mr. Cousins that the needs of the individual were not always taken into account by previous heads of state in the Soviet Union."[20]

Shortly after his return to the United States, Cousins asked for a meeting with Eisenhower. He got it on August 6, 1959. He told the president, naively perhaps, that "the Soviets will discuss any matters freely, if you talk to them as equals" and noted the many profound changes that had taken place in the five years since he had last been to the Soviet Union.[21] To Cousins, the conflict between the Soviet Union and the United States was "no longer ideological, but one of conventional balance of power." Eisenhower expressed his view that the Soviet people wanted peace, but they did not know how to go about getting it. Moreover, he said "their fate is in the hands of a few who are such hardcore Communists that it is difficult to discuss affairs rationally with them." The conversation ended with an appeal by Cousins for his ideas about world federalism.

There was no apparent reference to the ideas that led to Dartmouth, but it seems likely that it was at this meeting that the matter came up. During the Dartmouth conferences, Cousins attributed the idea for them to Eisenhower. But it appears to have come to Cousins during his 1959 trip to the Soviet Union. Rob Nelson spoke about this to Cousins' wife, Ellen, in 1993. She replied that

> it was Norman who went to President Eisenhower to propose the importance of a citizen gathering from both countries and it was characteristic of Norman always, in great modesty, and perhaps in great wisdom in my sense of it, not to claim credit for something and he said that he had always given credit for the Dartmouth beginnings to President Eisenhower, that she was certain that it was Norman who went to the President to propose this gathering and that the President had then confirmed that it was a very good idea.[22]

The idea may not have been Eisenhower's then, but his support for it is significant. Dartmouth came about with the blessing of government, not in opposition to it.

It is not clear whether Cousins followed his informal suggestions to the Soviet Peace Committee with a formal proposal, though several "initiatives" were made. In any case, in November Cousins received a three-page letter from Kotov and Nikolai Tikhonov, chairman of the Soviet Peace Committee, proposing a meeting of "public representatives of our countries." Some work was needed before Cousins and his Soviet colleagues could agree on who those representatives could be. The Peace Committee wanted to have a conference with the heads of American peace committees. Cousins insisted on emphasizing the "individual stature of the participants" instead and managed to convince his inter-locutors.[23] By January 1960 the Soviets had given conditional accept-ance to the conference.

In the meantime, Cousins discussed the idea of the conference with a number of other people. The Ford Foundation expressed interest. Philip Mosely was asked to work with Cousins.[24]

Mosely was remarkable in his own right. Before World War II, he was one of the few American scholars able to conduct research in the Soviet Union, spending the better part of two years in Moscow begin-ning in 1930 working on his dissertation. Through the remainder of the decade he taught at Princeton and Cornell Universities and did field research in the Balkans. During World War II he worked on pol-icy planning at the State Department, where he served until he returned to teaching at Columbia University in the fall of 1946. He became friends with most of the senior fraternity of Soviet specialists in the Foreign Service, including Charles Bohlen and Llewellyn Thompson, both of whom became ambassadors to Moscow in the 1950s and were important figures in the Kennedy administration. He thus became an important source for the connections with the U.S. government that Dartmouth had in the early 1960s. He was important to the growth of the newly important field of Soviet studies, helping found the Russian Institute at Columbia and serving as its director in the early 1950s. He became the director of studies at the Council on Foreign Relations in 1955. This was the post he held when the Dart-mouth conferences began.

In character he seemed to complement Cousins, and his impor-tance to the early Dartmouth conferences can scarcely be overesti-mated. Where Cousins was a fountain of ideas and energy, Mosely was a steadily flowing, calm stream of good sense and organization.[25] If Cousins was a man of many causes, Mosely was a man of few. Cousins was impulsive; Mosely, much more careful. Cousins was loquacious;

Mosely, a superb listener. Their differing qualities, brought together, made Dartmouth possible and kept it going through its first few years. Mary Kersey Harvey, Cousins' assistant at the *Saturday Review,* painted an eloquent picture of Mosely in a letter written several months after the second Dartmouth Conference. She spoke of Mosely's guidance at the conference, "deft, sure, and completely subtle," and described

> the pleasure—the complete and reassuring pleasure—of working with and witnessing in action a man fully but quietly in command of the situation whose motivations were as powerful and straight as his intellectual resources and knowledge.[26]

More than twenty-five years later, George Klebnikov described Mosely this way:

> He was very good at telling the Soviet participants exactly what he wanted them to know and what he wanted to convey and yet he had a marvelous manner, a bedside manner, and I never met a Soviet who didn't like him.

Klebnikov went on say that Mosely was able to

> speak truth in the eye, the Russian *govorit' pravda v glaza,* in other words, straight out, not mixing words. It was extremely popular with the Soviet side, and of course, he knew everything there was to know about them.[27]

A committee was formed to organize the conference and to write a proposal to the Ford Foundation. In addition to Cousins and Mosely, it consisted of Arthur Larson, then at the World Rule of Law Center of Duke University, and A. William Loos of the Church Peace Union. They discussed the idea in a meeting with senior officials at the State Department, who expressed their willingness to support it, "on a non-official basis."[28]

Preparations for the conference began in the spring of 1960. Participants were chosen and the agenda was prepared. Alice Bobrysheva describes the preparations on the Soviet side: each participant wrote a discussion paper on an assigned topic and the group consulted with both the Foreign Ministry and the Central Committee of the Communist Party.[29]

The conference was postponed, however, following the U-2 incident in May 1960, which also led to the cancellation of the second summit that had been scheduled between Premier Khrushchev and President Eisenhower. This would not be the last time that the fate of the Dartmouth Conference depended on the state of U.S.-Soviet relations.

THE FIRST DARTMOUTH CONFERENCE

The "First Informal U.S.-U.S.S.R. Conference" opened on the campus of Dartmouth College in Hanover, New Hampshire, on October 29, 1960. The Soviet delegation arrived the evening before at the Hanover Inn, a crenellated building on Main Street. Most of the Americans arrived the next day.

The American participants, chosen by Cousins, spanned the spectrum of American cultural and intellectual life. They included choreographer Agnes DeMille, playwright Russel Crouse, and Walt Rostow, who was then an advisor to presidential candidate John F. Kennedy. He would soon join the State Department and later serve as national security advisor to President Johnson. Mary K. Harvey served the conference as its coordinator. She was an editor, journalist, and writer who worked with Cousins at the *Saturday Review.* Mosely and Cousins were cochairmen of the delegation. Mosely was the expert on Soviet affairs for the Americans. Bobrysheva worked with Oleg Bykov on the Soviet side and Aleksandr Federov and Harris Coulter on the American as interpreters, using equipment rented from IBM during the formal sessions.

Another member of the American delegation, former senator William Benton, became an important figure in the early Dartmouth conferences. In 1960 he was publisher of the *Encyclopedia Britannica.* Almost two decades before he had made the company profitable. Much of his career after that had been dedicated to public service. He served as an assistant secretary of state shortly after World War II and was appointed senator from Connecticut in 1949. While in office he became a prominent opponent of McCarthy—he sponsored a resolution to have him expelled—before he was defeated in his bid for reelection in 1952.[30] The strength of the Soviet education system impressed Benton during his first trip to the Soviet Union in 1955. His book on the subject, *This Is the Challenge,* appeared when the flight of *Sputnik* shocked Americans and left them asking about the weaknesses of American education. Benton "felt that the book would help offset the lingering McCarthyite charge that I was 'soft on communism.'"[31] He was energetic and dedicated, but abrasive and, to use his own word, "tactless." While visiting Leningrad in 1964 (he rented a yacht to get there), he toured the bookstores of the city, accosting managers and seeing what people bought. One of his guides, evidently somewhat perplexed at this choice of activity, asked whether he was "a member of the ruling imperialist clique in America." Benton's answer: "You're damn right I am."[32]

Aleksandr Korneichuk was the head of the Soviet delegation and the dominant Soviet participant in the early Dartmouth conferences. He had been a protégé of Khrushchev's since the 1930s.[33] His wife, Wanda Lvovna Wassilewska, a Polish writer who came to the Soviet Union in 1939, often visited Khrushchev at home.[34] A member of the Central Committee of the Communist Party and the winner of five Stalin prizes, Korneichuk was a stalwart defender of the Communist Party. He would later describe with pride how he had scolded Aleksandr Solzhenitsyn, receiving the congratulations of writers who had kept silent.[35] Clearly no liberal or dissident, Korneichuk wrote plays that nonetheless contained limited criticism of the flaws of the Soviet system. He supported de-Stalinization and the thaw that occurred after Stalin died in 1953.[36] George Kennan and George Fischer, after lengthy conversations with him at the Hanover conference, were impressed by the substance and sophistication of what he had to say. Fischer described Korneichuk as "soft-spoken, with a pleasant plebeian pronunciation of Russian. He appears partly gay and partly soulful and sickly."[37] Indeed, he was in ill health, having come to the United States against the advice of his doctors.

According to Bobrysheva, the rest of the Soviet delegation was not distinguished.[38] It did, however, reflect a range of interests as broad as that of the U.S. delegation. Its members included a movie producer, a chemist, a composer, and a historian. Several had been to the United States before.

Late in the afternoon of Sunday, October 30, the participants crossed the Dartmouth Green to enter the Wren Room of the Baker Library at Dartmouth College for the first session. Earlier that day the Planning Group had decided that the conference would begin with an informal discussion of U.S.-Soviet relations in the context of the objectives of the conference. Participants began the discussion by noting that what distinguished the conference was precisely that its objectives did not include agreement about something specific. This made it unique among conferences between the two countries. It would be enough, they said, "if there was candid discussion, and the establishment of personal relationships among the participants."[39] They argued that public opinion was important: "Governments pay attention to citizens of good will." This, they felt, was how the conference could have influence.

The participants returned to the Wren Room the next morning to discuss the role that the United States and the Soviet Union could play in the economic development of what became known as the Third World. Many of the countries in the Third World were just then becoming independent as the colonial empires collapsed. In 1960 they were a focus of Cold War competition as the two superpowers sent economic and military assistance and tried to convince the new leaders of the superiority of their economic system. Indeed, the author of the American discussion paper presented at that first session, Walt Rostow, wrote *The Stages of Economic Growth* as a "Non-Communist Manifesto" to show how economic development would occur under the capitalist economic system.[40]

Speaking in the Wren Room, Rostow was frank in his opposition to what he saw as Soviet aggression in the Third World. In the spirit of the conference, he nonetheless called for such cooperation as was possible.[41] In the following sessions the participants discussed "the psychological texture of peace," how to create a "structured peace" (a phrase that brings to mind Cousins' proposals for world federalism), and how citizens can take part in developing foreign policy. But the high point of the conference came during the discussion of arms control.

The key figure in this discussion was Grenville Clark. A Wall Street lawyer born to wealth and a member of the Eastern elite in good standing, he gained considerable influence, though not fame, through "public service in a private capacity" and public advocacy of positions that his peers considered unorthodox, notably civil rights and "world peace through world law."[42] He had considerable influence on Cousins and, through him, the Dartmouth Conference.

In October 1945 Clark convened a conference in Dublin, New Hampshire, to discuss the prospects for world government. That conference brought together almost fifty prominent people who were then outside government. It may have served as a model for Dartmouth. Cousins attended it and heard Clark make an appeal for world government as a way to avoid a nuclear holocaust, an appeal that Cousins soon took up himself.

On Tuesday, November 1, Dartmouth participants in Hanover began a discussion of arms control. The two sides echoed the official arguments that had been made in Geneva for at least two years. The Americans insisted on the need for inspection; the Soviets resisted it as interference in their internal affairs, to use a stock phrase that became common later. Tempers rose. The exchange became angry. The seventy-seven-year-old Clark, until then silent, raised his massive six-foot frame. He asked to speak and then spoke eloquently. Cousins described it later:

> He began by saying he accepted fully the sincerity of the Soviet delegates to reduce and eliminate the dangers of war. He spoke of the enormous numbers of casualties suffered by the Russian people in the Second World War, some twenty million dead. He referred to the siege of Leningrad and the heroism of its people. He paid tribute to the Russian contribution to victory during the war. He spoke movingly and with great dignity. Then he told of the need to avert even greater wars in an age of nuclear weapons. He defined the basic principles that had to go into the making of a workable peace. He described the opportunity before leaders of public opinion in gaining acceptance for these principles. He called on both Americans and Russians to see the problem of disarmament in a larger and more historic setting than weapons alone. When he sat down, both sides gave him sustained applause.[43]

The mood of the conference changed after Clark's speech. Daniel Yankelovich would call it a "gesture of empathy," an action taken by one side that shows understanding of the other and lowers the defenses of both.[44] Such gestures raise the possibility that a true dialogue can begin; Clark's action did that. Clark's speech became a defining moment that gave Dartmouth personal, human value. No minds were changed at Dartmouth I, and, as Cousins later described it, the two sides spent the conference seated opposite each other, a physical manifestation of their approach to one another. This arrangement also reflected the opposition of their countries on the world stage. It did not change during the remaining three days of the conference, but a link had been forged among those who heard Grenville Clark.

During the conference, Korneichuk and Fischer spoke often, at length, in private.[45] Fischer's Russian was excellent, and he and Korneichuk felt a strong rapport, perhaps even kinship. Fischer's mother had been an interpreter for Soviet foreign ministers Georgi Chicherin and Maksim Litvinov; he himself had been educated in Soviet schools and had spent a year as an American officer in Ukraine during World War II.

After the conference the Soviet delegation went to New York, visiting the homes of Norman Cousins and Senator Benton on the way. They spent a week in New York, sightseeing and meeting with people, including Cousins, Loos, Shepard Stone, and Mosely. The Soviets attended a reception held for them by Averell Harriman and a party put on by Joshua Logan, the producer and director responsible for such movies and Broadway shows as *Bus Stop* and *South Pacific*. Boris Polevoi, Irina Lagunova, and Viktor Chkhikvadze went to Los Angeles, responding to an invitation given on the ship when they came to New York. They met with members of peace groups and Linus Pauling. From New York the entire delegation submitted a preliminary report to Moscow and received permission to hold another conference, which, it was hoped, would be held in Moscow or the Crimea the following May.[46]

The Soviets were interested in the views of John F. Kennedy, who was only a few days away from election as president. Korneichuk had conversations with two advisors to Kennedy, Harriman and Rostow, reports of which found their way to the candidate's eyes. During the conference, Korneichuk urged Rostow to "take disarmament seriously" as forces in Moscow might soon "make a movement toward peace impossible."[47] This conversation was probably on Rostow's mind when, in November after the election, he went to Moscow to discuss disarmament. Perhaps after meeting Korneichuk at his reception, Harriman wrote Kennedy that Korneichuk "asked me whether you would follow FDR's policies . . . he asked me how I thought you and Mr. Khrushchev would get along if you met. I said Mr. Khrushchev would find you were not interested in scoring points in a debate."[48] The last comment was, presumably, meant to contrast Kennedy with Nixon, who had scored points in the "Kitchen Debate."

It is likely that the detailed report on the conference that the Soviet delegation sent to the Central Committee was read with great interest—few such firsthand reports on the opinions of Americans were available. In mid-December, four members of the delegation—Korneichuk, Lagunova, Polevoi, and Modest Rubenstein—spoke about the conference to an overflow audience in Moscow's Central Lecture Hall, an event significant enough to be reported in the *New York Times,* which said the lecture was "good natured and sometimes amusing."[49] But another report notes the tendentiousness of some of the remarks.[50] Bobrysheva confirms that both moods were evident. She also notes that the tone of Korneichuk's remarks to the Moscow audience was different, more in line with Soviet propaganda, than the tone she had heard in New Hampshire.[51]

The difference suggests why many participants came to regard the Dartmouth conferences as important in a personal but intangible sense. During the conference, they were able to talk to one another about the issues between their countries and, no doubt, about matters of personal importance, in a way they could not when they left its somewhat rarefied atmosphere. George Kennan's reaction, described by Cousins in a post-mortem to participants a few days later, underlined both the rarity of the conversations and their value.[52] Few Americans had had as much contact with the Soviets as Kennan, yet he had never had as full and direct an exchange with "Russians of intellectual substance" as he had had during his one day in Hanover.

Leaving Dartmouth, the participants returned to the restraints of everyday discourse, where the feelings of personal goodwill toward individuals from the opposing side had little place and could yield only subtle influence. The Soviets also returned to the full constraints of their totalitarian political system (present but diluted at Dartmouth), which put strict limits on what could be said.

DARTMOUTH II: IN THE CRIMEA

Mosely and Korneichuk met in Moscow in March 1961 to plan for Dartmouth II, which took place two months later.

U.S.-Soviet relations were in flux when the conference met in May. John F. Kennedy had become president and was determined to make his mark on the U.S.-Soviet relationship. The Bay of Pigs invasion had taken place just a month before, but plans were being made for the summit meeting between Kennedy and Khrushchev in Vienna two weeks after the conference.

The number of participants on both sides was greater in the Crimea than in Hanover. The delegations were more expert in the topics discussed and more prepared for the discussions.[53] Eight Americans took part in both conferences; they included Cousins, Mosely, Benton, and Larson.

Grenville Clark was absent, but his coauthor, Professor Louis Sohn, participated. Margaret Mead, who in addition to her other anthropological work had written on Soviet attitudes,[54] took part. So did Marian Anderson, the great contralto of the Metropolitan Opera, also known for her civil rights work; Gabriel Hauge, who had been chairman of the Council of Economic Advisors under President Eisenhower; and Erwin Griswold, dean of Harvard Law School. This was also the first Dartmouth Conference for Paul Doty, a physical chemist from Harvard with an active interest in arms control issues. He became a Dartmouth regular and the American cochair of the Arms Control Task Force twenty years later. His involvement in the Manhattan Project as a graduate student left a strong impression on him, which led to a concern with arms control. He later became chairman of the Federation of Atomic Scientists and in that capacity attended the first Pugwash Conference in 1957. Beginning in 1960 he was an advisor to the U.S. government. At the time of Dartmouth II he was a member of the President's Science Advisory Committee.[55]

The two interpreters who accompanied the American delegation to the Crimea—George Sherry and George Klebnikov—became fixtures at the Dartmouth conferences into the 1990s. It was on Sherry's recommendation that Klebnikov was asked to take part in the second conference. They were both Russian-born Americans who worked as interpreters for the United Nations. Sherry became a senior officer working on special political affairs at the United Nations in 1962 and later deputy secretary-general for political affairs, but he continued to interpret for Dartmouth.[56] Klebnikov helped pioneer simultaneous translation at the Nuremberg trials. He became the chief interpreter at the United Nations and later retired as the director of translation services.[57]

They had contrasting personalities. Outside the interpretation booth, Sherry was voluble, Klebnikov taciturn. Inside the booth, their work showed impressive sophistication and skill. Owing to the respect they earned from the participants and the time they gave to the Dartmouth Conference, they—and Alice Bobrysheva, a Soviet counterpart—came to be treated virtually as participants themselves. Bobrysheva ceased to interpret after the first few conferences yet remained essential to them, becoming the executive secretary for the Soviet side.

Six of the Soviet participants in the first conference went to the Crimea for the second. Korneichuk returned as cochairman. There were several newcomers whose presence suggested the importance that the Soviet leadership accorded the Dartmouth dialogues. Academician Evgeni Fedorov was secretary general of the USSR Academy of Sciences and had once been an Arctic explorer. He was important not only by virtue of his position within the Soviet scientific community; he was also a significant figure in Soviet arms control efforts. As noted, he had taken part in the Conference of Experts in Geneva in 1958. The next year he led the Soviet delegation in the discussions of the Technical Working Group II, convened by the Conference of Experts to examine the matter of on-site inspections. At a meeting of the Academy of Sciences, he urged Soviet scientists to become more active on political issues.[58] Not one to stray far from the party line, he concluded the meetings of the Technical Working Group, which failed to reach an agreement, with a salvo attacking the scientific integrity of the American delegation.[59]

Retired major general Nikolai Talensky wrote about arms control and taught at the Military Academy of the Soviet General Staff. Shortly after Stalin's death, he had published one of the first articles revising Stalinist military theory.[60] It began an extensive debate on the need for such revisions. Later he argued that a nuclear war was unwinnable and that this made arms control necessary—including negotiations with the United States. This viewpoint, dominant in Soviet thinking at the time of Dartmouth II, placed him in what might be termed a moderate camp and made him a subject of attack after Khrushchev fell from power in 1964.[61]

Mark Mitin was the editor of the important journal *Voprosi filosofii*. The Soviet delegation also included two experts from the Institute of World Economy and International Relations (IMEMO), one of the increasingly important institutes of the Academy of Sciences that provided policy-oriented analysis to the Soviet leadership. One expert, Modest Rubenstein, was an economist. The other, Nikolai Mostovets, while nominally with IMEMO, was actually on the staff of the Central Committee of the Communist Party as head of the United States section.[62] One member of the delegation, Fedor I. Kozhevnikov, had been a member of the International Court of Justice until earlier in 1961; another, Vladimir I. Koretsky, had just been appointed to it. Together, they were able to offer the Soviet point of view on the arguments for world federalism argued by Sohn, Larson, and Cousins.

On Sunday, May 21, the American delegates, who had gathered in Moscow, climbed into fourteen black cars, two or three to a car, to be taken to the airport. They met the Soviet delegates there for the flight to Simferopol in the Crimea. From Simferopol they took buses for the three-hour ride with motorcycle escort through Yalta to Nizhnaya Oreanda. The sanatorium in which the conference took place stood on a hill overlooking the Black Sea. Peacocks strolled around the grounds, which were covered with spring flowers.

Cousins found this second conference somewhat more formal than the first, but he said that whereas in Hanover the two groups sat facing each other across the table, in the Crimea Americans and Soviets sat interspersed. This would have been by design of the organizers, who placed name cards at each place at the long rectangular table, covered in green, around which the delegates sat for the formal sessions.[63] Erwin Griswold noted that outside those sessions, at meals, for example, the two delegations mingled. They may not have done so with complete ease and freedom, but the spirit of this was caught by the humorous suggestion made at the end of the first day—unanimously agreed upon, according to the rapporteur's notes—that the conference "withhold nourishment from tables at which are seated only Soviets or Americans."[64]

Spouses were invited to attend the conference and to stay for the week following. As Bobrysheva notes, this was also a sign of the importance the Soviet authorities gave to the conference. Ordinarily only heads of state or leaders of communist parties were invited to bring their spouses.[65]

Bobrysheva describes many of the events that took place between sessions of the conference in almost idyllic terms. There was a boat trip from Yalta to Sevastopol and back, a visit to the youth camp Artek, and another to the Massandra wine collection. Film director Sergei Gerasimov directed Bobrysheva and other women along for the conference—American, Soviet, and Ukrainian—in cooking Siberian *pelmeni*. Bobrysheva leaves an impression of relaxed good feeling that stands in contrast to the tone of the conference's discussions.[66]

Griswold, writing during the conference, made a similar contrast. The Russians were frank, but they "all [hewed] close to the communist line," which he described as self-serving and hypocritical. Yet "the Russians there couldn't have been personally nicer to us, and there was a great deal of friendship and bonhomie."[67] An indication of the impact of the Americans on the Soviets was given in a letter from Academician I. I. Artobolevsky to Mosely in September. He wrote,

> I was very pleased to meet with outstanding American leaders in your intellectual life and to have the opportunity of carrying on numerous friendly talks with them. I was deeply impressed by their profound knowledge, their straightforwardness and frankness in stating their views, and by their great spirit of humanism toward all mankind, with which their comments were imbued. It was also a special pleasure to me to find that my American friends are gay and lively people who love and appreciate a sense of humor, and that, like us, they love art, music, and all beautiful things given to us by life.[68]

The agenda was longer than it had been at the first conference but covered much the same ground.[69] The discussion on the first day addressed the role of the citizen in international relations. It touched on American public opinion and the role of free speech in American society. This raised a theme that would be heard many times at the Dartmouth conferences. It is well to remember that the Soviet participants came from a society in which the party and the government had their hand in all aspects of public life. For many, it was literally inconceivable that markets, newspapers, or public opinion could operate without some real, if hidden, hand, guided by a cabal of capitalists. Not all the Soviet participants in Dartmouth had such a distorted picture of American society, but among their compatriots, even among senior policymakers, such a view was not uncommon.

Consequently, the idea that statements of journalists, politicians, or ordinary citizens appearing in the American media that decried

Soviet policies could reflect honest concerns rather than the attitudes of anti-Soviet circles of the ruling elite was foreign to the Soviet participants in Dartmouth. To them, it seemed that if the American government wanted to coexist peacefully with the Soviet Union, it could simply ban anti-Soviet statements. In their view, as the Soviet propaganda machine could exercise such control, surely the American machine could do the same. Indeed, Soviet participants tried to get the Americans to agree that the United States should pass a law that outlawed propaganda for war.

The second day opened with Doty's statement on the question of disarmament. He focused on the obstacles, listing three: Soviet support for conflicts in the Third World, the secrecy of the Soviet system, and the absence of agreement on a plan to ensure verification of any disarmament agreement. This list of obstacles, though presented in "a cool, dispassionate" manner, according to another American participant, struck at Soviet sensitivities. The Soviet participants responded defensively. Discussion on this issue, which continued through the day, became sharp.

An exchange between Senator Benton and Korneichuk illustrates the tone and shows how frank the discussions became. Benton gave a list of reasons why "the West suspects the Soviet disarmament proposals [to be] merely clever political propaganda." The day's discussions, according to Griswold's notes, then concluded after this exchange:

> *Korneichuk:* "I am much saddened to see that you call our plan . . . perfidious or clever. To repeat such words at our meetings is not conducive to the success of our meeting."
> *Benton:* "I didn't use the word perfidious. I said clever propaganda."[70]

Sharp discussions were not exceptional during the early conferences. As Klebnikov said later:

> It was extremely polemical. We looked at each other as dogs and cats, as aliens, as somebody who's come from the planet Mars and landed on earth and vice versa. There [were] a lot of . . . misunderstandings of course. Words don't have the same meaning and so on.[71]

In regard to Doty's first obstacle, the Americans saw an inconsistency between what the Soviets felt they could do to prevent a nuclear exchange and their willingness to support "wars of national liberation" in the Third World. In the mid- to late 1970s, détente began to founder as the American public came to see a similar inconsistency in Soviet policy.

Much of the disagreement over disarmament stemmed from the argument over whether disarmament had to precede a more general peace or follow it. This argument had plagued arms control negotiations for several years. The Soviets were unanimous in their support of general disarmament.[72] But the argument also found some support on the American side. Indeed, at the place of each participant at the opening session was a copy of a message to the conference from Grenville Clark that applauded Korneichuk for describing general disarmament as the "main and compelling task of our time."[73] The counterargument, made by Sohn, Clark's collaborator on the book *World Peace through World Law,* was that it was unrealistic to seek complete disarmament except as a long-term goal.[74] In this view, the arms control approach, as it was called at the time, which sought to address disarmament one step at a time, was more practical.

Most of the conference was spent discussing disarmament and the possibility of a test ban. The other topics on the agenda—the rule of law, aid to Third World development, the prospects for the improvement of relations, and the "education of the coming generation" received less attention. In contrast to the hostile attitudes toward American society that were often shown, a Soviet economist—probably Modest Rubenstein—caught the Americans by surprise by saying that the American economy was both resilient and not dependent on military spending. Writing a few weeks later, Cousins cited several instances in which the minds of the participants seemed to meet.[75] One American, he wrote, "spoke simply and eloquently about the primary place that a good society must accord the creative life of the mind, and of the need to keep material things from obscuring the importance of good books, music, art." This made an impression on several Soviet participants, who said privately at dinner that night that they had been moved by the statement. A statement by Marian Anderson at a folk festival one evening had a similar effect on her audience, which included the entire conference group. It is significant that these two instances of harmony and the idyllic events recounted by Bobrysheva took place outside the formal sessions of the conference.

Indeed, over the next thirty years, what took place informally at the conferences, outside the formal sessions, would prove to be an essential element of Dartmouth. Philip Stewart even called this the "real mechanism of the Dartmouth process." Whereas formal statements and discussions were bound by the constructs of Soviet politics in particular—but American politics as well—the informal parts came to create a "free space" in the minds of the participants. This space was gradually introduced into the conference itself. By the 1980s problems placed on the table at the formal sessions could be approached from this "free space," that is, with the politics of the two countries set aside. Real give-and-take on the issues could then occur in a way that was impossible in the formal sessions of the early conferences.[76]

During the discussions the participants developed a list of possible cooperative projects. The idea of a jointly produced movie was made real more than a decade later.[77] A proposed exploration of law for outer space prefigured treaties signed as a part of détente. Joint medical research on heart disease and cancer was also proposed. A historical commission "to clear up commonly perpetuated errors" and a proposal to divert a tenth of the cost of armaments to the developing world reflected more the temper of the conference than the reality of politics in Moscow and Washington (it was also a proposal made by the Soviets at the United Nations at about the same time).

Cousins drew several lessons from the discussions at Dartmouth II. In sum, he found the Soviets strikingly confident about their system. At the same time, he found them unexpectedly likely to respond to the needs of national interest and prestige rather than to the requirements of ideology.

Lessons that the Soviets drew had more immediate application to the U.S.-Soviet relationship. The newly opened Soviet archives show that reports about the Crimean conference found their way to the highest circles of the Soviet leadership.[78] The Soviets needed to find out what they could about the attitudes of President Kennedy, as the summit meeting between Khrushchev and Kennedy at Vienna was only weeks away. According to a report given to Khrushchev himself, Cousins told one of his Soviet interlocutors that the president's advisors were split, with hard-liners in the Pentagon and the CIA bent on opposing an improvement in U.S.-Soviet relations, even to the point of manufacturing provocations (as the advisors saw them) such as the Bay of Pigs invasion and the U-2 spy-plane incident.

Another report came from KGB sources at the Crimean conference. It would have been surprising indeed if the KGB had not had at least one of its men with the delegation. In this report the head of the KGB, Aleksandr Shelepin, told Vasili Kuznetsov, deputy minister of foreign affairs, about a conversation his source had had with Robert Bowie, the former chief of the State Department's Policy Planning Staff; Paul Doty, who was a member of the President's Science Advisory Council; and Shepard Stone, director of international programs at the Ford Foundation and a participant both at Hanover and in the Crimea. The Americans said that they had spoken to Walt Rostow and McGeorge Bundy, the national security advisor, before leaving for the Crimea. Rostow and Bundy had told the three that Kennedy wanted to use the summit both to learn where Khrushchev stood on fundamental issues and to bolster his faltering position with the U.S. public by establishing a personal relationship with the Soviet leader. At the summit itself Khrushchev was truculent, perhaps in part because of the perception gained from this report that Kennedy needed a good relationship with Khrushchev more than Khrushchev needed one with Kennedy.

Griswold reports an incident that suggests that a part of the KGB was disappointed in the results of the conference.[79] He left the conference early, on the morning of the last day, along with Doty, Marian Anderson, and Lloyd Reynolds, an economist from Yale. The next day he had lunch with Mikhail Kotov, two professors from the Moscow Institute of Law, and a Mr. Davidov, for whom Griswold gives no affiliation. Davidov worried Griswold. Before lunch, he took Griswold into the dining room, alone, and presented him with his passport (Griswold had probably given it up at the hotel, which was the standard procedure for visitors to the Soviet Union). This suggests that Davidov's true affiliation was with the KGB.

During the discussions with Kotov and the others, Griswold says, Davidov "questioned me quite sharply about the Oreanda Conference, and why we hadn't reached an agreement." At the conference, the Soviet participants had made suggestions about what to put in the final communiqué. The Americans, wanting to avoid having these conferences become tools of Soviet propaganda, ignored most of them.[80] As a consequence, the communiqué that resulted from Dartmouth II, like most of the statements for the conferences that followed, was a bland description of who took part and what topics were discussed, with expressions of hope for the improvement of relations. The Americans avoided saying that conclusions were reached that would further the Soviet propaganda line, but there can be little doubt that there was pressure on the Soviet side to have the conferences do precisely that. Davidov's disappointment is an indication of the interest that Soviet officialdom had in such an outcome, which would, after all, have made this transnational meeting useful to Soviet foreign policy.

Like Griswold, Senator Benton left the conference early, but he had a different experience in the day or two he spent in Moscow before going on to London. Yuri Zhukov, who had been the foreign editor of *Pravda* in the 1950s but was now "minister in charge of all foreign cultural exchanges," spoke with Benton for two hours, hoping, Benton thought, that the senator would pass along some of his ideas to Chester Bowles, undersecretary of state, and Edward R. Murrow, the eminent journalist who then headed the United States Information Agency. Benton did so, writing letters to both of them in his Moscow hotel.[81] The message to Murrow was about jamming broadcasts of the Voice of America (VOA). Jamming had stopped for a time before the U-2 incident, but Zhukov said that it had been resumed as the tone of the VOA broadcasts changed. He pointedly compared VOA broadcasts with broadcasts by the British and French, which were not being jammed, with the implicit suggestion that the United States might be better off if it followed the example of its allies.

Benton wrote Bowles in regard to Cuba and the forthcoming summit meeting in Vienna. Benton quoted Zhukov:

> The general situation is not so bad now. We are not using the mistakes of your government about Cuba. We are not dramatizing these or hammering these. Nor are we pushing hard in Ghana. We do not intend to use such mistakes being made by your government. We do not want to put President Kennedy in a bad position. Chairman Khrushchev immediately accepted the invitation from President Kennedy to meet with him. This was of course President Kennedy's proposal, but we do not want to feature the fact that it was his initiative. We are striving hard to develop a policy of cooperation. Naturally there will be no negotiations in the Khrushchev-Kennedy meeting. There are only two days. We understand this.[82]

Zhukov was clearly trying to explain Soviet statements to U.S. officials and suggesting that Soviet policy on the eve of the summit was moderate and cooperative. This was an example of Soviet use of a "back channel" to pass information to the U.S. government that could not be passed through more formal or open channels. It would be used during the Cuban missile crisis and become a distinguishing feature of U.S.-Soviet relations under Henry Kissinger. Several times in the coming years, the Dartmouth Conference and the people involved would become important vehicles for both countries when they found it necessary to use this kind of approach to each other.

After the conference, several of the American participants wrote about their impressions, spreading the word about the dialogue. Stuart Chase wrote an article on the conference for his local paper in Connecticut.[83] A. William Loos reported on both the Hanover and Crimea conferences to his board of directors at the Church Peace Union.[84] Mosely described the conference to State Department officials working as part of the Soviet and East European Exchanges Staff. He also wrote his senator, Thomas J. Dodd, who expressed skepticism about unofficial talks with the Soviets.[85] In addition, articles based on the press release and the press conference appeared in the *New York Times* and *Pravda*.[86]

Benton was especially active in spreading the word about the conference. In addition to writing to Bowles and Murrow, he wrote a series of three articles for the North American Newspaper Alliance. These were condensed into a single article by the *New York Times*.[87] They caused a stir among the Americans who had been at Oreanda.

The problem was that he cited a number of his Dartmouth colleagues, Soviet and American, by name, explaining their positions without having gained their permission to do so. This broke the understanding about confidentiality, which had been discussed at length before, after, and during the conference. The exchange of letters and the conversations among Mosely, Cousins, Hauge, Stone, and Benton's staff left the senator defensive and complaining, "Now I wish I had not written the articles."[88] He noted, however, that whatever the complaints from the Americans, the Soviets did not seem to mind the publicity, citing a recent telegram from Korneichuk as evidence.

This incident was important to the Dartmouth process. It firmly set narrow parameters for the citation of participants in the dialogues: they could not be cited by name; their positions at the conferences could not be publicized by other participants without their permission. This precedent did much to preserve confidentiality in future conferences, building trust among participants on both sides. It would be important in determining both the character of the conferences and their influence in the coming decades.

The participants in the Crimea agreed that a third conference should be held in six months. But it was not to be. The renewed crisis over Berlin that fall seems to have had no effect on Dartmouth, but the decisions of both countries to test nuclear weapons once again in the atmosphere forced a postponement. The new Soviet tests, which broke a two-year moratorium on nuclear testing, began in September. By American count, fifty atmospheric tests were conducted over two months. They were unprecedented in size and duration and culminated in a fifty-megaton explosion at the end of October.[89]

Cousins wrote Korneichuk and urged him to "dissuade the Soviet government from this dangerous course."[90] In an editorial in the *Saturday Review* he also expressed his long-held conviction that testing should not take place and spoke out strongly against the Soviet action, proposing a worldwide campaign of public protest. Korneichuk responded in the cold tone of a Soviet official, repeating arguments used by the Soviet government to justify the new tests.

The United States responded with underground testing in the fall. A series of forty atmospheric tests began in April. The third Dartmouth Conference, also scheduled for April, was postponed to October. As luck would have it, that same month, in the Crimea not far from Nizhnaya Oreanda, Khrushchev was struck by the idea of deploying missiles in Cuba.[91]

DARTMOUTH III: OCTOBER CRISIS

It almost seemed as if fate conspired to have the third Dartmouth conference take place in October. In the summer of 1961, Mosely and Cousins proposed to Korneichuk that the conference take place in January. But Mosely became ill and Cousins' travels kept him out of the office more than in, so that by early December the necessary arrangements had not been made. They cabled Korneichuk to explain and proposed an April conference.[92] So plans were made to hold the conference in the spring, at Airlie House near Warrenton, Virginia. But the conference was again postponed, this time at the behest of Korneichuk and his colleagues, as the conference would have coincided with the resumption of nuclear tests by the United States.[93] Mosely feared that the Soviet participants would feel compelled to issue public statements about the testing while they were on American soil. These statements would, he believed, require a response from the American participants. Such a situation could threaten to wreck the conference and, perhaps, end the dialogue.[94] Given how things turned out in October, the concern is ironic. After flirting with a September date, the two sides finally agreed to hold the conference in late October, at the Andover Inn, in Andover, Massachusetts, just north of Boston.

The Soviet participants arrived in New York on Thursday, October 18, two days after President Kennedy had been told that Soviet missiles were in place in Cuba, but several days before the news was made public. Korneichuk was unable to attend owing to ill health, so Academician Fedorov was again the chairman of the delegation. Only three of his Soviet colleagues had been at Dartmouth II in the Crimea: Rubenstein, Talensky, and the colorful and convivial Boris Polevoi, who had also been at Hanover. Among the nine new participants were two commentators from *Pravda*—Viktor Maevsky and Yuri Zhukov— and several other academics and journalists. A. D. Shveitser gained his first experience as a simultaneous interpreter at this conference, the first of many Dartmouth conferences that he attended. His Soviet colleague was Boris Belitsky, an interpreter for Radio Moscow. On the whole the delegates were younger than earlier ones had been. About half spoke English, which made communication easier. Unlike the American delegates who went to the Crimea with their wives, the Soviet delegates did not bring theirs.

After having spent Thursday in New York, the group traveled leisurely through New England to the Phillips Academy in Andover, stopping to see Yale University and Old Sturbridge Village on the way. They were accompanied by Mosely. In the meantime, in Washington President Kennedy had begun to meet frequently with his close advisors.

The press was trying to guess why. The conference opened on Sunday, October 21. Cousins was in the American delegation again, as were Mosely, Margaret Mead, Doty, Larson, and three other participants. Also present once again were the two interpreters Sherry and Klebnikov, and Mary K. Harvey, Cousins' close associate from the *Saturday Review.* She acted as secretary to this conference as she had for the two before. New participants included John Oakes, editor of the editorial page of the *New York Times;* Robert B. Meyner, who had been governor of New Jersey until earlier that year; and Thomas Coughran, executive vice president of Bank of America (International). While not formally a participant, David Rockefeller came to Andover to attend the final session, his first time at Dartmouth.

The conference met in the "paneled" Trustee's Room on the third floor of George Washington Hall at Andover Academy, the prestigious New England prep school that numbers both Presidents Bush, *père et fils,* among its alumni. The agenda, agreed to in March, was shorter than the agendas for the two previous conferences, but it contained the same basic issues: the United Nations and international law, arms control, aid to the Third World, and bilateral exchanges. Surprisingly, the discussions followed this agenda despite the pressure of events.

The conference went as planned on Sunday and through the day on Monday, with the discussion centered on the first item on the agenda, the United Nations. Outside the conference, tension rose as the press continued to note and speculate about the increased activity in Washington. Participants would have seen that morning's headline of the *New York Times:* "Capitol Crisis Air Hints at Development on Cuba; Kennedy TV Talk Is Likely." At the end of the morning session, Cousins observed, "It was clear from the course of the discussion the Soviet speakers were concerned about one question above all, the situation in Cuba."[95] About noon, Cousins announced that the president would speak that evening. A television set and equipment for interpretation were installed in the hall during the afternoon. The scene was set for Monday evening, October 22, the most dramatic in Dartmouth's history.

That night during dinner the participants watched President Kennedy announce to the nation that Cuba was being "quarantined"—blockaded—to force the evacuation of the Soviet missiles then being installed and to prevent the delivery of additional missiles that were on their way. He said that he was willing to risk a war "in which even the fruits of victory would be ashes in our mouth." The mood of the participants reflected that of the country. They were tense, troubled, and concerned.

Seeking a place free from hidden microphones, the Soviets withdrew to the courtyard of the school to discuss the situation. The two *Pravda* commentators, Zhukov and Maevsky, spoke first. They opposed having the meeting continue. The president's speech, they said, made the atmosphere intolerable. Academician Fedorov and Grigori Shumeiko favored having the meeting continue. Shumeiko was formally a member of the editorial board of the Soviet trade unions, but in fact he was a section head of the International Department of the Central Committee. They argued that the American participants were not responsible for the president's statement and that it was precisely in a situation like this that dialogue became most important. A heated argument followed. Fedorov called Ambassador Dobrynin in Washington for instructions. Dobrynin suggested that the Soviet participants continue to take part in the conference unless the Americans ended it.[96]

The ambassador must have left Fedorov with a great deal of discretion, for when the group reconvened, Fedorov said, in Cousins' account: "Gentlemen, we are in your hands." Following some discussion, Cousins said that he thought Fedorov was asking a direct question: "Did the Americans wish to continue?"[97] His compatriots thereupon raised their hands unanimously, without abstention, voting to continue the conference. In reply, the Soviets did the same. A debate on the crisis began that evening with Fedorov's defense of the Soviet action. It continued when the conference reconvened the next day. Over the next few days, the American participants monitored the breaking news on their transistor radios. At times, the sessions broke up as everyone ran out to catch special announcements on television.

On Tuesday, as the Soviet military was placed on alert and the Cuban military was mobilized, the Dartmouth discussions continued. The dialogue was sharp, vigorous, and full of disagreement as both sides stood behind the positions of their governments. Divided by the interests at stake in the Caribbean, they, like their governments, were nonetheless joined by the need to avoid a holocaust. Disagreements about the crisis and other topics on the agenda grew then and during the week. But so did the rapport among the participants. This was a basic quality of the Dartmouth conferences that followed, a quality essential to the success of the dialogues. As Cousins put it in his description of the Andover conference: "[T]here was no awkwardness or strain in raising any question, however severe, or in venturing any response, however pointed. It was possible to be forthright without being caustic, impassioned without being abusive, severe without being cutting. You could disagree and still retain your respect for the person you were disagreeing with."[98] This "spirit of Dartmouth" was forged in that paneled room by the heat of the Cuban missile crisis.

Much of the discussion focused on arms control and disarmament, as it had in the Crimea, with the difference that the situation in Cuba made the issue more immediate. As before, both sides were forthright in their criticism of each other. Curiously, the Soviet participants insisted that the Soviets sold the missiles to Cuba rather than retained them as their own, despite the implications, as Doty pointed out, that this had for the proliferation of nuclear weapons, which both countries wanted to avoid.

As at the Oreanda conference, participants spent a great deal of time discussing the meaning of the Soviet concept of peaceful coexistence. Mosely found this discussion more penetrating than at either of the two previous conferences. He thought that the Soviets left with a better understanding of why the concept disturbed Americans.[99]

Another discussion was about national goals. Fedorov and other Soviet participants asked why there was no single statement of American national goals to match what was contained in the recently approved Party Program. According to Mosely, "The American participants gave a lively and varied presentation of the primary role of individuals and of voluntary organizations and groupings of all kinds." The Soviet members, he concluded, "were intensely interested and seemed to gain a much better perspective on American society and ways of thinking, and a number of them spoke with special appreciation of this session."[100]

Given the gravity of the situation, it is not surprising that efforts were made to issue a joint statement. Cousins was the first to suggest that one be made, during the morning session on Wednesday. He proposed that the conference recommend a ten-day moratorium on action and that the General Assembly of the United Nations appoint a commission "to undertake an immediate examination of all facts" and recommend approaches to the settlement of the crisis.[101] Fedorov postponed discussion of Cousins' proposal at that session and the following one. After a meeting of the cochairmen that night, Cousins withdrew his proposal. The Soviets, however, having had a chance to meet, put one of their own on the table the next day. This was for a statement that urged a meeting between Khrushchev and Kennedy. By Friday night, however, it was clear that the two sides would be unable to agree on recommendations to make. The participants, therefore, held to the Dartmouth tradition that the conversations remain off the record and that no position be taken.[102]

On Wednesday, Father Felix P. Morlion, president of Pro Deo University in Rome, appeared at the conference. He had been in contact with Cousins in New York since the previous March and had asked for an opportunity to speak to the Soviets at the Dartmouth Conference. Arriving at the height of the Cuban missile crisis, he asked whether intervention by Pope John XXIII might be useful. Encouraged by both delegations, he called the Vatican. Hours later, he received word that the pope would like to propose that both the Soviet ships carrying weapons and the American blockade be withdrawn. But he would make the proposal only if both sides found it acceptable.

Both the Americans and the Soviets contacted their governments. Cousins spoke to Theodore Sorenson at the White House, who returned the call after speaking to President Kennedy. The president welcomed a papal appeal, Sorenson said, but thought the suggested proposal avoided the main issue, the missiles installed in Cuba. The leaders of the Soviet delegation called Moscow and reported back that Premier Khrushchev found the proposal acceptable. An appeal from Pope John for moral responsibility in the crisis was issued over Vatican radio at noon the next day, with no reference to the blockade or the ships.[103]

Father Morlion also discussed with the Soviet participants the possibility of further contacts between the Vatican and Moscow, suggesting that Cousins could be used as an intermediary to begin the exchange.[104] After the conference, in late November, Ambassador Dobrynin called Cousins to say that the Soviet authorities had approved the project proposed by Father Morlion and set a date for Cousins to visit Khrushchev on behalf of the pope. Cousins became an intermediary between Kennedy, the pope, and Khrushchev, which gave him and Dartmouth a small but significant part in the achievement of the Limited Nuclear Test Ban Treaty, a role that will be described at the end of this chapter.

Some discussion centered around a statement contributed by Grenville Clark on disarmament and "supranational peacekeeping."[105] This was his last contribution to Dartmouth.

The participants also took time to visit places of interest around Boston, such as Bunker Hill. At Harvard they were able to speak with students and faculty, an opportunity the Soviets used to gauge public opinion.[106] While this meeting took place, Zhukov and Maevsky stayed at Andover to write a long piece on the crisis for *Pravda*. When published, this article caused some concern among the Americans—it said that no Americans believed that Soviet missiles had really been installed in Cuba, a clear misrepresentation of the views of the Americans at the conference. Cousins confronted Zhukov and asked him to write a letter clarifying this to the *New York Times*. Zhukov refused.

After the conference, the Soviet delegates returned to New York by bus, stopping at Cousins' house in New Canaan, Connecticut, on the way. It was there that they heard the radio announcement of Khrushchev's agreement to remove the missiles from Cuba.[107] The delegates spent a few more days in the United States, attending meetings in New York and Washington. They flew home in the first few days of November.

When they returned to Moscow, the entire Soviet delegation appeared before the staff of the Central Committee's International Department. According to Shveitser, some of the participants who had told the Americans of their friendship now spoke about how unimportant those same Americans—those "pacifist intellectuals"—were and tried to impress the party functionaries with their vigilance toward their adversaries. As was clear after the Hanover conference, the tone of the Dartmouth Conference could not always be sustained after participants returned home. This was sometimes true for Americans, but it was doubly hard for the Soviets, who could deviate from the party line only at a significant personal cost.

Some hope was expressed after the third conference that a fourth conference would be held, but no dates were set or plans made. Two years passed before Dartmouth IV was held.

DARTMOUTH IV: DISCUSSIONS IN LENINGRAD

The next Dartmouth conference was held in Leningrad in July 1964. It is not clear from the documents available why the conference was delayed, but undoubtedly Philip Mosely's return to academia in September 1963 was important. Dartmouth had no institutional affiliation at this time on the American side—the Kettering Foundation would give it one later—and so the organization of the American part of the conference fell on the shoulders of a few individuals—primarily Cousins, Mosely, and Mary K. Harvey.

Mosely returned to Columbia University to head the European Institute and to serve as associate dean of the School of International Affairs. As he makes clear in his letters, he had less time for Dartmouth, having accrued a number of obligations he had to discharge, including writing a book.[108] He found that he had no time either to attend the fourth conference or to help organize it.[109] The latter duty fell to Larson and the newcomer Marshall Shulman, who was later an advisor to President Carter and head of the Harriman Institute at Columbia University.

Larson and Shulman made the necessary arrangements for the conference during a trip to Moscow in May and June 1964. Cousins helped with the arrangements as well. In early July, shortly before leaving for the Soviet Union, he flew to Washington to meet with McGeorge Bundy, President Johnson's special assistant for national security affairs. Bundy asked Cousins to transmit some points to the Soviets with the goal of keeping them out of the 1964 elections.[110]

Only three American participants returned to the conference—Cousins, Larson, and Stone, although Mary K. Harvey and the two interpreters Sherry and Klebnikov returned as well. The other thirteen Americans were new to Dartmouth. They included John Kenneth Galbraith, the prominent Harvard economist and former ambassador to India; Buckminster Fuller; Franklin Long, a chemist at Cornell, a

former assistant director for science and technology of the Arms
Control and Disarmament Agency, and a member of the President's
Science Advisory Committee; James Michener, the novelist; and Paul
Dudley White, an eminent cardiologist who had treated President
Eisenhower following his heart attack in 1955 (he also numbered
Grenville Clark among his patients). Norton Simon, owner of the
company that published Cousins' *Saturday Review*, also took part.
Cousins described Simon as "soft-spoken, reflective. . . . He followed
world affairs closely and had a deep concern about the response of the
individual to the stresses of his society."[111] Marshall Shulman took
Mosely's place as the conference's expert on the Soviet Union.[112]

The incident—Shulman, though he was highly regarded by Mosely, was the second choice. The first, suggested by Senator Benton, was Loy Henderson, one of the most senior Soviet specialists in the Foreign Service,
a peer of Kennan's. He had helped open the embassy in Moscow after
the United States reestablished relations with the Soviet Union in 1933,
serving as first secretary. He had just retired in January 1961.[113] Benton
discussed the suggestion with Undersecretary of State Bowles. Bowles
suggested to Benton that Henderson would not be right for the conference but that Shulman might be a good substitute. Henderson wrote
Benton to concur with Bowles, saying that

> [t]he Russians consider me as one of the most dangerous American
> undercover agents. I doubt whether they would give me a visa. Even
> if they did, my presence would place any group under a cloud.[114]

The incident suggests that the relationship between the Dartmouth
Conference and the U.S. government at the time was informally, unself-
consciously close. This was not regarded as unusual or inappropriate in the
era before Vietnam and Watergate. Those who took part in Dartmouth
were comfortable with officials; officials trusted those who took part in
Dartmouth. They knew one another and had access to one another, informally as well as through official channels. This was an important source of
Dartmouth's influence.

David Rockefeller also took part in the Dartmouth Conference
for the first time as more than a visitor. Cousins, who knew Rockefeller
both socially and as the banker for *Saturday Review*, was looking for a
prominent businessman to take part in Dartmouth. Philip Mosely had

known him as a vice president of the Council on Foreign Relations. A regular participant in Dartmouth through the middle of the 1980s, he may have been the most prominent American to take part in the conference, not least in Soviet eyes.[115]

At the time of the fourth Dartmouth Conference, the youngest of the six children of John D. Rockefeller, Jr., the son of the founder of the dynasty, was forty-nine years old.[116] He had been president of the Chase Manhattan Bank for four years, after having worked his way up through the organization. As that suggests, he considered himself born into responsibility as well as privilege. He was unfailingly polite, with the demeanor of a kind uncle. But his bland avuncular disposition rode on top of a disciplined, meticulous character. As he once told a son: "Whatever you do, do it hard enough to enjoy it, the important thing is to work and work hard."[117] He had seemingly limitless reserves of energy that allowed him to operate nonstop for sixteen hours a day. His energy and intellect led a president of Harvard to say, "I sometimes think he's got electricity in his head."[118] He was dedicated to his work at Chase, with a special interest in the international side of the bank's operations. But his interests ranged far and wide, from the work of Dartmouth to the development of New York City to modern art to collecting rare beetles.

Mosely invited Rockefeller to take part in the Crimea conference, but he declined.[119] He did, however, attend several sessions of the conference at Andover and was pleased at the result. In the spring of 1964 he asked two aides for their impressions of the conference then being organized and their advice on whether to attend. With little enthusiasm, they wrote that they saw "no reason for you not to go."[120] Nonetheless, to Cousins' surprise, he agreed to participate. He soon became a mainstay of the conference.

Almost half of the twenty-five Soviet participants had taken part in earlier Dartmouth conferences. These included Polevoi, Talensky, Gerasimov, Alla Masevich, and the two chairmen, Korneichuk and Fedorov. The twelve new participants included Nikolai Blokhin, president of the USSR Medical Academy and president of the Institute for Soviet-American Relations; Anna Boykova, deputy mayor of Leningrad; Aleksei Treshnikov, who, like Fedorov, was a polar explorer; Daniel Kraminov, editor in chief of the journal *Za rubezhom,* secretary of the Union of Soviet Journalists, and a former journalist for *Pravda;* Boris Konstantinov, president of the Physics Mathematics Institute in Leningrad, who, like Alla Masevich, was a physicist; and a historian, Isaak Mintz.

The discussions opened on Sunday, July 26, with disarmament as the topic. The signing of the Limited Nuclear Test Ban Treaty the previous August had raised hopes for movement on disarmament, and the discussion reflected that optimism, at least to a degree. The Soviet participants seemed more willing than they had been before to suggest compromises. The first such compromise was proposed by Talensky in the first session.[121] He suggested lengthening the first period of the Soviet plan for complete disarmament to three years. In retrospect—and to many of the Americans at the time—this hardly seems realistic; it is significant solely because such Soviet proposals had not been forthcoming before. Talensky, who had been noticeably liberal in the previous two conferences, also discussed the so-called nuclear umbrella, later called minimum deterrence. His description is memorable, particularly as it came at a time when the weapons buildup was continuing on both sides:

> All sorts of figures have been named as the minimum of weapons to be kept on both sides, down to just two bombs: one under the White House with the button in the Kremlin, and one the other way around.

Other proposals were made on arms control and on greater cooperation in cultural exchanges.

Another important topic of discussion in the first few sessions was the Multilateral Force (MLF) then being discussed by NATO countries. This was to be a nuclear force, probably on ship or submarine, with weapons supplied by the United States but with personnel from the NATO countries. The primary advocate of the MLF was West Germany. And West German participation was the major problem the Soviets had with the concept. Several of them expressed the fear that the Soviet Union had of a revived and revanchist Germany. Having suffered terribly at German hands during World War II, the Soviets saw the MLF as a way of giving their former enemy access to the ultimate weapon, aimed clearly at them. Some Americans objected to this characterization of the Germans. Cousins, however, responding to Talensky, who was less concerned about a Germany armed independently than about one armed through the MLF, argued that an independent Germany could provoke a general war.

The question of a Chinese bomb came up during this discussion. The attitude of the United States to China was in some ways like the attitude of the Soviet Union to West Germany: the country in question was regarded as a less rational partner of the other side, seeking to acquire a nuclear capability. Neither the Americans nor the Soviets at the conference could know that China was only weeks away from exploding its first atomic bomb.

Mark Mitin raised the issue, discussed in the Crimea, of the publication of American books like those by Herman Kahn. The bald editor of *Voprosi filosofii* found these "hair-raising" in what he regarded as their justification for nuclear war. In response, Cousins gave a spirited defense of free speech and the need for a multiplicity of views. This issue, raised before and raised here, would be raised again.

The Soviets, particularly Blokhin and Gerasimov, asked why so few Soviet authors were published and so few Soviet films shown in the United States. Fedorov noted that the Soviet authors who were published included the likes of Pasternak and Solzhenitsyn, who, he argued, were published because of "the sensation-quotient" of their works.[122] The Americans raised the parallel issue of the openness of Soviet society. Cousins and Franklin Long asked why the *New York Times* was not sold in Leningrad. Both sides argued that if each society were to have an accurate understanding of the other, the exchange of information and scholarly exchanges like those that were then taking place were essential. Problems with the exchanges at the time—their small size, the rejection of good scholars (including Shulman) for bureaucratic and political reasons—were also discussed in this context.

The problem of the information each side had of the other was regarded as important enough that proposals were made for a subcommittee to meet on the topic after the conference in Europe or elsewhere, or even for devoting the next conference entirely to the topic. Fedorov invited a portion of the American delegation to spend an extra few days in Moscow to discuss the issue.

Another question raised before and here was whether there should be a formal American organization to organize the Dartmouth

Conference and similar exchanges. Dr. Blokhin raised it in Leningrad. His organization, the Institute for Soviet-American Relations, had been formed three years before. It was one of the "Friendship Societies" established by the Soviets, ostensibly as nongovernmental citizens' organizations, to further the goals of Soviet foreign policy. Based in the Dom druzhbi—the House of Friendship—in Moscow, it was to be the Soviet half of a Soviet-American Friendship Society. It ran "nonofficial" exchanges, that is, exchanges conducted outside the official framework established by the 1958 U.S.-USSR governmental agreement.[123] According to a letter from the State Department to Cousins, the institute had tried to gain respectability by injecting itself into the officially sponsored exchanges that the Cultural Exchange Agreement of 1958 had provided for.[124] Blokhin's proposal at the Leningrad conference was preceded by an exchange between Tamara Yu. Mamedova, secretary general of the Institute for Soviet-American Relations, and Mosely, who had politely rebuffed the suggestion that an American counterpart organization be established. As Mosely rebuffed her, so Cousins rebuffed Blokhin, saying that the perceived political purposes of the institute roused suspicion. Other Americans, however, notably Galbraith and Charles Frankel, thought that it might be a good idea to form an American organization to assist the exchanges.

The Dartmouth conferences were always seen by Soviet institutions as opportunities for propagandistic advantage, reflecting the efforts of the Soviet Union since 1918 to use transnational organizations to further Soviet interests. The effort by Blokhin, Mamedova, and the Institute for Soviet-American Relations provides merely one example. But the determination of Cousins, Mosely, and colleagues both Soviet and American to minimize publicity and to issue public statements that were merely summaries of who attended and what was discussed helped keep the conferences useful and helped them retain their reputation among the policymakers with whom the participants conferred.

The leaders of the two delegations met at lunch on Friday, July 31. They agreed that a small group would meet in Moscow the following Monday to continue discussing the problems with the exchanges and to plan future activity of the Dartmouth Conference. They also suggested that three working groups be established. This suggestion can be regarded as foreshadowing the Dartmouth task forces that were set up in the 1980s. These groups would correspond rather than meet, unless a meeting before the next conference was deemed necessary. The topics they would address were trade, scholarly and other cultural exchanges, and information, by which was meant the media, books, magazines, and films.[125] These plans never became reality, however.

As at previous conferences, a number of events took place outside the formal meetings. The Americans were moved by a trip to Piskariovskoye Memorial Cemetery, where hundreds of thousands of the dead from the siege of Leningrad during World War II lie buried.[126] On Friday evening Buckminster Fuller and Fedorov spoke to the group on "glimpses of the future."[127]

In *The Critical Path,* Fuller describes the atmosphere of the conference outside the formal sessions:

> We all lived at the same hotel. The dining room had only four-place tables. As you entered, you chose quickly with which of the Russians you wished to sit. They were the first to reach the dining room. You tried to sit successively with each of the U.S.S.R. team members. The moment you sat down with a Russian, an interpreter moved in with you. . . .
>
> Our meetings consisted of (A) those lasting all day, every day, at which all the officially-to-be-considered points were discussed; and (B) the very small individual dining room and other casual meetings at dinner parties and receptions. At the latter it seemed as though all points of contention could be coped with in a manner satisfactory to all sides. At the formal all-day meetings, however, everyone seemed so intractable that nothing could be resolved.[128]

The longest excursion of the group began on Tuesday evening and went through Wednesday, when they cruised up the Neva River to Lake Ladoga toward the Valaam Monastery. The American group met informally to discuss problems with the official exchanges. Galbraith later wrote about a conversation he had on this trip with "an articulate and charming woman scholar from one of the Soviet institutes." She argued that Soviet citizens read their newspapers in greater depth than Americans, looking for nuances of meaning in what was said and what was not.[129] Unfortunately, the group never made it to Valaam. Korneichuk learned from the radio that afternoon that his wife had died. The boat returned to Leningrad, where

"Korneichuk in dark eyeglasses was the first to go down the gang-plank."[130] He left for Kiev. Fedorov took his place as chairman.

David Rockefeller was not along on the trip to the monastery. In the middle of the conference, on Tuesday, July 28, Rockefeller received word from Moscow that Khrushchev wanted to see him Wednesday afternoon.[131] That night he and his daughter Neva took the train to Moscow, arriving the next morning. He spent the morning talking business with A. A. Pskonov, the chairman of the State Bank; M. N. Sveshnikov, the chairman of the Bank for Foreign Trade; and E. Pekola, the minister of finance.[132] His conversation with Khrushchev lasted two and a half hours. Rockefeller called it "the most intensive conversation I've ever had with anyone."[133] While Neva took notes, they discussed trade between the United States and the Soviet Union, Soviet policy in Cuba, and the increasingly serious situation in South Vietnam. Rockefeller described the Dartmouth meetings as having gone "extremely well."[134] He also passed along the message that McGeorge Bundy had asked Cousins to give Khrushchev, "that it is important for the Chairman to keep out of the election."[135] According to Bundy, writing after he had read Neva's notes of the meeting, "Khrushchev indicated to Rockefeller that he understood the point and would behave himself." Bundy made the point that Rockefeller "did not bring the White House into his comment."[136]

Rockefeller briefed the new U.S. ambassador, Foy Kohler, in Moscow about what Khrushchev had said. On his return to the United States, Rockefeller sent President Johnson and the State Department copies of Neva's notes. Having requested an opportunity to discuss the meeting with Khrushchev, he met with Johnson on September 11.[137] Bundy wrote the president that the most interesting part of the discussion between Rockefeller and the president was on trade and the need for a settlement of the debt left over from lend-lease during World War II. Khrushchev expressed interest in trade, Bundy told the president, but said that a settlement could be made only if long-term credits were extended to the Soviet Union, as had been extended to other American allies: "From this and other evidence I conclude that Nikita simply does not understand the politics of East-West trade."[138] Bundy then suggested that Johnson ask Rockefeller whether he should write a note to Khrushchev telling him that the president heard from Rockefeller about the conversation. As Bundy put it, "This is exactly the sort of thing which created a sense of personal communication between Khrushchev and Kennedy, and I believe that such a sense of communication can be useful to us as time goes on." But no such communication took place.

After the conference, as the leaders had agreed at their lunchtime meeting on Friday, several of them went to Moscow. Activities there included a lunch for Galbraith and Rockefeller given by Foy Kohler and attended by a number of prominent Soviets. Rockefeller was also treated to a hydrofoil ride on the Moscow River with Vladimir Suslov, UN undersecretary for political and security affairs.

Cousins was miserable the last few days. He was exhausted, assaulted by the noise and fumes of diesel trucks, and, finally, frustrated as his driver became lost trying to find Fedorov's dacha outside the city on the night before the Americans left. Weakened by those experiences, he was struck by the full exhaust of a jet at the airport the next day. The cumulative result, he believed, was a disease that brought him close to death after he returned to the United States.[139]

DARTMOUTH, COUSINS, AND THE LIMITED NUCLEAR TEST BAN TREATY

Before this chapter on the early years of Dartmouth concludes, it will take a look at the contribution Dartmouth and Cousins made to the Limited Nuclear Test Ban Treaty. Most of their contribution happened outside the framework of the conferences themselves, between Dartmouth III and Dartmouth IV. This agreement, signed in 1963, was the first significant arms control agreement reached between the United States and the Soviet Union. The role Dartmouth played in this agreement was small but significant, and it speaks to the kind of influence that the Dartmouth conferences had on the U.S.-Soviet relationship during the Cold War.

The negotiation of a test ban began with the meeting of scientists and officials in Geneva in 1958 mentioned earlier. Much progress was made, but after 1960 the talks were stuck on the question of how to verify whether tests had been conducted underground. The technology of the time made it easy to detect tests conducted in the air, under the sea, or in space. The seismometers used to detect underground tests, on the other hand, could easily confuse the blasts from the tests with earthquakes. The Soviets were reluctant to allow foreigners to come into the Soviet Union to determine whether seismometer readings reflected earthquakes or nuclear explosions. The United States argued that such on-site inspections were necessary.

By late 1962 the Soviets had conceded that some inspections could be made, but disagreement remained over how many were to be allowed. There were two sources of the disagreement. One came from a conversation between a Soviet official and Arthur Dean, the chief U.S. negotiator at the test ban talks. The other was a conversation that took place in Washington in November, after Dartmouth III, when Academician Fedorov, chairman of the Soviet delegation, traveled to Washington for a few days of talks. This was not Fedorov's first opportunity to speak to American officials. He had, after all, been head of the Soviet delegation to the 1958 Conference of Experts. Nonetheless, Dartmouth provided him with an opportunity to hold these discussions in Washington. This was a small contribution but an important one.

Among those he spoke to was Jerome Weisner, special assistant for science and technology to President Kennedy. Weisner suggested that Khrushchev propose two or three inspections per year to President Kennedy as a negotiating ploy that would result in the two sides splitting the difference between their proposed number of inspections—the United States favored eight to ten—to reach an agreement for five or six inspections. But Fedorov misunderstood Weisner and thought that the latter had said that the United States would accept a proposal of three.[140] This helped confirm what Ambassador Dean had told his interlocutor, Deputy Foreign Minister Kuznetsov. Khrushchev wrote Kennedy in December, offering to accept two or three inspections each year. But Kennedy thought that number too small for Congress to accept, and talks on the matter in January came to naught, with Khrushchev, as he later told Cousins, feeling betrayed.[141]

In December Cousins traveled to Rome and Moscow to serve as an intermediary between the pope and Khrushchev, following the discussions Father Morlion had had at the Andover conference, recounted above. Feeling compelled to inform the U.S. government, Cousins spoke to Pierre Salinger, the presidential press secretary, who told Cousins that the president felt it necessary to speak to Cousins before he left for Rome and Moscow. President Kennedy told Cousins:

> I don't know if the matter of American-Soviet relations will come up. But if it does, he [Khrushchev] will probably say something about his desire to reduce tensions, but will make it appear there's no reciprocal interest by the United States. It is important that he be corrected on this score. I'm not sure Khrushchev knows this, but I don't think there's any man in American politics who's more eager than I am to put Cold War animosities behind us and get down to the hard business of building friendly relations.[142]

Bearing that message, Cousins flew off to Rome. From Rome he flew to Moscow. Two days later he spoke to Khrushchev in the Kremlin. Oleg Bykov, one of the Dartmouth participants, served as interpreter. Khrushchev said that several of the participants in the Andover conference had suggested that Cousins be invited to speak to him. It seems to have been their knowledge of Cousins, gained over the course of a week of discussion, rather than Cousins' reputation, gained over two decades of writing and activism, that gained Cousins his audience. Khrushchev addressed a number of topics for more than three hours. They included the nuclear test ban and the desire of both the United States and the Soviet Union for better relations.

Cousins' efforts on behalf of the pope had been successful, and in January Morlion proposed that Cousins return to Moscow on the pope's behalf. Cousins asked a presidential assistant whether a return visit could be useful. Secretary of State Rusk then invited Cousins to lunch. Rusk told him that he might suggest to Khrushchev that the negotiators be authorized to seek agreement on all points other than the number of inspections, with perhaps a summit meeting to follow at which Kennedy and Khrushchev could resolve that question.[143] Cousins then asked Ambassador Dobrynin to forward a request to Khrushchev for another meeting. The request was granted.

Before going to Moscow, however, Cousins met again with Kennedy. Kennedy asked Cousins to see if he could "get Premier Khrushchev to accept the fact that there had been an honest misunderstanding over the question of the number of inspections," in order to pave the way for a fresh start on the test ban issue. The president wanted the premier to know that he genuinely wanted a test ban treaty.

This was the message that Cousins took to Sochi, where he met with Khrushchev on April 12. Glenn Seaborg, who was the chairman of the Atomic Energy Commission at the time and deeply involved in the events that led to the test ban treaty, later wrote that this conversation "did more than explain history—it helped to make history."[144] In the course of the long discussion, Cousins made the points that Kennedy asked him to. By Cousins' account, it was hard to convince Khrushchev that a simple misunderstanding had occurred. Where Kennedy had thought it stemmed from a single conversation—between Arthur Dean and Kuznetsov—Khrushchev revealed that the exchange between Weisner and Fedorov had been one of two other important sources for the idea that the United States would accept three inspections. Cousins pressed him to accept the president's good faith. Khrushchev also said that he had had to spend considerable political capital to get the Council of Ministers to accept three inspections. Nonetheless, he was willing, he said, to accept Kennedy's explanation of an honest misunderstanding. He suggested they get moving toward an agreement.

Cousins saw Kennedy again when he returned to the United States. He recounted his conversations with Khrushchev and suggested that "perhaps what was needed was a breathtaking new approach toward the Russian people, calling for an end to the cold war and a fresh start in American-Russian relationships." He repeated this suggestion in a memorandum he prepared for the president the next day and in a conversation with Theodore Sorenson two weeks later.[145] Others may have made the same suggestion to Kennedy as well, but in any case, Kennedy's commencement speech at the American University on June 10 promised a new era of U.S.-Soviet relations. This changed the atmosphere in which the United States and the Soviet Union dealt with each other. Three weeks later Khrushchev indicated his willingness to accept a partial test ban treaty. A partial test ban, though less desirable to Cousins and many others than a comprehensive ban, avoided the inspection problem. In August the treaty was signed in Moscow.

It is difficult to separate the contribution of Dartmouth in making the treaty possible from that of Cousins, whose work on the test ban issue began in the mid-1950s. Nonetheless, it was Father Morlion's visit to the conference at Andover that set into motion the chain of events that led to Cousins' meetings with Khrushchev and Kennedy. And Morlion made the visit simply because the Dartmouth Conference existed. The conference had become a trusted avenue by which the Soviets could be approached. There were few conferences in the early 1960s. Over time, their continuation increased Dartmouth's influence. Finally, after gaining the confidence of Soviet participants who spoke with him across the conference table and informally, Cousins became a credible spokesman to Khrushchev. The premier himself told Cousins that it was because of the Soviet participants that Cousins was granted his first audience. In sum, Cousins' meetings happened because of Dartmouth. They gave Khrushchev and Kennedy a channel for important, indirect communications that helped create a brief thaw in the Cold War. Without them, the Limited Nuclear Test Ban Treaty, an important part of that thaw, might have been, at a minimum, delayed.

3 | The Rise and Fall of Détente, 1969–80

DARTMOUTH V: Rye, New York; January 13–18, 1969

DARTMOUTH VI: Kiev; July 12–16, 1971

DARTMOUTH VII: Hanover, New Hampshire; December 2–7, 1972

DARTMOUTH VIII: Tbilisi; April 21–24, 1974

DARTMOUTH IX: Moscow; June 3–5, 1975

DARTMOUTH X: Rio Rico, Arizona; April 30–May 2, 1976

DARTMOUTH XI: Jurmala, Latvia; July 8–13, 1977

DARTMOUTH XII: Williamsburg, Virginia; MAY 3–7, 1979

DARTMOUTH LEADERSHIP CONFERENCE: Bellagio, Italy; May 22–26, 1980

U.S.-SOVIET RELATIONS UNDERWENT GREAT CHANGES between Dartmouth IV and Dartmouth V. The earlier conference took place when Khrushchev was still in power. After he fell, U.S.-Soviet relations went into a tailspin as the new "collective leadership" of General Secretary Leonid Brezhnev and Premier Aleksei Kosygin proved to be more conservative than their flamboyant predecessor—conservative in that they preferred little or no change, avoided the "adventurism" that they said typified Khrushchev's leadership, and were more willing to hearken back to the Stalin era. The new leadership also began a massive arms buildup in an effort to ensure that the embarrassment of the Cuban missile crisis would not recur.

Relations between the countries also became sour after each sent troops into a smaller country. The United States intervention in Vietnam, of course, grew into full-scale war after 1964. The Soviets quashed the Prague Spring in 1968.

Both the Soviet and American organizers thought that the fifth Dartmouth Conference might be held in the fall of 1965, but by the summer of that year Korneichuk and Oleg Bykov were making it clear that, owing to the growing involvement of the United States in Vietnam, their superiors were forcing the postponement of the conference.[1] Twice each year after that the Americans renewed the invitation. It was not accepted.

But by 1969 the foundations for what became known as détente were being laid. The Nuclear Nonproliferation Treaty was signed in July 1968, and both sides were prepared to begin arms control negotiations. They were sidetracked by the invasion of Czechoslovakia. Richard Nixon, elected the previous November, would be inaugurated two days after Dartmouth V ended. The Soviet regime, in which Brezhnev was showing his colors as primus inter pares, was becoming increasingly willing to seek better relations with the United States. Soviet confidence grew as their buildup of strategic arms brought them closer to parity. As the growth of the Soviet economy slowed, Soviet decision makers began to perceive a need to import food and technology from the West. The usefulness of improved relations with the United States became clearer as relations with China worsened to the point that skirmishes took place along the border in the Far East.

Beginning with the conference at Rye, New York, in 1969, the Dartmouth Conference underwent numerous changes that gave it a new character. A number of new people attended Dartmouth V and Dartmouth VI who would become fixtures through the 1970s and well into the 1980s. The Ford Foundation, the funder through the first few conferences, reduced its funding of the conference, but its place was taken by the Johnson Foundation and the Kettering Foundation.

There was also a change in the perception of what made the Dartmouth Conference important. To Cousins and Mosely, Dartmouth's most important effect was on the perceptions of the participants. Cousins had this to say about Dartmouth I a few months after it took place:

> [T]he important thing about Dartmouth was that lines of communication were opened up. Human relationships were established. Each position had the name of a man attached to it—someone who would sit next to you at the breakfast table, enjoy a stroll with you on the campus, swap humorous or not-so-humorous stories, go over family pictures together, and marvel at nature's full bouquet. The hope, of course, was that a different frame of reference might be established—that problems would be considered not solely according to the national interest but according to their human interest.[2]

As Mosely put it in 1970:

> The immediate purpose of the conferences is to educate the participants themselves, not to influence the policy of either government. This purpose seems to have been achieved. Members of both sides have come to a better understanding of views on the other side, and why, and have learned to communicate better with participants on the other side. Beyond this, there may be some influence on government policies, but this is very indirect.[3]

Under the influence of James Gavin, however, the purpose became more clearly one of affecting U.S. policy directly.[4]

On the Soviet side, Georgi Arbatov and the Institute for the Study of the United States, formed only in 1967, rose to prominence. Indeed, from this time on, the institute (renamed the Institute for the Study of the USA and Canada [ISKAN] in 1975) became central to Dartmouth. Arbatov brought other members of his institute into the Dartmouth dialogues to the point where they sometimes dominated the Soviet delegations. ISKAN became a cosponsor of the conference along with the Soviet Peace Committee. It also provided the intellectual heart of the Soviet delegations, though the contributions from other Soviet institutions, such as the Institute of Oriental Studies and IMEMO, and individuals, such as Evgeni Primakov, were often significant.

Like ISKAN, the Kettering Foundation became involved in the Dartmouth Conference at this time. Kettering became an essential part of Dartmouth on the American side by providing financial, organizational, and intellectual support. It was established in 1926 by Charles F. Kettering, inventor of the electrical self-starter for the automobile. After the hiatus between 1964 and 1969, Dartmouth attracted the interest of Dr. James Read, a former UN deputy high commissioner for refugees and then vice president of the foundation. Robert Chollar, then president of the foundation and a former chairman of National Cash Register, also took a strong interest in Dartmouth. Through their involvement, the Kettering Foundation became a sponsor of the conference and so made an important contribution to its resumption. Like Gavin, Chollar wanted to make Dartmouth a more focused process for examining alternative responses to policy issues.

Kettering soon began to budget Dartmouth as if it were one of its own programs. Succeeding Chollar several years later, David Mathews would also play a strong supportive role. Mathews emphasized the role citizens play as political actors, in their own communities and in the interaction of countries, that is, of whole bodies politic. In 1973 Phillips Ruopp succeeded Read as vice president with responsibility for international affairs. He oversaw Kettering's role in Dartmouth for the next thirteen years, organizing the American side of the conferences. He attended all the conferences outside the Soviet Union plus Dartmouth IX in Moscow and Dartmouth XV in Baku. Robert Lehman succeeded him in 1986. It was Ruopp who made Philip Stewart, a professor at Ohio State University, executive director of Kettering's substantive leadership in Dartmouth—a role that he would play for the following two decades.[5]

Norman Cousins' connection with the Kettering Foundation began a few years earlier, in 1965, when the foundation took over the funding of the educational supplement of *Saturday Review* from the Ford Foundation.[6] He served as a Kettering trustee from 1967 to 1987. Kettering's support in collaboration with Cousins gave Dartmouth the long-term institutional and financial backing that it had lacked.

DARTMOUTH V: CHANGING OF THE GUARD

In June 1968 David Rockefeller spoke to Ambassador Anatoli Dobrynin, assuring him that the Americans were ready to proceed with a fifth conference. A month later, Dobrynin's office sent word that the Soviets were ready to proceed.[7] The conference was scheduled to open in September in Princeton, but the invasion of Czechoslovakia in August forced another postponement. The conference finally opened in January 1969. It took place at the Westchester Country Club in Rye, New York, a bucolic town on Long Island Sound about half an hour north of New York City.

Dartmouth V was Mosely's last Dartmouth Conference and Georgi Arbatov's first. Arbatov served regularly as the Soviet cochairman through the last full Dartmouth Conference, held in 1990. One of the most important figures on the Soviet side of the Dartmouth Conference, he was also one of the most complex. Writing after the collapse of the Soviet Union, he said that he had been a "rational believer" in the system:

> I confess without hesitation that I was not a secret "progressive" and "reformer," hiding my views in a closet and masquerading as a loyal Communist in front of others.[8]

In his public appearances, including those at the Dartmouth conferences, he seemed to others to be a strident, self-serving supporter of the system. Nonetheless, Robert Lundeen, who met Arbatov at Dartmouth conferences later on, when asked whether he thought Arbatov was an angry man or a man with an angry assignment, replied that he found the latter more accurate because,

> in a non-negotiating environment where he didn't have to make a point, he charmed the socks off you. . . . We were having drinks before dinner and kind of talking about some of the issues which in presenting himself he was much more relaxed and thoughtful, not confrontational because he didn't have to impress anyone.[9]

Estimates of the amount of influence he had varied. He did, however, have access to Brezhnev and was a protégé of Andropov.[10] Gorbachev teased Arbatov endlessly and sometimes cruelly but sought and respected his opinions.[11]

Arbatov's severe appearance at the conferences deserves further comment. Despite his strident public appearance, as head of ISKAN he had the crucial role of preserving a center of new thinking through the Brezhnev era and into the era of perestroika when he and those who thought like him became prominent in the evolving Soviet system.[12] Indeed, by bringing his subordinates to Dartmouth, he ensured that they would be exposed to American thinking.

Yet through the 1970s and into the 1980s, he and his colleagues hewed closely to the official line at the conferences. This was frequently frustrating to the Americans. Yet it was an unavoidable part of dealing with the Soviets at the time and well into the 1980s. Arbatov's explanation is worth quoting at length:

> In general I shared the values of my society, but I did not lose the capacity for independent thought. . . . Of course I could not escape being stultified to some degree. But somehow I did not become an idiot. I did not allow anyone to stuff my head with ideological trash, but could not avoid some degree of indoctrination either. And most important, though, I hope the reader won't regard this as immodest, I preserved my honor. Not in the sense that I rejected the system or defied it. I would not have survived if I had. And not in the sense that I did not make compromises. This was not only a matter of personal survival and well-being. If you felt that you had an opportunity to make an important contribution in foreign policy or regarding internal political and economic problems, you had to comply with the rules of the game and be ready to compromise on some other issues. . . . The final judgment can be made only when you weigh the achievement against the compromises you had to make.[13]

Arbatov could be speaking for a number of his Soviet colleagues here. It is not clear how much of what they said came from conviction and how much from playing the rules of the game. Some were undoubtedly true believers in the Soviet system. Many probably believed that it was necessary to present a united face in front of the enemy. But it is probably also true that many, Arbatov included, if they went over the transcripts from decades ago, would be hard-pressed to distinguish between words of conviction and words of compromise.

Yuri Zhukov chaired the Soviet delegation. He had been one of the two *Pravda* commentators at the Andover conference and the cultural exchange official who had spoken with Senator Benton in Moscow after Dartmouth II, using him as a back channel to American policymakers. Boris Polevoi returned once again. He was the only Soviet participant to attend the first five conferences. Nikolai Mostovets of IMEMO returned for his second conference. His previous experience had been at Dartmouth II in the Crimea. Several participants in the Leningrad conference made the trip to Rye: Nikolai Orlov, director of the Economic Research Institute of the Ministry of Foreign Trade; Anna Boykova, deputy mayor of Leningrad; Dr. Nikolai Blokhin; and Daniel Kraminov, editor in chief of *Za rubezhom*. Newcomers included, besides Arbatov, Viktor Karpov and Yuri Bobrakov, his colleagues at the institute; Vladimir Trukhanovsky, editor in chief of *Voprosi istorii;* and Igor Belyaev, an expert on Asia and Africa for *Pravda*. The staff that the Soviets brought with them included Dartmouth veterans Alice Bobrysheva and A. D. Shveitser. A friend of Shveitser's, Hans Vladimirsky, shared the interpretation duties. He had, according to Shveitser, "a vivid and unorthodox personality" that led him to be blacklisted by the KGB until Khrushchev's thaw made it acceptable to use him for interpretation.[14]

On the American side, Cousins and Larson were back. Like Polevoi, they had been at all of the earlier conferences. Cousins had recovered from the illness that had put him in the hospital after Dartmouth IV. Mosely escaped from his academic obligations to appear briefly at the country club. Norton Simon, Buckminster Fuller, and Leslie Paffrath, whose first conference had been Dartmouth IV, all returned. So did David Rockefeller. Harvard's Merle Fainsod took the role of Soviet specialist at Dartmouth V. Two senior publishing executives joined the American delegation at Rye. These were James Linen, chief executive officer of Time-Life, and Franklin Murphy, chancellor of UCLA and chairman of the board of the *Los Angeles Times-Mirror*. Murphy had also been at the Leningrad conference. Retired general James Gavin, now chairman of the board of Arthur D. Little, Inc., appeared for the first time. Gavin became a hero during World War II as the commander of the Eighty-second Airborne Division and served as ambassador to France in the Kennedy administration. By 1969 he had become widely known as an opponent of the Vietnam War. Other prominent figures who came to Dartmouth for the first time included George Kistiakowsky, who had been President Eisenhower's science advisor; Patricia Harris, who had been ambassador to Luxembourg but was then a professor of law at Howard University and would become its dean later that year; and Rosemary Park, vice chancellor of UCLA. Interpretation was provided, as so often before, by Sherry and Klebnikov. Among the observers was Richard Lombard, a lawyer who served as chairman of the Kettering Foundation's board of trustees.

The agenda was set a week before the conference in a meeting between Norman Cousins and the Soviet editors, Trukhanovsky of *Voprosi istorii* and Kraminov of *Za rubezhom*.[15] This was a much less formal way of deciding on the agenda than Dartmouth had seen before or would see again. Whereas the earlier conferences had addressed broad topics, the trio agreed to topics that were precise: exchanges, arms control, the United Nations, trade, Vietnam, and the Middle East.

Cousins opened the conference. Blokhin made the opening statement for the Soviet delegation. The discussion began by addressing the subject of exchanges. The conference seemed to start off slowly, with the morning session given mostly to statements by the Americans. The Soviets made most of the contributions at the afternoon session. Both sides addressed the obstacles to trade after Simon brought the matter up.

Arbatov's first contribution is worth noting, both because of his subsequent importance to Dartmouth and as a measure of the state of the U.S.-Soviet relationship at the time. He evinced deep suspicion of the motives that underlay American efforts to foster exchanges and trade:

> One underlying US policy is the so-called "erosion" of our social system. As a professional student of the United States I feel that this is a basic United States policy line and that it distorts all good proposals, including those regarding contacts. Professor Brzezinski speaks of promoting evolutionary changes in the Soviet Union. This is what underlies the United States policy of promoting cultural contacts and trade. The Republican party platform speaks of the Soviet system as something abnormal which can yield to the normal and refers to trade as a wedge for this purpose. This is how influential people in the United States *do* regard their policy and we must remain cognizant of this strategy as the framework within which exchanges are conceived. This is the *main* obstacle to contacts and cannot be ignored.[16]

Despite this suspicion, the Soviet position, as expressed by Arbatov and his colleagues, favored increasing both exchanges and trade. As they had before, the Soviets blamed the United States for placing obstacles in the way of both. And, as before, Americans argued with them, notably Larson and Cousins, two Dartmouth veterans.

The discussion of arms control was significant largely for what was not talked about. Much of the discussion focused on the nonproliferation treaty that had been signed six months before, but there was no discussion of either antiballistic missile (ABM) systems or multiple independently targeted reentry vehicles (MIRVs). The former had been an important topic at meetings of Pugwash and other groups as early as 1964, and both were important topics in the discussions leading up to the SALT talks that would begin in November 1969.[17] There were, in fact, no arms control experts on either side at this conference—no Paul Doty or Franklin Long on the American side, no Talensky on the Soviet.

Nonetheless, in view of what happened later, some of the statements given in the discussions are notable. Arbatov argued for the need for general and complete disarmament, but he added that "the arms race greatly hinders our own internal development" and offered a criticism of the dinosaurlike mentality of the Soviet military that might not have been expected.[18] Kistiakowsky made an argument for what came to called "sufficiency" in nuclear weapons policy. This was more than a decade and a half before analysts from Arbatov's institute began to make it in Soviet publications:

> Given the present state of military armaments, the concept of military superiority has no meaning. You can kill an individual and destroy his house only once. But what is important *is* the concept of "adequacy." *Responsible* people in both countries know that "superiority" is an impracticable catchword.

And, as they had at previous conferences, participants on both sides recognized the common interest of the two superpowers in arms control, a commonality of interest demonstrated clearly by the non-proliferation treaty.

On Thursday, the fourth day of the conference, delegates focused their attention on the two regional conflicts that had become significant in U.S.-Soviet relations—Vietnam and the Middle East. Regional conflicts had figured prominently in the discussions at the previous conferences, but they were more theoretical, focused on the Soviet concept of "wars of national liberation," with the two sides debating whether Soviet support for them would harm relations between the superpowers. At Rye participants from the two sides outlined the interests of their countries and their allies in the conflicts but did little more. Harry Schwartz, writing in the *New York Times* later in January, said he detected hints from the Soviet participants "that the Soviet Union would welcome some continued American military presence in South Vietnam after conclusion of a political settlement."[19]

In the second session of discussion of these conflicts, Norman Cousins brought up the Soviet invasion of Czechoslovakia and its effect on U.S.-Soviet relations, drawing a parallel between divisions in American society over Vietnam and divisions in Soviet society over Czechoslovakia. The Soviets tried to avoid discussing the matter and then, not unexpectedly, defended the invasion, arguing both that it was "done in the interests of Czechoslovakia itself" and that the invasion came about to forestall anti-Russian, revanchist plans of the West Germans.

Orlov opened the discussion on trade. He deplored restrictions the United States placed on trade with the Soviet Union and noted that trade was linked with the state of the relationship between the two countries. Rockefeller concurred that this link existed but argued that Soviet actions seen as expansionist undermined "our efforts at cooperation in trade." Other Soviet participants disagreed, pointing out that Soviet trade was higher with some countries in Western Europe despite disagreements between those countries and the Soviet Union.

Although the United Nations was on the agenda and was brought into the discussions several times, much less attention was given to it than at previous conferences. The absence of Grenville Clark and Louis Sohn may partially account for this, but even Larson and Cousins, committed federalists both, did not approach the topic with the sense of urgency evident in their remarks earlier in the decade.

According to Fuller, many of the Americans lived near the Westchester Country Club and so went home each night. He and Paffrath stayed at the club with the Russians. He apparently found the conversations less enlightening than in Leningrad at Dartmouth IV:

> I found that the young editor of *Pravda* [probably Belyaev] was the only Russian amongst them who seemed free to explore and discuss spontaneously the world's future prospects. Though obviously a faithful communist, his speculative thoughts seemed not to be bound within popularly established party line dogma.[20]

Shveitser describes Arthur Miller at the conference as quiet, sad, and introverted. He was then the international president of PEN. During the sessions, he spoke about the ignorance of Americans about the Soviet Union. There was, he noted, an imbalance in efforts to get Soviet literary works translated. He suggested that a translation agreement be reached between the two countries, but he also said, "You only *foster* our ignorance by what you do sometimes." One night, Miller asked Shveitser to join him at his table so that he could pass along a message that banning the books of dissident writers such as Sinyavsky and Solzhenitsyn was counterproductive as it simply increased their popularity.[21]

As had become customary, the Soviet participants spent time elsewhere in the United States after the conference. Most simply stayed for another week in New York City, where they saw Broadway plays and heard concerts. Mosely met informally with Zhukov and others for lunch or dinner during this week. Some of the Soviet participants flew to California, where Rosemary Park and Franklin Murphy arranged appointments with prominent Californians and where they had the opportunity to see the art collections of Norton Simon.

DARTMOUTH VI: MISPLACED OPTIMISM?

When the participants scattered after the Rye conference, there was hope for another session but no plans for one. Mosely would have liked the conferences to become annual events, but it was not to be.[22] Little planning was done in 1969 until Rockefeller, Cousins, Gavin, Lombard, and Mosely met after Christmas. Even so, Zhukov told Mosely in March 1970 that the Soviet participants would be too busy to hold a conference that year, and so the conference was put off until 1971.

The first thing decided about the conference, even before the approximate date or the membership of the delegations, was that trade would be on the agenda. As early as March 1970, a group at Chase Manhattan in New York and groups at the USA Institute and the Research Institute on Business Cycles of the Ministry of Foreign Trade in Moscow were preparing studies that, it was hoped, would serve as a basis for discussion.[23] A Soviet paper was delivered to Cousins, in Russian, in August. Zhukov had circulated the paper from Chase Manhattan among the Soviet Dartmouth group by December.[24]

The United Nations had been placed on the agenda by September 1970. Cousins was commissioned to write a memo about its reconstruction. A third item, new to Dartmouth and to international dialogue in general—the environment—was added in December. These topics were chosen, it appears, because they were regarded as less controversial than others. The absence of arms control is notable; it had been prominent at earlier meetings. With the SALT talks continuing and major strategic arms programs in progress in both countries, it was, if anything, more important in U.S.-Soviet relations than it had been before. The feeling may have been either that an unofficial dialogue could contribute little to what was being done in the official realm or that the issues would be too contentious to be fruitful.

The preparations for Dartmouth VI, unlike those for its predecessors, included papers on all three main agenda topics. As it turned out, Samuel Pisar, author of *Coexistence and Commerce,* published the year before, also prepared a paper for the conference. It was based on testimony he gave before the President's Commission on International Trade and Investment Policy. Charles Yost, who had been the American ambassador to the United Nations from 1968 to 1971, and Grigorii Morozov, chief of the International Organizations section of IMEMO, wrote papers on strengthening the United Nations. Fedorov wrote the Soviet paper on strengthening the environment. The American contribution was written by Thomas F. Malone, the dean of the Graduate School at the University of Connecticut and a former chairman of both the Geophysics Research Board of the National Academy of Sciences and the U.S. National Commission for UNESCO. The exchange of papers was regarded as useful for the conference, but it was hardly timely. Whereas the two trade papers (excepting Pisar's paper, which was an unsought bonus) were available months beforehand, the other two American papers became available in Moscow only two weeks beforehand, and participants saw the two Soviet papers only once they had come to Kiev.

As planning began for Dartmouth VI, some of the Americans expressed dissatisfaction with the composition of the American delegation at Dartmouth V. Immediately after the Rye conference, Larson said that the "United States delegation can no longer be a miscellaneous collection of eminent people from all walks of life."[25] He pushed for a clearer purpose and a more limited agenda. Dartmouth was evolving.

In September 1970, General Gavin was asked to take the chairmanship of the conference. After some thought, he took it. Beginning the next month, Gavin consulted with Henry Kissinger and officials in the State Department about the agenda and participants in the meeting. In March 1971, he and Robert Chollar met with Kissinger. The national security advisor told them that "from the White House point of view the Dartmouth Conference was a very good undertaking" and suggested the names of senators who might take part.[26] Kissinger also spoke in favor of opening up U.S.-Soviet trade relations.[27]

The American delegation to the conference in Kiev reflected General Gavin's concerns about the American delegation at the Westchester Country Club. Sixteen strong, most of the participants had significant experience working on foreign policy issues. There were no cutural figures like Marian Anderson or Arthur Miller. Indeed, Norman Cousins himself was not there. Only four had taken part in Dartmouth conferences before (Gavin, Kistiakowsky, Harris, and Rockefeller), and only Rockefeller had been to more than two. This was the first Dartmouth Conference to include sitting members of Congress—Senators Mark Hatfield, a Republican from Oregon, and Frank Church, a Democrat from Idaho. This was also the first conference for Charles Yost, who was to become a fixture at Dartmouth for the next decade. Besides his experience in the United Nations, he had had a distinguished career as a Foreign Service officer in Laos, the Middle East, and Eastern and Western Europe.[28] He was also a part of the dialogue with the Soviets carried out by the United Nations Association. Milton Eisenhower, the former president's brother, flew to the Soviet Union for the conference but had to leave early, owing to a death in the family. As at Rye, the Kettering Foundation funded the conference along with the Johnson Foundation. Kettering was represented by Chollar, Lombard, and Read. Mark Kasoff, chairman of the Department of Economics at Antioch College, attended the conference as a consultant hired to evaluate it, a result of the Kettering Foundation's "interest in the process of communication in such encounters."[29]

The Soviet delegation, in contrast to the American, included twelve participants from earlier conferences. They included Korneichuk, who served as chairman, Fedorov, Polevoi, Zhukov, Mostovets, and Orlov. Mostovets, nominally a researcher at IMEMO when he took part in Dartmouth II, was now on the staff of the Institute of the International Labor Movement. An observer at the conference described him as "direct from a Stalinist purge trial—quite belligerent, narrow and pedantic."[30]

Arbatov also attended, along with several of his colleagues from the Institute for the Study of the USA. Some of them were appearing at Dartmouth for the first time, filling out the huge, twenty-seven-member delegation. They included Deputy Director Vitali Zhurkin, who was to become a regular at Dartmouth. In his mid-forties at the time, he was described as "intelligent, sophisticated, and quick-witted," with excellent English. He had been with the USA Institute almost since it was formed but had spent most of his earlier career in India, working for Radio Moscow and the Foreign Ministry.[31]

Also appearing for the first time was Evgeni Primakov, who later became foreign minister and then prime minister of post-Soviet Russia. At that time he was a deputy director of IMEMO. Before then, he had been a journalist and a deputy director of the USA Institute. Primakov and Zhurkin were not unknown to each other. They were, in fact, collaborating on a book, to be published in 1972, in which they argued against military intervention in the Third World, finding that the risks of escalation into nuclear war were too great.[32]

Another new member of the Soviet delegation was Vladimir Petrovsky. At the time he was a senior researcher under Arbatov. He had been in the Foreign Ministry earlier and served in the UN Secretariat. Later he would become under-secretary-general of the United Nations and director general of the United Nations' Geneva office.

The American delegates met before the conference for two briefing sessions, one in New York, the other in London, and then flew to Moscow. They took a train to Kiev, traveling overnight in a "special, wood paneled railway car that was equipped with a steaming samovar and buffet that included the obligatory vodka and caviar."[33] They arrived in Kiev optimistic and ready for the opening of the conference in the October Palace on Monday, July 12.

But after the conference opened, the warm optimism of the Americans began to cool, matching the tone of the Soviet rhetoric. Korneichuk opened the conference with a speech that included extended citations from Brezhnev's recent report to the Twenty-fourth Congress of the Soviet Communist Party, which had been held in the spring. General Gavin responded in a straightforward, strong manner, saying that many Americans felt uneasy about Soviet actions, but that the American delegates saw the conference as an opportunity to "solve some problems."[34]

More time was spent discussing U.S.-Soviet trade than any other topic on that first day. Rockefeller opened by discussing the Chase Manhattan paper, coming to the rather pessimistic conclusion that "[a]s to prospects for the future, in all candor, no rapid expansion can be anticipated." He was followed by Pisar, who spoke of the internationalization of production and the gradual move toward a unified world market. He proposed a "charter for East-West trade relations," with some fifty points. This was not well received by the Soviets. Orlov, in particular, argued that the state monopoly on foreign trade and capital investment and state planning of the economy were immutable, suggesting that Pisar had not taken that into account. Pisar also mentioned the theory that the Western and Soviet social systems were converging. Both Arbatov and Zhukov objected. They saw no such convergence.

Orlov made the Soviet presentation on trade. Whereas Rockefeller had found obstacles to trade on both sides, Orlov and his colleagues blamed American restrictions alone for inhibiting trade. These restrictions, he said, had been established after World War II. He saw no sign of change. Rockefeller objected to the latter point, arguing that changes already put into place by the Nixon administration were significant and liberalizing.

The American side emphasized the role of public opinion in fostering trade with the Soviets. Senator Church in particular spoke of the constraints felt by himself and his fellow legislators in acting to reduce trade restraints, eliminate discriminatory tariffs, and extend most-favored-nation status to the Soviet Union. A majority of his constituents, he said, looked on the Soviet Union as a potential enemy and at trade as a means of strengthening an adversary.

The Soviets found little merit in this. They believed that public opinion was easily malleable. If American leaders wanted trade, there would be trade. Mostovets expressed the Soviet attitude in a crude form:

> Lack of trade should not be blamed on public opinion, because that opinion can be created. This unfavorable public opinion is caused not by the Soviet Union but by the ruling American circles.[35]

Discussion of the United Nations took place the next morning. It took less time than had originally been planned. Like the discussions about the United Nations at Dartmouth V, this discussion lacked the urgency that had been apparent in the first few Dartmouth conferences. Yost and Harris, both of whom had served on the American delegation to the United Nations, noted that people in the United States were showing a growing lack of confidence in it. Morozov argued essentially that few changes were needed in the United Nations' structure or machinery. Petrovsky echoed this attitude in objecting to several changes proposed by Yost. In particular, he emphasized that the Security Council, where the Soviet Union held a veto, should not be bypassed.

This was the first Dartmouth Conference to discuss environmental issues. At the time, these issues were not a part of official state-to-state dialogue between any two countries. Even as a domestic concern within the United States, environmental issues had not yet won the universal acceptance they enjoy today. Perhaps partly because the environment was a new topic to many of the participants, some saw this discussion as one of the highlights of the conference. Kasoff found the dialogue to be "crisp, general, complete, with a fairly apolitical flavor." To Rockefeller, however, the session did not seem productive.

This may have been because participants tended to describe environmental problems without suggesting how to solve them. There was, however, one notable exception. Malone, who prepared the American paper, suggested that an international environmental institute be formed. He provided a detailed outline of its purpose, functions, and structure. It was to be a huge organization, with 300 researchers working in a central institute, and another 400 working in four regional institutes spread throughout the world. The Soviets were not enthusiastic about this proposal, and the final communiqué describes it as solely an American proposal worthy of further study.

The Soviet paper, prepared by Fedorov, was remarkable for its optimism, a reflection of Soviet thinking on environmental issues. He seemed to reject the Malthusian logic common in the West, epitomized by a study issued by the Club of Rome that suggested that the supply of resources, particularly food, would be outrun by the growth of population. He conceded that there was a limit to the amount of resources available to mankind. He declared that he and his Soviet colleagues were as impressed with the importance of environmental problems as their American colleagues.

Fedorov's remarks at Dartmouth VI suggest the logic of the Soviet position on environmental issues that led to the sometimes horrifying outcomes that became all too evident after the Soviet Union collapsed.[36]

The problems were seen, at least by those at Dartmouth VI, but the solutions were believed to be too readily at hand, easily available to those who decided to do something about them through existing institutions. Sometimes these solutions were the stuff of fantasy. For example,

> [a] definite optimum for the Earth's population does not necessarily mean restricting the size of Earth's population in general. It is highly probable that earlier than that, it will become possible to create large inhabited cosmic bodies or to utilize other planets for living purposes.[37]

Later Fedorov referred to the plan to divert the flow of Siberian rivers from the north to the south in order to provide irrigation water for Central Asia. This idea was seriously considered into the 1980s before being dropped as both too expensive and too threatening to the environment. But these proposed solutions to environmental problems suggest the basic Soviet position on the environment. As stated by Fedorov, this was that "not conservation and stabilization of [the] natural environment, but expedient and planned transformation of it should become our goal and purpose." Planning and public ownership of natural resources, Fedorov thought, made it possible to use natural resources most effectively for the good of mankind. No one argued with him at Dartmouth VI.

The last two sessions of the conference, held on Wednesday and Thursday, were given over to current issues in the relationship. Kasoff found these discussions unproductive, with too much familiar rhetoric coming from both sides. And indeed, their beginning was unpromising as Zhukov read a paper that simply rehashed sections of Brezhnev's reports to the Twenty-fourth Congress. The two sessions touched on a variety of topics. Yost took exception to Primakov's comments on the Middle East, given the day before, arguing that the Soviets had "not taken adequate account of all interests involved," the interest of the Israelis in particular. Throughout these sessions, in fact, Kassof found

> Yost to be by far the star performer, trying to be sensitive to all parties concerned on each of the issues. His comments were rational, low keyed, and provided the basis for compromise.[38]

Arbatov and others spoke about arms control and the European security conference proposed by the Soviets.[39] Arbatov asked whether any of the American participants would be interested in discussing European security with a committee of the Supreme Soviet in Moscow to which he had been appointed. The war in Vietnam was brought up by Gavin and discussed by others. Gavin accused the Soviets of sending arms to the hot spots in the Middle East and Vietnam. Zhurkin responded by arguing that the Soviet Union sought a political solution. He urged compromise over Vietnam, with a "neutralist regime" in South Vietnam a desired result.

Pisar had been bothered by the tone of the meeting. He had commented on the first day about the conference going off course. Now he thought that "between the Soviets' gratuitous assault and the Americans' offended silence" the conference could collapse. He caught Gavin's eye and then went to him and whispered, "[C]ould we step outside for a minute?" Church followed them.

> "Don't you think," I asked when we had closed the door behind us, "it's about time someone talked back to them?"
> Gavin shrugged. "Oh. It'll blow over."
> "Don't be so sure," I said.
> I drew a deep breath, suddenly feeling afraid I was going too far. "Listen! I think I know a thing or two about the Russians, and at this rate they're going to walk all over us and that's not going to do this conference any good." [. . .]
> Frank Church, who until then hadn't said a word, broke in. "Sam is right, we should answer them. I'm sick of listening to their endless barrage on Vietnam, too. I have been on the public record on this issue for a long time and we certainly don't need any lessons from them."
> "Jim," I added, after a brief silence, "I'd like to answer them."
> The general grew thoughtful, concerned. Then he said calmly, putting his hand on my shoulder, "Okay, let them have it. Good luck."[40]

Pisar then spoke at length "from a personal point of view."[41] He had heard an anti-Semitic undertone in the remarks of the Soviet delegation and believed it stemmed, at least in part, from the current pressure from Soviet Jews to be allowed to emigrate to Israel, pressure that had aroused international concern and, in turn, Soviet concern about the support given to Soviet Jews in the United States linked, it seemed, to American support of Israel. A prisoner at Auschwitz as a child, he spoke to those concerns and of the roots of anti-Semitism in Russia and asked for understanding of those Soviet Jews who wanted to go to Israel. But then he closed with an affirmation that

> [t]he similarities between the [United States and the Soviet Union] are striking. . . . The two countries are more similar than France and Britain, even though those have the same social structures. One should stop repeating the old dogmatic formulas day after day, but rather take a pragmatic approach and look at areas of common agreement in the fields of trade, science, the United Nations, the true framework of the agenda. The rhetoric can be dispensed with.[42]

He finished by proposing a trip to Babi Yar, the site of the massacre of Soviet Jews on the outskirts of Kiev by the Nazis during World War II. It was then unmarked and, owing in part to Yevtushenko's poem, a symbol of the state of Jews in the Soviet Union. After the session the American delegates asked for a bus and went there. Much to Pisar's surprise, soon after they arrived, a second bus drove up with the Soviet delegates. He found their arrival "deeply moving." His impression was that "these hard-boiled types" had joined the Americans "in a pilgrimage that went against the official grain." But it seems unlikely that the pilgrimage was made without higher approval. And the reference to "hard-boiled types" shows how great the distance between Americans and Soviets was.

Pisar's speech and the trip to Babi Yar helped improve the atmosphere, much as Grenville Clark had at Dartmouth I. A cruise that afternoon helped relax things further. There was but one day left, however. Most of the work was done. With the stresses of the previous few days in mind, two suggestions for restructuring Dartmouth were made that prefigured Dartmouth's future.

Yost made the proposal, which Rockefeller seconded, that future conferences make greater use of "small, informal groups." He found the abrasive polemics of the formal statements of the plenary meetings to be regrettable and suggested that smaller, more relaxed, less formal groups would allow personal friendships to develop. His UN experience suggested that this would make the conference more successful.

Korneichuk agreed "more time should be devoted to small groups and informal contacts." But he also thought that it would be valuable to have continuing contacts between conferences, rather "than for all to go home, forget about these matters for a couple of years, and then come together again." He suggested that a committee of correspondence be established with three or four members from each side to continue the work of Dartmouth between conferences. This suggestion was made periodically during the years that followed. It became a reality in the task forces created in the 1980s.

Both suggestions recognized that the success or failure of Dartmouth depended on the relationships between the participants. Yost and Korneichuk both recognized that Dartmouth worked on two levels. The people who came embodied—literally—aspects of the society they came from. They could not divorce themselves from the environment they returned to after the conference ended. But they were individuals, too, representing themselves. It was as individuals that they could build a bridge between the two hostile societies, if such a bridge could be built. But they saw that, if it could be done, it could only be done over time and with a continuing effort.

Gavin, Church, Yost, and Rockefeller left Kiev in the middle of the press conference that followed Dartmouth VI to fly to Moscow for a 3:00 P.M. meeting with Premier Aleksei Kosygin. They met in the same office of the Kremlin where Rockefeller had met with Khrushchev six years before.[43] They discussed a range of issues that included arms control, the environment, and trade. Kosygin proposed a pilot trade project arranged through the State Committee on Science and Technology, whose deputy chairman, the Americans discovered, happened to be his son-in-law, Dzherman Gvishiani. Before this, according to Gavin, Gvishiani had expressed interest only in large projects that required amounts of capital far larger than American firms were interested in investing at the time.

On returning to the United States, Gavin held a further conversation with Ambassador Dobrynin and a commercial counselor at the Soviet embassy. Dobrynin told Gavin that Kosygin's answer to the Dartmouth group was the Soviet answer to a query from the Commerce Department about projects the Soviet Union would be interested in entering into with the United States.[44] Gavin then met with Secretary of Commerce Peter Peterson and then with Undersecretary of State John Irwin and three assistant secretaries.[45] Gavin and Rockefeller spoke about the conference over dinner with Secretary of State William Rogers and in a meeting with Kissinger.[46] Peterson and Kissinger expressed interest in the idea of a pilot project. Peterson also discussed the relaxation of trade restrictions. Irwin and the three assistant secretaries were interested in the conference, but "they made no contribution or comment of any substance." No single pilot project seems to have been undertaken. Fruitless though these meetings may have seemed, however, they took place on the eve of the dramatic increase in U.S.-Soviet trade that accompanied détente. The conversation with Kosygin might have helped open the doors that made that increase possible.

DARTMOUTH VII: RETURN TO HANOVER

General Gavin came away from Dartmouth VI dissatisfied with the course of the discussions. He did not return to Dartmouth VII. According to notes made by David Rockefeller, "He cited [the Soviets'] frequent off-the-agenda statements, their bullying language, their frequent changes of chairmen, their overstuffed delegation, their anxiousness to draft an early communiqué, and their failure to provide some amenities that had been offered at previous conferences."[47] Other participants found the Kiev conference to be an improvement over Dartmouth V.[48] But as they said in the last session in Kiev, many felt that further improvements could be made. As a result, Dartmouth VII was a much different conference than its predecessors.

The transition in the leadership of the conference, evident at the two previous conferences, continued. Mosely and Korneichuk had both died early in 1972. And although Cousins is prominent in the pictures of the conference, he was there only as an observer, not as a participant. While he never lacked for things to do or places to be, in late 1972 even his prodigious energy was being taxed. He quit *Saturday Review* shortly after new publishers bought it in 1971 and turned his efforts to creating a new magazine, *World.*

Dartmouth VII marked the first appearance of Phillips Ruopp. It was also the first attended by Philip Stewart, who quickly became essential to the Dartmouth conferences. The rapporteur of this conference and many that followed, he was a young professor of political science at Ohio State University who had received his Ph.D. from Indiana University seven years before. He brought a new analytical rigor to the reports about the conference. In these reports he examined the structure, process, and achievements of the conferences in detail not heretofore seen. In a short time he became the chronicler of Dartmouth, producing transcripts of the conferences and long analytical memoranda that told what had happened, explained why, and, when necessary, suggested how the conferences might be improved. He was also, de facto, the manager of Dartmouth. More than any other individual, he maintained continuity between conferences.

Zbigniew Brzezinski, then director of the Russian Institute at Columbia University, came to Dartmouth VII, the first of two Dartmouth conferences he attended. By 1972 he had gained a strong reputation as a scholar of the Soviet Union and the Soviet bloc. But he was branching out beyond the confines of this specialty. He served on the Policy Planning Staff of the State Department for two years in the Johnson administration and had recently written two books on topics far from those on which his reputation was based. One, *The Fragile Blossom,* was on Japan. The other, *Between Two Ages,* posited the approach of a new age of technology.[49] The latter book and the thinking done by David Rockefeller led the two to become instrumental in founding what in 1973 became the Trilateral Commission.[50] This work brought Brzezinski into contact with Jimmy Carter after he was elected governor of Georgia in 1970. Carter brought Brzezinski and his incisive mind to the National Security Council in 1977, the second participant in the Dartmouth Conference (after Walt Rostow) to become national security advisor.

Members of Congress took part in the Hanover conference, as they had in Kiev. This time, however, they came from the House of Representatives: John Brademas, a Democrat from Indiana; Peter H. B. Freylinghausen, a Republican from New Jersey; and Morris K. Udall, a Democrat from Arizona.

The American delegation also included Hedley Donovan, editor in chief of Time, Inc., and James Billington, a professor of history at Princeton who later led the Wilson Center for International Scholars at the Smithsonian Institution. He is now librarian of Congress. Three senior business executives filled out the trade group, along with Rockefeller: Lauris Norstad, chairman and director of the Owens-Corning Fiberglass Corporation; Donald Kendall, chairman of PepsiCo, which was in the forefront of trade with the Soviet Union, and Michel Fribourg, chairman and chief executive officer of Continental Grain, which had been involved in the recent, massive sale of grain to the Soviet Union; the first since 1963. Howard Raiffa, director of the International Institute for Applied Systems Analysis (IIASA), was a member of the environmental group. The IIASA was founded earlier in 1972, when twelve academies of science signed a charter creating it. Raiffa, a mathematician trained in game theory, had worked toward creating it, following an initiative suggested to McGeorge Bundy by President Johnson when Bundy left government to head the Ford Foundation in 1967.[51] Father Felix Morlion, whose presence at Andover had led to the papal message during the Cuban missile crisis and to Norman Cousins' mission as intermediary among Kennedy, Khrushchev, and Pope John XXIII, was again an observer.

Several of the Soviet participants also returned. Primakov and Arbatov did not. Polevoi was there, once again. Fedorov returned to chair the environmental work group along with Harrison Brown, his American counterpart, who had also been in Kiev. Mostovets and Zhukov were back again. Nikolai Orlov chaired the trade work group, sharing those duties with David Rockefeller. The newcomers included Anatoli Gromyko, the son of the foreign minister, but there as a staff member of the Institute for the Study of the USA. Anatoli was much like his father, according to the defector Arkadi Shevchenko: "He possessed the same tenacity, excellent memory, attention to detail, and dry manner."[52]

As a counterpart to Yost, the Soviets included Nikolai Federenko in their delegation. He was a former ambassador to the United Nations and to Japan, but his heart lay in China. "An elegant man," reserved and soft-spoken, according to Shevchenko, a former subordinate, he was given to "long hair, flashy clothes, and bow ties." For this reason and others, the Soviet foreign minister distrusted him.[53]

The conference returned to the Dartmouth College campus. It took place at a time that might be regarded as the height of détente, a few months after the summit that took place in Moscow the previous May. A number of agreements had been signed, including the first SALT agreement and an agreement on basic principles of relations between the two countries.

The structure of this conference differed from that of previous conferences. Instead of being held solely in plenary session, the conference broke up into "work groups" after the opening session to discuss trade, political issues, and environmental issues. Plenary sessions were held in the middle of the conference, to exchange information about the progress made in the work groups, and at the end, to adopt the conference communiqué.[54] As at Dartmouth VI, papers were prepared to give the work groups a basis for discussion. The new structure seemed to work well. Participants concluded that the dialogue was more focused and extended than at previous conferences and that disputes that stemmed from ideological differences gave way to dialogue on the substance of issues.[55]

The political work group was more balanced than the other two groups. Like Yost and Federenko, the former ambassadors to the United Nations, most participants had a counterpart on the other side. The exception was in the case of disarmament. There was no Soviet expert on disarmament who could be the opposite number of George Rathjens, an MIT professor and participant in Pugwash who was a prominent opponent of the American ABM system, Safeguard.[56] Civilian experts on military matters were scarce in the Soviet Union; there was no one like Talensky available to come to Hanover in 1972.

The political work group discussed the variety of accords that had been signed in Moscow the previous May and negotiations then under way that seemed to be transforming U.S.-Soviet relations. Both sides believed that the transformation was occurring. Although continuing disagreements between the two countries were acknowledged, this was the height of optimism about détente. They were moving from an era of competition and mere "peaceful coexistence" to one of cooperation. As a Soviet participant put it, "A new era of international cooperation has begun."

The Soviet delegates, like the Soviet government, focused on the principle of "equality of the sides." Indeed, they saw this principle as "the cornerstone of a stable U.S.-U.S.S.R. relationship in all spheres."[57] And they saw it embodied—recognized—in the new relationship that was being established. In their view, the Soviet Union had now become the equal of the United States. They believed that their new status would bring with it benefits in all fields.

The dialogue of this group ranged over several topics that had held center stage at previous Dartmouth conferences. These included disarmament and "the United Nations and world order." Other topics included European security, Vietnam, and the Middle East. Vietnam in particular aroused little controversy, probably because the involvement of the United States was reaching an end. Both sides favored increasing use of the United Nations, but neither delegation favored changing the charter.

The Soviet delegation was uniformly enthusiastic about the SALT I agreement, signed in May. The agreement had two parts. The treaty to limit ABM systems excited no controversy from the American side. But the same could not be said about the agreement to limit offensive weapons. The problem that some on the American side saw was essentially that that agreement simply froze the missile programs of the two countries in place, and for a limited time. Meanwhile, both sides were allowed to, and did, continue their development of offensive weapons systems, including MIRVed warheads. The Soviet side did not view this as a problem with the agreement, as some Americans did, but they did ask why the Americans continued weapons development after SALT I was signed.

The Americans in the political work group identified the conflict between the concepts of "equal security" and "sufficient security" as a central problem. The difference was that in the world of nuclear deterrence, where everything depended on how each side perceived the balance, what was equal to one side might seem a deadly imbalance to the other. Efforts to achieve equal security, therefore, could be like balancing a brick on a nail, with a minute margin for error, particularly given that the two sides had asymmetrical forces: the Soviets were strong in land-based missiles; the United States had more numerous and effective bombers and submarine-based weapons. If it were believed, however, that the balance was robust, that a few weapons would suffice to deter an attack, then both sides could feel more secure and further arms control agreements would be easier to achieve.

The debate over this issue would be played out on both sides over the next decade and a half. But in 1972 the Americans at Dartmouth argued that only a few skeptics in the United States rejected the sufficiency argument. The Soviets rejected it totally. They found the concept arbitrary and "obfuscating," and seemed to suspect that it was part of an attempt to justify an American search for "security through an absolute preponderance" of force.

The agreements reached in this work group were less substantive than those reached by the other two groups. They included recognition of the "need for deliberate speed" in reaching arms control agreements and of the "potential for peace" in the negotiations then going on over security and arms control in Europe.

The trade group discussions took place not only in the aftermath of the agreements at the May summit, but also following an agreement on trade made a few weeks before. This contained provisions for Soviet payment of the lend-lease debt from World War II and a number of other provisions designed to facilitate trade.[58] The agreement spoke of a goal of tripling trade in three years. The discussions also came on the heels of "the great grain robbery," in which the Soviets, taking advantage of secrecy on the part of both Washington and Moscow, were able to acquire millions of tons of grain at bargain prices.[59] This suggested to many in the United States that economic relations with the Soviets could become as competitive, as much a zero-sum game, as political relations had become.

The Soviet participants in the trade group focused on the need for the United States to grant the Soviet Union most-favored-nation (MFN) status, an issue that Senator Henry Jackson, among others, knowing how important this was to the Soviets, was linking to the issue of Jewish emigration. This was also an issue in the discussions of the political group and clearly something the Soviet delegation came primed to talk about. As James Billington put it, "They vehemently and repeatedly insisted that MFN was the absolute pre-requisite to everything."[60] The Americans tried to explain why it was an issue in the American polity, though most of them favored extending it to the Soviets. In the end, the group found room to agree to support the approval of MFN by Congress.

The other idea that Billington saw the Soviet participants prepared to push was a Soviet-American Chamber of Commerce. The Soviets had established similar chambers with the Finns, the British, and the French. It was to serve as a place to exchange information, chart trade, and increase contacts between Soviet officials and American businesspeople. Rockefeller brought up the idea of having a trade "subcommittee" of the Dartmouth Conference. Most of the participants agreed that the two cochairmen would select the subcommittee members, who would meet regularly. The agreement to create these two bodies was the chief concrete result of Dartmouth VII. The subcommittee was stillborn, but Donald

Kendall later became the American cochair of the U.S.-U.S.S.R. Trade and Economic Council. The council was reconstituted in 1993, after the collapse of the Soviet Union, as the U.S.-Russia Business Council.

These two initiatives were designed to increase the supply of information, which the Americans saw as critical to the development of economic relations and trade in particular. The Soviets asserted that the quantity of information that the Soviet Union was making available was more than sufficient. Indeed, they presented Rockefeller with a copy of the most recent statistical yearbook as proof. With the grain deals made earlier in the year in mind, moreover, one of the participants, "While observing that it was his 'personal opinion,' . . . argued that the 'substantial information' already provided the United States by the Soviet Ministry of Agriculture and other ministries 'is detrimental to our own trade interests.'"[61]

The Americans suggested in counterpoint that the information available was not as useful as was needed. In particular, it was not timely. For example, official data on the size of the 1972 grain crop were still not available at the time of the conference. By implication the Soviets agreed that the usefulness of the information available could be improved.

The trade group discussed other obstacles to increasing Soviet-American trade. Among them were difficulties in getting enough capital from private American banks to finance the amount of trade anticipated and projects of the scale that was being contemplated, the inconvertibility of the ruble, the complexity of bureaucracy in the Soviet Union, and the need to negotiate trade deals with senior officials. Not all the Americans saw the last as a problem. The Soviets in general saw no problem as insurmountable and pleaded for optimism about the prospects for trade, seeing in pessimism itself an obstacle to be overcome.

Stewart found the discussions of the environmental work group to be the least satisfactory at Dartmouth VII. A broader range of opinion was expressed there than in the other groups. This may have been, he suggested, because the composition of the delegations differed greatly. The American side was made up of people such as Gordon McDonald, a professor of environmental science at Dartmouth College, and Harrison Brown, the American cochairman. Most had scientific expertise on some aspect of the environment. The first administrator of the Environmental Protection Agency, William Ruckelshaus, also a participant in the conference, had, of course, built up a certain amount of expertise since his appointment in 1970. His expertise was supplemented by that of two of his assistants who attended as observers. On the Soviet side, in contrast, only the chairman, Fedorov, "possesses any scientific competence." Blokhin had been important in fostering cooperation between the two countries in medicine, but he had no counterpart in the American delegation. The rest of the Soviets, as Stewart put it, "must be seen simply as representatives of the Soviet Peace Committee whose influence is primarily limited to the readers of their literary and journalistic writings."[62]

Looked at in the light of more than a quarter century of experience in environmental matters, however, the dialogue contains several points of interest.[63] The discussions took place against the background of both the thirty agreements on scientific cooperation signed at the May summit in Moscow and the dire predictions that emanated from many Western studies of environmental problems, which saw trends in the growth of population and resources leading to a Malthusian nightmare of poverty, hunger, and starvation.[64] Consequently, many of the Western comments expressed a sense that there were, indeed, limits to economic growth and to population. As before, the Soviet side was more sanguine on most environmental issues, even contending at one point, bluntly, that there were no limits to growth.

However, they brought up the matter of the potentially irreversible damage to the biosphere stemming from the increased use of energy. The thermal pollution produced, they said, could change the earth's climate in undesirable ways. They emphasized the need for "global cooperation" in managing this problem. The Americans agreed that this was a problem and were, if anything, more pessimistic about the potential it held for catastrophe. On the related issue of environmental pollution, the Soviet side took a broader view of its causes, seeing them in industry in general, which created radiation, noise, and cancer-causing chemical compounds, as well as dirty air and water. The Americans had a more limited view, seeing the principal source of pollution in the burning of fossil fuels. The prescience of the concern both sides expressed over thermal pollution—foreshadowing some of the concern over global warming—was equaled by the American sense that an energy crisis in the United States was imminent. This was just a year before the crisis triggered by an increase in oil prices by the OPEC countries.

As might be expected, propaganda was not absent from the Soviet remarks. In particular, the need to reduce arms expenditures and end war in order to make resources available to work on environmental problems ran as a constant theme through the Soviet parts of the dialogue. Also, as at Dartmouth VI, the superiority of the Soviet system in taking care of the environment was touted, nonsensical as that seems today.

The two sides agreed that further collaboration on environmental problems should take the form of research. This was a disappointing outcome to some of the Americans. One can imagine that Fedorov and some of his colleagues came to be disappointed as well, as their calls for the more efficient use of energy and efforts to reduce existing sources of pollution were ignored in the Soviet Union.

DARTMOUTH VIII: DÉTENTE, BUT NO TRUCE

A year and a half elapsed before Dartmouth VIII met in a convention center outside Tbilisi, the capital of Georgia. The euphoria in U.S.-Soviet relations that still reigned in December 1972 had subsided. Support was growing for the linkage of trade and Jewish emigration enshrined in the Jackson-Vanik Amendment then before Congress. During the October 1973 war in the Middle East, American forces were placed on alert to oppose the introduction of Soviet troops in the Middle East. This showed in dramatic fashion that American and Soviet interests were far from congruent. Nonetheless, the glow had yet to leave détente entirely. One summit meeting had just taken place in Washington in the summer of 1973, and another one was coming up in June.

In Tbilisi, as at Hanover sixteen months before, there were three work groups. Once again, one group discussed political issues. The mandate of the trade group was expanded to include other economic issues. And the environmental group became the science group, addressing a greater variety of issues. The American members of these groups began work long before the conference opened, as more effort was made to prepare the delegations for the conference than had been made before.

A number of papers were prepared for the American delegation. They were to identify significant issues in U.S.-Soviet relations in order to focus and stimulate discussion at the conference.[65] But as the papers often reflected the viewpoint of the authors about what was important rather than a consensus among the participants, and as there was sometimes no consensus at all in any case, the papers failed in their intended goal. Similar problems were encountered on the Soviet side. So it was agreed that each side would prepare a single paper on the problems that détente would encounter over the next five years. This was the theme of the conference.

The American paper was to have sections from each of the work groups. Professor Thomas Malone, who was now the director of the Holcomb Research Institute at Butler University and chairman of the science group, convened a seminar at the National Academy of Sciences in January 1974 in an effort to reach agreement on how to approach the issues to be addressed by the group. The delegates to the Tbilisi conference were joined by other experts.

The political group also met beforehand, although only three of the delegates were able to attend. They reached consensus, however, on how to approach the issues their group would address. These included arms control, European security, naval competition, the United Nations, public opinion, and the Middle East. Stewart developed the final draft.

The economics group, led by Rockefeller, was made up of people who were already in close contact. They already knew each other's views and, in fact, largely agreed with each other, so they did not feel the need to meet to draft their paper. They left it to one of their number to prepare their section.

The three sections were joined together into a single paper, which was sent to the Soviet participants. They, in their turn, had also prepared a paper. This was made available to the Americans at a planning meeting held in New York three weeks before the conference opened.[66] As often before, the preparations included a "high-level" briefing on U.S.-Soviet relations. This briefing "reflected a new awareness at the highest levels of administration foreign policy-making of the importance to both sides of the informal mechanisms of Dartmouth."[67]

Finally, the American participants flew to Moscow and from there to Tbilisi. The conference took place at a resort outside the city. Sixty-seven people attended the opening session, the first of two plenary sessions at the conference. Unlike at Dartmouth VII, there was no plenary session halfway through. It was dropped at the suggestion of the

Soviets. The participants sat at a large rectangular table to hear the mayor of Tbilisi and the two cochairmen, Zhukov and Cousins, make their opening remarks.[68] Senator Kennedy also addressed the opening plenary session before returning to Moscow.

Joining the American delegation once again, and leading it, was Cousins. His new magazine, *World,* merged with the old as the new owners of the *Saturday Review,* having failed in their effort to change it, sold it to its longtime editor. Pisar, Rockefeller, Yost, Malone, and Donovan also returned, giving the delegation a solid core of people with Dartmouth experience. Landrum Bolling, who was executive vice president of the Lilly Endowment, Inc., attended for the first time; he would remain involved with Dartmouth for more than a decade. His extensive experience in the Middle East had begun at the end of World War II. He had been working with the American Friends Service Committee since 1968.[69] He came to Tbilisi directly following a trip to the Middle East, where he had had discussions with government officials in several countries.

Paul Doty was also back for his first Dartmouth Conference since Dartmouth III. He had continued to discuss arms control issues with the Soviets in the interim as head of the Soviet-American Disarmament Study Group (SADS), which was established by the Committee of the Academy of Arts and Sciences in Cambridge. As he put it, in 1973 "these extracurricular activities were legitimized . . . when I became director of the program on science and international affairs at Harvard."[70]

As at Dartmouth VII, two senators attended the conference. Hugh Scott, a Republican from Pennsylvania, wrote a report on his experience for the Senate Committee on Foreign Relations.[71] As noted, Edward Kennedy, his Democratic colleague, attended as well but only for a day. Another Democratic senator, Stuart Symington, had been invited, but illness led him to decline.

The Soviet delegation was large, as it usually was when the conference was held in the Soviet Union. There were twenty-five Soviet participants, and another eleven men attended as "advisor consultants." Of these thirty-six people, fourteen came from the two main foreign policy institutes in the USSR Academy of Sciences, IMEMO and Arbatov's USA Institute. These included both Arbatov and Primakov, absent from Dartmouth VII. Fedorov was also back to serve as cochair for the science work group. Blokhin returned to join him in that group. Oleg Bykov, who had interpreted at Dartmouth I and for Cousins and Khrushchev in 1963, was now a head of section at IMEMO. This was his first Dartmouth Conference since Rye. Zhukov returned as well to serve again as head of the Soviet delegation. Another veteran, Mostovets, had been appointed recently to an important position in the Soviet policymaking hierarchy. He was now head of the U.S. section of the International Relations Department of the Secretariat of the Communist Party's Central Committee. As Stewart put it, "Mr. Mostovets is directly responsible for both supervising the execution of Party policy (i.e., Soviet policy) toward the United States, and for supervising the preparation of policy recommendations to be considered by the Central Committee or Politbureau in all issues affecting Soviet-American relations."[72]

In his analysis of the conference, Stewart divided the Soviet delegation into two groups. One group, consisting of policy advisors and administrators, included Arbatov and his colleagues from the Institute for the Study of the USA, Primakov and his colleagues from IMEMO, and several other participants. The other group was the "propaganda and public relations group." The chairman of the Soviet delegation, Zhukov, was a prime example. Stewart found this group to be increasingly, disturbingly active at Dartmouth VIII. Its members sought, as a number of their predecessors had, to make Dartmouth an instrument of Soviet foreign policy. An example of this was the proposal—made before and here again—for an American counterpart to the Institute for Soviet-American Relations.

Now that the conferences were well into their second decade, one of the characteristics of the Dartmouth dialogues had become an awareness that the conferences were linked, that they were each part of a process, though that process had yet to be clearly defined. Consequently, the issue of what to do between conferences in order to facilitate the dialogue that took place at the conferences was addressed again. One proposal that was adopted was for a series of meetings to be held between conferences. Small numbers of delegates would meet to discuss specific problems.

An indication of the changes that the dialogues were making possible was an incident that took place during a reception at the Kremlin held after the participants returned to Moscow. Aleksei P. Shitikov, chairman of the Council of the Union, one of the two chambers of the Supreme Soviet, responded to a question with a denunciation of Henry Kissinger's shuttle diplomacy, then taking place between Israel and Syria. Yuri Zhukov interrupted him. Stewart, who speaks fluent Russian, heard Zhukov say, in an aside that the interpreter did not pick up: "Your statements on this are now out of date. We have already gone beyond this position in our Dartmouth discussions." The incident suggests that the Soviet delegates were not mere mouthpieces for the Kremlin line; their opinions were undergoing some change during the Dartmouth discussions.

The structure of the Tbilisi conference was much like that of its predecessor, though with two plenary sessions, rather than three. The work of the conference was concentrated in the work group discussions, held over two days. As usual, there was ample time given to informal activities outside the conference that would allow the participants to get to know both one another and the republic of Georgia. The oppor-tunities for informal contacts were somewhat limited, however, because the Soviet delegates ate and slept far from the conference center.

Rockefeller and his fellow businessmen seem to have been the focus of special attention. Rockefeller, James Ferguson, president of General Foods, and William Hewitt, chairman of Deere and Company, were the guests of Mikhail Zakhmatov one night for dinner at a small restaurant on a lake outside the city. Zakhmatov was young, a chief of section at the USA Institute, with an interest in economic matters. He had been prominent in the discussions of the trade group at Dartmouth VII, sometimes suggesting clear, generational differences with the older Orlov, the Soviet cochairman. He was not one of the participants in Dartmouth VIII but attended as one of the Soviet advisor consultants.[73] After the conference Ambassador Stoessel held a reception for Rockefeller, Ferguson, and Hewitt at Spaso House in Moscow, attended by Arbatov. This followed a meeting with Stoessel and embassy staff attended by the entire American delegation. This meeting gave Rockefeller an opportunity to brief the American officials on the results from the economic work group.[74]

The discussions of the political group suffered from a surfeit of Soviets.[75] The six Americans were confronted with twenty-four Soviets, including eight advisor consultants. The Soviet delegation this time included three experts in military affairs, Mikhail Milstein, Zhurkin, and Genrich Trofimenko, and two experts on the Middle East, Primakov and Belyaev. There were also four experts on European affairs, V. I. Gantman, Oleg Bykov, Dmitri Ermolenko, and Vikentii Matveev. Their expertise was not matched on the American side, but their presence suggested that European matters were now a high priority of the Soviets. The political group was clearly the most important to the Soviet organizers. The result of having a large number of people in the group, however, was that the atmosphere was more formal than in the meetings of the other two groups. There were also fewer opportunities for extended exchanges among participants.

Milstein frequently took part in Dartmouth dialogues through the 1970s and 1980s. Born before the Soviet Union was formed, he was orphaned by it at an early age, when his parents were exiled to Siberia and died there or on the way. Like Arbatov, he distinguished himself during World War II. Wounded during the war and decorated for his courage, he entered military intelligence and attained the rank of general. He was dedicated to the Soviet state, as he showed even in private conversation in the late Gorbachev period. The Soviet Union was, for him, a replacement for the parents who had died.[76]

The political group discussed both arms control and European affairs. On arms control, both sides expressed their concern that while limitations on strategic arms had been agreed to as a part of SALT I, arms reductions had not, so the arms race continued. On European affairs and the efforts to reduce both conventional and tactical nuclear weapons, the two sides agreed, "Military détente is a sine qua non for political détente in Europe."[77]

In the discussion of the Middle East the two sides seemed to agree on little, save that the disengagement of military forces was important, that the United Nations should have a role, and that the proposed Geneva conference would be significant. A point related to the importance of the Geneva conference, which would include the Soviet Union in the peace process in the Middle East, was the concern expressed by the Soviet delegates that Henry Kissinger, in his efforts to broker a peace through "shuttle diplomacy," was not treating the Soviet Union as a full partner in the search for peace. This was a theme that would have particular significance for Dartmouth in the coming years. This expression of concern was also an indication—one of several in the Dartmouth conferences during the mid-1970s—that a purpose of Dartmouth for the Soviets was to push for the full benefits that they believed should derive from their newly attained nuclear equality with the United States.[78]

As before, discussion touched on the role of public opinion in foreign policy. As might be expected, the hopes of the Americans that there would be some discussion of public opinion in the Soviet Union were disappointed. They tried again to explain the composition of American public opinion and why support for détente was decreasing. While the Soviets suggested ways to manipulate that opinion, the Americans suggested that the solution to this problem could be resolved through policies and agreements that the public saw as beneficial.

The group also discussed conflicts in Southeast Asia, the U.S.-Soviet relationship in the Indian Ocean, where the naval presence of the two countries was being expanded, and the continuing problem of China. The Soviet paper prepared before the conference and the discussions at the conference affirmed the importance of the United Nations. Cousins took heart from this, but the approaches of the Soviets and the Americans to the United Nations differed significantly. The Soviets complained about the growth of UN activity on social and economic issues, according to Stewart, but the Americans stressed that the United Nations' importance on issues stemming from the scarcity of resources was increasing.

In the discussions in the economic group, the Soviet delegates were more willing to discuss the prerequisites of trade than they had been at Dartmouth VII. They were less inclined to focus on MFN status, although the central importance of this issue to the Soviet delegates remained apparent. The Americans suggested that the lack of MFN status was more a psychological barrier than a real one as most Soviet goods could not be successfully marketed in the United States anyway. The Soviets saw what they regarded as ungenerous terms offered by American firms and lending institutions as a continuing, significant constraint. They implied that this was due to a lack of political will in the U.S. government. The Americans argued that these economic institutions were private and separate from the government. They, in their turn, saw the monopolistic nature of Soviet economic institutions and the secrecy with which they habitually operated as hindering the expansion of trade. Leasing arrangements and international banking consortia were also seen as ways to minimize the barriers to trade that had been described, such as the ban on private ownership.

The Soviets expressed interest in joint ventures in the Third World. This was an idea pushed by Pisar, who thought that instead of exporting arms to gain political influence, the two countries could cooperate in programs to improve health, education, and agriculture.[79] He called his idea "transideological enterprise." Pisar saw his Soviet colleagues blanch when he suggested that this would require an ideological truce, but the economic sessions were distinguished by generally free give-and-take and a lack of dogma on the Soviet side.[80]

The discussions of the science group differed little from those of the environmental group at Dartmouth VII. As Stewart saw it, the approach of the Soviet group members to the discussions "consisted primarily of receptive listening and pointed probing in response to American proposals and ideas." In truth, the Soviet participants, as before, saw little need for changes in their country's policies that affected the environment. Moreover, they insisted that there was no crisis in the world's supply of energy or resources. The Americans believed more strongly that the world's biological and economic resources were limited. Nonetheless, cooperative research was still welcomed by both sides. And in keeping with their desire, expressed time and again in the Dartmouth discussions, to be dealt with as an equal in international affairs, the Soviets expressed interest in participating in the network of international agricultural research institutions that was being formed. They never took part in the activities of this network, however. This may have been at least partly because this network, which became the Consultative Group for International Agricultural Research (CGIAR), was associated with the World Bank.

During the final plenary session, the role and structure of the Dartmouth Conference became the subject of the discussion. Cousins saw an important change in the purpose of the conference. Whereas it had been important in the early days simply to broaden the dialogue at a time when official contacts were minimal, the conference could now "explore ways of resolving specific issues."[81] The Soviets also saw a need for the conference to serve as a means for strengthening public support for improved Soviet-American relations.

With these purposes in mind, the two delegations discussed how to change the structure of the Dartmouth Conference. Most of the proposals came from the Soviet side, which suggested to Stewart that they were part of a planned, concerted initiative. The idea of a permanent American counterpart to the Institute for Soviet-American Relations was raised again, but the proposals that received the most attention were for some less formal means of filling the gap between conferences, perhaps with one or more working groups with just a few participants. As the conference ended, there was informal agreement among the participants that this was the next step that Dartmouth should take.

Primakov recalled in his memoirs that during the conference the Soviet side decided to invite the Americans for an evening with a Georgian family.[82] He received permission to do this from the first secretary of the Georgian Communist Party—Eduard Shevardnadze, who later became Gorbachev's foreign minister and president of Georgia—and then arranged to have Rockefeller, Senator Scott, Yost, and Donovan go to the apartment of his wife's aunt, Nadezhda Vasilevna Kharadze. She was a professor of music and a former prima donna with the Tbilisi opera. As Primakov puts it, however, she "lived modestly," like most members of the Georgian intelligentsia. The group walked up to her fourth-floor apartment in the dark—there was neither lift nor light—and sang songs until the Americans left at 3:00 in the morning. According to Primakov, Rockefeller later spoke of that evening often.

The day after the conference ended, Rockefeller met with Premier Kosygin, as he had in 1971. They spoke for an hour and a half, mostly about economic issues. These included the problems of the American balance of payments and energy—this was the time of the first energy crisis in the United States, stemming from the dramatic increase in oil prices by OPEC.[83] Kosygin asked Rockefeller a number of questions: whether the good grain harvest in the United States would bring prices down, what Rockefeller thought of the prospects of the dollar and interest rates, and what Rockefeller thought about the Japanese and European interest rate problems. They discussed how to lower energy prices.

Rockefeller brought up the matter of U.S.-Soviet economic cooperation as discussed by the economics section at Tbilisi. The section, he said, had agreed that the U.S.-USSR trade council should conduct some studies that would address the possibility of such cooperation. Kosygin agreed but added that the details would have to be worked out.[84] The premier then asked what he described as a private, off-the-record question about cooperation between the United States and the Soviet Union on building nuclear power plants for export. "Through this method," he said, "we could corner the market and force oil prices down." He emphasized that this matter was confidential and preliminary. Rockefeller proposed exploring the matter with Kissinger and William Simon, then head of the Federal Energy Office in the White House, but Kosygin demurred, proposing instead that Rockefeller wait to move the matter into official channels until after Kosygin and his "colleagues" discussed the matter further and prepared a paper for Rockefeller. Rockefeller could then reply—orally, Kosygin suggested—through Ambassador Dobrynin.

Rockefeller was not the only participant to speak with a Soviet leader. Senator Kennedy spoke with Brezhnev before flying to Tbilisi. He spoke with Foreign Minister Gromyko as well. Senator Scott met with Brezhnev in the Kremlin on April 26, the day the conference ended. Brezhnev and the senator spoke for two hours, covering several topics, including the *Apollo-Soyuz* space mission, which Senator Scott said he had discussed with Mikhail Suslov in 1971, and the arms control negotiations. Brezhnev spoke of the Soviet Union's need for "international cooperation" to exploit its natural resources, oil and gas in particular. They discussed the trade bill then before Congress, which was the subject of the Jackson-Vanik Amendment, and the linkage between trade and human rights.

DARTMOUTH IX: DÉTENTE EBBS

As planned, the ninth Dartmouth Conference was to be a small affair, not a full-fledged conference at all, but simply a meeting of the "Executive Steering Committee." After Dartmouth VIII, a steering committee established among the Americans made five proposals for activities that could take place before the next full-fledged conference.[85] The Soviet side responded with a proposal for an open, informal discussion on how to strengthen Dartmouth. The discussion would also include an exchange of views on economic relations, the Middle East, and arms control. No formal papers were to be exchanged beforehand. The Americans accepted the Soviet proposal, pleased with the idea of doing something between conferences.

The Americans prepared a single paper for themselves that addressed the three broad topics about which views were to be exchanged. As they had expected, the Soviet participants in the conference wanted to see this paper, and so they received translations of the two sections on economic relations and arms control and copies of the original analyses used to draft the Middle Eastern section.

The American delegates met in New York before the conference, as they had before Dartmouth VIII. A high-ranking State Department official briefed the group on current relations with the Soviet Union. The delegates then held a "lively, informed, and informing exchange" on the issues. A number of materials on détente and translations of articles by Soviet observers in the USA Institute and IMEMO were made available so that the American participants could know the views of their Soviet counterparts. Most of these Soviet pieces argued in favor of détente, so Stewart found the inclusion of an article by a Professor Sobolev in the journal *Rabochiy klass i sovremenniy mir* to be especially important. The article reflected the views of Soviet hard-liners. Focused on the competitive aspects of détente, Sobolev's piece explained that it was a ploy to weaken Soviet society. The article was essential to the preparations of the American side for the discussions.

There were ten American delegates to the conference. Five of them had been at Dartmouth VIII: Bolling, Cousins, Read, Rockefeller, and Stewart. Three had been at Dartmouth VII: Brzezinski, the Kettering Foundation's Chollar, and George Rathjens, the MIT professor and expert on arms control. There were also two newcomers: Lawrence Brainard, an economist at Chase Manhattan, and Richard Furlaud, chief executive officer and chairman of the board of Squibb Corporation.[86]

On the Soviet side, Zhukov, Fedorov, and Blokhin attended the conference only briefly. Zhukov was at a conference on the reduction of nuclear weapons in Stockholm, Fedorov was negotiating an agreement with the United States not to use environmental modification in war, and Blokhin was able to attend only the last session. Arbatov was the Soviet cochairman. Most of the rest of the Soviet delegates were familiar to their American interlocutors. They included Primakov, Mostovets, Zhurkin, Trofimenko, and Bykov. About a dozen people formed a core of the Soviet delegation, present most of the time. The rest came and went through the three days the conference met. On average, there were about twenty-five Soviet delegates present at each session to face the ten Americans. Many became available only because the conference was held in Moscow, a virtue of holding a conference in a capital city. Arbatov, in fact, took advantage of the location of the conference to rotate groups of experts in, expanding the number exposed to the dialogue.[87] This was all to the good from both the American and Soviet perspectives. On the other hand, the diverse obligations that a capital creates kept many of the Soviet participants from becoming fully engaged in the dialogue or available for the private conversations that had been valuable at earlier conferences. Stewart noted that only about four Soviet participants were able to join the Americans for lunch or dinner.[88]

Dzherman Gvishiani was one Soviet participant who would have been unlikely to come had the conference been held outside Moscow. He was the deputy chairman of the State Committee on Science and Technology whose name came up in Rockefeller's conversation with Kosygin in 1971. More important, particularly in the Soviet context, he was Kosygin's son-in-law, with whom the premier shared a home.[89] Gvishiani had intended to come to Dartmouth VIII and had, in fact, written a paper for the conference that was published in the conference brochure afterward. But illness had prevented him from coming to Tbilisi.

The conference opened with a discussion of current threats to détente. In the United States, opposition to it had been growing, as the vote on the Jackson-Vanik Amendment suggested, though it was by no means dominant in American public opinion. The Americans wondered whether opposition to détente had also been growing within the Soviet Union. They started the conference asking for an explanation of the Sobolev article.[90] Arbatov could not explain it—he had not read the article—but he assured the Americans that the views expressed were contrary to those of the Soviet government.

With that, the discussion moved to the other items on the agenda. Four other topics were to be discussed: trade and economic relations, the Middle East, arms control, and ways to strengthen Dartmouth. This set of topics was smaller than the agendas of previous Dartmouth conferences, but it prefigured the task forces that would be created a few years later. Notably absent were discussions of scientific or environmental issues. The Soviet steering committee had indicated to the Americans that cooperation on these issues had progressed far enough that there was no need to include them on the agenda.[91] Nor were other regional conflicts included—Vietnam had been settled by the complete victory of the North the previous spring, but Angola was becoming a major issue in Soviet-American relations as the Soviet-backed faction was approaching victory with strong and open Cuban support.

The discussion of trade came after the Jackson-Vanik and Stevenson Amendments to the Trade Reform Bill had been passed by Congress and signed into law by President Ford the previous January. This legislation in effect placed strict limitations on U.S.-Soviet trade. Both sides expressed hopes for continued improvement in trade relations. The Soviets argued that American firms had become less competitive. The Soviet Union, they said, could go to firms in Europe and Japan instead. Zakhmatov, on the other hand, was pessimistic, arguing that MFN status, limited by the Jackson-Vanik Amendment, and credits from the Export-Import Bank, limited by the Stevenson Amendment, meant everything to the expansion of trade. Arbatov found this comment unconstructive and told him so.[92] This was a sign that the Soviet side was less set on marching in lockstep than it had been earlier.

Brainard, the Chase economist, thought that the major result of the conference was the willingness of the Soviets to discuss the problems and prospects of joint ventures.[93] His notes show that this willingness was shown mostly by Arbatov and his colleague Evgeni Shershnev from the USA Institute. The latter made the Soviet statement on trade in counterpoint to Rockefeller. Brainard found this to be a significant change in policy, although he noted that the Soviets were still talking about creating such ventures as experiments and that it would be five years before "practical" joint ventures became a reality. This prediction proved to be optimistic.

But Arbatov took joint ventures seriously. In later years he put what he learned about them at Dartmouth and elsewhere to practical use. His commitment to them became evident in the late 1980s, after Gorbachev began his efforts to reform the Soviet economy. Arbatov helped influence the first law on joint ventures and worked tirelessly with American firms to create them.[94]

The discussion of the Middle East came in the context of Kissinger's shuttle diplomacy in the region, which had pointedly excluded the Soviet Union. The Soviet participants did not overlook this exclusion. One reason for it was the inability of the Soviet Union to carry any influence in Israel. Much of the conversation indirectly focused on this point. The Soviets complained that the Israelis did not take seriously their offer to facilitate a settlement by helping guarantee Israel's borders; the Americans suggested that Soviet resumption of relations with Israel might be in order. The Soviets, however, replied that this step could only follow Israeli withdrawal from the lands occupied during the Six Day War. Brzezinski suggested that the United States and the Soviet Union issue a joint statement in which they defined what they regarded to be the essential aspects of a durable peace between the Israelis and the Arabs.

Rathjens opened the discussion of arms control with an argument that agreements should reduce arms rather than simply freeze the balance of offensive weapons. This was a criticism commonly made in the United States of the agreement reached between Brezhnev and President Ford at Vladivostok the previous November. The Soviets at Dartmouth IX were more impressed by the recognition, as they saw it, of the Soviet achievement of nuclear equality. The discussion showed agreement over the general notions that the two sides had an equal right to security—a Soviet delegate called it a right to equal insecurity—but disagreement over almost everything else. To an American suggestion that the two countries do more to share their strategic thinking and cooperate in studying strategic concepts, the Soviets replied that relations between the two countries were not yet advanced enough to discuss such matters in detail.

The last session of the conference was spent discussing ways to improve the Dartmouth conferences, once again showing a self-consciousness absent from the early conferences. Several proposals about how to proceed were made, but there was general agreement that some form of activity by small groups between conferences continued to be desirable. Task forces, they said, could be formed to discuss détente, the Middle East, and arms control. Another group could discuss the effectiveness of Dartmouth. In his final statement, Arbatov said, "[W]e definitely will have a meeting in the fall of smaller groups." He named two topics that were "explicitly acceptable to the Soviet side": making Dartmouth more effective and the "process of détente."[95] The two sides agreed to exchange letters on the matter of these task forces and to hold Dartmouth X in the United States the following spring.

As usual, David Rockefeller had a panoply of meetings while he was in Moscow. They included another meeting with Kosygin, which took the place of a meeting with Brezhnev, canceled owing to an illness.

TASK FORCE EXPERIMENTS

As promised in Moscow, two task forces met late in 1975. As has been seen, for several years now many Dartmouth participants thought that some kind of small meeting held between conferences would be useful. It would allow the dialogue begun at the conferences to continue and, perhaps, deepen. The two meetings held in New York in December were experiments designed to do just that. The subject of one, the future of Dartmouth, might have been expected, given the dialogue on the topic at Dartmouth IX and the remark of Arbatov that the topic was acceptable to the Soviets. The subject of the other, the Middle East, could not have been predicted as easily. But the meeting proved to be one of the more important in the history of Dartmouth.

In December 1975 six people met at the St. Regis Hotel on Fifth Avenue in Manhattan to address issues in the Middle East. This task force included Cousins, Yost, and Bolling on the American side. Their Soviet counterparts were Vitali Zhurkin and Aleksandr Kislov of the Institute for the Study of the USA and Igor Belyaev, a vice director of the Africa Institute.[96]

Both groups gave their summary of the situation in the Middle East and what they believed should form the elements of a settlement of the Arab-Israeli conflict. They found that they had much in common, including skepticism about whether either unilateral action by the United States or the Soviet Union or the actions then being taken through the United Nations could bring a settlement. They then played a game, as Bolling put it. What if their governments had asked them to draft a resolution for the Security Council to consider? They began with the principles contained in Security Council Resolution 242, passed in 1967 after the Six Day War. After much debate they created a draft resolution. It included what Bolling described as a modest proposal, affirming both the right of Israel to exist as a secure and independent state and the right of the Palestinians to govern themselves. The participants agreed to forward the draft to both governments. The ideas contained within it were elaborated on at both Dartmouth X and Dartmouth XI.

At Dartmouth X and later, the Soviet participants noted that the task force discussions in the St. Regis Hotel had influenced a rethinking of official Soviet policy on the Middle East. Primakov later also told Harold Saunders that these conversations had a significant influence on the Soviet government. He added that they had influenced the Soviet draft of a joint statement by Secretary of State Cyrus Vance and Foreign Minister Gromyko at the United Nations in October 1977.[97] At Dartmouth XVI in 1988, one of the Soviet speakers also suggested that some of the ideas in the joint statement came from a document published at the Brookings Institution a week after the meeting in New York by a group that included one of the American participants in the task force discussions and Brzezinski.[98] The codirector of the Brookings group happened to be Yost. It is understandable that the two documents would be similar. The exchange at the St. Regis would have given participants a sense of what the other side could accept. Apparently the Brookings draft came to the attention of Gromyko and, perhaps, Brezhnev. It is not known who saw the paper drafted at the St. Regis Hotel; we know only, through the statements of Primakov and others, that it influenced Soviet policy.

The statement produced at the United Nations in October 1977 set out the views of the two cochairmen of the Geneva conference on the Middle East on the objectives of the conference were it to reconvene for the first time since it first met in December 1973. The conference would have established a framework for negotiation of the Middle East conflict. Both superpowers would have played key roles. The idea for the statement came at the initiative of the Soviets, who produced a draft that Brzezinski described as moderate.[99] The views expressed in the draft were similar to those expressed in the meetings at the St. Regis. When issued, the statement was bitterly denounced by the Israelis. The United States soon began to back away from the statement, and any practical effect it might have had died when Sadat's dramatic trip to Israel the next month placed resolution of the conflict between Egypt and Israel outside the framework of the Geneva conference. The October statement, an all-too-rare example of U.S.-Soviet cooperation in a conflict in the Third World, long remained the high point of superpower cooperation in the Middle East.

Examining what influence Dartmouth might have had here shows how complex influences on policy can be. Bolling told Harold Saunders, an old acquaintance who then directed the Bureau of Intelligence and Research at the State Department, about the St. Regis meeting.[100] Saunders was interested in knowing what had happened but found the results parallel to advanced U.S. thinking as reflected in the Brookings report, published a week later. Yost was a key figure in both groups, and what he learned from the St. Regis discussions may have found its way into the Brookings document.[101] It was that document that apparently came to the attention of Soviet decision makers and was incorporated into policy more than a year and a half later. Yet the assessment of Primakov and, possibly, his Soviet colleagues from Dartmouth that the St. Regis paper influenced policy suggests that the paper's influence came more directly.

Beyond the papers, the ideas may have been transmitted through people who carried them. Bolling later briefed presidential candidate Jimmy Carter on the Arab-Israeli conflict. Two other people in the Brookings study became important officials in the Carter administration. Brzezinski became President Carter's national security advisor. He hired William Quandt as his chief Middle East staff member. The St. Regis discussions, therefore, may have had two paths of influence— through Bolling directly to Carter or through Yost to the Brookings group and thence through Brzezinski and Quandt to affect the policies of the Carter administration. In any case, the discussions seem to have added something to the climate of opinion in which the Carter administration formulated its policies on the Middle East.

The other task force—the Task Force on Process—examined ways to make the Dartmouth Conference more effective. By effective, the members meant that Dartmouth would be better able to increase understanding and cooperation between the two superpowers, particularly when it came to solving problems affecting not only the United States and the Soviet Union, "but all mankind."[102] These task force discussions made it clear that the purpose of Dartmouth had expanded yet again. At Dartmouth I, simply having a dialogue that opened lines of communication was an important achievement. Under General Gavin, the purpose became more ambitious. He wanted the conferences to influence policy. Dartmouth was to help expand the dialogue between the two countries in order to foster greater agreement on issues important in the bilateral relationship. The purpose now included having the two countries work together to find solutions to problems affecting mankind in general.

The task force discussed all aspects of the conferences, from preparation to implementation, and the participants expressed satisfaction with how Dartmouth had evolved. Many of their recommendations amounted to no more than continuing to do what was being done—continuing the plenary plus work group format, for example. There were two exceptions.

First, the Task Force on Process considered task forces to be an essential part of the preparation for the full conferences. The idea was to convene them to discuss specific issues, spend no more than a year investigating the issue, and then have them disband after preparing a report to the full conference. Although the Americans, in particular, tried to convene a task force like this, they could not. Probably because the timing was bad—Dartmouth XI would leave a sour taste in the mouths of some—money for such projects was becoming scarce, and the topic chosen by the task force, world food policy, was not of equal interest to both sides, as was to become clear later. But the success of the work group format that had been adopted by Dartmouth made it almost inevitable that task forces would become an important part the Dartmouth process.

Second, the task force said that the membership in the delegations should be diversified to include people from a broader set of institutions, more women, younger delegates, and greater "geographical diversity." The latter was not defined, but it probably meant that the Soviet delegation should include more people from outside Moscow and the American delegation should include more people from outside the Northeast Corridor.

The Task Force on Process also did much of the preparatory work for organizing Dartmouth X. The structure of that conference largely followed its recommendations. It suggested that each side prepare papers on each of the topics on the agenda, as they had done at Dartmouth VII. This was done. The task group also set the agenda for Dartmouth X. There were nine major items. As had become usual, many of them were issues that were then prominent in the bilateral relationship. They included détente, an evaluation of the Helsinki accords signed the previous year, arms control, economic relations, and the Middle East.

The American side proposed two other issues, energy and the environment. This was part of an effort to have Dartmouth discuss issues that were important, but not yet prominent in Soviet-American relations. The acceptance by the Soviet steering committee of the proposal to place these items on the agenda was regarded as a significant accomplishment in view of this goal.

The conclusions reached by both task forces were tentative and regarded as subject to approval by the steering committee and Dartmouth X. The Soviet participants were especially reluctant to consider the documents produced by the task forces, which showed areas of common interest, to be joint proposals. This reluctance led some of the Americans to doubt whether the task forces could help make Dartmouth more effective. On the other hand, the participants from both countries believed that the discussions in the task forces had been "substantially more effective" and even found that the tentative conclusions reached suggested that the format could be useful in preparing for the full conferences.

DARTMOUTH X: CONVERSATIONS IN THE DESERT

Preparations for Dartmouth X began in October 1975 when the steering committee met at Chase Manhattan Bank in New York. Nine people came. All had been at one of the two previous conferences: David Rockefeller, Landrum Bolling, Robert Chollar, Norman Cousins, Paul Doty, Thomas Malone, Sterling Wortman, James Read, and Philip Stewart. These men can be considered to be the core of Dartmouth at the time. Three—Rockefeller, Cousins, and Doty—had been associated with Dartmouth for more than a decade.

These men were determined to improve the ability of the Dartmouth Conference to lay a basis for cooperative action by both the

Soviet Union and the United States that could solve problems they faced in common. Détente was no longer in full flower, but it still bloomed. It was still easy to be optimistic about the possibilities for cooperation. To the steering committee, it was no longer enough to find common ground. That had been done. Dartmouth had to show ways to act on it. The preparations the steering committee determined upon reflected this. These preparations had three parts: (1) two interim meetings held that had been agreed on at Dartmouth VIII; (2) decisions made about the structure and content of the preparatory papers; and (3) organization of the meeting held to prepare the American delegates for the conference.[103]

The interim meetings were discussed earlier. The preparatory papers were put together by the chairmen of the four groups that were expected to meet during the conference. The Task Force on Process, when it met in December 1975, recommended that each group prepare a separate paper, like the papers written for Dartmouth VII, rather than a single paper for the entire delegation like that written for Dartmouth VIII. The American papers were prepared by Stewart, on political issues; Doty, on arms control; Bolling, on the Middle East; and Richard Gardner, on "global cooperation." Gardner, new to Dartmouth, was a professor of law and international organization at Columbia University Law School. His paper discussed issues such as environmental problems, world food shortages, and Third World development. Stewart noted later that the Soviet papers rarely went beyond identifying issues and describing official proposals for solutions. Zhurkin commended the papers by Gardner and Stewart for putting current problems in the perspective of the future course of U.S.-Soviet relations.

The preparatory meeting for Dartmouth X was held in New York on April 16. Helmut Sonnenfeldt, counselor for the State Department, briefed participants for about forty-five minutes on official views of Soviet-American relations and related issues. He stressed that fora such as the Dartmouth Conference were important at a time when the perceptions, interests, and objectives of the superpowers diverged. After Sonnenfeldt's presentation, participants discussed what the conference should focus on and who should "take the lead" on certain topics.

The conference opened at the end of April in Rio Rico, Arizona, a resort in the mountains rising from the Sonoran desert, south of Tucson close to the Mexican border. The isolation of Rio Rico placed Dartmouth

X in stark contrast with Dartmouth IX, where the distractions of Moscow had the delegates coming and going throughout the conference. Residing in a single facility and taking advantage of the amenities of a resort, delegates had many chances to converse informally.

The two delegations were much more equal in size than they had been at Dartmouth IX, with twenty Americans coming to Arizona to talk to sixteen Soviets. As now seemed to be the rule, most of the delegates had been to Dartmouth conferences before. The delegations included Bolling, Brzezinski, Yost, Rockefeller, and Cousins on the American side and Arbatov, Primakov, Mostovets, Zhukov, and Zhurkin on the Soviet. Stewart was again the rapporteur for the conference and Phillips Ruopp provided organizational support. Joining them on staff for the first time was Patricia Coggins. She would gain the respect and affection of everyone involved with Dartmouth over the next two decades as she made the arrangements for virtually everyone and everything on the American side. Zakhmatov attended this conference as an observer rather than as a participant, owing to his new position as counselor in the Soviet embassy in Washington.

The new American participants included three figures intended to add depth to the arms control work group. They were Harold Agnew, director of the Los Alamos Scientific Laboratory, which conducted research on nuclear weapons; Barry Blechman, then a young, respected analyst for the Brookings Institution; and Paul Warnke, who had been assistant secretary of defense. Regarded as a dovish, strong advocate of arms control, Warnke, quick-witted and controversial, would have a prominent role in the arms control efforts of the Carter administration. Marshall Shulman returned to the Dartmouth Conference for the first time since Dartmouth IV. He was now director of the Russian Institute at Columbia University, a position once held by Mosely. Gardner, of course, wrote the preparatory paper on global issues. A colleague of Brzezinski, he was also a friend of Cyrus Vance, who served Jimmy Carter as secretary of state and was a member of the Trilateral Commission.[104]

The new Soviet participants included Stanislav Borisov, a deputy finance minister, who came as the Soviet cochairman for the group that discussed global issues, replacing Fedorov. Boris Runov was not new to Dartmouth—he had taken part in Dartmouth VIII and Dartmouth

IX—but his importance to the conference increased over the next two years as the world food problem gained prominence on the agenda of the conference. He had been a deputy minister of agriculture since 1970. In his early fifties, he had earned a doctorate in agricultural sciences, spoke fluent English, and had been agricultural counselor in the embassy in Ottawa during the 1960s. He attended Iowa State University as an exchange student in 1960 and had been to the United States several times since.[105]

Before the conference the American side expressed its concern over the quality of the Soviet representatives intended for the arms control work group. Indeed, when the delegation appeared at Rio Rico, there was no Soviet working on arms control with the stature or expertise of Doty, Agnew, Warnke, or Blechman.

To be fair, this was probably partly because until the 1980s almost all of the arms control expertise in the Soviet Union remained in the military. People like Talensky, who was himself a retired general, were the exception rather than the rule. The ignorance of even basic technical information among the civilians had been clear to those involved in the negotiations over SALT I.[106] Indeed, Stewart's complaint about the Soviet delegates to Dartmouth X—that they were well read in the American literature on arms control but knew little about Soviet programs and weapons systems—was, as he acknowledges, precisely the same complaint that American negotiators had about their Soviet civilian counterparts. Some of the Americans suggested that they respond to the Soviet failure to send their best experts by not attending themselves. But owing at least in part to the dissatisfaction of the Americans, the Soviet delegation came to the conference especially well prepared to discuss these issues. The discussions proved useful after all.

The arms control work group was to have been one of four at the conference, according to the arrangements agreed to by the Task Force on Process. This was to give the conference a structure similar to those of Dartmouth VII and Dartmouth VIII, and the conferees came to Rio Rico expecting arms control to be discussed separately, with Doty serving as American cochairman and a paper he wrote helping to frame the discussion. But as a result of American protestations about the weakness of the participants in the arms control group, that group was combined with the political work group, giving the conference only three work groups.

As so often before, Cousins opened the conference. Like the rest of the conference, his address focused on détente. He noted the problems with it that had arisen but argued that détente was needed and that the problems could and would be solved. Zhukov and Arbatov replied for the Soviet delegation, with Arbatov speaking in English. They explained the Soviet approach to détente as outlined by Brezhnev at the recently completed Twenty-fifth CPSU Congress.

Two more plenary sessions were held during the conference. One came in the middle of the conference, as at Dartmouth VII. It focused on reports that the work groups were preparing. This proved to be a way of giving the participants a sense of taking part in all the work groups, not just their own, and improved the coherence of the conference as a whole. The reports were also a useful way to make the discussions more concrete. One Soviet participant who, Stewart wrote, had been prone to giving long polemical orations at previous meetings simply distributed copies of his remarks to his work group rather than read them.

The group that worked on political issues, having had its agenda expanded by the inclusion of the arms control group, found itself unable to discuss fully all the issues on its agenda.[107] It gave short shrift to the United Nations. On the other hand, it covered a wide range of arms control issues. Group members on both sides spoke in favor of a comprehensive ban on the testing of nuclear weapons and expressed concern about both the proliferation of nuclear weapons and the continuing development of weapons systems. The support that the Soviets gave to allied movements in the Third World, as in Angola, was a matter for disagreement here, as it had been at the first few Dartmouth conferences.

The group on the Middle East picked up where it had left off in December. Its membership was somewhat different, however, with Primakov present and Belyaev absent. Nonetheless, the group reaffirmed the recommendations made in New York, favoring "joint or parallel" action by both the United States and the Soviet Union and recognition of the national rights of both Israelis and Palestinians.[108]

The third work group discussed a range of "global issues" that included energy, food, and economic cooperation. The last issue had originally been part of the brief given to the group that discussed political issues but was reassigned to lighten that group's load after it was given arms control issues. The group agreed that the two countries should cooperate on joint research on the mining and use of coal and called attention to the possibilities of nuclear fusion as a source of energy. It recommended greater cooperation in international bodies working to increase agricultural production, such as the Food and Agriculture Organization of the United Nations and the CGIAR, which had been discussed by the science group at Dartmouth VIII in Tbilisi. The discussion of economic cooperation noted the increase in U.S.-Soviet trade, but it included, predictably, the failure of the United States to grant the Soviet Union most-favored-nation status.

There was also discussion of three possible links between the Soviet Union and the rest of the world economy: a convertible ruble, membership in the General Agreement on Tariffs and Trade (GATT), and membership in the International Monetary Fund (IMF). In each case, the Soviet participants found a reason not to bring the Soviet Union closer economically to the rest of the world. They (and the Americans) noted the incompatibility of a convertible currency with a centrally planned economy. There was clear reason given why the Soviet Union could not join GATT; this was recognized as a political decision that had not been made. As for the IMF, the Soviets objected to the system of weighted voting, which gave the wealthier countries (they did not include the Soviet Union) greater power within the organization. The "new international economic order" was also discussed, but the Soviets argued that this was a matter between the West and the South. In other words, they saw it as a problem for the imperialist and former colonial powers, which bore guilt for what had happened in the Third World. The Soviet Union, as it did not share that guilt, they argued, would deal with the South bilaterally, as it was doing in its economic relations with India.

By the time of the third and final plenary, each work group had completed its paper. Stewart described the papers as "the first jointly developed and approved, relatively detailed statements of the results of the discussions to be produced in ten Dartmouth Conferences." These papers also formed the basis for the final communiqué for the conference. As most of the work on this communiqué had, therefore, been done before the final session, agreement on the text came quickly, leaving time for discussion about the Dartmouth process as a whole.

This gave the communiqué a different character from the communiqués issued at the early conferences, which were meant merely to inform the public in the most general terms about what was discussed at the conferences. The communiqué from Dartmouth X, in contrast, gave much more detail and was intended to be more substantive.

Given the prominence that the issue of Jewish emigration from the Soviet Union had at the time, owing to the link of that issue with trade made through the Jackson-Vanik Amendment, it may have taken some courage for Arbatov and Zhukov, the two Soviet cochairmen, to meet with leaders of the Jewish community in Tucson.[109] As might have been expected, they discussed Soviet policy on providing exit visas to Soviet Jews. The dialogue appears to have been polite, but as might also have been expected, the two sides did not see eye to eye.[110]

After the conference, the Soviet delegates returned east, spending several days in Washington. While there, they and the leadership of the American delegation met with a variety of officials from the State Department and elsewhere in the administration. The Soviet delegates had lunches with members of the House International Relations Committee and the Senate Committee on Foreign Affairs. An informal gathering was also held at the Smithsonian Institution.

DARTMOUTH XI: WONDERLAND ON THE BALTIC COAST

The approach of the Carter administration to relations with the Soviet Union was a cause of some consternation to the Soviet leadership. It had gotten along well with the personalities in the two Republican administrations that preceded Carter; it understood their approach to the world and the Soviet Union. But now the Soviet leadership found itself faced with people who had come into office, in part, by defining themselves in contrast to their predecessors. These people approached the Soviets accordingly. The most telling example of this may have been the new arms control proposal given to the Soviets by Secretary of State Vance in a visit to Moscow in March. Having reached agreement with President Ford at Vladivostok not long before, the Soviets found that agreement scuttled and replaced with a set of proposals that seemed to be self-serving, promising advantages to the Americans that the Soviets were by no means ready to accept. They rejected the package out of hand, to the surprise and dismay of the Carter administration.

Moreover, the new administration placed an emphasis on human rights that seemed to the Soviet leaders to be aimed directly at them. This focus on human rights was a key part of the new administration's approach to foreign policy and one that set it apart from its predecessors. It was not aimed exclusively or even primarily at the Soviet Union, but it stemmed from the new president's highly moralistic view of the world. This was of little comfort to the Soviet leaders, who saw this as an assault on them and the Soviet system.

The steering committee for the American side met on April 7 to prepare for Dartmouth XI.[111] Bolling, Cousins, Doty, Malone, Wortman, Read, and Stewart attended. John Wilson and Donald Green, both of whom were from Chase Manhattan Bank, also came. Their boss, David Rockefeller, was there for the last hour. Several reports were made to the committee before it opened a discussion of the agenda and participants in the coming conference. Cousins described his Writers' Conference, an attempt to bring Soviet and American writers together.[112] He intended to link this new project with his old one, Dartmouth. Bolling and Cousins described visits to Washington to speak to Brzezinski and Philip Habib, undersecretary of state for political affairs and a close friend of Secretary of State Vance. Both Brzezinski and Habib had been enthusiastic about the prospect of a Dartmouth Conference at this time. Brzezinski even seemed to consider attending himself, though that was unlikely given his position.

Read reported to the steering committee on a proposal for a Food Task Force. By now, this proposal had had a long history. At the end of Dartmouth X the two sides agreed to put together a task force to discuss "joint measures in the application of science in agriculture to enhance agricultural productivity."[113] In its conception it was one of the task forces meant to be convened according to recommendation of the Task Force on Process that met in December 1975. It was discussed at the Kettering Foundation in October 1976. A proposal was sent in December to Boris Runov, Soviet vice minister of agriculture. The Soviets did not respond to the proposal, but in April the U.S. steering committee, with a little reluctance, decided to make food policy the subject of one of the four work groups at Dartmouth XI. Runov and

Zhurkin both agreed with Read and Stewart to place the matter on the agenda of the coming conference. The highly technical nature of the topic as the Americans conceived it was shown by the comment that Runov "did not fully understand the implications of nitrogen fixation research or why it should be discussed among policymakers, as well as among scientists." Indeed, the approach to the topic was much more arcane and technical than were even the arms control discussions with their extensive use of an acronym-laden jargon. That jargon, at least, was a part of the public discourse on the issue. Terms such as "nitrogen fixation" had not escaped the pages of scientific journals. Later in April, some of the American organizers of the conference, including Read and Stewart, decided to take food policy off the agenda of Dartmouth XI. They intended, however, to pursue the topic through a task force. But there was no response from Runov and the proposal died, although efforts to include food policy on the Dartmouth agenda continued to be made, and Runov himself took part in Dartmouth XI.

Two days after the meeting of the steering committee, on April 9, Read, Stewart, and Cousins spoke with Arbatov at the Soviet Mission in New York. He brought the Soviet version of the conference agenda, which held little to surprise the Americans. Read and Stewart then flew to Moscow, where they spoke to Zhukov, Zhurkin, and Neil Zubkov at the Soviet Peace Committee. They spoke of holding the conference on Lake Baikal, at a center that had been built for the visit of President Eisenhower that had been aborted by the U-2 spy-plane incident.

The conference actually took place at Jurmala, a resort on the Baltic Sea, not far from Riga, Latvia. There were three work groups this time, as at Dartmouth X. The work group on the Middle East had its scope expanded to include other regional conflicts, especially in Africa, where Soviet assistance to the MPLA in Angola and the Mengistu regime in Ethiopia was adding to the existing strains on détente. Another work group focused on arms control issues. This amounted to a narrowing of the agenda from Dartmouth X, where arms control and political issues were combined. The agenda of the third group was also narrower than it was in Arizona, focusing exclusively on economic cooperation and trade. The scientific and environmental issues that had been addressed at the conferences held earlier in the decade were now to be discussed only in their economic context.

The participants on the American side once again included several Dartmouth regulars, though fewer than had returned for recent conferences. Cousins came, though he had expected to be finishing up with the Writers' Conference. Rockefeller also returned. So did Doty, who had become director of Harvard's Programs for Science and International Affairs; Donald Kendall, chairman of PepsiCo; and Bolling, now president of the Lilly Foundation.

Two former senior officials from the Ford State Department attended. One was Helmut Sonnenfeldt, counselor in the department, who had briefed the participants in the preparatory meeting before they flew to Rio Rico. The other was Joseph Sisco, who had served as undersecretary of state and had been prominent in the Middle Eastern efforts of the previous few years.

In a sense they replaced the participants who had gone into the new administration, for the relationship between the Americans who took part in the Dartmouth conferences and the Carter administration was unusually close. Besides Brzezinski and Warnke, the appointees of the new administration included Shulman, who became the State Department's lead Soviet expert, and Gardner, who was appointed the ambassador to Italy. Another participant in Dartmouth X not present at Jurmala, W. William Miller, chairman and chief executive officer of Textron, became chairman of the Federal Reserve Board in 1978 and secretary of the treasury in 1979. President Carter had offered that post to Rockefeller earlier but was turned down.[114] Also in 1979, Herbert York, new to Dartmouth, became the chief U.S. negotiator at the talks on a comprehensive test ban. In a sense, he was continuing the work that had been so important to Cousins during Dartmouth's early years.

York was a former director of the Lawrence Livermore Laboratory and the first director of defense research and engineering in the Eisenhower administration. The others new to Dartmouth included Vernon Jordan, executive director of the Urban League, later a close advisor to President Clinton, and Rita Hauser, a lawyer who had taken part in the Brookings Study Group on the Middle East.

Participants on the Soviet side included, as before, Arbatov, Zhukov, Primakov, and Zhurkin. As at Tbilisi, the Soviet delegation included a number of "advisors" in addition to the participants. Among these were Arbatov's son, Aleksei, an analyst at IMEMO and later the deputy chairman of the Defense Committee of the Russian State Duma. By late 1983 he would become the head of the newly created disarmament section of IMEMO.[115] In post-Soviet Russia he became a member of the Yabloko party, a prominent deputy in the Duma, and deputy head of its Defense Committee. Another advisor was Apollon Davidson, a specialist on Africa at the Institute of World History. Davidson would have a long association with Dartmouth.

Held against the backdrop of the downturn in relations with the Soviet Union that accompanied the first months of the Carter administration, Dartmouth XI was "the most unreal, the most like a visit to Alice in Wonderland," according to York, a veteran of numerous trips to the USSR, including one for a Pugwash conference.[116] It was almost certainly the most difficult Dartmouth Conference of the decade, though Chollar said that he had seen worse at earlier conferences. Even Cousins, in a generally optimistic account of the conference, spoke of some of the exchanges in the early sessions as being "a little overheated perhaps."[117] One American participant in the conference wrote, "The Soviet delegates were aggressive, and in some cases acrimonious, in their criticism of the present administration and its policies in regard to human rights, arms control and economic cooperation."[118] The discussion sometimes took a turn not taken since the early 1960s. For example, Mikhail Kotov, secretary of the Soviet Peace Committee (and one of the propaganda and public relations group, to use Stewart's category from Dartmouth VII), responded to a remark by Sonnenfeldt by saying, "What kind of secrecy can there be . . . when 150 million people in our country have signed an appeal for disarmament?"[119] Stewart himself wrote that the Soviets showed bad form: "Once again they used the sessions to build support for Soviet foreign policy objectives and not to solve bilateral problems."[120]

Interestingly, given that Brzezinski had been a participant in Dartmouth IX and so had to have been known to several members of the Soviet delegation, this same participant noted that Carter's "appointment of Zbigniew Brzezinski as National Security Advisor is regarded as unfavorable to U.S.-U.S.S.R. relations, and Brzezinski was contrasted unfavorably with Henry Kissinger."[121]

What York found most unreal was the discussion of Soviet dissidents. Hauser raised the question of Anatoli Sharansky, who had been

arrested but not yet tried. Arbatov assured her that he would receive a fair
trial, but Hauser pointed out that no one accused under the same statute
had been found innocent. York "watched Arbatov literally blanch, but he
made no further comments."[122] And indeed, Sharansky was later found
guilty and sentenced to a decade in prison. In the Soviet perspective, it
seemed to Shveitser, the Soviet interpreter at the early conferences who
had returned for this one, that the Americans launched an "all-out offensive on human rights in the Soviet Union" at this conference.[123]

This was, indeed, the first conference at which human rights had
a major place in the discussion. As recounted above, Arthur Miller had
brought the persecution of dissidents up in an informal conversation
with Shveitser at Rye in 1969, but Dartmouth XI was the first conference at which it was discussed in a formal session. This was a reflection
of the times. Jimmy Carter was the first president to place human rights
issues at the center of foreign policy, and the importance of Basket 3 of
the Helsinki agreement signed in 1975, under which the Soviet Union
and the other signatories incurred some obligations on human rights
issues, was just now becoming clear. The Soviet participants, like Soviet
officialdom in general, were probably caught off guard. Certainly, as
John Wilson noted, they were "somewhat bewildered by the employ-
ment of human rights in the field of foreign policy."[124]

Despite the conflict, there remained areas of substantial and even
surprising agreement. One of these was Africa, which was discussed
extensively in the regional conflicts work group. The Soviet participants
agreed to a statement that external forces ought to avoid actions that
could make the situation worse. Bolling said that meetings of this group,
which included Sisco and Hauser, began with a harsh tone emanating
from the Soviets, who complained about the new administration and its
human rights policy. But the discussion improved and became one of the
best that Bolling had experienced.[125] Their conclusions built on what had
been agreed to at the St. Regis Hotel and in Rio Rico: the two superpowers should issue a statement affirming their support for "just and fair
principles" in a peace in the Middle East and their commitment to pro-
tecting the rights of both Palestinians and Israelis. The group also concluded that the Soviet Union and the United States should try to reconvene the Geneva Conference, prefiguring the joint statement made by
Vance and Gromyko less than three months later.

The Arms Control Task Force wrestled with the problems that had left the negotiations for SALT II deadlocked. Participants traded accusations about who was responsible. Doty linked the American decision to develop the cruise missile to Soviet efforts to strengthen their air defenses, but the Soviets saw the cruise missile as only the beginning of another round of the arms race. In the end both sides agreed on little but that a SALT agreement was desirable.[126]

The work group on economic relations discussed the failure to grant MFN status to the Soviet Union and the lack of Export-Import Bank credits, as it had at the previous two conferences.[127] As before, the Soviet side seemed to believe that overcoming these obstacles to expanded trade was simply a matter of will on the part of the administration and that the will was not there. Indeed, they were suspicious of the intentions of the Carter administration, particularly after it denied Control Data Corporation a license to export the Cyber 76 computer to the Soviet Union. The American delegates argued that the Ford administration would probably have done the same thing, but they could not convince their Soviet colleagues of that.

The Soviet hard-currency debt was discussed at length. The Soviet delegates argued that the debt was, at bottom, insignificant. The Soviet Union, they said, had a good history of repaying its debt and much of the debt incurred was for projects designed to earn foreign currency. The effort to report on this discussion in the work group's paper and the final communiqué of the conference brought out a sensitivity to the issue on the Soviet side. The Soviet delegates wanted the paragraph on the discussion removed from the group's report. In the end it was retained, but the word "debt" was changed to the phrase "extension of hard currency credits." Wilson concluded, "Apparently debt is not an acceptable word in a communiqué directed to the Soviet public."[128]

A discussion of areas of possible cooperation touched on the energy and food issues that had been a part of the mandate of the environmental and global issues groups. The delegation also discussed the possibility of joint ventures again, but any interest the Soviets had shown in them before was gone. Joint ventures, they said, "did not fit in well with the Soviet scheme of economic organization."[129] To Wilson, what did not fit was the concept of joint ownership inherent in the idea of a joint venture.

Compensation agreements, where ownership was not in question, were much to be preferred.

As at many of the previous conferences, personal contacts were extensive. They by no means reflected the contentiousness that seemed to dominate much of the formal part of the conference. For example, Jordan and Sonnenfeldt, both first-time participants in Dartmouth, played tennis each morning with Milstein and Zhukov. Jordan gave a lighthearted report on this competition at the final plenary.

That plenary was followed by an impromptu meeting of the American delegates, who discussed the difficulties with the conference, including not only the tone of the discussions, but also what they regarded as changes in the agenda and structure of the conference made unilaterally by the Soviets. Chollar listed what he described as failures of the American delegation. These included allowing the agenda to be changed and the plenaries to be extended more than the Americans had intended. He and others expressed their belief that communications among the American delegates during the conference were inadequate.

DARTMOUTH XII: DIFFERENCES AT WILLIAMSBURG

The American leadership of Dartmouth met early in 1978 to discuss the future of Dartmouth in general and the next conference in particular. They proposed that the conferences be held about eighteen months apart and that Dartmouth XII be held in the United States in April 1979.[130] It was, in fact, held in early May in Williamsburg, the colonial capital of Virginia, which had been restored by the Rockefellers.

Chollar attended again and led the American side, along with Cousins, who was leaving the new *Saturday Review*. He would no longer be the editor of a magazine. The dean of the UCLA medical school approached him that year with an offer to join its faculty. The invitation had been instigated by Franklin Murphy, chancellor of UCLA and a participant in Dartmouth IV and Dartmouth V. Cousins jumped at this chance to pursue what he called his "obsession" with medical science and the ability of the body to heal itself; he began a new career at the age of sixty-two.[131] But this could not keep him away from Dartmouth. Nor was Bolling able to stay away, despite a move to the

Council on Foundations, where he was now chairman and chief executive officer.[132] Hedley Donovan, editor in chief of Time, Inc., was back for his first conference since Dartmouth VIII. Rockefeller, a constant at Dartmouth since his brief appearance at Andover in 1962, Yost, and Doty filled out the list of people returning.

The participants once again included members of Congress, for the first time since Dartmouth VIII in Tbilisi. The American delegation included Senators Charles Mathias, a Republican from Maryland, and Paul Tsongas, a Democrat from Massachusetts who became a contender for the presidential nomination in 1992, and Representative Stephen Solarz, a Democrat from New York. Charles Whelan, a former member of the House, also took part.

Doty, chairman of the work group on political relations, was joined by Chollar, Donovan, Mathias, Yost, and three new participants. Retired general Royal Allison, a fighter pilot in World War II, had been the representative of the Joint Chiefs of Staff at the SALT I talks. Herbert Scoville, Jr., worked on arms control for eight years at the Central Intelligence Agency and then for another six as an assistant director at ACDA. He was a founder of both the Arms Control Association and the Arms Control Program at the Carnegie Endowment for International Peace. Jan Lodal worked on arms control issues on Kissinger's National Security Council staff but in 1979 was executive vice president of American Management Systems, a firm he helped found.[133] The Soviets in the political relations group were all Dartmouth veterans. Zhurkin was cochairman. His colleagues were Arbatov, Bykov, Milstein, and Zhukov.

The most prominent issue in their discussions was SALT II. Negotiations of the treaty were in their final phase—the last pieces of the agreement fell into place the Monday after the Williamsburg conference closed—and the battle over ratification was already heating up.[134] Arbatov and his colleagues found a lack of strong public support of the treaty within the United States. They also noted contradictions among the opposition, with some of the opponents to the treaty saying that it went too far and others arguing that it did not go far enough. General Allison expressed concern about whether the treaty was evenhanded, or would be perceived as evenhanded, because it allowed the Soviets, but not the Americans, to have 308 "large" missiles. This referred to the

SS-18, the largest missile in the Soviet inventory, to which there was no American equivalent. It was seen by many to be a special threat to the U.S. force of ICBMs because of its size and would remain a problem for the next twenty years. It was discussed "vigorously" in the sessions of the work group and in private discussions between Allison and Arbatov.[135]

During the meetings Allison also read an account given by an American congressman of a discussion with a Soviet military officer. The officer said that the United States had best get used to the idea that it would be threatened now that the Soviet Union had achieved military superiority. To Allison, "The Soviet side reacted in a way which gave me the impression that there was sufficient truth in the allegation that it disturbed them."[136]

Not all of Allison's American colleagues shared his concerns about the SALT II treaty as it had been negotiated or about Soviet attitudes toward the balance of forces. This much is clear from Cousins' account of the meetings of the group.[137] But it was significant for Dartmouth both that the Soviet members of the work group were able to hear this point of view in constructive, lengthy discussions and that Allison, after it was over, was impressed by "the level and seriousness of Dartmouth XII deliberations."[138]

The Soviet participants in the work group on the Middle East were also veterans of earlier Dartmouth conferences. Primakov was back as cochairman of the Middle East group, joined by Kislov and Mostovets. He was no longer a deputy director at IMEMO, having been promoted to director of the Oriental Institute. Primakov's American counterpart, once again, was Bolling. He was joined by Cousins and Solarz and three new colleagues, all from academia. Roger Fisher was a conflict resolution specialist from Harvard, J. C. Hurewitz was director of the Middle East Institute at Columbia University, and Paul Jabber was a professor at UCLA.

The discussions of this group focused on the role—or lack of it—of the Soviet Union in the Middle East following the dramatic initiative of Egypt's President Sadat that took him to Jerusalem in 1977 and the Camp David agreement reached in September 1978. The Soviet delegates in Williamsburg were pessimistic about the chances that a treaty between Egypt and Israel would work, arguing that it would simply polarize the Arab world, much of which had reacted to the agreements reached between Israel and Egypt with suspicion and some dismay. In the end, the group members acknowledged differences in their views, but they affirmed a view of a possible settlement similar to the one outlined in the previous Dartmouth discussions of Middle Eastern issues.

A separate work group was devoted to conflicts in southern Africa. The five Americans in the group were new to Dartmouth. Tsongas has already been mentioned. Charles Whelan had served on the Subcommittee on African Affairs of the International Relations Committee when he was in the House. The cochairman of the group was John Stremlau, assistant director of international relations of the Rockefeller Foundation. A young scholar, he was an expert on Africa, having published a study of the Nigerian civil war.[139] He would become one of the essential figures in the Dartmouth process during the 1980s. After working with him for several years, Stewart noted that he had "an outstanding ability to direct the discussions into productive directions."[140] Professor Robert Legvold was a well-respected student of Soviet affairs at Columbia University who had written on Soviet policy in Africa.[141] He would later follow Mosely and Shulman as director of the Russian Institute after it was renamed for Averell Harriman. Jim Hoagland was, and still is, a journalist at the *Washington Post.*

Their Soviet counterparts were all from the academic institutes and did not have the same expertise in African affairs as their American colleagues.[142] Vladimir Gantman, a department chief at IMEMO, was the cochairman. He had been to every Dartmouth Conference since the return to Hanover in 1972. His expertise lay primarily in European and theoretical issues. His compatriots in the group were Valentin Berezhkov and Vsevelod Oleandrov, both of whom were scholars under Arbatov at ISKAN. At the time, Berezhkov was the representative of the institute in the Soviet embassy in Washington. It was the first Dartmouth conference for both of them.

This was the first Dartmouth discussion given over solely to the issues at stake in southern Africa. The two superpowers had come to be involved in conflicts in Namibia, Angola, Zimbabwe, and Mozambique, all of which occurred in the dominating shadow of a South Africa whose abhorrent system of apartheid was itself threatened with unrest. The Americans pointed out that the American public was less willing to support joint action with the Soviets owing to their perceptions of actions of the Cubans in the region. Both delegations stressed the potential role of the Organization of African Unity in the region and emphasized the dangers that could stem from the proliferation of nuclear weapons in Africa. They also agreed that the two countries had a joint interest in maintaining the sanctions that had been put in place against the white government of Ian Smith in Zimbabwe/Rhodesia.

The fourth and last group focused on the perennial topic of economic cooperation. Most of Rockefeller's American colleagues in the group had a professional interest in agriculture. David Williams, chairman of the Resource Sciences Corporation, was the exception. Those who had been at the Rio Rico conference knew him. He had been their host. His interest was in energy rather than agriculture as he had recently signed a major contract to build a pipeline in Siberia.[143] Donald Paarlberg was an agricultural economist at Purdue University who had served as an assistant secretary of agriculture and a special assistant to the president. Roy Harrington, an engineer, was a product planner at Deere and Company, the manufacturer of farm machinery. The chairman of Deere, William Hewitt, had been a participant in Dartmouth VIII. Harrington was recommended because he had substantial international experience working on food problems.[144] Sylvan Wittwer had been a part of the steering committee on a proposal for a Food Task Force. An environmentalist, he was director of the Agricultural Experiment Station at Michigan State University and a professor of horticulture. Shortly before his affiliation with Dartmouth he had served as chairman of the National Research Council.

Their Soviet counterparts were all Dartmouth veterans, with the exception of the cochairman, Vladimir Alkhimov, who was chairman of the board of the State Bank of the USSR, and Revold Antov, a chief of section at IMEMO. Runov clearly shared an interest in agriculture with most of the Americans in the group. The interests of the rest were more general. Stanislav Borisov, a deputy minister of finance, had been the cochairman of the group at Rio Rico. George Shchukin had been at Rio Rico. Now vice president of the U.S.-USSR Trade and Economic Council, he had been the chairman of the Soviet Purchasing Committee.

Yuri Bobrakov, a scholar from ISKAN, had been a participant at Dartmouth as long ago as Dartmouth V, at Rye.

Given the backgrounds of its members, it was not surprising that a large part of the discussion in this work group was on agricultural issues, showing a residual interest in the issues that had led the American side to press for a Food Task Force. Members emphasized ways in which cooperation might be increased in agricultural research and agricultural assistance to the Third World. The two sides made a variety of proposals. Participants also discussed, not for the first time, the negligible role that the Soviet Union played in the activities of the Food and Agriculture Organization of the United Nations and the international centers for agricultural research that had been established around the world. The Americans expressed the hope that the Soviet Union would come to take part more fully.

When the group discussed trade, the now perennial topic of the failure of the United States to grant the Soviet Union MFN status came up again. The Americans also talked about the difficulties that American firms encountered when trying to work in the Soviet Union. These included costly, time-consuming difficulties in negotiating projects and frequent changes made in project specifications by Soviet partners. The potential for cooperation in finding sources of energy to substitute for petroleum, like Soviet natural gas, was discussed at length. According to Cousins, it was apparent that the Soviet participants believed that a planned world economy was the only means through which the world could avoid economic instability. They expressed anxiety about the euro-dollar market, a thoroughly unplanned economic phenomenon, with $500 million floating between countries with virtually no government control.[145]

U.S.-China relations figured prominently in private discussions, though they were not on the agenda of the conference and were not discussed during the formal sessions.[146] The Soviet participants expressed concern that recognition of China by the United States was part of an effort to play China and Russia against each other. Their anxiety was raised not just by the recognition of China, but also by the outbreak of war between China and Vietnam that followed soon after Deng Xiaoping's visit to the United States in January and February 1979. They echoed the charges made by the Soviet government that Deng must have told his interlocutors about the invasion to come and gained at least tacit approval of it. The Americans who were approached by their Soviet colleagues responded by expressing their concern about the dangers of Sino-Soviet confrontation and their belief that stability in the world required that tensions be reduced among all three powers.

THE DARTMOUTH LEADERSHIP CONFERENCE

At the end of Dartmouth XI, the cochairmen had an informal agreement not to hold a full plenary session for another two and a half to three years, although smaller task forces could meet in the interim. Between then and December 1979, some work was done to establish task forces that would continue the discussions on the Middle East and Africa. This new emphasis on smaller groups reflected concerns by Chollar and the Kettering Foundation that the results of the larger meetings did not justify their growing costs. The smaller groups, however, particularly the group that met in the St. Regis Hotel to discuss the Middle East, had proved their worth.[147]

But in the last week of December, Soviet troops marched into Afghanistan. They killed the leader of the government, Hafizullah Amin, and established a new government. Thus began a war that would be a bleeding sore for the Soviet Union for the next decade, affecting not just U.S.-Soviet relations, but internal Soviet politics as well. The invasion and the American response effectively killed whatever was left of détente. That response included the boycott of the 1980 Olympics in Moscow, deferral of the vote on ratification of SALT II, and an embargo on grain sales to the Soviet Union. It amounted in many respects to holding the Soviet Union at arm's length, pointedly not continuing business as usual. It suggested to the American organizers that the continuation of the Dartmouth conferences should be examined.

Stewart discussed the matter individually with the members of the advisory group through the beginning of January. He favored holding a small meeting on neutral territory. Dartmouth tradition would have the next meeting in the Soviet Union, but American policy made this seem inadvisable. John Stremlau found that the Rockefeller Conference and Study Center in Bellagio, Italy, was available in May and tentatively reserved it. The advisory group itself met on February 4. Stewart sought and got the opinion of two Dartmouth alumni serving in the Carter administration—Shulman in the State Department and Brzezinski at the National Security Council.[148] They both believed that a small meeting would be useful at that time. Finally, the advisory group decided to take advantage of the opportunity Stremlau had found and to hold a small meeting at Bellagio. This was the only Dartmouth event to be held outside the borders of the two superpowers.

Most of the people who gathered there for what came to be called the Dartmouth Leadership Conference had been associated with Dartmouth before. The Americans were Bolling, Doty, Stewart, Stremlau, Yost, and Donald Green, an aide to David Rockefeller who had helped prepare for Dartmouth XI, now a vice president at Chase Manhattan Bank responsible for economic analysis of the Soviet Union.[149] David Williams, who took part in Dartmouth XII a year before, returned. The only American new to Dartmouth was Stanley Hoffman, a distinguished scholar, expert on European, particularly French, politics from Harvard University. Cousins, now on an academic schedule himself, was no doubt immersed in life at UCLA.

The Soviet delegation included Primakov, Zhukov, and Zhurkin. Arbatov attended though he had suffered a heart attack only six months before.[150] Half were new to Dartmouth. Valentin Falin, the ambassador to West Germany through much of the 1970s, was first deputy head of the International Information Department of the Central Committee.[151] No liberal, he nonetheless became head of the International Department under Gorbachev and later was again the ambassador in Bonn. Mikhail Pankin was from the Ministry of Foreign Trade. Ivan Ivanov was a deputy director at IMEMO, as Primakov had been. Oleg Sokolov was a professor at the Institute of International Relations.

The agenda had just three items. Participants were to assess the state of U.S.-Soviet relations, discuss the ground rules for those relations, and examine the future of the Dartmouth Conference. They discussed these in the context of five topics. Two of them, arms control and economic relations, had been standard topics at Dartmouth since the first conference at Hanover. The other three topics were about regional conflicts in the Third World, which were the proximate cause of what was seen as the end of détente. Afghanistan and the Middle

East were discussed separately. Cooperation and competition in the Third World became a topic by itself.

The discussion began with the invasion of Afghanistan.[152] The Soviets defended it as a response to a security threat. They linked the Soviet feeling of insecurity that led to the invasion to the improvement of U.S. relations with China that had been evident throughout 1979, involving the visit of Deng Xiaoping to the United States and formal recognition of the People's Republic of China.

A theme that ran through this discussion was the need for parity as a superpower with the United States. In the Soviet view, the United States should not try to forbid the Soviet Union to do what the United States allowed itself to do. This reflected, among other things, continued Soviet frustration that nuclear equality did not translate into equality across the board. The model the Soviet delegates sought to impress on the Americans was Soviet behavior following the bombing of Haiphong harbor in 1972. Why, they asked, were the Americans going to let a similar event, peripheral to the U.S.-Soviet relationship, interfere with good relations between the two countries? The Soviet Union had, after all, welcomed Nixon to Moscow despite the bombing. They also expressed concern that the American response to the invasion of Afghanistan, which was tougher than they appeared to expect, was the beginning of a campaign to mobilize American popular support for a more aggressive foreign policy. They wanted out of Afghanistan, the Soviet delegates said, but they also made it plain that they would not withdraw unless they could be certain that a secure regime loyal to Moscow would remain.

The Americans expressed concern that the invasion of Afghanistan might be part of an escalating pattern of Soviet involvement in the Third World that ran through Angola and Ethiopia. The long-term security interests of the Soviet Union in the world were unclear: Were they limited? Or global?

On arms control, the Soviet delegates saw the failure of SALT II as a signal that the United States was, at least for the time being, pursuing military superiority. The Soviets proposed that, in the absence of ratification, the protocol and treaty that made up SALT II simply be extended by two years. The National Security Council expressed strong interest in this.[153]

The two sides also argued over the deployment of new missiles in Europe. This issue had come to the top of the agenda after the decision made by NATO in 1979 to deploy Pershing II missiles and cruise missiles in Europe in response to the deployment by the Soviets of SS-20 missiles. Each side argued that their opponent's deployment was an inadmissible improvement over existing forces that threatened the nuclear balance in Europe. The discussion at Bellagio broke no new ground.

The two sides found extensive common ground in their discussion of the Middle East. The two countries faced rising militarization and political radicalization in the Arab world as a result of the new-found oil wealth, stressed the Soviets. They also pleaded that they had little influence over allies like Syria. Both delegations agreed on the need for cooperation between the United States and the Soviet Union in pursuit of peace in the Middle East.

On the last point in the discussion, conflict and cooperation in the Third World, the Americans proposed four principles of restraint and four principles of cooperation. The Soviets responded that more consultation and restraint were needed, but that the principles embodied in the agreement signed at the May 1972 summit on bilateral cooperation and the prevention of war were probably adequate. Both sides seemed to agree on the threat that distant conflicts in the Third World posed to the relationship: they threatened to pull the superpowers in though they had little real strategic significance to either country.[154]

In the discussion of economic relations the Soviets repeated the themes of equality and mutual threat. They emphasized that they wanted to be equals in the world economy. They also told the Americans that they wanted to prevent the formation of other cartels like OPEC because of the harm they could do to Soviet as well as American interests. The American response was to say that with responsible behavior the Soviets could achieve the stable and ordered world economy that they sought.

On May 25, after the dinner that closed the "consultation," Doty spent an hour and a half talking to Falin, continuing a conversation they had begun in April.[155] In May they discussed many of the same issues that they had touched on with their colleagues in the preceding few days. Falin made the suggestion that the United States and the Soviet Union should jointly provide leadership for a transition from the use of existing reserves of energy, such as oil and gas, to fusion and other, novel, forms of energy. He continued by saying, "We should undercut the appetites of those plotting to profit on a rapidly developing oil shortage." Falin assured Doty that an incident in Sverdlovsk—an outbreak of anthrax— that many believed was caused by a spill of biological warfare agents was caused when "uninspected meat had gotten to a café and most of the customers had become ill and many died." He ended discussion of this topic by saying heatedly, "That is the way it was and you should tell President Carter that the Soviet Union will let its reputation for all time stand on that." The fear of those who thought that biological agents were at fault was later borne out.[156]

Arbatov and Zhukov met with Brezhnev on their return to Moscow. They told the Soviet leader what their American interlocutors at Bellagio had said about Afghanistan, suggesting that it was ruining détente and helping the extreme right as the elections in the United States approached. They suggested that the Soviet Union might make the symbolic gesture of reducing their forces by 10 percent. The next day, Andropov chewed Arbatov out for taking this initiative.[157] Brezhnev was little better than an invalid at this time, and nothing seems to have resulted from the meeting. Nonetheless, this account confirms that what was said at the Dartmouth meetings still got to the top of the Soviet hierarchy, at least part of the time.

Three weeks before the November elections, on October 15, Stewart held meetings in Washington with Brent Scowcroft and William Hyland, both of whom were out of government at the time, and Marshal Brement, who was Brzezinski's principal assistant working on Soviet bloc issues on the National Security Council staff.[158] Stewart briefed them on the Bellagio consultation. He also asked for their comments on the future of the Dartmouth dialogue, particularly in the event that Ronald Reagan won the election. All spontaneously spoke about the value of Dartmouth. Hyland and Brement both suggested that the conferences would become more effective if government officials were invited. Stewart and Phillips Ruopp had suggested that an experimental format be used to try out this idea. Scowcroft, who had contacts in the Reagan camp, said that he believed a Reagan administration would be skeptical about the benefits of dialogue, but that there would be highly placed people who would see its value and facilitate it. He, Hyland, and Brement all expressed strong support for the Dartmouth idea.

The decision to postpone the full Dartmouth plenary, coinciding as it did with the end of détente, and the consultation at Bellagio, coming shortly before the advent of the Reagan administration, marked the end of one era in Dartmouth's history, as it did in U.S.-Soviet relations. The role of Dartmouth in the new era was uncertain.

4 | A New Cold War and the Beginnings of Perestroika, 1981–88

DARTMOUTH XIII: Moscow; November 16–19, 1981
DARTMOUTH XIV Hanover, New Hampshire; May 14–17, 1984
DARTMOUTH XV: Baku; May 13–17, 1986
REGIONAL CONFLICTS TASK FORCE
ARMS CONTROL TASK FORCE
POLITICAL RELATIONS TASK FORCE

THE AMERICAN ORGANIZERS OF THE DARTMOUTH CONFERENCE looked at the arrival of the Reagan administration with trepidation. The new president arrived with a set of hard-line attitudes toward the Soviet Union that seemed to be at odds with the emphasis that Dartmouth placed on improving relations. It appeared likely that there would be less official dialogue and that misperceptions would increase as a result.[1]

Moreover, Reagan brought with him a group of people unknown to the Americans who had been taking part in Dartmouth. Heretofore, Dartmouth had benefited from close relations with both bureaucrats and decision makers in the executive branch of the U.S. government. The apparent absence of such ties threatened to make the conference less relevant in terms of direct, short-term influence on policy. The Soviet participants would of course recognize this, just as they would perceive that the views of the American participants simply did not reflect those of the new administration. Why, then, would they want to take part in the dialogue?

Paul Doty saw parallel trends at work in the Soviet Union. Conservative forces there, he believed, were gaining influence as détente collapsed. And with this, he thought, Arbatov and ISKAN were losing influence as well.[2] The decline of détente hurt the institute. So did what Doty saw as Gromyko's opposition to ISKAN.

Moreover, there were now other dialogues with the Soviets that seemed to be doing much of what Dartmouth had long tried to do. They were engaging many of the same, limited number of figures whom the Soviet authorities permitted to have this kind of access to Americans. Cooperation had been close between the organizers of the Dartmouth conferences and the Soviet-American Parallel Studies Program conducted since 1969 by the United Nations Association of the United States and the USSR United Nations Association.[3] The National Academy of Sciences had put together the Committee on International Security and Arms Control (CISAC) in 1979, a successor to Paul Doty's SADS, which had been active in the 1960s. The Central Committee of the CPSU approved contacts between CISAC and the USSR Academy of Sciences in December 1980 and the Soviet government gave the first meeting semiofficial status.[4]

The decline of détente, the arrival of the Reagan administration, and the multiplication of exchanges led the core of people associated with Dartmouth to reevaluate the Dartmouth process. They raised no questions that had not been raised by Stewart and others earlier, but the new situation that the Dartmouth conferees found themselves in following the Bellagio conference gave these questions a salience that they had not had before. The results of this reevaluation were changes that made the Dartmouth process of the 1980s quite different from what it had been in the 1970s.

The advisory group met in Washington in February to plan, not just for Dartmouth XIII, scheduled to take place late in the year, but for the Dartmouth process as a whole. They believed that Dartmouth had to broaden its base of support. That support had always been narrow. The Kettering Foundation, the Rockefeller Foundation, and the U.S. International Communication Agency (the once and future United States Information Agency) had funded Dartmouth XII. But funding by the latter two was sporadic at best. The Ford Foundation had long since stopped funding Dartmouth, following its practice of providing only seed money to projects. The Lilly Foundation had provided some money, but it stopped at about the time Bolling moved on. No reliable source of funding other than the Kettering Foundation had presented itself. This was a matter of some concern.

The plan discussed in February 1981 included sponsorship of Dartmouth by a consortium of universities, a three-year commitment of funds from a wider array of foundations, and an approach to the business community for funding. Both the Mershon Center at Ohio State University and the John F. Kennedy School at Harvard had been approached and expressed interest.

In May Bolling spent a few days in Moscow asking people associated with Dartmouth about its value and making preparations for Dartmouth XIII, which the Soviets had agreed to host in November. He found that the Soviets he spoke to seemed to prefer the larger, more visible full-scale conferences than smaller meetings like the Bellagio conference, though the latter had already been chosen as a model for Dartmouth XIII. Despite the proliferation of meetings with other nonofficial groups, they found that Dartmouth was distinguished by its flexibility in form and substance, continuity of membership, and what Bolling described as "a certain, not-well-defined quality or tone to the meetings that makes them less formal, less professionally focused, more open and free-wheeling than other efforts at Soviet-American dialogue."[5]

The importance of the continuity of membership reflected the importance of the personal aspect of Dartmouth. Because the participants knew one another well, they could minimize ideologically charged huffing and puffing in the discussions and approach a real dialogue on the issues at hand.[6] Bolling's quotation of Kislov, the Middle Eastern expert from ISKAN who had taken part in the meeting at the St. Regis Hotel in December 1975, makes this clear:

> The more we meet, the more easy it is to discuss the most difficult and delicate issues. If we meet only once in two or three years, we, in effect, have really very little contact and, therefore, have difficulty in maintaining the personal confidence needed for frank discussions.[7]

Kislov also made a case for more frequent meetings, as the Americans had discussed for some time.

Bolling found that this was a time of some personal hardship for a number of the Dartmouth regulars. Zhukov, like Cousins and Arbatov, had suffered a heart attack. Primakov suffered the sudden, devastating loss of his twenty-five-year-old son shortly before Bolling arrived in Moscow. Later in May, Yost died. In the obituary he wrote, Arbatov praised Yost as "an able and often tough polemicist," notable for his wisdom, and said, "To me personally Charles Yost was an old friend, and that friendship was very dear to me."[8] This expression of friendship of a Soviet official for an American was unusual and gives one more indication of how important the personal aspects of Dartmouth had become.

In April Yost had written a letter to Rockefeller expressing his concern about Dartmouth, which he felt was "slowing down ominously."[9] Part of the reason for it, he felt, was that "the founders and most prestigious members" were unavailable in 1981. By these he meant Cousins, still recovering from a heart attack, and Rockefeller. He pointed out how important Rockefeller had been to Dartmouth. So did Phillips Ruopp in a memorandum to David Mathews, the new president of the Kettering Foundation, in May.[10] By this time Rockefeller had taken part in ten full conferences and many smaller meetings among the American participants. He had helped attract a number of participants, especially from the business world, and had given Dartmouth access to, among others, Lyndon Johnson and Kosygin. As Ruopp wrote, "It is his imprimatur that establishes Dartmouth's credibility in a number of circles both inside and outside of government." Yost urged Rockefeller to provide leadership to Dartmouth. Mathews was to meet him to find out how much he was willing to give to Dartmouth, considering the many other claims on his time. As will be seen, Rockefeller remained a constant in Dartmouth and an important element of continuity as the conferences entered their third decade.

DARTMOUTH XIII: BEARING A MESSAGE

A small meeting of Dartmouth participants had originally been scheduled to take place in Moscow in March, with a full plenary session scheduled for November. But the Dartmouth Advisory Committee consulted with the new administration, and on the advice of Richard Pipes, the prominent Harvard historian who was then on the staff of the National Security Council, and Walter Stoessel, then at the State

Department but previously ambassador to the Soviet Union, this small meeting was postponed to May. The administration's approach to foreign policy would be more fully developed at a later date, they said.[11] Secretary of State Alexander Haig thought the dialogue would be more useful if it took place still later in the year.[12] Finally moved to November, this meeting became Dartmouth XIII, much as a small meeting became Dartmouth IX in 1975. Dartmouth XIII was slightly bigger—there were fourteen Americans rather than ten—and the format of the meeting was already set up to include both plenary and work group sessions.

Two of the American participants in Dartmouth XIII who came to Dartmouth for the first time quickly became essential to the Dartmouth dialogues and remain so today. David Mathews had recently become president of the Kettering Foundation, replacing Chollar. A youthful president of the University of Alabama and secretary of the Department of Health, Education, and Welfare under President Ford, he brought a classicist's training and a profound sense of the importance of dialogue and deliberation to the work of the Kettering Foundation. He found that importance reflected in Dartmouth and quickly gave it his strong support.

Harold Saunders had just left the government after a distinguished career working on Middle Eastern issues on the National Security Council staffs of Presidents Kennedy, Johnson, and Nixon and in the State Department under Presidents Ford and Carter. He came to Dartmouth with experience in government at its highest levels and as a witness to the transformation of the seemingly intractable conflict between Israel and Egypt. That transformation, through Sadat's actions and the dialogue that produced the Camp David agreement, was a powerful influence on his thinking.

Saunders saw in Dartmouth a strong potential to ameliorate the conflict between the superpowers that seemed so strong in the early 1980s and to foster cooperation between them in the Middle East and elsewhere. He came to see the Dartmouth deliberations as elements in a process that could make it possible to ameliorate conflicts between countries and even within countries. He later used his Dartmouth experience to describe such a process in terms that were applicable elsewhere.[13]

Other prominent Americans who took part in Dartmouth for the first time included Harrison Salisbury, the *New York Times* reporter, now editor emeritus, who had written extensively on the Soviet Union when posted to Moscow and after; William T. Coleman, President Carter's secretary of transportation; and Seweryn Bialer, who renewed the connection between Dartmouth and Columbia University established by Mosely. Antonia Chayes, undersecretary of the air force in the Carter administration, was becoming a prominent expert on conflict resolution and arms control. Deere and Company was represented at Dartmouth once again, this time by its president, Robert Hanson. Brent Scowcroft was not new to Dartmouth, having given briefings and advice to Dartmouth people many times before as a government official, but this was his first conference as a participant.

The remainder of the American delegation were familiar faces. Bolling and Stremlau returned for the discussions on U.S.-Soviet relations in the Third World. Doty came to talk about arms control. Stewart, a constant presence since 1972, also took part. Rockefeller in the end did find the time to give to Dartmouth, as Yost had asked.

Many of the American participants met in Washington on October 12 and 13 for a series of briefings on U.S.-Soviet relations. Far from putting the Dartmouth Conference at arm's length, as had been feared, the policymakers at the highest levels of the administration gave the briefings. They included General David C. Jones, chairman of the Joint Chiefs of Staff; Stoessel, now undersecretary of state; and Joseph Twinam, deputy assistant secretary of state for Near East and South Asian affairs.

On October 13 some of the participants met with Secretary of State Haig. He suggested to them that they emphasize four points at the coming conference.[14] First, the tough policy of the Reagan administration toward the Soviets reflected a consensus in the United States; it was not an aberration. Second, the American public gave strong support to the increase in defense spending that the administration was pushing through Congress. Third, the United States did want improved relations with the Soviet Union, but improvement had to come on the basis of reciprocity, and the Soviets had to show restraint in their policies in the Third World. Fourth, while the Soviet buildup in strategic nuclear arms had made Americans skeptical about arms control, the Reagan administration did include people who were seriously interested in it.

The other officials who briefed the group added to the points raised by Secretary Haig. On arms control, they suggested that the Dartmouth participants emphasize the asymmetry and imbalance in strategic forces and the need to cooperate to improve verification. They also suggested that the administration, which was not interested in a comprehensive test ban, would nonetheless push ratification of the Limited and Threshold Nuclear Test Ban Treaties. SALT II and further SALT negotiations, they said, were on the back burner, but progress on the negotiations over theater nuclear forces was essential to an improvement in relations. On regional conflicts, they talked about Afghanistan, the Persian Gulf, and the conflicts between Ethiopia and Somalia and in Angola. They urged Soviet restraint in all these areas and said that the United States was building its forces in the Gulf in response to Soviet actions. The briefers were clearly trying to use the Dartmouth Conference to send a message to the Soviets. In effect they were saying, "We are ready to engage you in serious dialogue, but it will be on different terms than before."

On Saturday, November 14, the American group flew to Paris. The following morning group members attended a briefing arranged by the Atlantic Institute. They heard a policy director of the French Foreign Office, a European specialist on nuclear weapons in Europe, and others give the European perspective on relations with the Soviet Union. Then they met among themselves to prepare for the conference in Moscow, where they arrived the next day.

Most of their Soviet interlocutors were known to them from previous Dartmouth conferences. They included Arbatov, Zhukov, Primakov, Boris Runov, Kislov, and Zhurkin. Evgeni Fedorov returned after several years' absence. The Central Committee staff was represented by Mostovets, his colleague Viktor Sidenko from the International Department, and Falin from the International Information Department. For the first time, an active military officer took part. This was General Major Viktor Tatarnikov from the General Staff. Gennadi Gerasimov was also a participant. He was then a commentator for Novosti but later became the press spokesman for Gorbachev. In all, the Soviet delegation had nineteen participants.

The conference opened in Moscow on November 16, the same day that a Central Committee plenum opened and the day before a meeting of the Supreme Soviet began. Just three broad issues were addressed this time: political relations, arms control, and the activities of the two superpowers in the Third World. Even though Fedorov was back, environmental and scientific issues were left off the agenda. Nor were economic issues discussed at length, despite the presence of Rockefeller and Hanson among the Americans and of Runov and Alkhimov among the Soviets.

As the two sides discussed the relationship between the United States and the Soviet Union in the Third World, they realized that their disagreements remained. The Soviets grudgingly acknowledged that Soviet actions in the Third World had an effect upon U.S.-Soviet relations in general through American public opinion, but they insisted that the Third World was unimportant to the bilateral relationship. They continued to reserve the right to support "wars of national liberation." And while the Americans once again expressed support for the establishment of a neutral nonaligned government in Afghanistan, the Soviets supported the idea of a nonaligned government that was more or less pro-Soviet. The Americans understood this to be contradictory. Curiously, the two sides agreed that it might be necessary to recognize spheres of influence in order to regulate the competition between the two countries. But they could not agree on where the spheres should be. The Soviets proposed that the West recognize Afghanistan and the Middle East as the Soviet spheres; they would leave the Persian Gulf and Western Europe to the United States.

The discussions of political relations focused on the principles of relations formally agreed to by Nixon and Brezhnev in 1972. These discussions were difficult, as Doty reported at the plenary session.[15] The Soviets were concerned with both political and military equality and with equal security. They feared that the United States under Reagan's leadership had abandoned the idea of equality, seeking superiority in arms. This was shown in the failure to ratify SALT II and the revisions to it suggested by the Reagan administration. They found these to be radical. The Americans, they felt, also sought to exclude or isolate the Soviet Union in the Middle East, Afghanistan, and other regions. The Americans were equal in their suspicion of Soviet motives, particularly in the Soviet arms buildup that had continued since the 1960s.

The discussion of arms control was influenced by the speech President Reagan made on November 18, the day before the conference closed. The president proposed what he called the "zero option" for theater nuclear weapons. This meant the complete elimination of the weapons in Europe. The United States would not make the deployments of Pershing II missiles or ground-launched cruise missiles that it was then planning; the Soviets would destroy their old SS-4s and SS-5s and the new SS-20s. The immediate response of the Soviet participants in Moscow was to brand the speech an effort to upstage Brezhnev, who was about to go to West Germany, and to undercut arms control proposals that he had made. Arbatov called it a "super propaganda document."[16] The day before Reagan's speech, the Americans at the conference had laid out the logic of the president's proposals. After the speech, the Americans emphasized that the president had created an opportunity and had diverged sharply from past rhetoric on the issue. One American participant at the conference, and Rockefeller in private discussions with Alkhimov afterward, emphasized that Reagan's speech was conciliatory and represented a serious opportunity that should be taken at face value.[17] According to Stewart, "These exchanges appear to have directly influenced the subsequent Soviet reappraisal of the US position."[18]

The last day of the conference produced what would prove to be the most significant change in the structure of the Dartmouth conferences since the first one. Stremlau, Stewart, and Rockefeller met with Zhurkin and two of his colleagues after the plenary session had concluded. They agreed to convene two task forces for two or three sessions before Dartmouth XIV, which was expected to occur in the spring or fall of 1983. These task forces would meet several times before the plenary conference and would include between six and eight people. The topics they would discuss were not specified in the agreement, but Rockefeller understood that one would continue the talks on arms issues and the other would "discuss the development of 'codes of conduct' and long range cooperation in the Third World."[19] They became the Arms Control and Regional Conflicts Task Forces, which were soon an essential part of the Dartmouth process.

After the conference, summaries of the conference proceedings were sent to Stoessel and General Jones. Reportedly, Antonia Chayes, who would have known the general from her recent experience at the

Pentagon, had also told him about the discussions. In any case, Jones found the summary valuable. As he wrote to David Mathews:

> The Soviet perceptions contained in the report closely parallel their current negotiating stance in the INF talks and other arms control forums. I will make it a point to have some of my key planners and advisors read the report in detail. I believe we can learn a few things from its timeliness and the fact that many of the views expressed are unencumbered by political overtones.[20]

THE TASK FORCES BEGIN: REGIONAL CONFLICTS

American participants in the Dartmouth process met in New York in January 1982. The month before, martial law had been declared in Poland, effectively ending the threat to the Soviet-supported regime by Solidarity, at least for the time being. Some, particularly Hyland and Bolling, expressed concern that if the task forces agreed to at Dartmouth XIII met as had been scheduled, it would send an inappropriate signal to the Soviets. Neither, however, was categorically opposed to holding the meetings. A majority of the people present—Saunders, Bialer, Doty, and Stremlau—argued that dialogue was all the more important at a time of crisis in U.S.-Soviet relations.[21]

A few weeks later, Zhurkin met with Stewart and Doty at Harvard. They came up with an agenda and a format for an interim meeting with only six or seven participants on each side. They proposed that a meeting be held again at Bellagio. The format they proposed also resembled the format for the Leadership Conference held nearly two years before. Poland was to be central to the discussion, which would also include issues of arms control and regional conflict, all under the single rubric of "Problems of International Security in the 1980s," proposed by Zhurkin.

But none of this happened, and it is not clear why, although dissipation of the sense of crisis over Poland assuredly contributed to the change in plans. Whatever the reason, in April, when the Bellagio meeting was to have taken place, Zhurkin called Stewart to propose that the Soviets and the Americans begin to work toward convening the task forces. The first meeting, he said, should take place in September or October. A few days later Stewart wrote Saunders and Seweryn Bialer, asking for their reaction to an outline of the agenda, the concept of the regional conflicts task force, and a list of proposed participants.[22] And within a few months, this important new element in the Dartmouth process came to be.

The first meeting of this task force took place sooner than anticipated, in late August 1982. The American participants met in London before flying to Moscow. They opened their stay in Moscow with breakfast at the American embassy. The first session was devoted to a general discussion of current U.S.-Soviet relations. Two senior, long-standing Soviet participants in Dartmouth insisted on attending it. Saunders later said that

> somebody raised a point in the opening meeting and I asked a serious question in response and Primakov just said right out in the meeting, "Why don't you hold that question until we get up to where we're going [Suzdal] and we get rid of all these politicians?"[23]

As Saunders recalled, sometime during this task force meeting Zhurkin was discussing the relationship between Soviet actions in regional conflicts and the end of détente. He, a deputy director of ISKAN, respectfully gave what he understood to be Arbatov's point of view and then said, "[N]ow I'll tell you what I think."[24] These disagreements were not aired often, but they suggested rumblings beneath the unanimity on the surface that would lead to the outpouring of opinion under Gorbachev. After the session, the task force boarded a bus and drove to Suzdal, an ancient Russian town about 200 miles northeast of Moscow.

The American delegation had five participants; the Soviets had six. Stewart also attended to serve as rapporteur, as he had at so many conferences before and would at so many meetings after. Saunders was the American cochairman; Primakov, his Soviet counterpart. Both were experts on the Middle East; both would be central to the work of the task force for the next several years. Bialer and Stremlau provided their expertise. Flora Lewis, a columnist on foreign affairs for the *New York Times,* based in Paris, was there to add her knowledge of European issues. She had reported on Europe for a variety of publications since World War II and written a column on the United States and world affairs since 1967. Another consideration in selecting her was "the desire to expose to this dialogue a particularly perceptive observer who could contribute effectively to the 'networks of influence'" that the organizers "deliberately tried to create in selecting participants."[25]

William D. Rogers was the Latin American expert on the American side. An attorney by profession, he had served as deputy coordinator of the Alliance for Progress under Kennedy. His expertise was valued highly enough that both Republican and Democratic administrations pulled him from his practice and acceded to conditions he had set for service.[26] Kissinger twice asked him to become assistant secretary of state for inter-American affairs. Rogers refused the first time, as he would not work under President Nixon. But the day after President Nixon resigned in 1974, Kissinger called again and Rogers accepted, with conditions. He later became undersecretary of state for economic affairs. Secretary of State Vance's deputy, Warren Christopher, asked Rogers to serve as mediator between the ruler of Nicaragua, Anastasio Somoza, and the opposition in 1978. Once again Rogers set conditions; once again they were accepted, and he served as mediator despite Somoza's objections. He also helped with negotiations in Panama.

The Soviet delegation came entirely from the institutes attached to the Soviet Academy of Sciences. Primakov brought two colleagues from the Institute of Oriental Studies, Aleksandr Chicherov and Apollon Davidson. The latter had attended Dartmouth XI, and he would later become the Soviet Africanist on the task force, although he would not begin to attend meetings regularly until after the Baku conference— Dartmouth XV—in 1986. It is possible that he was kept from attending them, particularly the meetings abroad, because—a rarity among the Soviet participants in Dartmouth—he was never a member of the Communist Party.[27] Anatoli Glinkin from the Institute of Latin America was Rogers' counterpart. The delegation was filled out by Nikolai Kosolapov, deputy editor of *Mirovaya ekonomika i mezhdunarodnaya otnosheniya*, the journal of IMEMO, and Evgeni G. Kutovoy, a researcher at ISKAN. He was soon named a deputy director and worked in the Department of International Organizations. Arbatov, Falin, and Milstein joined this group for the opening session in Moscow.

The opening discussion in Moscow, according to Saunders, allowed "a venting of feelings" about current relations between the superpowers.[28] Following this necessary prelude, most of the discussions in Suzdal were devoted to "a candid and systematic review" of the situation in several regions of the world.[29] An entire day was spent discussing Europe. Then a half-day each was devoted to Africa, Latin America, and the Middle East. Together, these sessions surveyed the current and potential trouble spots in U.S.-Soviet relations. There were many of these. One was the controversy over European oil pipelines. The Reagan administration sought to impose sanctions on European firms that provided equipment for Soviet pipelines then being built to bring petroleum westward. Another was Poland, where the imposition of martial law had forced the Solidarity movement underground. Unrest in Nicaragua was thought to be inspired, supported, or both by Cuba. The civil war continued in Angola, and a host of problems involved the superpowers in the Middle East from Lebanon through the Persian Gulf to Afghanistan.

Stewart noted that at the end of the discussions Zhurkin evidently concurred with the assertions that the Americans had made for years that what happened in the Third World, in Angola, Afghanistan, and elsewhere, did influence the U.S.-Soviet relationship. As Saunders and Stewart put it:

> [I]n more than ten years of dialogue, no Soviet had openly made such an admission, in spite of both the evidence and endless American attempts to establish that such a relationship exists as a matter of fact, not rhetoric.[30]

It is not clear whether Zhurkin's belief was shared by many in the Soviet policymaking institutions, but this remains a significant change nonetheless, a recognition of an important reality in the U.S.-Soviet relationship.

But the most important outcome of the Suzdal meetings for the Dartmouth process arose from the discussions that took place on the last day. In discussing the last item on the agenda, "Rules of the Game or Principles of Managing U.S.-Soviet Relations," the participants took as their starting point the Agreement on Basic Principles of U.S.-Soviet Relations signed by Brezhnev and Nixon at their summit meeting in Moscow in 1972.

The Basic Principles Agreement had been written at the behest of the Soviets. Like many of the communiqués that were written at the end of the Dartmouth conferences, it was taken more seriously by the Soviets than by the Americans, who considered it too general to be useful as a guide to policy.[31] Two things in the agreement were important to the Soviet side. First, it affirmed "peaceful coexistence" as the basis for U.S.-Soviet relations, using that Soviet term and thereby, they thought, legitimizing the term and the concept. Second, and more important, the text included the recognition by the United States that the Soviet Union had achieved not just military parity but equal political and diplomatic status in the world.[32] The American perception of the meaning of the agreement was different enough that Alexander George, an American scholar who took part, found it to be in reality "only a pseudoagreement." No effort was made to put the principles stated in the agreement into practice. By the end of the 1970s it had become a dead letter.

Nonetheless, it offered the Soviets and the Americans meeting in Suzdal a starting point for discussing what the basis of U.S.-Soviet relations should be. It proved to be a valuable analytical tool. With the idea behind the Basic Principles Agreement as their guide, Saunders and Primakov independently presented a list of suggested principles during the discussion of the issues in the Middle East. These were discussed at Suzdal and became the basis for the agenda at the next meeting, held in January.

The "Primakov draft" had six points. Three were negative—the two sides would renounce the use of force in regard to each other, oppose efforts to achieve military superiority, and, in their activities in third areas, renounce "interference in internal affairs of other nations." Two points called for dialogue to define the sphere of common interests and to seek solutions at times of crisis. A last point urged the two countries to act together to curb the proliferation of nuclear weapons. These points paralleled those made in the 1972 statement. But Primakov and his colleagues did not include the term "peaceful coexistence" or a statement referring explicitly to the equality of the two superpowers. The fact of that equality was certainly implied, however.[33]

The American draft, presented at Suzdal and amended after discussions among the American members of the task force the next month, was more elaborate. A page-long preamble was followed by nine points. In general, the statement focused more on expressing the authors' understanding of the interests of the two superpowers than in setting parameters for their actions in regard to each other. So, for example, where Primakov had the two sides "renounce . . . the use of crises in confrontation with each other," the American draft said that the two sides "have a common interest in preventing the processes of change from becoming crises in U.S.-Soviet relations." The Americans, and perhaps their Soviet colleagues as well, believed that it was enough at that point to try to understand the reasons—the perceived interests—that lay behind the behavior of the two superpowers.

The American statement differed also in its focus on the activities of third forces—international organizations, regional organizations, and "foreign forces." This seems to have come from the tendency of the Americans at Dartmouth, and perhaps policymakers in Washington as well, to be less willing than their Soviet counterparts to insulate the bilateral superpower relationship from other events and forces.

Despite these differences, the two statements of principles were close. Saunders believed they could serve as the basis for a common document. Indeed, the Soviet participants asked the Americans to draft a document that would meld the two statements that would at least illuminate their differences and that perhaps both sides could accept.[34]Primakov promised to send what he called clarifications in response to such a draft. Saunders received one by telegram on October 1 along with a proposal that the second meeting be held in January.

That meeting was held at Amelia Island, a resort off the Atlantic coast of Florida, a few miles north of Jacksonville. This was the first Dartmouth meeting of the post-Brezhnev era. Brezhnev had died the previous November. His place was taken by Yuri Andropov, the former head of the KGB, and a mentor of Arbatov. Almost seventy when he became general secretary and plagued by illnesses that would first incapacitate and then kill him after not much more than a year in office, Andropov nonetheless tried to rejuvenate the Soviet economy and end what would come to be called the "era of stagnation." He would only partly succeed.

The American delegation at Amelia Island was unchanged from that at Suzdal. On the Soviet side, only Primakov and Chicherov returned. There were three new Soviet participants, but they were a distinguished group. Georgi Kim was one of Primakov's deputies. The other two newcomers would become significant figures in post-Soviet Russia. Aleksei Arbatov, Georgi's son, was now an expert on security affairs at IMEMO. Like Davidson, he had first come to Dartmouth at Dartmouth XI at Jurmala in 1977. He had already published a book on nuclear security issues. Andrei Kokoshin, then at ISKAN, was becoming a civilian expert on military affairs and would become a leading advocate of the reform of military doctrine under Gorbachev. After the Soviet Union collapsed he became Russia's only civilian deputy minister of defense before becoming secretary of the Defense Council and then secretary of the Security Council, a powerful post.

The agenda at this second meeting of the task force was based on the issues raised by the statements of principles with the ideas of elaborating on the principles and seeing how they might be applied in specific situations. As Saunders put it, the idea was to use the principles as "take-off points for a discussion which would illuminate each government's limits of tolerance as defined by important interests in specific past and potential crises."[35] The task force discussed social change and revolution, nonintervention and the nonuse of force, scenarios for crisis prevention, and mechanisms for conflict management. A final session was given to the triangular relationship between China, the United States, and the Soviet Union.

Writing in early 1985, Saunders said that the Amelia Island meeting might have been the least conclusive of the meetings of the task force.[36] But, he said, the discussion of the statements of principles did bring to the surface several differences in outlook between the superpowers. They looked at social and political change differently. They regarded the possibility that revolutions could be reversed differently. The discussion brought out asymmetries in the interests of the two countries in different regions. Moreover, neither side was willing to forgo options by making a commitment to an agreement to abide by an abstract set of principles. With these differences delineated, the effort to define a set of principles for conduct was suspended. In the eyes of the American participants, the exchange had made the point that clear disagreements about meaning, many unspoken, meant that some of the familiar phrases in foreign policy pronouncements were of little practical use as guides to interaction.

A brief but useful exchange on the situation in Afghanistan took place during the session on nonintervention. As a basis for discussion, the scenarios for crisis prevention were developed around possibilities for conflict over Iran. Saunders and Stewart found that the discussion of these possibilities presented a telling example of the strengths and weak-

nesses of the dialogue.[37] In the introductory exchange, American participants made the point that the Soviet invasion of Afghanistan had raised
deep concern that the Soviet move could be a first step toward the oil of
the Persian Gulf. That concern had led to serious military contingency
planning in the Pentagon. Two Soviet participants said that Soviet troops
had moved into Afghanistan in response to American aid to Afghan
rebels. A U.S. participant responded: "I sat in the White House situation
room on every occasion when we did decide to provide military assistance. Not one of those decisions was made before the Soviet invasion."
A third Soviet participant replied: "A friendly government was in trouble,
and we moved in to help it." With that exchange, the discussion returned
to the Persian Gulf, but U.S. participants felt that the exchange had established a standard of factual exchange in the dialogue.

Returning to the conflict management scenarios, the two sides identified the interests of their countries in Iran. They suggested that any
change in the situation there could lead to a crisis between the superpowers as they would be ready to use whatever means were necessary to
defend those interests. This was not a conclusion that the public statements of two governments would have made obvious, yet the members of
the task force could come up with no proposal that was likely to be attractive or effective enough to head off a crisis, should it develop. Saunders and
Stewart felt that the development of alternative approaches to such potential crises was an approach that the task force could usefully adopt, albeit
not one that could be achieved easily or rapidly.

In a later discussion, speakers on both sides agreed that fewer
means of communication were being used at that time—the beginning
of the Reagan administration—than had been available before. Both
sides noted the absence of a back channel such as the one between
Kissinger and Ambassador Dobrynin. The Soviets complained that signals they were sending were not being received in Washington. One
American participant reported conversations with the American
ambassador in Moscow in which he said that he felt unable to communicate with the Soviets productively. There was a general need felt
at Amelia Island for developing some kind of continuing dialogue
among highly placed figures, perhaps in office, perhaps out of office. In
any case, it would be off the record, like the Dartmouth conferences,
but, unlike them, it would have official government sponsorship.

The progression made from the presentation of the list of principles at Suzdal to the discussion based on those principles at Amelia Island meant that there was formal continuity between meetings, something new to Dartmouth. Participants also set aside the development of principles of conduct as a useful approach and explored focusing on crisis scenarios as a method of work that might reveal deeper interests that would govern U.S.-Soviet relations. Moreover, the Americans wrote and the Soviets apparently concurred that it would be useful to have these meetings occur regularly. They hoped to have them occur more than once each year. The next two would meet in January or February 1984, then again as a part of Dartmouth XIV, now scheduled for the following May.[38] Each of the next few meetings, the conferees said, would focus on one particular region, with the first meeting in 1984 devoted to the Middle East, the second to Latin America and the Caribbean.

As it turned out, like the first meeting of this task force, the third meeting took place earlier than anticipated, in late November rather than in late January. This time, the American delegation changed. Lewis and Rogers did not return. Their places were taken by Alexander George and Robert Neumann. George had worked for many years at the RAND Corporation before going to Stanford. He had produced a distinguished body of work on how states react to conflict and how international conflict might be managed. Neumann had also taught political science in California (at UCLA) but had gone on to become ambassador to Afghanistan, Morocco, and Saudi Arabia. He was also the head of the transition team of the new Reagan administration for the State Department, after which he began his appointment in Riyadh. Moreover, he had direct access to Vice President George Bush and, according to Stewart, reported to him after each meeting in which he took part.[39] He brought to the task force not only insight into the thinking of the Reagan administration, but rare wisdom and wit.

In contrast, Primakov was the only member of the Soviet delegation at the previous two meetings to return for the third. Zhurkin also took part in this meeting. Among the people attending for the first time was Sergei Rogov. Mustached, tall, and eloquent, today he writes commentaries on foreign affairs for *Moscow News* and other Russian newspapers. He has succeeded Arbatov as head of ISKAN. Aleksandr

Bovin, a commentator for *Izvestiya,* had worked for Andropov as one of the "Group of Consultants" to the Secretariat of the Central Committee in the 1960s.[40] Arbatov had led that group. He and Bovin were close friends. Despite his independent and even unorthodox views, Bovin later became a speechwriter for Brezhnev.[41] Fedor Burlatsky, who wrote for *Literaturnaya gazeta,* had been an advisor to Khrushchev and preceded Arbatov as head of Andropov's "Group of Consultants" in the 1960s. Both were advocates of détente, and both became important in the development of Gorbachev's approach to foreign policy later in the decade.

The other Soviet participants in this meeting were Vladimir Nosenko, Oleg Kovtunovich, and Irina Zviagelskaya, three researchers from the Institute of Oriental Studies; Igor Belyaev, another commentator for *Literaturnaya gazeta,* who returned for the first time since 1975; Grigori Morozov from IMEMO; and Oleg Buyanov, secretary of the Soviet Peace Committee.

In the opening session the participants discussed the general state of U.S.-Soviet relations. The focus of the meeting then became the problems of the Middle East. The discussion was remarkably nonideological, particularly when contrasted with the discussions at previous Dartmouth meetings. No Soviet participant quoted at length from an official document, as Zhukov had done at Dartmouth VI. Indeed, the general secretary, Andropov, was hardly mentioned. The "deideologization" of foreign policy that took place under Gorbachev was prefigured in the content of these discussions: the Soviet delegation sounded much like the American in its description of the problems of the region and the interests of both superpowers.[42]

Before and after the Moscow meeting, the U.S. team met in the United States with about twenty specialists in Middle Eastern and Soviet affairs from the State Department, the National Security Council staff, congressional staffs, and private organizations. It also had smaller meetings in the State Department and the White House.[43]

The Americans came to the meeting with ideas for an intellectual framework for the discussions. This was not a new effort; Saunders in particular had a framework in mind when he joined the Dartmouth process. The discussions at the first two meetings that came out of the discussions of the 1972 Basic Principles Agreement used that agreement to structure the examination of superpower relations in regional conflicts. But the effort to use the task force dialogues to build an analytical framework in which to look at regional conflicts was to become an increasingly important part of the work of the Regional Conflicts Task Force.

The Americans presented two sets of ideas for a framework in Moscow. First, in the opening presentation, the American speaker argued that a useful concept of the national interest must have two components. One was an analytical statement of objective interests, which was something that researchers, analysts, or a Dartmouth dialogue could develop. But, the speaker noted, national leaders work in the political realm and see an additional dimension of interests. They have to respond to different political forces in their bodies politic and must make the choices needed among competing interests. They must allocate their attention and the resources available among them in ways that may seem nonsensical to those who define interests in any one area in objective terms. One senior Soviet participant rejected this approach, saying that the Soviet Union had only objective interests. The American speaker noted that even the Soviet leader had constituencies, but he left that idea for his Soviet colleagues to consider.

The other part of the framework was provided by Alexander George, who presented a set of principles for the management of conflict.[44] This brought out the Soviet suspicion that conflict management was a nice-sounding term that overlay efforts by the United States to exploit conflicts to their own advantage. As the discussion continued, the Soviet participants seemed to come around to the idea that the concept could be useful, at least in the Dartmouth context.

The Soviets made it clear at this meeting of the task force that they valued the access the American side had to policymakers in Washington. One of the Soviet participants, Primakov, spoke privately to two of his American colleagues, delivering a message about the situation in Lebanon that he intended to go to official circles.[45]

U.S. forces were deployed there at the time, and the Syrians were firing at U.S. reconnaissance aircraft. Primakov made several points about Soviet interests in Syria, stated "in such a way and with such precision that [his message] was clearly initiated or authorized by the Soviet government." In its essence, the message was to make it known in Washington that Soviet radar deployed for the defense of Syria (with

Soviet personnel) could not distinguish between American and Israeli air-craft because Israelis flew U.S.-made aircraft. If an American aircraft were shot down, therefore, U.S. policymakers should not interpret the act as aimed at the United States.[46] Primakov suggested later that U.S. policy toward Syria changed that month, when the United States used "all avail-able channels" to tell the Syrians that they did not intend to escalate mil-itary action against them. He made no mention, however, of any contact between Soviets and Americans, official or nonofficial, on the matter.[47]

THE TASK FORCES BEGIN: ARMS CONTROL

Originally scheduled to take place in December or January 1982 some-where in the eastern United States, the first meeting of the Arms Control Task Force took place in late April 1983 in Denver. Doty and Arbatov were the cochairmen. Stewart was again the rapporteur. The rest of the American members had extensive experience in government.

Arnold Horelick had worked at the Central Intelligence Agency as national intelligence officer for the Soviet Union and Eastern Europe during the Carter administration. He went from there to the RAND Corporation, where he stayed well into the 1990s. At the time of the first meeting of the Arms Control Task Force, he was helping to found the RAND/UCLA Center for Soviet Studies. Horelick brought three qualities to the task force, according to Stewart. One was his under-standing of arms control issues. Another was his access to President Reagan. Lastly, he was a participant "who actively searches for and pro-motes ideas which may open the door to removal of major roadblocks to serious arms reductions."[48]

William Hyland also had experience in the CIA, where he served before joining the staff of the National Security Council in 1969. He went from there to the State Department in 1973 as director of intel-ligence and research (he was succeeded by Saunders). He became deputy national security advisor in 1975 under Scowcroft but left the government in 1977.[49] In 1983 he was at the Carnegie Endowment for International Peace. He subsequently became editor of the journal *Foreign Affairs.* Two years later, Stewart wrote that Hyland had "a par-ticular ability to seek out and articulate conceptual bridges that often have helped to join otherwise seemingly irreconcilable positions."[50]

Scowcroft, a retired air force general, also served on the National Security Council staff as Kissinger's deputy and succeeded him as the national security advisor under President Ford (Hyland became his deputy). He was a rare figure in American foreign policy in being almost universally liked and respected. Robert Gates, who worked closely with him for several years when Scowcroft was President Bush's national security advisor, says that he was "trusted as no other National Security Adviser has been trusted" and describes his "lack of egotism and his gentle manner," but notes that he nonetheless "had his own strong views and he would advance and defend them stubbornly."[51] Scowcroft was, by his own admission, cautious. A strong supporter of the tough policy the Reagan administration adopted toward the Soviet Union, he nonetheless thought some of the rhetoric excessive.[52]

David Jones had retired from the air force the previous June. He had been chief of staff of the air force and then chairman of the Joint Chiefs of Staff. He earned his wings during World War II, flew bombers in Korea, and later served with NATO in Europe. As noted, he had briefed the American delegation going to Moscow for Dartmouth XIII and later found the discussions of arms control at the conference to be valuable.

The Soviet members of the task force all came from ISKAN. In addition to Arbatov, they included Kokoshin and Milstein, two of the institute's experts on military affairs, and Zhurkin and Evgeni Kutovoy. All had taken part in Dartmouth discussions before, with Kokoshin and Kutovoy also having attended meetings of the Regional Conflicts Task Force.

Two days before the meetings began in Denver, the American delegation was briefed in Washington by James Timbie, assistant to the director of the Arms Control and Disarmament Agency (ACDA), and Kenneth W. Dam, deputy secretary of state. Lawrence Eagleburger, the undersecretary of state for political affairs, had recommended to Secretary of State George Shultz that the secretary meet with the members of the task force, but both Shultz and Eagleburger had flown to the Middle East. All the same, the importance with which the administration regarded the Dartmouth discussions was clear.

An important element in the Denver discussions stemmed from

President Reagan's appointment, earlier in 1983, of Scowcroft as the head of the President's Commission on Strategic Forces. The commission issued its report on April 6, just three weeks before the Arms Control Task Force met in Denver. It questioned whether the United States' nuclear arsenal faced a "window of vulnerability" owing to the Soviets' buildup of their own arsenal that had begun in the 1960s. The existence of such a window had been argued strenuously by the Reagan administration. The report also proposed the development of a single-warhead missile to replace the multiple-warhead MIRVed missiles that had been developed in the early 1970s, arguing that this would make the American land-based missile force more secure. At the same time, the commission made a recommendation for how to deploy the biggest of these MIRVed missiles in the American arsenal, the MX, until the smaller missile, the Midgetman, could be developed and deployed.[53] The deployment of these missiles was an important issue at the time as it was felt that silos such as those used for the Minuteman might be too vulnerable and that other, mobile, means of deploying them were expensive with their effectiveness unknown.

This last recommendation may have been the most important for the administration, which was fighting hard for funding for the MX in Congress, but the rest of the commission's conclusions stoked the fires of discussion in Denver. The implications of creating a force of single-warhead missiles rather than MIRVed missiles were discussed at length. This was a fairly new approach to creating stability in the arms race. Neither side yet had fixed ideas about it, which made the Denver dialogue all the more important.[54]

The other major topic was the deployment of intermediate-range missiles in Europe. There were the three-warhead SS-20s, which the Soviets began deploying in the mid-1970s, and the Pershing II and cruise missiles that NATO was planning to deploy in response. Negotiations over the control of these weapons began in the fall of 1981. By the spring of 1983 they had reached an impasse. Both sides at Denver agreed that a new approach of some kind was needed, but they could not find one. The idea of deferring deployment of the Pershing II and cruise missiles was raised, but people on both sides agreed that a deferral by itself, without changes in the approach to the talks or in the political situation surrounding them, would yield nothing.

Horelick subsequently discussed the meeting with the chief negotiator in the Strategic Arms Reduction Talks (START), General
Edward Rowny. Rowny had taken General Allison's place in the SALT
talks in the 1970s but resigned in protest when the agreement was
signed. He continued to take a hard line on negotiations even after he
joined the Reagan administration. Fairly or not, he was regarded by the
Soviets as stubborn and unyielding. Nonetheless, he was interested in
what Horelick told him about what had been said in Denver and asked
for a summary of the discussions. Stewart quickly typed up some notes
and sent them.[55]

The task force met again in Moscow the following March. By this
time U.S.-Soviet relations were in a deep freeze and tenser than at any
time since the invasion of Czechoslovakia in 1968. The destruction of
Korean Air flight 007 over Kamchatka in September 1983 was followed by bitter denunciations by each side of the other. More ominously, arms control talks over strategic weapons and theater nuclear
weapons stopped two months later with no prospect of renewal. Konstantin Chernenko replaced Andropov as general secretary of the
CPSU in February 1984. He was ill, as Andropov had been, and had
achieved prominence primarily by serving as a yes-man to Brezhnev.
The prospects for change within the Soviet Union and in its relations
with the West seemed distant.

The March meeting of that task force gained special importance
because Scowcroft carried a personal message from President Reagan to
the new general secretary, Chernenko, with the authority to say more.[56]
Chernenko had written to Reagan in February shortly after he became
general secretary and, among others things, suggested that the sides
engage in "a dialogue" to "search for common ground."[57] The national
security advisor, Robert "Bud" McFarlane, wrote a policy memorandum
on February 24 in which he suggested that personal exchanges about a
wide range of issues be intensified. The question of using Scowcroft came
up in a meeting with the president and senior members of the National
Security Council in the residential quarters of the White House on
March 1. McFarlane thought the Soviets might respond to messages sent
outside official channels, and so the message from Reagan was prepared.
In order to ensure that the official nature of the message was understood,
Shultz told Ambassador Dobrynin in Washington about it, and the

American ambassador in Moscow, Arthur Hartman, told the Foreign Ministry.

However, the Soviets were suspicious of a message delivered this way. Hartman was asked by one official why an unofficial channel would be used if the message was important. More significant, perhaps, the Soviets understood this to be an effort to go around Gromyko. Whatever the reason, they allowed only Scowcroft to meet with Viktor Komplektov, a deputy foreign minister. Scowcroft refused to deliver the letter to an official that unimportant. So the mission backfired, making the Soviets more suspicious of American motives than before and making a thaw in relations more difficult to bring about.

This suspicion by the Soviets may have colored the discussions of the task force, or it may have been the general gloom that lay over the public U.S.-Soviet relationship in general (the suggestion that dialogue might be useful was, after all, made by private correspondence between Chernenko and Reagan and was not a part of the public dialogue). In any case, that gloom spread over the deliberations of the task force. Summing up the lessons of the meeting, Stewart reported that the Soviets trotted out a new line at the meeting that depicted the deployments in Europe "as a vehicle for humiliating the Soviet Union" that raised "the danger of war."[58] He found the Soviets rigid and almost irrational and feared that the struggle over intermediate-range nuclear forces (INF) had done long-term damage. This was communicated to several senior administration officials at a briefing held the next month in preparation for Dartmouth XIV, which would be held in May.

The American members of the task force at the March meeting were the same as at the previous two, except that Bialer also took part. The Soviet delegation included two new members from the scientific community. They were both physicists-turned-administrators, liberals in the Soviet system, and old friends. Both had also taken part in discussions with the Committee on International Security and Arms Control of the National Academy of Sciences in Washington the previous year. They also shared an aversion to antiballistic missile defense, Soviet and American. This was especially important in the aftermath of President Reagan's proposal for the Strategic Defense Initiative (SDI), made in March 1983.[59]

Evgeni Velikhov, the head of the Kurchatov Institute of Atomic Energy and vice president of the Soviet Academy of Sciences,[60] had been awarded a Lenin Prize for his work on high-powered lasers. By this time he "had firmly launched himself in the front line of opposition to SDI."[61] In truth, this meant opposition not merely to the American program, but also to Soviet efforts to move in the same direction. In 1983 he founded the Committee for Soviet Scientists for Peace, Against the Nuclear Threat. He named Roald Sagdeev and another Dartmouth participant, Kokoshin, as his deputies.

As a nuclear physicist, Sagdeev had been kept along the fringes of the Soviet military-industrial complex, but he had avoided being swept into its "mailboxes," the top-secret installations such as Arzamas-16 where the work on nuclear weapons was done. In 1984 he was the director of the Space Research Institute of the Academy of Sciences and a member of the Supreme Soviet. An ethnic Tatar, rather than a Russian like most of his Soviet colleagues, he later followed Andrei Sakharov's path into dissent. An evocative picture from a meeting of the Supreme Soviet in October 1988 shows him voting alone—arm raised, mouth drawn tight, the lights of the hall reflected in his glasses, dismay showing in the face of the man seated to his left. At that time the Supreme Soviet was still a rubber-stamp legislature, and any such act of opposition was both unexpected and dangerous.[62] He is now director of the East-West Center for Space Science at the University of Maryland and a senior associate at the Center for Political and Strategic Studies in Washington. His marriage to Susan Eisenhower later provided a human highlight, full of hope-giving symbolism, of the end of the Cold War.

DARTMOUTH XIV: TENSIONS REDUX

The gloom that had settled into U.S.-Soviet relations the previous summer remained in the spring of 1984, when the Dartmouth Conference returned to Dartmouth College for Dartmouth XIV. The experience of the Arms Control Task Force meeting in March and the failure of the Scowcroft mission that was a part of it brought home to the participants how cold the Cold War had again become. Yet a significant contrast could be made with the late 1960s. At that time, tensions in the relationship over Vietnam and Czechoslovakia, and other issues as well, had led to the postponement of Dartmouth V for five years. Yet in 1984 both the Soviet and American governments felt it important enough for a dialogue of some sort to continue that Dartmouth activities—the task force meetings and the full, plenary conferences—were not even delayed, though official negotiations were canceled.

On April 11 and 12, about a month before the conference, the American participants were briefed by three officials from the Reagan administration: Lawrence Eagleburger, undersecretary of state; Thomas Simons, who was then head of the Soviet desk and chief expert on the Soviet Union in the State Department (he was put in charge of assistance programs to the former Soviet states in the Clinton administration); and Jack Matlock, who then worked on the staff of the National Security Council. Matlock would later become ambassador to the Soviet Union and then take part in the Dartmouth process himself.

The meeting opened with a discussion over dinner led by Eagleburger of the current state of the relationship between the superpowers; it continued the next day with briefings by Matlock and Simons.[63] All three briefers were pessimistic about the chances for change in the immediate future. The Soviets, they said, were unlikely to do anything that might help Reagan be reelected that fall. The Reagan administration, in its turn, would do nothing to increase economic relations with the Soviet Union. Discussions of Third World conflicts "have been dry holes," they said. They expected the Soviets to suggest merging the START and INF negotiations by early 1985 and believed that the United States might well agree. But that approach, they said, was so complex that there might be "no new arms agreements during Reagan's second term." They also expected turmoil in Soviet foreign policy during the rest of the 1980s, making some containment necessary, and foresaw that the Soviet economy would suffer from "carrying the burden of global power."

But not all was gloom and doom. Eagleburger spoke at length on the question of why the Soviets should trust or deal with Reagan.[64] In effect he outlined a change in the thinking of the Reagan administration. He said that President Reagan had come into office with three priorities: first, economic recovery; second, rearmament and healing relations with friends and allies; and third, dealing with the Soviet Union. By the spring and summer of 1983 Reagan felt his accomplishments on the first two priorities were such that he could afford to go on to the third and deal with the Soviet Union. But his move toward negotiations was brought to a halt by the destruction of the Korean airliner in September. Nonetheless, the briefer concluded, "In US political terms, there is now a better basis for negotiations than has existed in more than ten years."

Having been given that twinkle in the dark of the relationship, the American participants made their way to Hanover to meet their Soviet colleagues. Most of the members of the two task forces took part in Dartmouth XIV. Indeed, the Regional Conflicts Task Force counted Dartmouth XIV as one of its regular meetings. All of its members were there except for Alexander George—Saunders, Bialer, Lewis, Rogers, Stremlau, and Neumann. Scowcroft, whose time was taken with official duties, was not in Hanover, but his colleagues were—Doty, Horelick, Hyland, and Jones. Other Dartmouth veterans also returned for the conference. Mathews was formally the American cochairman of the conference, though he generously ceded the role to Cousins. Bolling, now president of the Ecumenical Institute for Theological Studies, south of Jerusalem, was there. So were Antonia Chayes and, as so often before, David Rockefeller. Cousins, still teaching medical students at UCLA, made his first appearance at Dartmouth since Dartmouth XII. William Coleman, who had attended Dartmouth XIII, also returned.

There were a few new faces as well. Rockefeller was able to attract Robert Lundeen, chairman of the board of Dow Chemical, and Daniel Yankelovich, one of the premier students of public judgment in the United States and a pioneer in the field. He developed the focus group, now a ubiquitous tool in research on public opinion. Both came for the first time but not the last.

Unlike the American delegation, the Soviet delegation was not dominated by members of the task forces. But most of the Soviet delegates were Dartmouth veterans, including members of the task forces who had been most closely involved in Dartmouth: Arbatov (who was the Soviet cochairman of the conference), Primakov, Zhurkin, and Milstein. Rogov also came, for his first full Dartmouth conference. Also attending were Runov, deputy minister of agriculture; Kislov, who had been at the St. Regis Hotel; and Stanislav Borisov, deputy minister of finance, who had first come to Dartmouth at the Rio Rico conference.

Newcomers included Valeri Pekshev, a deputy chairman of GosBank, the central bank of the Soviet Union; Sergei Tarasenko, a deputy department head in the Foreign Ministry; Vladimir Gantman, a section head in Arbatov's ISKAN and a participant at several Dartmouth conferences during the 1970s; and Konstantin Sarkisov, a section chief at Primakov's Institute of Oriental Studies. In all, half the Soviet delegation came from ISKAN. Of the other six participants, four came from the Soviet government.

As the plenary began, the atmosphere was filled with tension, reflecting the tension between the two governments. It was not clear how, or even whether, the tension could be lifted. As often with Dartmouth, however, simple human concerns made it possible to begin the dialogue. In their opening remarks, Cousins and Arbatov agreed that it was good to be together, ready to talk. Both had suffered life-threatening illnesses. As it happened, public television during the meeting broadcast a program on Cousins' struggle to overcome his illness, a struggle that was the source of much of his thinking about the relationship between mind, body, and spirit, which made his experience all the more real to the delegates.

There were three work groups at the Hanover conference.[65] As noted, the Regional Conflicts Task Force conducted one of its regular meetings at Hanover. The arms control group combined its discussion of arms control issues with a discussion of political relations between the superpowers. As the presence of Rockefeller and Lundeen might suggest, the topic of the third group was economic relations.

The regional conflicts group had two items on its agenda—how U.S.-Soviet relations play themselves out in regional crises, and the prospects for a common approach to a settlement in the Middle East. The focus of most of the discussion was on the latter, the Middle East. Both sides agreed that Soviet participation in efforts to resolve the conflicts in the region was needed if an effective settlement was to be reached. But the Soviets complained that the U.S. government had excluded them systematically, mentioning the failure to follow through on the joint effort launched in October 1977. The Americans argued that the Soviets had not shown themselves able to contribute to a settlement. They said that the Soviet Union had put support for its Arab allies above taking steps toward a balanced settlement. In addition, the parties involved had shown little interest in having the Soviets involved in a

settlement process. The Soviets echoed, repeatedly, an old refrain, arguing that as the Soviet Union was the nuclear equal of the United States,
it had to be treated as a political equal. The American cochairman,
somewhat exasperated at this, asked one of his American colleagues, not
associated with policy in the Middle East, to explain American attitudes.
The colleague was blunt: "As long as the Soviet government sends its
opponents to gulags or confines them to psychiatric hospitals, it will not
be regarded as a political equal by Americans." The subject was dropped.

Much of the group's discussion of political relations followed previous paths. The Soviets blamed the United States for the decline of
détente. They made the same argument their colleagues made in earlier
meetings of the Regional Conflicts Task Force, complaining that the
United States failed to recognize political equality, even though the
Soviets had gained military parity. The American response was not
unified. One American put the onus of the collapse of détente on the
Soviet Union. Another said U.S.-Soviet relations followed a cycle of
action and reaction. Still another argued that détente had never had a
firm political foundation in the first place; it came about because of developments outside the control of either superpower.

One of the Soviet participants expressed opinions that seemed to
belong to the coming Gorbachev era. He was remarkably even-handed
and called for major changes in policy on both sides. "What is required
[now is] not the timid steps of the 1970s," he said, "but a total reversal
of traditional forms of behavior." Small steps have "no effect," he continued, when there is no trust in the "intentions of the other side." He
concluded by noting "that we have on both sides arsenals of space-age
weapons controlled by stone-age emotions."

In the discussion on arms control the Soviets complained that the
United States was not serious and pointed to the deployments of missiles in Europe as a prime example. Several Americans echoed the briefer
in April who had said that in 1983 the Reagan administration had come
to feel able to address arms control issues with the Soviet Union.

Part of the discussion at the conference focused on the effect of
public opinion on foreign policy. As in the previous discussions of the
topic, the focus was on American public opinion. Yankelovich, who may
know more than anyone about American public opinion, explained the
public's views of the major issues in the relationship. He argued that in

the United States, public opinion often influenced foreign policy. Indeed, he said, for many political leaders, "public opinion is the strongest single element in policy judgment." The data he had showed that the invasion of Afghanistan had acted as a watershed, moving American public opinion against the Soviet Union. But dramatic changes in public attitudes had occurred before and would occur again. Disapproval of the Soviet Union, which had been between 85 and 90 percent in the 1950s and 1960s, had plunged to 30 to 40 percent in the 1970s. Moreover, whereas the nature of the challenge had been perceived as ideological in the 1950s, the public now saw it as stemming from Soviet military power.

He also addressed the question of whether American public opinion was formed independently or was primarily shaped by policymakers. He found no simple answer to that question. The public leaned on the interpretations of others in forming its attitudes toward foreign policy. Nonetheless, his conclusion was that "[p]ublic opinion more often influences foreign policy than the leaders influence public opinion on foreign issues."[66]

Soviet views about the role of public opinion in the foreign policies of the United States and other capitalist countries had been important in Soviet foreign policy since 1917, when the two tracks that were hallmarks of Soviet foreign policy were first established. One was the track of state-to-state relations and official diplomacy. The other was, from the Western perspective, the track of subversion. This track, embodied in the Comintern in the 1920s and 1930s and characterized by support for communist parties, front organizations, and sympathizers, was based on the idea that Western public opinion was to some degree malleable, at least in the long term.

A strong thread in the opinion of the Soviet leadership, however, had long been that, despite phenomena such as the active opposition of elements of the American public to the Vietnam War in the 1960s and the nuclear freeze movement of the early 1980s, American foreign policy was dominated by an entrenched elite that was immutably hostile to the Soviet Union and its goals.[67]

By 1984 Soviet opinion about the role of the public in the Reagan administration's foreign policy was divided. In one view, which had Marshal Nikolai V. Ogarkov as its most prominent spokesman, public opinion had little or no effect on how the United States approached the Soviet Union. This was similar to the views often expressed at Dartmouth conferences that the actions of the Soviet Union during the 1970s could have no effect on the United States' Soviet policy. Proponents of this view advocated responding "symmetrically" to the Reagan administration's military buildup, including SDI, with a buildup of Soviet forces. The other view, led by Foreign Minister Gromyko, instead sought to respond through diplomacy and appeals to public opinion.[68] Its proponents assumed that American policymakers were at least partially susceptible to the pressure of public opinion.

This second view may not have been entirely new—it can be questioned whether Gromyko, an old dog, had learned a new trick. But the policies advocated by those who held this view, which eventually included Gorbachev, in effect meant that for the first time since World War II the Soviet Union would rely on foreign public opinion to forestall a developing military threat. It would not rely solely on the real and perceived capabilities of its own military. The Soviet participants who heard Yankelovich's presentation probably had this in mind as he spoke.

Three issues were addressed by the work group on economic relations: general trends in the world economy, the effects of these trends on the American and Soviet economies, and ways to reactivate trade relations between the two countries. The dual deficits that the United States ran at the time—in the federal budget and in trade—were an important element in the discussion. The Soviets expressed concern about how these deficits affected global interest rates, the increase in which led to an increase in the indebtedness of developing countries. This indebtedness, like the deficits, was a major concern of the time, with major debt crises developing in Brazil and Mexico, although these crises had causes other than simply the deficits run by the United States. One Soviet speaker emphasized that global trends such as the increase in interest rates were becoming increasingly important in Soviet planning as the Soviet economy was becoming more closely integrated into the world economy.

The discussion about how to increase trade and economic cooperation was the first to take place in several years. This made the discussion significant, but the lines of the discussion were familiar. One Soviet speaker said that the conditions needed for large-scale trade included unconditional most-favored-nation status. An American noted the not-always-beneficial importance of human rights concerns, embodied in the Jackson-Vanik Amendment, in the American approach to trade. Other Americans noted the obstacles to trade that came from the "complex and cumbersome" Soviet bureaucracy and the obstacles to trade that came from American efforts to restrict the transfer of technology to the Soviet Union. This was an important element in the Reagan administration's trade policy.

THE REGIONAL CONFLICTS TASK FORCE, NOVEMBER 1984 TO APRIL 1985: A THAW BEGINS

During the summer and fall, relations between the United States and the Soviet Union began to thaw. The change began with the visit of Foreign Minister Gromyko to Washington after his annual speech at the United Nations in September. On this visit he met with President Reagan as well as his American counterpart, Secretary Shultz. It marked the first time he had been in the White House since the invasion of Afghanistan. In the words of Shultz, these meetings "marked a new turn in the superpower relationship."[69]

In July, shortly before the thaw began, the Soviets issued a statement calling, once again, for an international conference to resolve the Arab-Israeli conflict. This was a recurring theme, both for the Soviet government and for the Dartmouth Conference. It was the subject of the task force meeting at the St. Regis Hotel in 1975. At the third meeting of the Regional Conflicts Task Force, in late 1983, it was discussed again. At that time, a Soviet speaker responded to American complaints that such a conference was unworkable by saying that it was simply the third stage of a process, following discussions between the Soviet Union and the United States and discussions between the two superpowers and their friends in the region. That notion of a process was absent from the July statement. With that background in mind, the Regional Conflicts Task Force met in Leningrad in November 1984 to discuss the Middle East.

The American side included three regular members of the task force—Saunders, Neumann, and Stremlau—and a newcomer, Philip M. Klutznick. Klutznick had been international president of B'nai B'rith and president of the World Jewish Congress. He was invited to give the Soviets—who had no official relations with Israel—a firsthand account of the realities of Israeli politics and their influence on the United States. It is not known who took part on the Soviet side, except, as usual, Primakov. Klutznick describes them as journalists and scholars from ISKAN and Primakov's institute.

The American delegation met twice before the task force meeting—in Washington in October and in Paris en route. They met with Ambassador Hartman in Spaso House for an informal dinner and briefing before boarding the night train to Leningrad. After their return, Hartman sponsored a lunch that was attended by both delegations and officials from both governments. Klutznick stayed in the Soviet Union for a few days to speak to Arbatov, meet with Jewish leaders, and search for his family roots.

The discussions in Leningrad revolved around the approach put forward in the Soviet message in July.[70] In addition to a focus on an international conference, the Soviet idea was to seek a comprehensive settlement. The Soviets also expressed bitterness over the exclusion of the Soviet Union by the Americans from peace efforts in the Middle East. They asserted that those efforts had utterly failed.

The American approach, in contrast, was to look at the conflict as a process, with an international conference as an option that could happen at one, late stage. The Soviets understood this to mean that their approach was being ignored. Consequently, following a visit to the Piskariovskoye Cemetery, the powerful monument to those who died in Leningrad during World War II that the Americans had also visited at Dartmouth IV, the Soviet members of the task force took aim at American and Israeli policy in the Middle East and fired away.

That happened halfway through the three-day meeting. But by the end of that day, the meeting began to change course. The tension began to subside. The Soviets asked the American side for a picture of what the total process leading to a settlement might look like. This request marked a key point for Dartmouth that reflected changes and a greater flexibility in official Soviet thinking.

The Americans provided a framework for dialogue the next day. It noted points that the two sides agreed on, including the importance of action by both superpowers and the need to improve the political environment before a settlement could be reached. The Americans then outlined a process characterized as "a multi-stage U.S.-Soviet consultation coupled with soundings in the region." The Soviets were skeptical about this approach but finally concluded that it was "natural" and "made sense."

At this meeting, Primakov asked Saunders and Neumann to meet in private late one evening. Noting that the warning about Syria he had given the year before "had obviously been delivered," he delivered another message, translating from notes he had in Russian. He made several points that together emphasized the dangers in the superpower relationship at the time—dangers coming from within a Soviet Union reacting to a set of American policies seen as uncommunicative and threatening. He said that the Soviet Union did not want war in the Middle East and was prepared to be flexible there. It is not clear whether this message influenced American policy.[71]

The next meeting of the task force, in April 1985, at the very beginning of the Gorbachev era, showed that both the cracks in the ice that covered the U.S.-Soviet relationship and the growing sophistication of the discussion in the Dartmouth dialogues depended on who was involved. This sixth meeting of the task force came about following an invitation extended by the Latin American Institute to the task force through William Rogers. This was another one of the regional institutes, like ISKAN, attached to the Soviet Academy of Sciences. That the institute took the initiative to have the meeting suggests that there was some prestige to be gained from association with the Dartmouth Conference, prestige that Dartmouth may have shared with other forums that allowed direct contact with Americans.

The meeting differed from its predecessors in a number of ways. The way it came about was one. Another was the participants. On the American side, continuity with the earlier meetings of the task force was embodied in Saunders, Stewart, and Rogers. The other two Americans were new to Dartmouth. Susan Kaufman Purcell was director of the Latin American Program at the Council on Foreign Relations. Robert Leiken was a senior fellow at the Carnegie Endowment for International Peace.

On the Soviet side, only Zhurkin was a veteran of Dartmouth. He was accompanied by a colleague from ISKAN, Viktor Kremenyuk, and a researcher from IMEMO, Nikolai Zaitsev. Kremenyuk, a sector chief at ISKAN, later came to be highly regarded as a specialist on conflict resolution, a rarity in the Soviet Union. The rest of the Soviet participants were senior members of the Latin American Institute, chosen by its director, Viktor Volsky.

The scholars from the Latin American Institute did not impress the Americans, who found them to be narrow specialists, without a broad conception of either how foreign policy is conducted or the U.S.-Soviet relationship. They also seemed weak as scholars. On the whole, while contributions made by the trio from ISKAN and IMEMO were good, "the contributions made by the group from the Latin American Institute were of lower quality than we are used to."[72]

The result was that as far as the Americans were concerned, the discussions were filled with polemics and "outmoded cliches about U.S. policy in Central America." Indeed, at one point, when an American speaker described efforts that the United States had made to liberalize the Somoza regime, Volsky pointedly pulled off his headset "and refused to listen." During the next coffee break, Saunders took him to task. He then apologized. The Americans missed the rapport that had been built in earlier meetings with the likes of Primakov.

It should be noted, however, that an expert on Latin America who looked at the memorandum written by the American participants came away feeling that they had "adhered very closely to the official U.S. line, and almost acted as if they were government spokesmen."[73] He said, for example, that they seemed to identify with a proposal made by President Reagan when, days later, the House of Representatives rejected it.

For the Americans, the meeting succeeded mainly in creating a clearer picture of the Soviet position. They found the Soviets unable to understand the American position on the reversibility of Marxist-Leninist regimes. The Americans categorized this position as a willingness to accept revolution provided that the new regime remained accountable through a free, democratic political process. The Soviet position, they felt, was to provide support in ways that made the revolution irreversible. A half-day discussion on the burden of foreign debt that had come to crisis in Latin America showed that the Soviets saw themselves as participants in the international financial system with no interest in its collapse. The Americans also sensed from some of the statements made that the Soviets were feeling some economic pressure owing to the support they were giving their Third World allies. And a discussion of the proposal that President Reagan had made shortly before, which was to have the two sides in Nicaragua sit and talk to each other, garnered a reaction that suggested to the American members a real reason for the Soviet concern about the U.S. approach to Nicaragua. A Soviet speaker described a version of the domino theory in which the United States sought changes in the structure of all Marxist-Leninist governments, beginning with Nicaragua and ending with the Soviet Union: "The emotion-laden statements on this issue suggested that we were seeing behind them the Soviet reaction to US statements over the years which seemed to be directed at changing the character of the Soviet regime itself."[74]

The task force meeting was accompanied by meetings between American members of the task force and senior Soviet officials. The group met with Vadim Zagladin, a first deputy director of the International Department of the Central Committee, and several members of his staff. They began with a discussion of the coming arms control negotiations and SDI (Zagladin showed no concern about the latter, arguing that the Soviets could overcome it at far less than the cost to build it) and then moved on to the situation in Central America.

Rogers met with Vladimir N. Kazimirov, chief of the First Latin American Department of the Foreign Ministry, who blamed the United States for tensions there and said that it was up to the United States to reduce them. Saunders met with Kazimirov's counterpart on Middle Eastern issues, Vladimir Polyakov, chief of the Middle East Department in the Foreign Ministry. The focus of their meeting was an exchange of information about the state of the conflict between the Arabs and Israel. Polyakov asked Saunders several times about the Israeli reaction to a recent meeting between Arafat and King Hussein of Jordan. They also discussed the reaction of the PLO to the agreement that Arafat had made. The Soviet position on the conflict, as Polyakov described it, remained focused, as it had for more than a decade now, on a "Middle East Conference" in which the Soviet Union would have a significant part.

THE ARMS CONTROL TASK FORCE, DECEMBER 1984 AND NOVEMBER 1985: A THAW CONTINUES

The thaw in U.S.-Soviet relations continued to develop while the Regional Conflicts Task Force met in Leningrad. That week, a week

after Reagan's reelection, it was announced that arms control negotiations would begin again in January 1985 with a meeting between
Gromyko and Shultz. As Eagleburger, Matlock, and Simons had foreshadowed in April, the negotiations on START and INF would be
combined. SDI would be included as well.

The Arms Control Task Force met again in early December in
Washington. The American team was the same one that had gone to
Moscow in the spring, with Bialer added. Hyland was now the editor
of the journal *Foreign Affairs;* Scowcroft was listed as the chairman of
the President's Commission on Strategic Arms, the appointment he
had received the previous January.

The Soviet team once again included Georgi Arbatov and Milstein.
Two other members were new to the task force but not to Dartmouth—
Rogov and Trofimenko. The last member of the group was Timur Timo-
feyev of the Institute of the International Labor Movement.

The discussions covered the range of arms control topics that were
on the agendas of the two countries at the time.[75] SDI was discussed at
length, the first time the task force had an opportunity to do so, as
Reagan had announced the initiative after its meeting in March and the
task force did not formally meet at Hanover. Skepticism about the technical feasibility of the program was expressed on both sides. Some speakers on each side also seemed to believe that the research would produce
some deployable weapons, though not, perhaps, the entire system envi-
sioned by the president.[76] The Soviets looked at the entire matter with
"the deepest distrust" and without the confidence shown by Zagladin a
few months later. Reagan had assured the Soviets that he would make
the technology for SDI accessible to the Soviets, but one Soviet speaker
asked: "If you don't sell microcomputers to us, how are we to believe you
will exchange this very sophisticated technology?" Another, perhaps less
skeptical of the feasibility of SDI than others, likened SDI to MIRV and
the cruise missile, two programs that did not have limitations negotiated
until research had ended and deployment begun. The members of the
task force wrestled with the question of how to negotiate arms control
agreements within the five years that Reagan said would be devoted to
research before a decision on deployment was reached. They reached no
firm conclusion on whether agreements were possible or what kind of
agreements might be reached.

The task force also discussed the possibility of developing forces made up of single-warhead missiles to replace the MIRVed forces that had been deployed in the 1970s. Speakers on both sides saw some value in this but believed that SDI, verification problems, and, above all, the cost of such a program limited the possibility. The INF talks were another major topic for discussion. The Soviets asserted that the forces of the British and French had to be brought into negotiations. The task force also discussed questions about compliance with existing agreements that were raised, above all, by the construction of a radar system at Krasnoyarsk that seemed to American observers to have an ABM capability, the continuing extension of the unratified SALT II agreement, and the Multilateral Balanced Force Reduction (MBFR) talks.

Before the task force meeting an incident occurred that underlined the continuing importance of Sherry and Klebnikov to Dartmouth. It has not been noted in these pages, but these two continued to interpret for Dartmouth discussions through the 1970s and into the 1980s. They had been present at all the meetings since Dartmouth II in 1961, a record matched by no one. Klebnikov had retired in 1983 as director of the UN Interpretation Service. Sherry had served as an assistant secretary-general at the United Nations. In 1984 he was a senior fellow of the UN Institute for Training and Research.

Shortly before the meeting of the task force, the American members met with an official of the National Security Council, who insisted that the meeting be for "principals only." This was interpreted to mean that Sherry and Klebnikov were excluded. They found this highly embarrassing. After discussing the matter with Doty, Stewart, and Pat Coggins, they wrote a letter in February to Ruopp at the Kettering Foundation saying so, urging that he or Mathews write a letter to a senior official "to avoid a recurrence of this kind of misunderstanding."[77]

Sherry was not present at the next meeting of the task force, which took place in Moscow over Thanksgiving the next year. Klebnikov and William Krimer were the interpreters for that meeting, which focused on SDI. The American delegation was largely unchanged from before: Doty, Horelick, and Jones, with Stewart once again as rapporteur. Neither Hyland nor Scowcroft came. Walter Slocombe was the sole addition.

Trained as a lawyer and a student of Soviet politics at Oxford, he had served on the staff of the National Security Council under Kissinger but worked in the McGovern presidential campaign in 1972. In the Carter administration he became a senior advisor on arms control matters in the Defense Department, having made a strong impression on the secretary, Harold Brown.[78]

The Soviet delegation, as usual for meetings in Moscow, was large and not limited to members of the Arms Control Task Force. Half of the fifteen members were veterans of earlier task force meetings: Georgi Arbatov, Kokoshin, Milstein, Trofimenko, Zhurkin, and the two scientists Sagdeev and Velikhov. The delegation also included Primakov and Zhukov, who had been absent from Dartmouth since the conference in Moscow in 1981. The rest included Aleksei Arbatov and two military officers on active duty with the General Staff of the Army: Colonel Geli Batenin and Colonel General Nikolai Chervov. General Chervov was head of the Treaty and Legal Affairs Directorate of the General Staff, which was responsible for arms control. Batenin was assigned to the propaganda section of the Central Committee.[79]

The task force meeting took place shortly after the first summit meeting between Gorbachev and Reagan, at Geneva. Also present in Geneva for the summit were the "Gang of Four," as the press called them. These were Sagdeev, Primakov, Arbatov, and Velikhov—all Dartmouth veterans. They had been sent along to brief the press on behalf of the Soviet delegation.[80] That summit was marked by disagreements over arms control issues. It became in its essence an opportunity for the two leaders to become acquainted. The summit did not figure in the task force discussions in Moscow.

Instead, task force members focused their attention on proposals from Horelick and Jones for an approach to arms control negotiations that would, they thought, take into account the interests of both countries in regard to SDI.[81] Both speakers assumed that a complete ban on research on antiballistic missile systems was impossible, though the official Soviet position was that such a ban should be imposed. One of them proposed that assurances be made to the Soviets that the United States would not break the ABM treaty by deploying an ABM system, assurances that would be good for the lifetime of any agreement on the reduction of offensive weapons. They could take the form of reaffirmation and clarification of the ABM treaty or an amendment of the article on abrogation of the treaty, so that either side would have to give several years' notice, rather than merely six months', the time agreed to in 1972. The other proposal was to link reductions in offensive arms to adherence to the ABM treaty, the idea being that reductions of, say, 5 percent per year could be made while adherence was regarded as satisfactory.

These proposals were made on the first day. The Soviets thought about them overnight and asked numerous questions about them the next day. From the questions asked it was clear that the proposals were taken seriously. There was even a sense that the Soviet participants were working through the issues as colleagues of the Americans rather than as representatives of the Soviet government. One statement in particular brings this out:

> If we are to try to persuade our people that this is reasonable, there is a strong argument you could use with your authorities. With a ban on field testing, an important role is acquired by computer simulation and modeling by the U.S. where you have a real advantage. This can all be done without proceeding to field testing. *We will try to conceal this fact from our authorities.*[82] (Emphasis added.)

The idea that the Soviet participants would in fact conceal an important idea from their authorities cannot be taken seriously, but the spirit of the comment is an important indication of the sentiments with which at least some of the Soviet participants approached the discussions.

Two weeks later, on December 9, Doty, Jones, and Slocombe had an appointment with Paul Nitze, who was then an ambassador at large, giving advice on arms control. The Americans left the conference in Moscow with the impression that the Soviets, too, would report its results to senior officials.

THE POLITICAL RELATIONS TASK FORCE, JANUARY 1986: A NEW APPROACH

The idea for a third task force was developed through 1985. It was to explore the interrelationships among the different facets of the relationship between the United States and the Soviet Union and look at both the prospects for the relationship and the obstacles to an improvement.[83] The idea was floated before Zhurkin in the spring. He agreed both to have it and to chair it for the Soviet side. But owing to a shortage of resources and time, the meeting came at the cost of the meeting of the Regional Conflicts Task Force that was to have been held in the fall.

The timing of the meeting was fortuitous. It opened at the end of January 1986 in Moscow. This was two months after the Geneva summit, about two weeks after Gorbachev had made a significant proposal for arms control, and about three weeks before the opening of the Twenty-seventh CPSU Congress. That Congress in many respects signaled the end of the shakedown period of Gorbachev's leadership and marked the beginning of perestroika, Gorbachev's effort to "restructure," or reform, the Soviet Union. The arms control proposal was significant both in itself and as an olive branch extended toward the United States. In its essence it called for the abolition of nuclear weapons in fifteen years. Most people in the U.S. government did not take it entirely seriously; the call for reductions was regarded as favorable, but the call for the abolition of nuclear weapons, combined with other elements of the package drawn from previous Soviet positions, made the proposal seem to be largely propaganda. In any case, it took the U.S. government more than a month to respond, long after the Political Relations Task Force meeting had ended.

The American members of the task force included Cyrus Vance, former secretary of state; Yankelovich; and Howard Swearer, president of Brown University. The rest were all veterans of Dartmouth. Bialer, the American cochair, was joined by Saunders and Stewart, who again served as rapporteur.

As the meeting was held in Moscow, the Soviet delegation was large. For most, this was by no means the first Dartmouth meeting. Zhukov was there again. So were both Arbatovs. Other veterans included Primakov, Sagdeev, Falin, Milstein, Trofimenko, and Vladimir Petrovski from the Ministry of Foreign Affairs. Petrovsky had been at the Rio Rico conference. Bobrysheva, now senior researcher at ISKAN, served on staff. The newcomers included Nikolai Shishlin, a section head in the Propaganda Department of the Central Committee, and Georgi Shakhnazarov. In the list of participants in the meeting, Shakhnazarov was listed as president of the Soviet Association of the Political Sciences. He was, however, like Shishlin, also an official of the Central Committee, serving as deputy chief of the Department for Liaison with Communist and Workers' Parties of Socialist Countries. More significant still, he later became an aide to Gorbachev and an expert on relations within the Soviet bloc.[84]

The topics that the task force addressed covered the gamut of issues in U.S.-Soviet relations.[85] They included the political context for those relations plus arms control, regional conflicts, and economic policy. They were notable for disagreement among the Soviet delegates, as when one speaker said the world was bipolar and one of his compatriots said, emphatically, "The bipolar world is finished." There was also apparent convergence between the Soviet position on some issues and the approach of the Americans, at least when compared with the conferences of the 1960s. For example, several Soviet speakers referred to the need for verification of arms control agreements. One said:

> The linking and cementing elements here include verification. This must become an essential integral part of the process. In addition to national technical means, we should use international measures of verification, including on-site inspection.[86]

Several Soviet speakers emphasized the need to conceive of security as "common security," taking into account the "security dilemma," in which the more one side feels secure, the less does the other. This concept is common in American political science, but it was foreign to Soviet ideology. One Soviet statement described this as "a new approach," another as a "political reconceptualization." This was becoming an important element in Gorbachev's "new political thinking." It was a marked change from most of what the Americans had heard before from their Soviet colleagues, to whom the idea that the Soviet nuclear buildup and activities in the Third World affected American perceptions and actions was almost literally inconceivable.

The discussion of common security was but one example of what seemed to the Americans to be "evidence of serious Soviet efforts at rethinking and re-evaluating many of the elements of Soviet foreign policy."[87] More evidence could be found throughout the discussions of the task force. In general, the Americans found their Soviet colleagues to be more open than ever before to new ideas and information. A new era in U.S.-Soviet relations was approaching.

DARTMOUTH XV: "WE DID NOT COME HERE TO COMPLIMENT ONE ANOTHER"

Just as there had been changes in the U.S.-Soviet relationship in the two years since Dartmouth XIV, so there had been changes in the Dartmouth process when Dartmouth XV met in Baku in May 1986.[88] The previous December, at a meeting of the International Planning Group of the Kettering Foundation in Dayton, Mathews had outlined five tasks for Dartmouth, which was viewed as a prime example of what had recently been defined as "supplemental diplomacy."[89] He believed it important to seek a balance between experts and public leaders, which he defined as "individuals with significant constituencies." He was also concerned about the relationship between the task force meetings and the plenary conferences and with creating bridges between the Dartmouth process and the public.

Mathews was also thinking about the need to engage the public in discussions of foreign policy. It was clear at the time that the relationship between the Soviet Union and the United States was changing. The public would be prepared to support these changes only if it was engaged in making them. Any foreign policy that was created only by experts and officials, particularly one as important to the American polity as policy toward the Soviet Union, would rest on shifting sand. A role that Dartmouth could play, Mathews and the others involved in planning the conferences believed, was to provide a means of engaging the public through these public leaders.[90]

The rest in the group, which included Stewart, Ruopp, and Robert Kingston, concurred in the importance of these tasks and agreed that no less than half the American delegates to the plenary conferences would be public leaders. At least three of the five American members of the new Political Relations Task Force were such leaders. The group also agreed that the members of the task forces would be people with specialized knowledge—both experts and public leaders—and that the chairs and one or two members of each task force would take part in the plenary conferences. It was also decided, however, to phase these changes in after Dartmouth XV.

These decisions strengthened the dual nature of the Dartmouth process. The task forces were already following a somewhat different path, owing to their smaller numbers and the differences that their discussions had acquired because they took place more frequently and had a narrower focus. The December meeting amounted to a formal recognition of these differences. Henceforth, the membership of the task forces and the general, plenary meetings would differ, with only a few members of the task forces taking part in the larger meetings. Lastly, the plenary meetings would be designed to appeal to larger audiences than the task forces.

The conference took place in Baku, the capital of Azerbaijan, at a time of important change within the Soviet Union. At the Twenty-seventh CPSU Congress, Gorbachev showed that he had consolidated his power in the Soviet Union and had begun many of the changes that became known as perestroika. Among these was a wholesale change in the foreign policy apparatus. This had begun with the appointment of Shevardnadze as foreign minister the previous July, but the mass change in personnel only began at the Congress in February. There was also a toughening of policy in the Third World on both sides. The United States began to supply aid to the forces of UNITA in Angola, who were opposed to the Soviet-supported government of the MPLA.[91] In April President Reagan decided to supply UNITA and the mujahideen in Afghanistan with Stinger surface-to-air missiles. The decisions in March to send American ships into the Black Sea, which was regarded as an aggressive gesture by the Soviets, and in April to bomb Libya contributed to a coolness in U.S.-Soviet relations. Soviet policy in the Third World had been marked by support for military offensives in Angola and Afghanistan the previous fall. In early May, it replaced the passive Babrak Karmal with the former head of the secret police, Najibullah. This was an ambiguous move that the CIA interpreted as one of a string of hard-line Soviet activities and the State Department found a bad signal.[92] Also, on the night of April 25, three weeks before Dartmouth XV began, the top blew off the Number 4 reactor at Chernobyl, spewing radiation across Europe and demonstrating, among other things, the dangers of nuclear power in even a peaceful form.

Twenty-six Americans came to Baku for Dartmouth XV. They included seventeen participants, six interpreters, among them, as ever, Sherry and Klebnikov, and three staff members from the Kettering Foundation, Coggins, Lehman, and Ruopp. Richard Lombard, a

trustee of the foundation who had been an observer at several conferences in the 1970s, accompanied the delegation as an advisor. Most of
the nine public leaders in the delegation had taken part in Dartmouth
before. The nine included Mathews, John Buchanan, a former Member
of Congress from Alabama, Antonia Chayes, Yankelovich, and two
journalists—Katherine Fanning, editor of the *Christian Science Monitor*,
and Harrison Salisbury. They also included three businessmen—
Rockefeller, William Hewitt, former chairman and chief executive officer of Deere and Company (he had also served as ambassador to
Jamaica), and Lundeen, retired chairman of the board of Dow
Chemical. Most of the experts were also Dartmouth veterans. They
included Doty, Saunders, Bialer, Horelick, Neumann, Stewart, and
Stremlau. Susan Purcell, who had participated in the Regional Conflicts
Task Force meetings in Moscow the previous spring, also came.

The Soviet delegation included twenty-seven participants.
Bobrysheva came as a staff member, as did three officials from the
Soviet Peace Committee and a secretary-typist. Zhukov from the Peace
Committee and Arbatov once again served as cochairmen. Several
Soviet participants had recently taken part in the work of the task
forces. Milstein, Zhurkin, and Sagdeev all returned, as did Davidson,
the expert on southern Africa. Primakov was back as well, in his new
capacity as director of IMEMO. As IMEMO was a more prestigious
institute than the Institute of Oriental Studies, this was a sign of his
growing importance in the Soviet hierarchy.

Unlike at the early Dartmouth conferences, several of the Soviet
participants came from party and governmental institutions. This reflect-
ed, among other things, the value placed on Dartmouth by the Gor-
bachev administration. Dimitri A. Lisovolik was the chief of the USA-
Canada section of the International Department of the Soviet Central
Committee. Nikolai Shishlin, deputy head of the subdepartment on
International Information, also came from the Central Committee,
Major General Yuri Lebedev served on the USSR Armed Forces General
Staff. Sergei Chetverikov was a deputy head of the USA Department of
the Ministry of Foreign Affairs. The delegation also included Nikolai
Baibakov, then a state counselor of the USSR Council of Ministers but
until the previous October the powerful chairman of the State Planning
Agency, GosPlan. Yuri Balandin was a deputy director of the USSR State

Committee on Agriculture (GosAgroprom). This organization was a product of Gorbachev's reforms, formed in November 1985 to be the central authority for the production of agricultural products.[93]

As with earlier conferences held outside Moscow, the Soviet delegation included representatives of local institutions, in this case three deputies of Azerbaijan's Supreme Soviet and an academic, director of the Institute of Philosophy and Law of the Azerbaijani Academy of Sciences. One of the deputies, Ramiz Mekhteyev, was chairman of the Central Committee of Azerbaijan's Communist Party. Another was the chairman of Azerbaijan's Friendship Society.

As usual, the conference opened with a plenary session. Several people on both sides noted the absence of Cousins. He had been involved in organizing the conference and had planned to attend but was hospitalized after the pressure system of an airplane he was traveling on malfunctioned and his doctors forbade him to take long flights. He ended up sending a message to the conference, as Grenville Clark had done at Dartmouth II in the Crimea and Dartmouth III at Andover. Mathews read it to the gathered participants. In much of the letter Cousins once again made the argument, central to his thinking since the atomic bomb fell on Hiroshima, that these new weapons made it necessary to change the organization of the world, or, as he put it, history "teaches us that common needs have to serve as the basis for common institutions." As one of the Soviet participants pointed out shortly after the statement was read, Cousins' ideas were similar to the thinking about mutual security then current in the Soviet Union. Cousins also included an eloquent summary of the purpose of Dartmouth:

> Our role is to raise questions and seek answers that do not ordinarily come up in the official exchanges. We can speak and think in a larger context. We are not obligated to defend every action or decision that occurs on the official level. We can afford to think in terms of historical principle. We need not shrink from the moral issues that often [underlie] the political problems or confrontation.[94]

This was followed by opening statements from members of the three work groups. The conference then broke into those smaller groups. One, on political relations and arms control, combined the work of two of the task forces as the Soviet participants on both task forces were almost the same. Another group discussed regional conflicts. The third group, as at most of the preceding Dartmouth conferences, discussed economic relations.

Much of the work of the first group focused on arms control. Members discussed the issues surrounding strategic nuclear forces, intermediate nuclear forces, and SDI, all then subject to negotiation. Other issues, such as the comprehensive test ban and conventional arms, also came up. The presence of General Lebedev appears to have made a difference, but the discussion, according to a Soviet participant, "didn't go beyond good will and decency."[95] What they were able to agree on, in fact, were the most general points—for example, that an agreement should lead to reductions in capability, that the resulting capability would be equal for each side, and that it would improve stability. An American was "surprised by the insensitivity of each to the concerns and processes of the other." Nonetheless, he found that it was "not . . . an empty exercise because we got beyond positions to interests." He also found that

> [o]ur group was most comfortable in reviewing long-term positions and presently tabled positions. They were most comfortable in seeking technical compromises, and in this they were most often imaginative. But, this group was less willing to talk of process, of concerns that create negotiating impasses.[96]

Disagreement was rampant in the discussions, but participants found it useful to air their differences and to exchange ideas. As it turned out, according to Stewart, summarizing the conference later in the year, several of these ideas found their way into proposals made at the Reykjavík summit in October.[97]

At Baku the regional conflicts work group spent one session on each region—the Middle East and Afghanistan, southern Africa, and Latin America. These discussions, particularly those on the Middle East, built on the work done at the meetings of the task force held earlier. According to a Soviet speaker, the two sides were close to agreement on four points: that regional conflicts threaten peace, that restraint is essential, that joint or parallel actions by the two superpowers are essential in these conflicts, and that there should be no linkage between regional crises and arms control; they should not be put in opposition to each other. The sense of agreement on these points stood in sharp contrast to the lack of agreement over regional conflicts from Dartmouth I through the conferences of the 1970s. Group members also felt that the two superpowers were not far apart in regard to southern Africa, despite the Reagan administration's recent embrace of UNITA in Angola.

But there was little agreement over Nicaragua, where the United States was concerned about Soviet support for the Sandinista regime and a scenario in which other Central American states, including Mexico, fell like dominos to Soviet-supported insurgents emanating from Nicaragua. The Soviets found these fears exaggerated.

The most interesting disagreements were over Afghanistan. The Americans argued that the Soviets were unrealistic in insisting that the regime in Kabul—now led by Najibullah—had to be "consolidated irreversibly." The Soviets preferred a settlement based on a strengthened and broadened government in Kabul, but they asserted that any settlement would be possible only if the United States stopped providing aid to the mujahideen and guaranteed that such aid would not be revived. Indeed, an effort by one American to lay out a framework for discussing the issue analytically was dismissed by one of the Soviet participants because it left out the issue of American aid. That, he insisted, was the main issue. Soviet participants even argued that before the Soviet invasion the opposition to the Kabul regime gained much of its strength because of American aid. Saunders, who had been the assistant secretary of state responsible for Afghanistan at the time, tried to disabuse them of that notion. The arguments were strongly felt and sharply expressed on both sides. They even spilled into the final plenary session, which was largely given over to calm descriptions of what the work groups had accomplished. Nonetheless, an expert on Afghanistan who was not at Baku but who joined the Regional Conflicts Task Force at its next meeting would later write:

> In retrospect, as a member of the Dartmouth team, I am inclined to suggest that the meeting in Baku (during which I was not yet a team member) signalled [that] a change was at least in the realm of the possible concerning this regional conflict. From that point, it is possible to track steady progress in the US-USSR dialogue on Afghanistan, both within official and unofficial circles.[98]

One of the most interesting exchanges on Afghanistan took place between two senior Soviet participants. One argued that Afghanistan was the subject of current UN-sponsored negotiations and, therefore, should not be discussed in the task force. In amicable disagreement, his colleague made the counterargument that it should be discussed. Such disagreement among the Soviets, amicable or not, was still rare, particularly over a topic as important and sensitive as Afghanistan.

Despite the hard arguments made about Afghanistan and other issues, there were indications both that the dialogue was no longer conducted by two opposing sides and that the growing personal relationships among the members of the group were openly influencing the course of the dialogue. In a discussion of southern Africa, one Soviet speaker, a specialist on Africa (which means that it was probably Davidson), concluded that "the situation in southern Africa is an important issue. This is not your Iraq. Nor can South Africa be compared to any Arab country. This is a developed, industrial power." One of his compatriots replied: "Why are you so against Iraq?"[99] The challenge implied by the question is remarkable, reminiscent as it is of the harsh responses that the Soviets sometimes gave to their American interlocutors. It clearly shows that by Dartmouth XV the Soviets were no longer coming to the conference ready to march in lockstep through the issues at hand. Another revealing exchange took place during the discussion of Central America:

> SOVIET SPEAKER: In the first place, do I understand the American speaker to be saying that everyone has the kinds of neighbors they deserve? That is the way I understand the speaker. We have many hostile neighbors.
>
> AMERICAN SPEAKER: No, I didn't say that. No, no.
>
> [ANOTHER] SOVIET SPEAKER: No that is not what was said. She said that we have accustomed ourselves to unfriendly neighbors and the United States has not. They were always in a unique position. You see, I defended you.
>
> AMERICAN SPEAKER: I will return the favor sometime.[100]

The second Soviet defended not only the American speaker but also a "deideologized" interpretation of world politics that placed the influence of geography ahead of class. He also prevented his colleague from "scoring points" in the debate with the Americans. This would have been unthinkable a decade before.

Joint ventures had a prominent place in the discussions of the work group on economic relations, as they had had at Dartmouth conferences during the period of détente in the 1970s. At that time, the interest the Soviets had expressed was tentative. They were interested only in experimenting with joint ventures, and mostly in conducting these experiments in the Third World at that. In Baku in 1986 the Americans brought up the topic. The Soviets did not jump at the chance to discuss it but were willing to nonetheless. One, in fact, said he thought that "joint ventures are the best form of economic cooperation." A proposal by another American, probably William Hewitt, for a joint venture based on a pesticide plant, was favorably received.

Much of the rest of the discussion centered on trade and covered old ground. The Soviets continued to harp on the absence of most-favored-nation status and complained about trade restrictions in general. Much of the Soviet discussion of economics, in fact, was of the effects of politics on economic relations. One of the Soviet speakers said that he thought the volume of trade between the Soviet Union and the United States should be similar to that between other industrialized countries. Echoing a theme of the discussion, he attributed the failure to reach that level to an absence of trust.

Some of the comments from the Soviet participants indicated that they did not believe that the Soviet economic system was in dire straits. An expert on Soviet agriculture, probably Balandin, was upbeat about it. Another participant said that, technologically, the Soviet Union was not behind the United States at all:

> By the way, we hear from American colleagues that the Soviet Union is significantly behind in the technological sphere and now it's time to catch up, and so on. All this is not quite so. We have our problems, of course, but these are problems of further growth, problems that have to do with future development. But, as my Soviet colleague said yesterday [at the plenary session], in the course of all these years we have been developing at a faster rate than even the Western countries in the technological area.[101]

The problem, he said, was with a cumbersome bureaucracy that hindered the implementation of "technological achievements."

During the conference, the two sides discussed the value of increasing access of prominent Americans to Soviet media. According to Stewart, this led, six months later, to "the first Soviet-American discussion on Afghanistan and the Middle East before a national Soviet television audience."[102] In addition, the Americans proposed that the Dartmouth Conference open itself up to engage in a public dialogue between participants and citizens. Arbatov supported the idea, which became reality two years later at Dartmouth XVI.

THE REGIONAL CONFLICTS TASK FORCE, NOVEMBER 1986: AFGHANISTAN WITH GLASNOST

The ninth meeting of the Regional Conflicts Task Force became one of the most significant. It was held in Moscow in November 1986, a month after the Reykjavík summit. The summit produced little work of significance on regional conflicts, in contrast to the revolutionary agreement on arms control that was almost reached. But Primakov headed a subgroup on regional conflicts and engaged in intense negotiations with Assistant Secretary of State Rozanne Ridgeway.[103]

Most members of the American delegation at the Moscow meeting were old hands, having taken part in several meetings of the task force. Saunders chaired the meeting again and Stewart was the rapporteur. Stremlau provided his expertise on southern Africa and Purcell her knowledge about Central America. The only new member of the American delegation was Thomas Gouttierre. He added his expertise on Afghanistan to that of Neumann, who had served as ambassador in Kabul. Gouttierre was dean of International Studies at the University of Nebraska at Omaha and director of the Center for Afghanistan Studies. When young, he had been a professional pastry chef in his family's bakery, earning a master's baker certificate. He had then spent a decade in Afghanistan, serving as a Peace Corps volunteer, a Fulbright fellow, and executive director of the Fulbright Foundation. He coached the national basketball team and came to speak Dari (Afghan Persian) fluently. He has even had his poetry in the language published.[104] It was while in Afghanistan that he first met Neumann, who was then the ambassador. Before Gouttierre joined the task force, Saunders wrote:

> I talked to a number of my colleagues in the State Department about him, and he received high marks from everyone. He does consider-

> able work with the Afghan Resistance in the field of education, so I
> hope the Soviets will not hold that against him. But I am inclined to
> let them worry about that.[105]

Gouttierre's contacts with those fighting the Soviets proved not to be a problem in the discussions.

Saunders' queries about Gouttierre were only one of several sets of contacts with U.S. government officials that task force members made before the meeting in Moscow. This was, of course, not unusual for Dartmouth, but these contacts may have had special importance for this meeting. Several were with officials working on Afghanistan. Undersecretary of State Michael Armacost called Saunders in August, before a Soviet delegation visited Washington and as he was preparing for the Reykjavík summit.[106] At the preparatory meeting of the American delegation in October, participants met with Armacost; Deputy Assistant Secretary Arnold Raphel, "who led the U.S. team in recent Moscow talks on Afghanistan" and in 1987 would become U.S. ambassador to Pakistan (he was killed with President Zia ul-Haq in an airplane crash in July 1988); and Ron Lorton, director of the South Asian section of the Bureau of Intelligence and Research of the State Department and several of his colleagues (on internal Afghan dynamics). Lorton and his colleagues focused on the internal dynamics of the situation in Afghanistan. Also present was Thomas Simons, one of the senior advisors on Soviet affairs.[107] Purcell held conversations on her own with government officials about the situation in Latin America.

The Soviet delegation in Moscow, a large one, came from the academic institutes. The exceptions were Sergo Mikoyan, the son of Anastas and editor in chief of the journal *Latinskaya Amerika,* and Vladimir Oryol, the first vice president of the Soviet Peace Committee. Unlike with the American delegation, Primakov was the only veteran of Dartmouth. Among the significant newcomers were Vladimir Lukin, then a section head at ISKAN, later the Russian ambassador to the United States, and now an influential member of the State Duma; and Vitali Naumkin, who would become a fixture of the task force through the 1990s and beyond. Two of the new participants were experts on Afghanistan. Yuri Gankovsky would be described by the Indian newspaper *Blitz* later that month as Gorbachev's "special adviser on Afghanistan."[108] Gouttierre wrote that

Gankovsky is the head of the Near and Mid East Department of the Institute of Oriental Studies, USSR Academy of Sciences. During a private two-hour meeting Gankovsky confided that he thought that he did not have substantial input into Soviet Afghan policy. He also was concerned that those who were making Soviet policy were not getting all the facts. Gankovsky was the one Soviet who seemed to have an appreciation of Afghan culture and tribal structure.[109]

He seems to have had a professional rival in Viktor Korgun, a senior researcher at the Institute of Oriental Studies of the USSR Academy of Sciences. Korgun considered himself more influential in Soviet policy than Gankovsky. He spoke to Gouttierre in fluent Dari but, according to Gouttierre, "displayed a condescending attitude toward the Afghans."[110]

Other topics were discussed at length at the Moscow meeting. Much time was spent on the Middle East, southern Africa, and Nicaragua, and participants regarded the discussions as fruitful. But the most important issue at hand was Afghanistan. It could not have been obvious to the Americans before the meeting, but Soviet policy in Afghanistan was at a crossroads that November. Indeed, on the last day of the formal meetings of the task force, November 13, a Politburo meeting was held at which Gorbachev pushed for formally notifying the Afghan government that the Soviets would begin their withdrawal "in one or a maximum of two years." In December, when Najibullah came to Moscow, he did just that.[111]

Soviet policy was changing, and it was changing dramatically. Some indications of this, such as Gorbachev's description of Afghanistan as a "bloody wound," had been clear at Baku. Since then, Gorbachev, in a speech made in Vladivostok in July, had emphasized making efforts at "national reconciliation" in Afghanistan and other regional conflicts, and the Afghan government had begun efforts to "broaden its base."

The Dartmouth participants discussed both concepts—national reconciliation and a more broadly based government—at length in regard to both Afghanistan and the other conflicts on the agenda. The Americans, particularly Neumann and Gouttierre, argued that a broader-based government did not necessarily mean a government of national reconciliation. The latter, they argued, had to include the mujahideen. The Soviets insisted, as had Gorbachev, that it could not include forces hostile to the government. The Soviets also argued that the Soviet presence in Afghanistan was necessary to ensure stability and to avoid a bloodbath. Primakov in particular argued that the Soviet Union needed "a calm, neutral, friendly and stable" Afghanistan.[112] He and others argued that the United States was preventing a settlement of the conflict through its support of the mujahideen and pressure on Pakistan not to come to an agreement.

These arguments were made not only in the formal discussions of the task force but also in a lengthy, lunchtime discussion initiated by Korgun. Tarabrin, Mikoyan, and Gouttierre were all there, speaking a mixture of English, Russian, and Dari.[113] A significant exchange took place that hinted that the Soviets might be willing to accept a one-year timetable for the departure of their troops from Afghanistan, rather than the three- or four-year one that the Afghan government had put on the table at the Geneva negotiations.

Afghanistan was also the focus of two meetings at the International Department of the Central Committee. The American participants met with two staff members of the department, Karen Brutents and Vadim Zagladin. The latter had met with task force members in November 1984, when his attention was focused on SDI. Brutents, a deputy chief of the department, was the International Department's main expert on the Third World.[114] Zagladin was now the first deputy chief and was himself a significant analyst of the Soviet role in the Third World. Their meetings with the American members of the task force and the meeting with their boss, the chief of the International Department, Anatoli Dobrynin, were significant as signs of the growing openness in the Soviet Union as Gorbachev's policy of glasnost began to take hold.[115] According to Zagladin, the department was also taking on a different role than it had taken before. It was becoming more engaged in global policy and broadening its contacts, rather than focusing more on the international communist movement.[116] Both he and Brutents made many of the same arguments that their colleagues had made in the task force meetings, but Neumann was impressed that Zagladin did not reject a suggestion that a new, expanded Afghan "governmental authority" be created that would be acceptable to the resistance. Saunders and Stewart found it significant that Zagladin spoke of Afghanistan "as a problem of finding a road to an internal political settlement which would give the resistance reason to lay down their arms and the refugees to return," rather than defining it as strictly a bilateral problem with the United States, the line commonly argued as recently as Baku.[117]

The meetings at the International Department were not the only sign of glasnost that the task force members saw. Before they returned to the United States, Saunders, Neumann, and Stewart joined three of their Soviet colleagues—Primakov, Korgun, and Aleksandr Kislov, a deputy director at IMEMO—in a forty-five-minute debate about regional conflicts that was broadcast the following Monday, preempting part of the regular news program.[118] This was a rare privilege at the time, one extended by the Soviets only to the likes of President Reagan and Senator Ted Kennedy.

Following the meeting, Primakov and Gankovsky accompanied Gorbachev to India along with two other Dartmouth alumni, Arbatov and Falin. This was one more sign of their rising importance in the Gorbachev era.

In January 1987, before he moved to the Brookings Institution, Saunders reported the results of the Moscow meeting to Armacost and Raphel. It should be noted that this was not done secretly; Saunders informed Primakov that he had done so.[119]

THE ARMS CONTROL AND POLITICAL
RELATIONS TASK FORCES, DECEMBER 1986:
IN THE WAKE OF REYKJAVÍK

Three weeks later, at the beginning of December, two task force meetings were held back-to-back in Washington. A group of nine Soviets came; all took part in both meetings. Arbatov once again headed the delegation. His compatriots included six colleagues from ISKAN: Kortunov, Milstein, Aleksandr Nikitin, Rogov, Trofimenko, and Zhurkin, all of whom had taken part in Dartmouth discussions before. The two new Soviet members of the two task forces were Vladimir Baranovsky from Primakov's IMEMO and Colonel Vitali Ganzha from the USSR Ministry of Defense.

The discussions in both task forces were dominated by the results of the two-day summit at Reykjavík. The results of this meeting between Reagan and Gorbachev may not have had much importance for U.S.-Soviet relations in regional conflicts, but they were central for the course of arms control negotiations and the U.S.-Soviet relationship in general. The two leaders came close to an agreement that would have been revolutionary. It would have halved the number of strategic nuclear weapons in five years and eliminated the intermediate nuclear forces in Europe. The two sides agreed to eliminate all nuclear weapons in ten years. But these conditions were contingent on an agreement on SDI. The Soviet proposals included a period in which neither side could withdraw from the 1972 ABM Treaty, one of the suggestions discussed by the Arms Control Task Force, but each side held firm on SDI. President Reagan would not agree to conditions that would in essence end SDI; Gorbachev insisted on them. Consequently, no agreement was reached, and Gorbachev left Iceland angry. Both Americans and Soviets were bitterly disappointed, and the disappointment had not entirely dissipated by the time the task forces met. But the near miss was stunning. It redefined the possible in arms control.

All but one member of the American delegation to the meeting on arms control had been a part of the task force before. Doty, Stewart, Chayes, and Horelick had all been at Baku. General Jones returned again, as did Scowcroft. Walter Slocombe came for his second meeting. The new member was Edward Warner, an analyst of the Soviet military at the RAND Corporation. Also taking part were two of the most respected congressional voices on military affairs, Les Aspin from the House and Sam Nunn from the Senate. This marked the return of members of Congress to Dartmouth, renewing a practice begun in the 1970s. It was also part of the effort begun before Dartmouth XV to have Dartmouth include more public leaders.

The themes of the Soviet new thinking were prominent in the discussions, particularly the idea of common security and the need to consider the perceptions of the other side.[120] Some attention was paid to differences in military doctrine between NATO and the Warsaw Pact. The argument was made that the two doctrines were incompatible. (The Soviet government had made this argument publicly in the previous few months.) The change in the approach taken by the Soviet side, both at Dartmouth and in Soviet policy in general, was shown by the response of a Soviet participant when asked why the Soviets had not accepted the zero option when first proposed, though they had in essence accepted it at Reykjavík. Rather than replying in a tone of self-righteous defensiveness, as would have been typical earlier, the Soviet speaker said, "We did not understand the real situation at that time and made a few mistakes." They were now, he said, more flexible and less rigid and had "a much higher level of thinking and understanding."

Arbatov was an important member of the Soviet negotiating team at Reykjavík. He took part in the all-night session chaired by Marshal Akhromeev, the Soviet chief of staff, and Nitze that produced many of the key formulas agreed to by the leaders the following day.[121] (Two other Dartmouth alumni took part in those sessions—Velikhov and Falin.) Arbatov brought a copy of the proposals made by the Soviets at Reykjavík to the Washington meeting and made a presentation about them. He went over the proposals with Stewart beforehand.[122] This is a measure of the cooperation that was growing between the two sides at Dartmouth. Earlier in Dartmouth's history—and at dialogues other than Dartmouth at the same time—it would have been unlikely for such documents to be discussed outside the Soviet delegation until the presentation was made.

These proposals formed the basis for the discussions on limiting nuclear arms and SDI. The two sides explored the reasons for the failure that Reykjavík was perceived to be. Analogies were made with the proposals for SALT that Secretary Vance took to Moscow in early 1977: the Soviets were unprepared for such radical changes from the previous course and so rejected them out of hand; the Americans were surprised by Gorbachev's proposals in Iceland and found them hard to accept. One American argued that the Soviet draft on ABM testing—the issue that the two sides could not agree on—was somewhat vague and confusing. Another found that the goals of the two sides in regard to SDI were incompatible but that structurally the proposals of the two sides were similar.

The day after the Arms Control Task Force finished its discussions, the Political Relations Task Force opened its meeting. While the Soviet delegation remained from the earlier meeting, among the Americans, only Stewart stayed. The rest of the Americans were new. Bialer was the American cochair. He, Saunders, Yankelovich, Vance, and Stewart had taken part in the January meeting of the task force in Moscow. Buchanan and Salisbury had been at Baku. Four members of Congress also took part. The Speaker of the House of Representatives, Tom Foley, attended part of the meeting. Senator Paul Simon and Representative Stephen Solarz were there for the discussions on the first day, and Al Gore, then a senator from Tennessee, was there on the second.

The first day, Simon and Solarz were invited to open the meeting by giving their analysis of current American politics and its effect on U.S.-Soviet relations.[123] They identified three important events. First, the Democrats had just regained control of the Senate. They predicted that this would lead to at least some additional, incremental movement on arms control. Second, the Iran-Contra affair was just beginning to heat up, and the fear, expressed by the Soviets as well as the Americans, was that the affair would make it difficult for the Reagan administration to do anything significant in relations with the Soviet Union by both distracting the administration and weakening it. The third event was the Reykjavík summit. Both congressmen commented on the administration's failure to consult with allies before negotiating the far-reaching proposals made at the summit. One of them believed that Reykjavík had "set back the prospects for an arms control agreement" and hoped that both sides would back off from many of the proposals made. He felt that these could not be ratified by the Senate. In contrast, a Soviet speaker commented that Reykjavík had "made it possible to discuss the entire range of Soviet-American security relations and other relations."

The changes under way in Soviet thinking were discussed at length over both days of the meeting. Simon and Solarz raised the question of the credibility of those changes, saying that many Americans were not yet convinced that the changes then beginning were more than propaganda. Other American participants echoed this thought. To their surprise, the Soviets accepted this concern as legitimate and were willing to discuss it rather than to simply dismiss the doubt implied as not worth mentioning. In a similar vein, one of the Americans said that a Soviet colleague with whom he spoke in January had told him flatly that the new thinking had no effect on Soviet thinking about the Third World. But, the American continued, that had changed.

As in the discussions of the Arms Control Task Force, particular aspects of Soviet thinking were analyzed in detail. This was particularly true, again, of the idea of "common security." Another point made was that Gorbachev "even went so far as to question the primacy of the class interest," a difficult breach with the past to make. And, indeed, the dialogue at this and other Dartmouth forums in the mid-1980s underlined how far from pure class analysis the Soviet participants had come.

A question about what the Soviets would have done differently in the 1970s elicited an interesting analysis of détente and its end from one of the Soviet participants who appears to have been involved in arms control issues. He described the SALT I delegation as "absolute innocents" (but the Americans were not much better) and said that the United States had thought about arms control earlier than the Soviet Union and had come to the SALT talks with more ideas. He was critical of much of Soviet policy at the time, particularly of how the SS-20 issue was handled. In 1977, he said,

> both sides lost an opportunity, or contributed to [losing an] opportunity. Your people caught us unprepared and in a situation when Brezhnev was not so active as before. And you know, the Vance proposals of March 1977 had to go to people who were under him, which always . . . makes issues more difficult to solve. And then you had Brzezinski who did know how to make our people jerky and nervous. And he prepared everything in a most awful way.

Without intending to, Al Gore dominated most of the discussion on the second day, partly because of his position in the American political process and partly because he offered a unique, well-thought-out perspective on U.S.-Soviet relations.[124] He began with an analysis of current American politics that echoed what his colleagues had said the day before, but he then suggested that in regard to Reykjavík and similar matters, public opinion would follow expert opinion, and the experts had said that they wanted to know more. As for the U.S.-Soviet strategic relationship, he said:

> I just feel that if you are in a room—speaking abstractly—with a chair, a lamp, a table, and a rattle-snake, your attention is not going to be evenly distributed among those objects. You are going to be obsessed with the rattle-snake. And you are not going to look at the table and a chair and a lamp. . . . There are many possible paths for [the United States and the Soviet Union] to take. One possible path is life-threatening. And so we are obsessed with this possibility and we do not pay much attention to the other possibilities. What is it that draws our attention to this one possibility? It is the fear of the first strike. It is the fear of attack.

Gore continued: "[O]ur fear of a first strike, and I think yours, is made up of a few bare facts and wild imaginings. And a lot of times we spend a great deal of effort arguing about the illusions and the imaginings."

In that context he discussed SDI, which he said had two versions—a complete shield against all Soviet nuclear weapons, and a barrier that would merely complicate any Soviet calculations for a first strike:

> In the case of SDI, expert opinion has not corrected public opinion. The first SDI alleged to be capable of stopping any kind of nuclear destruction, in the view of experts is totally unrealistic. But that view of the experts has not led to a withdrawal of support from SDI, because expert opinion is that the second SDI is, or might be, in our interest.
>
> And why is that? The second SDI is designed to frustrate a Soviet first strike and without dwelling on a subject I discussed earlier, it really does come back to the same seminal fear. An American frustration with this seeming Soviet ability to gain an advantage from a counterforce attack, even though that fear is irrational, has led to support for the second version of SDI.

Much of the discussion from that point had Gore's rattlesnake—the thing feared—at its center, with some disagreement and discussion about what the people in both countries actually feared.

The following February, the Kettering Foundation sent copies of the reports on these task force meetings to senior members of the U.S. arms control delegations in Geneva. Max Kampelman, the head of the delegation for the START talks, said he found them useful. He was impressed that one of the themes was common security, a point he had been emphasizing, and was interested in what appeared to be inconsistencies with what his interlocutors in Geneva had said. The most striking discrepancy was with the statement that with the elimination of intermediate missiles in Europe, there was no need for short-range missiles in Eastern Europe.[125]

Others were less impressed with the proceedings, seeing the Soviet contributions as more propaganda than substance. Michael Mobbs, assistant director for strategic programs at the U.S. Arms Control and Disarmament Agency (ACDA), writing for Kenneth Adelman, its director, was "struck by the Soviet effort to project a new image of unusual openness and flexibility." "Unfortunately," he continued, "we have yet to see the Soviets translate this new 'openness' into concrete proposals at the negotiating table."[126]

In February the Kettering Foundation put together a series of workshops to discuss the meetings of all three task forces with U.S. government officials. Speaker Foley was the host for a breakfast at the Capitol to which a number of senators and representatives were invited. The previous afternoon a briefing was held at the Foreign Service Institute for almost thirty "working level" officials from the State Department and the CIA.

THE ARMS CONTROL TASK FORCE, JULY 1987–JANUARY 1988: THRESHOLDS AND DENUCLEARIZATION

The Arms Control Task Force met twice more before Dartmouth XVI convened in April 1988. Before then, the "package" of arms control proposals brought forth at Reykjavík and discussed by the task force in December was unwrapped. The first part of the package was the INF negotiations. The essential elements of an agreement that would bring the number of intermediate nuclear forces on both sides to zero were in place by the time the task force met in July. It met again in January 1988, a month after the INF Treaty was signed at a summit meeting in Washington.

Two weeks before the July task force meeting, the American members were briefed on developments in arms control in a series of meetings at the State Department. They were told about the issues remaining on INF. Negotiations on strategic arms—the START talks—were stalled, with strategic defense the main sticking point, as it had been at Reykjavík. Conventional arms negotiations were also stalled, as they had been for twelve years.

Most of the Americans who flew to Moscow for the meeting had also taken part in the previous meeting of the task force. This included longtime participants Doty, Stewart, and Jones as well as Chayes and Warner. Instead of Horelick and Slocombe, the delegation was filled out with Scowcroft, returning for the first time since the task force met in December 1984, and Ashton Carter, a renowned expert on arms control who was then deputy director of Doty's Center for Science and International Affairs, which was now a part of the Kennedy School at Harvard.

The Soviet delegation was led, once again, by Arbatov. It included Zhurkin, Milstein, and Baranovsky, all of whom had been at the two previous meetings of the task force. Sagdeev and Shishlin both returned after having missed the December meeting in Washington. The Soviet delegation included another officer serving on the General Staff, Captain Yuri Beketov, a section head in the Arms Control Department. One of Shishlin's colleagues, Vladimir Tulinov, another section head from the Central Committee staff, attended, as did Gennadi Stashevsky, deputy head of the Arms Control Department of the Foreign Ministry. Genrikh Borovik represented the Soviet Peace Committee, which was still a cosponsor of Dartmouth. President of the committee, he was a widely read journalist who had been a correspondent for Novosti in New York in the 1960s.[127] The last member of the delegation was Aleksandr Vasiliev, from ISKAN.

As usual, the discussions covered the range of arms control issues on the U.S.-Soviet agenda, from START to SDI to INF to chemical weapons and conventional forces. Through the course of the meeting, two things stood out.[128] As they had over the previous two years, participants tried to square the circle that was the link between strategic defense and offensive nuclear weapons. Most of this discussion covered ground that had already been plowed through many times, either at previous conferences or in public discussions in the preceding months. But following a suggestion from the Soviet side, they also tried to devise "thresholds" for the exotic technologies that might come to be deployed as a part of SDI. These thresholds could be used to define what kinds of research and testing might be permitted under an agreement such as the one outlined at Reykjavík that traded limitations on the research, testing, and deployment of defensive weapons for cuts in offensive arms. The thresholds suggested were technical in nature—it was suggested, for example, that a threshold be established on the brightness of lasers, expressed in "watts per steradian." Other ways of limiting lasers were discussed as well, such as the dimensions of the mirrors they would need. The group also suggested thresholds on the energy of nuclear reactors on satellites and the altitude of kinetic weapons.

The attitudes of the two sides toward the elimination of nuclear weapons were in striking contrast. The complete elimination of nuclear weapons was a goal subscribed to by both Gorbachev and Reagan, but only the Soviet members of the task force took it up. They argued that nuclear weapons are in their essence irrational and that human survival demands a nuclear-free world. Some seemed skeptical about the argument, but most seemed to make it wholeheartedly. They did note, however, that not everyone in the Soviet military accepted it. The Americans, on the other hand, reflected the consensus among experts that it was unrealistic to seriously consider putting the nuclear genie back in the bottle. These attitudes affected the discussion of most issues. For example, the Soviets, but not the Americans, saw INF as a step toward denuclearization. One of the issues outstanding after the INF Treaty was the fate of seventy-two Pershing 1a warheads that were still in the hands of the Germans. The Americans, at the Dartmouth meeting and in Washington, were unwilling to negotiate these away (in the end the West German government solved the problem by unilaterally giving up the warheads).

Limitations on conventional weapons were discussed at this meeting of the task force, as they had been at all previous meetings. The main focus of the earlier discussions, however, had always been on the limitation of nuclear arms. In large measure this reflected the reality of negotiations, where any progress made had been in negotiations on strategic and intermediate nuclear weapons. In contrast, the MBFR talks had stagnated for more than a decade, unable to get past the fundamental difficulties of determining what forces and weapons to include and how to count them.

By the time the Arms Control Task Force had finished its meeting in Moscow in July 1987, the Americans had become convinced that Soviet proposals made in the fall of 1986 made progress on conventional arms reductions possible. Moreover, they believed, as Stewart wrote:

> It is not an overstatement to suggest that further progress toward a fundamental change in the U.S.-Soviet relationship will rest centrally upon our [mutual] ability to increase the sense of security of both sides through substantial conventional reductions in Europe.[129]

Stewart suggested that Dartmouth could help "conceptualize a framework" for an agreement on these reductions. He suggested that an expert on conventional arms reductions be added to the task force and that steps be taken to make task force members more knowledgeable about the issues involved. To that end, Robert Blackwill, who had just retired as the ambassador to the MBFR negotiations and was working on a book at Harvard, was invited to join the task force.

That November, the Kettering Foundation sponsored an all-day seminar on conventional arms control in Washington. Experts on conventional arms control were invited to discuss the issues at stake with the task force members.[130] They went over all the steps toward agreement taken by both NATO and the Warsaw Pact. But suspicions remained about how genuine the Soviet moves were. One conclusion was that "the new tone evident in Soviet thinking has at least one objective, undermining Western stability." It was also noted that concepts such as "reasonable sufficiency," which had been prominent in Soviet discussions of arms control issues, "have found no manifestation in concrete proposals as of this date." Nonetheless, the participants concurred that there were good reasons for the Soviets to make a unilateral reduction of conventional forces in Europe. Indeed, they felt that such an announcement might well be the next major event in the conventional arms arena.

THE REGIONAL CONFLICTS TASK FORCE, MAY 1987: AFGHAN ASIDES AND PROCESSES DEVISED

While the United States and the Soviet Union were edging toward an agreement over INF through most of 1987, they were doing little about regional conflicts other than exchanging rhetoric.

In contrast, the Regional Conflicts Task Force was more productive and, indeed, showed signs of moving its dialogue to a new level. It met in May at the Graylyn International Conference Center in Winston-Salem, North Carolina. The center was a long stone building near the campus of Wake Forest University that resembled a Renaissance manor house.

The members of the task force gathered in Washington before going to North Carolina for a limited session on the Arab-Israeli peace process. Most knew one another well. All six Soviet participants had been a part of Dartmouth before. Four—Primakov, Kislov, Robert Markaryan, and Vladimir Moskalenko—had been at the meeting in November. Davidson had been at Baku. Volsky was regarded as a "freshman," but he had been at the meeting on Latin America held in April 1985. On the American side, only William Quandt was new. He had worked on Middle Eastern issues on the National Security Council staff, first with Saunders (1972–74) and then under Brzezinski. Now a colleague of Saunders at the Brookings Institution, he joined the group for the session in Washington on the Arab-Israeli conflict. The rest, save Gouttierre, who had joined the task force at its last meeting, had taken part in at least four task force meetings, and all had been in Moscow the previous November.

Little of what was said during the first sessions of the full meeting at Graylyn was new.[131] The Soviets still pushed for a comprehensive settlement in the Middle East but said that the Soviet Union would not negotiate with the mujahideen in Afghanistan, despite the appeal of Najibullah's government for a government of national reconciliation.

What was new suggested the withdrawal to come. The Soviets discussed in dispassionate terms the prospect of a bloodbath in Afghanistan after they withdrew. They gave their estimate that half a million would "be in jeopardy" and asked whether that estimate was accurate. The Americans thought it was high. Primakov indicated that Soviet foreign policy would become more active once Soviet troops were out of Afghanistan: "We've given up hibernating in the Middle East. . . . Once our troops are out of Afghanistan, our potential will be increased."

An interesting series of exchanges concerning Afghanistan followed the dinner of the first full day of meetings. Each suggested an unexpected openness by the Soviet members to the prospect of troop withdrawal. On the way back to their rooms, Primakov took Gouttierre aside under a large stairway at Graylyn and declared: "Look, Tom, we are aware that we cannot win the war in Afghanistan without unacceptable loss of life on both sides." He continued by positing the following: "Do you think the US government would offer cooperation to the USSR in getting its troops out of Afghanistan?"

Gouttierre, in only his second Dartmouth meeting, was taken aback by these comments, but he recognized that Primakov's statements constituted a moment of note. He replied that, as he was not an official member of the U.S. government, he could not authoritatively offer what might be its position. But, he added, the U.S. government might take the stand that the USSR had gotten itself into Afghanistan and would have to get itself out.

Gouttierre quickly followed that he believed strongly it was not the U.S. government's objective, in seeking the removal of Soviet troops, also to seek military advantage in Afghanistan. Gouttierre expressed his conviction that American pronouncements indicating so were sincere:

Afghanistan should resume its policy of neutrality between the United States and the Soviet Union; each of the two powers should respect that position; the United States did not intend to establish a military presence in Afghanistan once Soviet troops were withdrawn. He added that it was only reasonable to assume that, in the near future, Afghan public opinion would likely favor the United States over the Soviet Union.

Primakov replied: "From a policy standpoint, these opinions are constructive. This is what we need to know. Thank you." With that, the discussion ended.

Shortly thereafter, Markaryan invited Gouttierre to take a walk on the grounds of Graylyn. Markaryan talked passionately about the suffering experienced by both Soviets and Afghans in the war. He offered that it was possible the Soviet Union was ill advised to have involved itself in such a way in a country like Afghanistan, which, apparently, was not ready for the type of revolutionary change proclaimed by the People's Democratic Party of Afghanistan (FDPA) following its coup in April 1978. He amplified the tragedy of suffering with examples from the history of the Caucasus peoples, with specific reference to his own ethnic origins.

After chatting for nearly an hour, the two returned to Graylyn, where they were met by Apollon Davidson. He, too, invited Gouttierre for "a walk and conversation." Over nearly two hours, Davidson decried the loss of life on both sides in Afghanistan. He described in an emotional and graphic discourse the suffering of himself, his family, and his friends during the siege of Leningrad during World War II.

These three exchanges, coupled with those in dialogue sessions earlier that day, persuaded Gouttierre that certain elements within Gorbachev's circles appeared resigned to the inevitability of a Soviet withdrawal from Afghanistan.[132]

The last session of the meeting, however, was described by an American speaker as "this interesting session, different from others we have had." The Soviets, in the course of the three days of meetings, had referred in several ways to the idea that the two superpowers should approach their relations as something other than a zero-sum game. This was an idea that had become a constant in the algebra of the Soviet new political thinking. One of the Soviet speakers—probably Primakov—laid out four steps that described a process for making a transition from zero-sum to positive-sum relations. This process began with each side determining its own interests and ended with the two sides acting in accordance with a consensus on the interests they held in common.

This four-step process resonated with ideas that Saunders had been ruminating over for some time. Just as the task force in its earliest meetings had tried to go beyond the immediate, specific problems the two countries faced in regional conflicts, Saunders now offered a general framework for examining the relations of the two countries in the Third World. He conceived of interests in human terms, speaking of the understanding of Soviet interests in world politics that he derived from the visit of the task force to the Piskariovskoye Cemetery in Leningrad in November 1984, walking with Igor Belyaev, a Soviet member of the task force who had a grandfather and an uncle buried there. He conceived of the relations between the superpowers in human terms as well, as a relationship between polities, not merely relations between powers. This relationship contained conflict as well as consensus. It was built on the experience that both sides had gained in acting with and against each other in the global arena. He offered this construct as a model for the task force and suggested that the task force could serve as a laboratory from which lessons might be learned that could be applied to the greater relationship. His colleagues, Soviet and American, seemed to agree.

An essential aspect of Saunders' approach was that the positions of the two countries and events in the regions should be looked at "analytically." In the transcripts of Dartmouth meetings held before and after 1987, his voice can be heard frequently making an appeal for participants to do that rather than trade accusations or repeat arguments received from higher authority or the general discourse. The time was past when such discussions held value; an analytical discussion was the first step to a clear understanding of the conflicts on the agenda and the improvements in the U.S.-Soviet relationship that he thought the Dartmouth conversations could help achieve.

Several meetings with American policymakers followed the meeting in Winston-Salem. The evening following the closing session, the participants returned to Washington to dine with members of Congress. The next day, task force members spread across Washington to discuss issues with members of Congress and their staff and with officials from the executive branch. Primakov, Kislov, and Markaryan, joined by Saunders, Stewart, and Neumann, met with Armacost to discuss Afghanistan and the Middle East.[133] One of the meetings was between one of the Soviets, probably Davidson, and the head of the South African desk at the State Department. The position of the diplomat was, in the eyes of his Soviet interlocutor, "very hard line," particularly in regard to Angola, which the American asserted had no legitimate government. The Soviet found the spirit of the conversation to be contrary to what he found in Dartmouth discussions.[134]

Gouttierre had been invited to a meeting of an intergovernmental task force on Afghanistan at the State Department to inform its members about the status of the Dartmouth discussions on the Soviet-Afghan War. Gouttierre indicated that the United States government might consider making contingency plans for a Soviet troop withdrawal from Afghanistan by sometime in 1990. In the main, the task force met this suggestion with considerable skepticism. Members of the various Soviet affairs units represented there were particularly skeptical. (At a similar meeting that took place approximately one year later, some weeks after the USSR had set a withdrawal date of February 1989, the chairman recalled the exchange of the previous year.)[135]

THE SOUTHERN AFRICA TASK FORCE, APRIL 1984–SEPTEMBER 1987: NEW THINKING, OLD THINKING

This task force met again in the fall to discuss the conflicts in southern Africa. This was the third meeting of a task force convened to discuss U.S.-Soviet relations in the region. Stremlau organized a series of these discussions after being approached by Boris Asoyan, a young, ambitious expert for African affairs.[136] At the time, Asoyan was a deputy director of the Institute for African Studies of the USSR Academy of Sciences. He had been a journalist, reporting for *New Times* in Tanzania, but by 1987 he was working on the staff of the Central Committee. At the time of the third meeting on southern Africa he had become deputy head of the Second African Department of the Foreign Ministry.

The first meeting was held in Moscow in April 1984 under the auspices of Asoyan's Africa Institute; Stremlau's employer, the Rockefeller

Foundation, funded it. It was intended to be similar to the meetings of the Regional Conflicts Task Force but was not a Dartmouth meeting. Nonetheless, several once and future participants in Dartmouth meetings took part. Robert Legvold, a Sovietologist from Columbia University, had been at Williamsburg for Dartmouth XII in 1979. A colleague of Neumann's at the Center for Strategic and International Studies (CSIS), Helen Kitchen, was the director of the African Studies Program there. She would become a regular member of the Regional Conflicts Task Force. Stephen Low, a former ambassador to Zambia, was director of the Foreign Service Institute. Donald McHenry had been the U.S. ambassador to the United Nations. Like Kitchen and Neumann, he had found a home at CSIS. Most of this team returned for at least one of the other two meetings of the task force.

The Soviets, in this task force as in the others, put less emphasis on continuity of membership than did the Americans. Asoyan attended this first meeting, as did Arbatov, Evgeni Tarabrin, and Kremenyuk; both of the latter came to later meetings of the Regional Conflicts Task Force to be the Soviet counterparts of Stremlau. The Soviet participants also included Anatoli Gromyko, director of the Africa Institute, and several officials of the Foreign Ministry. Among these was Vladilen Vasev, who would become deeply involved in the 1988 accords that led to the end of the conflict in Namibia and the removal of the Cubans from Angola.

The discussions at this meeting and the two later meetings had South Africa and apartheid at their center. They also addressed two other conflicts, in Mozambique on one side of the continent and over Angola and Namibia on the other. In all three conflicts, insurgents were challenging the governments—the African National Congress and other organizations in South Africa, SWAPO in Namibia, RENAMO in Mozambique, and UNITA in Angola. The last two were supported by South Africa and opposed by the Soviets. Beginning in 1986, the United States gave support, including Stinger missiles, to UNITA in its battle against the MPLA, which had been backed by Cuba and the Soviet Union since 1975. In 1981 the United States had launched a policy of "constructive engagement" with South Africa, intended to help these conflicts move toward resolution, but the step away from complete, open opposition to apartheid made it controversial.

The discussions mirrored those held at other Dartmouth meetings at the time. U.S.-Soviet relations were held to be at an all-time low.[137] One Soviet speaker, perhaps Arbatov, said that it was not Soviet behavior in regional conflicts that doomed détente but "the American political process." The Soviets also echoed the official line on the Lusaka Agreement between South Africa and Angola and the Nkomati Accord between South Africa and Mozambique, which was to be uncharacteristically sanguine about agreements that were signed over Soviet objections and brokered by the United States. It reflected the points made by task force participants that Africa was not a high priority for either superpower and that this was a region where neither wanted a confrontation.

Because of the access provided by their Soviet counterparts, the American participants had meetings with Africanists at ISKAN and the Foreign Ministry. The officials they met at the Foreign Ministry, like the participants from the Africa Institute, were enthusiastic about these talks. Their interlocutors at ISKAN, however, found the subject peripheral to their concerns and the discussions not particularly useful.

After the meeting, Anatoli Gromyko sent a cable suggesting that a second meeting be held but under the aegis of Dartmouth. Stewart asked Zhurkin, who was still at ISKAN, about the possibility of holding some Dartmouth task force meetings on southern Africa. Zhurkin did not think it a good idea. The Soviet side, he argued, had neither the people nor the resources for such meetings. The Americans thought about going ahead without ISKAN but, given the importance of Arbatov and ISKAN to Dartmouth, decided not to. They did agree, however, that Saunders and Stewart would take part in the next meeting and that the Kettering Foundation would help organize it (but the Rockefeller Foundation would fund it).

The second meeting of the Southern Africa Task Force, therefore, like the first, was not a Dartmouth meeting. It was held in Tarrytown, New York, in the Hudson River Valley not far from Sleepy Hollow. Stremlau and Viktor Goncharov, a deputy director of the Africa Institute, were chairmen. Stremlau found Goncharov to be "a fairly creative thinker." Andrei Urnov, recently promoted to become the head of the "Black African Sector" of the International Department of the Central

Committee, proved to be, along with Asoyan, "one of a few competent Soviet policy intellectuals" working on Africa.[138] The discussions covered much the same ground covered in Moscow the year before. Like that meeting, and like many other Dartmouth discussions, it was significant mostly for the chance the participants gained to get firsthand insight into the thinking of the other side and to strengthen personal contacts with participants on both sides.

The third meeting, held at the Institute for African Studies in September 1987, was a regular meeting of the Regional Conflicts Task Force. Aside from Saunders and Stewart, however, the American participants were the same as those who met in Moscow in 1984—Stremlau, Kitchen, Low, and McHenry. There was one addition, John Marcum, a professor at the University of California at Santa Cruz and one of the most highly regarded experts on Angola.

The Soviet delegation had far fewer people from the earlier meetings. It was led by Gleb Staruchenko, who, like Goncharov, also present, was a deputy director of the Africa Institute. Asoyan was included once again, as was Davidson, who was becoming a regular member of the Regional Conflicts Task Force. According to Stremlau, Gromyko had fired Davidson—the two had little liking for each other—and so Davidson had moved to the Institute of General History, where Primakov protected him.[139]

The members of the Soviet delegation represented a range of views in the Soviet debates over foreign policy in general as well as over policy in southern Africa in particular. Stewart described them as forming three groups.[140] Two members of the delegation, Ambassador Sergei Slipchenko and Staruchenko, were from "the old, confrontational, polemical school." A second group was made up of several younger participants from the Africa Institute and the Foreign Ministry who represented newer schools of thought. The last group was made up of more senior officials from the Central Committee and the Foreign Ministry. They listened attentively and helped move the discussion along but contributed little of substance. Stewart and Stremlau both praised Asoyan for, as Stremlau put it, leading "the charge to open the debate among the Soviets."

Few Soviet participants had had experience with the approach that Primakov, Saunders, and others had developed since 1982 in the meetings of the Regional Conflicts Task Force. The hope had been that the two groups had learned "how to talk about the issues" during the first two meetings about southern Africa. As it was, the task force spent the first day setting out the facts about the situation in the region. Then Saunders stepped in to begin to move the participants toward an effort to devise steps for solving specific problems. All recognized that both sides were working for the elimination of apartheid in South Africa, though they differed in how they favored doing it. There was some discussion about a joint statement of principles in regard to South Africa.

At the end of the second day, Asoyan suggested privately to Stewart that the two sides write down the ideas about a political solution in southern Africa that the task force had discussed. Stewart, Stremlau, and Saunders drafted the American version and discussed it with their colleagues over breakfast the next morning. It was typed out on a word processor, and Stremlau presented it at the beginning of the session. Davidson and Asoyan presented their versions immediately after. The documents, particularly the American summary, set off a lively exchange among the Soviets. Stremlau wrote, "We Americans could hardly get a word in." Attention was paid to the use of economic sanctions—a lever not available to the Soviets because their economic presence in South Africa was insignificant—and the role of violence in any transformation of the South African regime. The Soviets clearly recognized that their lack of diplomatic relations and, they asserted, the lack of economic ties with South Africa limited their influence and the means available to them to foster change in the region.

Stewart found that the meeting affirmed the value of the approach to dialogue that had evolved in the regular meetings of the task force.

THE REGIONAL CONFLICTS AND POLITICAL RELATIONS TASK FORCES, FEBRUARY 1988: AFGHANISTAN AGAIN AND PROBLEMS WITH PERESTROIKA

As in December 1986, in February 1988 two task force meetings were held back-to-back. This time they werre in Moscow, and the meeting of the Political Relations Task Force was preceded by a meeting of the Regional Conflicts Task Force rather than the Arms Control Task Force.

Unlike in 1986, in 1988 there was little overlap of participants—only Stewart and Saunders on the American side, and Oryol, first vice president of the Soviet Peace Committee, took part in both meetings.

The central issue before the Regional Conflicts Task Force was, once again, Afghanistan. One Soviet participant estimated that 70 percent of the discussions were devoted to it. Five of the Soviet participants were experts on Afghanistan or related subjects: Primakov, Kislov, Korgun, Markaryan, and Moskalenko, all of whom had taken part in earlier task force meetings. The delegation was filled out by three of the leaders of the Soviet Peace Committee—Borovik, Oryol, and Secretary Igor Filin—and by three other regional experts—Davidson for Africa, Glinkin for Latin America, and Vladimir Babak, a section head at IMEMO. The American delegation was the same as it had been in the two meetings in 1986: Neumann and Gouttierre with their experience in Afghanistan, Saunders and Stewart, and Stremlau and Purcell, who contributed their knowledge of the conflicts in Africa and Latin America, respectively.

The group met a week after Gorbachev had made a speech announcing that the Soviet withdrawal from Afghanistan would begin on May 15, provided that an agreement was signed by March 15. Gouttierre spoke of his visit to resistance forces in Peshawar the previous month. He brought with him to both Peshawar and Moscow a proposal for resolution of the conflict there that was intended to allay the concerns expressed by the Soviets at the meetings in Graylyn in 1987 over the possibility of a bloodbath following a Soviet withdrawal and the development of relations with the postwithdrawal Afghanistan. The proposal had two parts. The first was the establishment of an interim government, replacing the Najibullah regime, before the Soviets withdrew. The second part, labeled the political track, was intentionally not clearly defined, but it had as its objective the development of a more permanent regime to replace the interim government.

Gouttierre summarized the situation he found in Peshawar. This served as a basis for the discussions.[141] Primakov led the questioning of Gouttierre, most of which was about the details of what he had found. The Soviets were no more reassured by American arguments that a bloodbath would not occur than they had been in 1987. They still insisted that a government of national reconciliation based on the

Najibullah regime had to be formed, even though Gouttierre insisted that the lack of legitimacy of the PDPA regime had made that option unlikely to succeed. The tone of the discussion left some Americans feeling that the task force had taken a step backward.

Meetings outside supplemented the discussions about Afghanistan that took place during the meeting of the task force.[142] Gouttierre and several participants from the Political Relations Task Force met with Yuli Vorontsov, the first deputy minister of foreign affairs. He had himself just returned from Pakistan (Vorontsov was later the Russian ambassador to the United States). Gouttierre also met with Aleksandr Oblov, the chief of Afghanistan affairs at the Foreign Ministry, and one of his subordinates, Simeon Gregoriev. The meeting, conducted in Dari, lasted about three hours. Immediately after, Gouttierre met with Gankovsky, Davidson, Korgun, and several specialists on Afghanistan and Pakistan for another three hours at the Institute of Oriental Studies.

Unfortunately, the idea of an interim regime must have sounded to Vorontsov, Primakov, and the other Soviets suspiciously like the official position of the United States, which was dedicated to the replacement of the Najibullah regime. The idea had been put on the table by the United States and Pakistan, though in a somewhat different form than that presented by Gouttierre. In any case, the Soviets felt that they could not abandon the Najibullah government; they had to preserve it in some form. Gouttierre, on the other hand, believed that the regime had almost no chance of survival without Soviet troops to prop it up. The Soviets were also reluctant to oppose Najibullah about arrangements for what would happen after the Soviets withdrew.

As noted, much less time was spent discussing conflicts other than Afghanistan than at earlier meetings. Some time was spent in the formal sessions on Latin America and southern Africa but none on the Middle East. Those interested in the region spent at least one lunchtime discussing the conflicts there.

In this regard, it should be remembered that the meetings of these task forces, like all Dartmouth meetings, were notable not just for the exchanges in the formal sessions, which were easy to record, but also for what was said outside them, on coffee breaks, at meals, and during other informal meetings. The task force meetings no longer included excursions like the visit to the cemetery in Leningrad that was such a powerful experience for the Americans in 1984, as it had been for those attending Dartmouth IV in 1966, or the cruise from Sevastopol to Yalta at Dartmouth II. But the times between sessions continued to be essential to the success of these meetings. On the last day of this meeting in Moscow, an American said:

> [T]here's an awful lot of product that comes out of the coffee breaks. I have found that the coffee breaks permit people to sit down and sort of chat around an issue, or explore other elements relating to the issue that time doesn't permit necessarily in exposing one's ideas in a formal table setting.[143]

This extra "product" that came from the coffee breaks and other informal discussions was especially important in the Regional Conflicts Task Force. Participants on this task force had become more or less constant on both sides by the beginning of 1988. The group had met more often than the other task forces, so that members knew one another and one another's positions fairly well. As a result, according to Saunders, as quoted by another American speaker,

> in his [Saunders'] view, never in the history of our relationship in Dartmouth, or perhaps even in the US-Soviet relationship, has conversation across cultural and ideological divides achieved such a level of discourse, such a high level of communication of real interests, real differences, and analysis together of the potential consequences of our differences, or at least clarification of those differences.[144]

Another first for Dartmouth was the agenda for the meeting of the Political Relations Task Force, which met after the Regional Conflicts Task Force dispersed. For the first time, the agenda focused entirely on domestic economic and political conditions within the two countries. This was in recognition of both the ever more rapid pace of perestroika in the Soviet Union and the presidential election campaign in the United States.

The American delegation was mostly new to both the task force and Dartmouth, in contrast to the delegation of Americans just departed. Stewart, Saunders, and Bialer had been at all three meetings. Mathews and Lundeen, now the chairman of the board of Techtronics, had both been at Dartmouth XV. Mathews, of course, had been close to Dartmouth since coming to Kettering several years before. The newcomers included two politicians, Nancy Johnson, a

Republican representative from Connecticut, and Charles "Mac" Mathias, the former senator from Maryland (also a Republican). Last but not least was Mortimer Zuckerman, editor in chief of *U.S. News & World Report.*

The Soviet delegation included several people who had been at the first or second meeting of the task force. Only Zhurkin and Arbatov had been to both. In addition, as often happened, several Soviet participants came to only one or two of the sessions, but those returning included Falin and Andrei Kortunov, Radomir Bogdanov, Sagdeev, and Shishlin. Lukin had taken part in the Regional Conflicts Task Force in 1986. Bobrysheva was a participant for the first time rather than an interpreter or staff member. She had come to Dartmouth with the Soviet Peace Committee; she was now a senior researcher at ISKAN. Also notable were Georgi Sturua, then a sector head at IMEMO but later a prominent commentator in the Soviet and Russian press, and Nikolai Shmelev, an economist at ISKAN, head of the department that studied the American economy. Shmelev was pushing to make economic perestroika more radical. In fact, in 1987 he had labeled the foundations of planning "economic romanticism" and during 1988 suggested that the Soviet Union borrow tens of billions of dollars to buy Western machinery and consumer goods.[145] More than an analyst, he had also published several works of fiction.[146]

Shmelev seems to have given the frank, concise report on the economic aspects of perestroika that became the center of the discussion on the first day.[147] The report said bluntly that the Soviet Union was in a "pre-crisis situation" that could be improved through a gradual process that would last more than a decade. His listeners considered his account to be optimistic, but he described three obstacles that had to be reckoned with: inertia in the economic system itself, resistance by bureaucrats, and a lack of understanding on the part of the populace based on their fear of inflation and unemployment. The Americans brought attention to the need to make prices correlate more closely to real costs and demand as they do in a market economy, but much of the discussion was focused on the obstacles to perestroika that the speaker outlined, particularly the resistance that would be offered by "18 million" bureaucrats. An American speaker, a businessman who may well have been Lundeen, adduced from his experience with joint ventures elsewhere that the Soviet Union and the United States would see the benefits of their joint economic relationship in no less than "a couple of decades." "If we think in terms of less than that," he said, "I really believe that we are making a big mistake."

In both economics and politics, the Soviets saw perestroika as a difficult, open-ended process with much yet to be learned. They saw problems in political reform that stemmed from a lack of consensus about the problems faced as well as from the inertia and resistance mentioned in the case of economic reform. One factor that was not seen as a problem was the increase in national feeling within the Soviet Union. This was, on the contrary, seen as positive.

There was a lengthy discussion of the American economy, which was growing at the time but facing deficits in trade and the federal budget. The consensus seemed to be that optimism about the economy was in order; U.S. economic problems seemed manageable. In contrast to the Soviet economic problems, they seemed solvable if the political will was there, and not insuperable if it was not. Johnson and Mathias in particular made this clear. The apparent decline in the competitiveness of the American economy was seen as a problem rapidly disappearing.

The implications of the changes both countries were undergoing were not discussed in depth. The sense seemed to be that U.S.-Soviet relations were in flux, just as Gorbachev's Soviet Union was. The participants seemed to suggest that the complexity of the relationship was becoming clearer, but improving, with even the military-industrial complexes on both sides far from monolithic.

A proposal for a Soviet-American Peace Corps, made by one of the Americans almost as an aside, stands out for its rarity. The participants in the Dartmouth conferences of the 1960s and 1970s wracked their brains for such projects on which the two superpowers could cooperate, but by the mid-1980s Dartmouth participants no longer had to. Whereas before contact was rare and cooperation rarer, the calming effect of détente and then the burst of glasnost and the concomitant explosion of contact between West and East made cooperation between Soviets and Americans increasingly common. Consequently, the search for discrete, often small-scale areas of cooperation in the Dartmouth conversations gave way to broader concerns about how the two governments and bodies politic could interact and join together in actions that would help each other grow and prosper, as well as avoid the confrontations that had been at the center of concerns expressed since the first conference in Hanover.

5 | The Peak of Glasnost and Collapse, 1988–91

DARTMOUTH XVI: Austin, Texas; April 25–29, 1988
DARTMOUTH XVII: Leningrad; July 22–27, 1990
REGIONAL CONFLICTS TASK FORCE
ARMS CONTROL TASK FORCE
POLITICAL RELATIONS TASK FORCE

BY 1988 GORBACHEV, WITH THE ADVICE AND SUPPORT of the new thinkers from ISKAN, IMEMO, and elsewhere, had begun to transform the Soviet Union. That had been clear in the discussions of the Political Relations Task Force in February. His new approach to foreign policy was having an equally profound effect on the U.S.-Soviet relationship, as could be seen in the recent meetings of the Regional Conflicts and Arms Control Task Forces. A treaty on intermediate nuclear weapons, signed by Gorbachev and President Reagan in Washington in December 1987, was a benchmark of the improvement in those relations. They were becoming warmer than anyone but a dreamer could have imagined possible a few years before. Little did anyone know that the newfound warmth of a day in spring was also the fading warmth of dusk in autumn.

DARTMOUTH XVI: "A MOVABLE AFFAIR"

In this warm atmosphere Dartmouth held its most ambitious conference, a cross-country extravaganza that flew the participants from New

York to California, by way of Austin, where the conference itself was held. As had been suggested at Dartmouth XV, there was a public dialogue with ordinary American citizens, held during the California part of the conference. Robert Kingston and Robert Lehman of the Kettering Foundation went to Moscow separately in July 1987 to get the Soviets to agree to this plan. They also suggested, as had Mathews in a letter to Arbatov, that the growing changes in the Soviet Union might make a parallel dialogue with the Soviet public possible. Arbatov was excited at the prospect. He suggested that public discussions in the Soviet Union could parallel those taking place in the United States. They could, he said, culminate in a spacebridge a couple of months before the conference met.[1]

A month before the conference, on March 13, 1988, a long letter appeared in the newspaper *Sovetskaia Rossiia,* written by Nina Andreeva, a heretofore unknown teacher in Leningrad, defending Stalin and decrying criticism of the past. The publication of this letter was seen as part of an assault on glasnost and perestroika. It took almost three weeks for Gorbachev and his allies to begin their response. It came after a Politburo meeting held on April 4 and took the form of what one of Gorbachev's aides called "a tornado of antistalinism" that began with an article in *Pravda* the next day.[2] As one of the Soviet speakers in Austin said:

> [I]t was precisely after those two publications [the articles in *Sovetskaia Rossiia* and *Pravda*] came out that we have been noticing an outburst of discussions and statements on the key problems of the development of perestroika.[3]

This tornado found its way to Austin and had a dramatic effect on the Soviet side of the discussions. To begin with, "at the last minute," that is, in all probability, after the Politburo meeting of early April, Arbatov asked to have the conference agenda changed to focus on "three current trends in the Soviet Union—glasnost, democratization, and perestroika."[4] The effects of glasnost had been seen in the task force discussions since the Baku conference two years before, but now some of the constraints that remained on discussion of the changes and criticism of the past lifted. Indeed, the Soviets probably felt encouraged to speak in favor of Gorbachev's reforms, to the point that the floodgates were opened. In the plenary sessions, at least, descriptions of the problems of the Soviet Union and the efforts to solve them came in torrents.

Many of the people in the twenty-nine-member American delegation had had long experience in the Dartmouth Conference. These included such core members as Stewart, Mathews, Saunders, Stremlau, and Rockefeller. Having the conference in Austin attracted several people associated with the University of Texas, including Barbara Jordan, whose unmatchable eloquence made her stand out as a member of the House Judiciary Committee when it debated whether to impeach President Nixon. The conference also brought Walt Rostow back to Dartmouth. Now a professor of political economy at the University of Texas, he had taken part in the first conference, in Hanover.

The Soviet delegation was a mixture of the old and new. Arbatov was the Soviet cochairman, as at so many conferences before. He was joined once again by Zhurkin. Long Arbatov's deputy, he was now the head of the newly formed Institute of Europe. Sergei Plekhanov, a deputy director of ISKAN, proved himself able to cross the cultural divide in California by playing jazz piano and American spirituals. His command of English made him a favorite among the journalists who covered the discussions in Newport Beach. Rogov made his second appearance at a plenary Dartmouth Conference, although, like Sagdeev, he had been a regular on the Arms Control Task Force. Shmelev reappeared, as did Kortunov and Lukin. Boris Grushin soon became one of the foremost Russian pollsters, a kind of Russian version of Yankelovich. Viktor Linnik, a commentator at *Pravda* in 1988, became a correspondent for *Pravda,* rose to become deputy editor, and was elected editor by the staff after publication was suspended following the destruction of Russia's parliament in 1993. He remains an active, conservative voice in the Russian press as editor of the version of *Pravda* that was renamed *Slovo* in November 1998.

The conference in Austin began at the LBJ Museum and Library at about 3:00 on Monday, April 25. All the meetings took place there and in the School of International Affairs nearby. There were more plenary sessions than at earlier conferences, five in all, one on each day of the conference. Four task forces also met between the plenary sessions, on Tuesday, Wednesday, and Thursday. Three of the task forces—on arms control, regional conflicts, and political relations—continued discussions that had been taking place between Dartmouth plenary sessions through the decade. An Economic Relations Task Force also met, continuing work that had been done at the plenary conferences. Political relations at this time essentially meant the U.S.-Soviet relationship as a whole.

The dialogue in the plenary sessions was characterized by an unprecedented candor. This was noticeable by the second day, when an American participant, perhaps Cousins, congratulated "our Soviet colleagues for the most remarkable and revealing exchange that has taken place since these conferences began."[5] Other American speakers made similar remarks. The remarks by the Soviet delegates were extensive. The changes taking place in the Soviet Union were the focus of most of the plenary sessions.

Arbatov said the changes since Baku were greater than between any other two Dartmouth conferences, and the speeches of the Soviet delegates made this clear. While some said that their delegation was largely explaining the changes to the Americans, it became clear to some American observers that they were also explaining them to their compatriots, and even to themselves. As Chris Carlson, an observer from the Kettering Foundation, put it:

> They were clarifying their own personal views about the changes going on within and around them. They expressed personal feelings and views, in some cases guardedly, in others with forthrightness and candor, disagreed with each other and changed their minds.[6]

Another American observed:

> Did you see how the generals were taking notes when the Soviet academics spoke, and the academics were taking notes when the economists spoke? They were as engrossed by what they were hearing as we were.[7]

The Americans were often amazed by what their Soviet colleagues said. But they were skeptical as well. Cousins was the first to express this skepticism in the plenary sessions. More than halfway through the second plenary session, on the second day of the conference, he cited a story told to him by Khrushchev during their conversations in 1962 or 1963. It was about suggestion boxes, placed in Soviet factories, following the example taken from American business. But the Soviet boxes were never filled, owing to "habits of fear." Khrushchev, Cousins said, found that this habit was deep seated. With this in mind, Cousins asked whether the necessary fundamental reforms had been made and cited the as-yet-untouched structure of the Soviet Communist Party in particular.[8] In response, Shishlin spoke of the need for reform of the party and suggested that a multiparty system might be seen five or ten years hence. In the event, his optimistic reply was too pessimistic: both reforms would be seen in the next year and a half.

Most of the focus of the plenary was on the situation within the Soviet Union. But during the third plenary session, on Wednesday, April 27, one of the Americans, a student of Soviet affairs, noted that in reading the Soviet press,

> [w]e do not see in your internal discussions of world politics, and certainly of your own foreign policy, anything approaching the sharp analytical critical acuteness that we see in the domestic dialogue.[9]

In responding, Lukin, Mikoyan, and Arbatov concurred with the American.[10] Two of them unintentionally echoed Khrushchev as recounted by Cousins. One suggested that those who wrote on Soviet affairs held themselves back, influenced by habits formed under restrictions now lifted. Another argued that the political culture had not yet changed enough to allow a full discussion of foreign policy problems. But all saw these things changing. Linnik, on the other hand, saw the cause for the discrepancy in the greater consistency of Soviet foreign policy. His question of whether the United States had made the admission of error in Vietnam that it demanded the Soviets make in regard to Afghanistan was followed by a politely blistering response from Bialer.[11]

The third session closed soon thereafter. That afternoon the participants received a tour of the LBJ ranch not far away and enjoyed a Texas barbecue, the kind of social event that had been common early in Dartmouth's history but was becoming rare.

The remaining two plenary sessions took on a somewhat different character. The fourth session began with descriptions of the major points of view found in the American presidential campaign. The American delegation contained people who were close to three of the campaigns still active at the end of April. Neumann described the views of Vice President George Bush; Chayes described those of Governor

Michael Dukakis, who would soon be the Democratic nominee; and Milton Morris, director of research at the Joint Center for Political Studies, spoke about Jesse Jackson. John Buchanan, a critic of the religious right, began by saying: "I am Jerry Falwell." He then humorously presented the views of the religious right in a way that made the necessary points without eliciting an unnecessarily defensive reaction from the Soviets. During the entire presentation of the views expressed during the campaign, the Soviet participants took extensive notes.[12]

They had not taken notes in Dartmouth discussions like that before. This was itself a reflection of the changes that had taken place in the Soviet Union and in the U.S.-Soviet relationship—never before had the Soviets shown so much interest in American politics. Marxist-Leninist ideology had predisposed the Soviets to see American politics as a show run by a monolithic elite. But the changes fostered by glasnost discouraged such a simplistic view of the United States. The arguments made by Soviet participants during the 1970s and earlier in the 1980s that it was impossible for American public opinion about the Soviet role in Third World conflicts to influence the greater relationship were symptoms of this kind of thinking.

The last plenary session began with another description of American public opinion by Yankelovich. The session concluded with summaries of the discussions in the task groups and of what had happened in the course of the conference. The experience of the task groups had been much different from what had been seen in the plenary sessions. Whereas a sharp exchange such as occurred between Linnik and Bialer stood out for its rarity in the plenary, differences of views were much more common when the smaller groups met.

This was probably most apparent in the meetings of the Regional Conflicts Task Force. Saunders described these meetings as the most unproductive to date. He concluded: "We still don't understand each other and there was no evidence of new thinking." A possible reason for this feeling was that Primakov was not present, one of the few times that he had missed a task force meeting. Primakov had a special rapport with Saunders that Kislov did not, and the discussions clearly suffered from his absence.

The task force devoted itself almost exclusively to the question of Afghanistan. There was good reason for doing so, as the Geneva

Accords had been concluded on April 8 and signed on April 14, less than two weeks before the task force met. The Soviet withdrawal was to begin on May 15, which was less than three weeks away. It was to last nine months, with half the troops coming out in the first three.

A source of strong disagreement between the two sides was the future governance of Afghanistan. Gouttierre, who made the first presentation outlining the situation there, argued that the regime of Najibullah was both illegitimate and doomed. The conflict in Afghanistan, he said, would continue after the Soviet withdrawal began. The resistance, having achieved its goal of getting the Soviets out, would not rest until its second goal, the end of the Kabul regime, was achieved.

The Soviet argument was precisely the opposite. Moskalenko, who like Kislov had recently returned from Afghanistan, replied that Najibullah and the PDPA regime had acquired legitimacy within Afghanistan. And, in the words of one Soviet speaker, "The Kabul regime cannot be overthrown by flicking one's thumb." The only reasonable approach, they continued, was the road of national reconciliation. In this context that meant a coalition government that included the Najibullah regime. To accept any other option, they argued, would mean acquiescence to the use of force.

The American response to that option was that a coalition government might be desirable, but the lack of legitimacy of the government in Kabul made it unrealistic. Moreover, such an option could not be forced on the Afghans. Both sides agreed that any resolution of the conflict within Afghanistan had to come from the Afghans themselves. It could not be imposed from outside. But in the end the two sides remained far apart.

The same spirit of disagreement could be found in the discussions of the Arms Control Task Force. Several topics were discussed, but the main focus was on the limitation of conventional arms. The Soviets expressed some fear that the inauguration of a new president, whether Bush or Dukakis, would break the continuity of the arms control process and impede progress, much as had happened at the beginning of the Carter administration in 1977. An American speaker, perhaps Chayes, sought to allay these fears by assuring the Soviets that Dukakis would consult with the Soviets. Unlike in 1977, there would be no surprises.

But the disagreements came over the issue of denuclearization and the fate of Soviet proposals made in 1986. The official Soviet position, stemming from Gorbachev's speech in January 1986 and repeated in speeches by Shevardnadze, was that nuclear weapons in Europe should be removed entirely. The Americans questioned even the desirability of this, arguing that the balance of forces would be more stable if some, even if fewer, nuclear forces remained.

The arguments over denuclearization were calmly reasoned. The fate of earlier Soviet proposals for the control of conventional arms was, however, an excuse for some old-style polemics from the Soviet side. At least one Soviet speaker said that the United States preferred that the situation not be changed. This exchange underlined the evidence from the plenary sessions that perestroika had yet to completely transform the relationship between the two countries.

There was also a discussion of the idea of asymmetrical reductions in conventional arms. This becomes especially interesting when seen in light of Gorbachev's speech at the United Nations made at the end of the year, when he announced that the Soviet Union would make a number of unilateral moves, including a reduction of its forces by 500,000 men. About half of these were to come from Eastern Europe and the western part of the Soviet Union. In April, well before that speech, everyone in the Arms Control Task Force discussions recognized that it was unrealistic to expect a one-to-one withdrawal of the tanks or troops that faced each other across the border between NATO and the Warsaw Pact. That would simply allow the Soviets to retain or even increase their advantage in ground forces. On the other hand, it seemed unlikely that the Soviet military could be sold on the idea that, for example, the United States would withdraw two divisions while the Soviet Union withdrew thirteen. It seemed more reasonable, particularly to the Soviet participants, for Soviet reductions in ground forces to be matched by some reduction in forces where the United States had superiority, in air forces, for example.

There was greater harmony in the discussions of the task force on economic relations. This group was smaller than the others, with only four members on the Soviet side and six on the American. Their discussions on the first day were largely about how to improve economic relations between the two countries, put in the context of the opening presentation by a Soviet speaker. The views of the speaker, by his own admission, were unconventional, which suggests that it may have been

Shmelev. Whoever it was, he outlined what the Soviets needed to do to make the Soviet economy an open economy. This was a task, he said, that required gaining access to foreign markets for both exports and imports and making the ruble convertible. The problem of gaining access was almost solved. Full convertibility, however, was a long-term problem; it required price reform and could not be expected "before the end of the next decade." That now seems a remarkably long time frame, particularly when outlined by a reformer who was in many respects radical in the Soviet context. But events were racing at a speed that overwhelmed the ability of most reformers, indeed, almost anyone analyzing the Soviet Union, to keep up.

An American speaker opened the session by expressing the hope that joint ventures, a topic of Dartmouth discussions for a decade, could now be achieved. In those discussions, joint ventures were seen as a means to the improvement of U.S.-Soviet relations. Speakers on both sides now argued that an improvement in economic relations awaited an improvement in political relations. Yet they also sought practical measures for assisting Soviet reform. Their efforts, and the discussion on the second day, came to center on business training. They discussed existing programs in the Soviet Union and the United States. They considered the best way to provide such training, whether, for example, it should be primarily theoretical or practical. These discussions had two concrete results. First, some of the American participants contributed to the efforts to draft the Soviet law on joint ventures published in November 1998. Second, Arbatov introduced Stewart to Alberts Kauls, the chairman of Adazi Agrofirm. He urged the chairman to invite the Kellogg Company for urgent discussions of joint ventures. This led to the formation of Kellogg Latvia in 1992. Stewart worked for Kellogg from 1993 until his retirement in 2001.

The Political Relations Task Force may have been the most successful. It certainly lasted longest. Steven Strickland observed that "the fact that the Political Relations Task Force kept talking when the others had stopped attracted those from the other groups to come on in and have another shot at it."[13] They would have come primarily from the Arms Control and Economic Relations Task Forces, which ended early. Indeed, Shmelev was listed as a member of the Political Relations Task Force as well as the Economic Relations Task Force. Mathews, the

American cochair of the group, noted that the discussions of the Political Relations Task Force had a different quality than others both in Austin and later in California in that they "got down to immediate public concerns," which is to say that they did not focus merely on the concerns of the foreign policy elite. But, he continued, they "dealt with those concerns that special interest groups have."[14]

The discussion was free flowing. No agenda had been prepared in advance and "the operative dynamic," as Strickland put it, was "every Soviet participant's irrepressible desire to unburden himself of a personal view of perestroika." He found three themes in the discussion. One was the need for new terms to characterize the relationship between the superpowers that was being formed, terms that would "match the altered pictures of 'the other' which are now entering our minds." A second theme, brought up by Bialer, was that the American public would see perestroika through the lens of human rights. The Soviets, unlike in the past, accepted this notion but sought to broaden the definition of human rights, as the Soviets—and others—had long done, to include matters such as economic status. The third theme came from Cousins toward the end of the discussions: how the two sides would deal with the Eastern European countries as they came under the influence of perestroika. The answer of one of the Soviet speakers to this question suggested what the expectations were just a year and a half before the Berlin Wall was torn down:

> The build-up of the common European home will require greater openness on our side, as well as from the West. . . . In what form will the openness develop? It will probably develop on the basis of two blocs. Both blocs will preserve their integrity but, at the same time, they will actively interact with each other.[15]

After the conference closed in Austin, on April 29, most of the Soviet delegates and a few of the Americans flew to Newport Beach, California.[16] The next day they began four days of discussions with members of the American public. Though it had been recognized since the first meeting in Hanover that it was important to reach public opinion, this was the first time that Dartmouth had opened itself up and tried to reach the public directly. It was, as Bob Kingston called it, "a grand experiment."[17]

This effort, in fact, began in Austin, where several delegates took part in a public session that demonstrated what the dialogue was like. This session was filmed and broadcast twice on The Learning Channel, which served about 13 million homes. An edited version of the session became the center of a videotape about the Dartmouth conferences put together by the Kettering Foundation for use in college courses.[18]

In Newport Beach, the Soviet delegates spent three days meeting at the breakfast table and the Ping-Pong table as well as the conference table with twenty-five participants in the National Issues Forums (NIF). The participants came from seventeen states, from New York and California to Wisconsin to Florida. They were united by their NIF experience, which included discussions that year of the superpower relationship. Eighty NIF participants from Orange County also attended the discussions.

Sunday, May 1, was mostly given over to several orientation sessions to prepare the participants, especially those from NIF, who were new to the Dartmouth process, for the discussions the next day. Those discussions began with a plenary session that included a report by Yankelovich on earlier results of NIF. In the afternoon the participants broke into five small groups for detailed roundtable discussions. These discussions, indeed, the entire dialogue, focused on the changes occurring in the Soviet Union. As in Austin, this was in contrast to most previous Dartmouth discussions. It left the Americans astounded and encouraged to hear the Soviets criticize their own society in strong terms and to affirm the need for change. Not all, however, were convinced that the changes were as far reaching as their Soviet interlocutors said. George Kessinger, the president of Goodwill Industries of Orange County, summed it up when he said, "I'd like to see more evidence," but "If half of what they say is true, there's an amazing thing going on."[19]

At Dartmouth XVI, a greater effort was put into using television to spread the word about the conferences than had been made before.[20] Not only was the film based on the session in Austin aired twice on The Learning Channel, but also one of the sessions at Newport Beach was videotaped for broadcast over the Public Broadcasting System. Four Soviet delegates took part: Zhurkin, Plekhanov, Shishlin, and Arbatov. The American participants were Julie Zimet, general manager of a moving company in El Paso; Deborah Rinehart, a dairy farmer from Wisconsin; Greg Gonzales, a mechanic from Denver; and Kessinger.

Hodding Carter, spokesman for the State Department during the Carter administration, was the moderator. The tape was edited and broadcast over 200 stations on May 22, shortly before the summit meeting between President Reagan and Gorbachev in Moscow.

A sign of the time, or perhaps a reminder that the United States and the Soviet Union always had a basis for something less than the total hostility that sometimes seemed to be the hallmark of their relations, was the encounter between Vladimir Kabaidze and Frank Parent at Disneyland.[21] They had both been young soldiers fighting through Germany in the spring of 1945, more than forty years before. Parent, ignoring orders, rowed across the Elbe to meet the Soviets on the other side. Among them was Kabaidze. They ate together, drank together, sang together, and exchanged addresses on a ruble and a deutsche mark. The latter was used by an American acquaintance of Kabaidze and friend of Parent to arrange the meeting.

On May 4, after the public sessions ended in California, the Soviet participants flew to Washington for several days of meetings. At the Brookings Institution they met with experts from Congress, the CIA, the State Department, universities, and think tanks. Twenty-five experts from around Washington attended a session at the Center for Strategic and International Studies. Robert Oakley and Dennis Ross of the staff of the National Security Council and Edward Djerejian, deputy assistant secretary of state, attended a separate meeting at the Brookings Institution on May 5 to discuss the Middle East. On Capitol Hill, Soviet delegates exchanged views with fourteen members of the House of Representatives, including such luminaries as Les Aspin, later secretary of defense; Benjamin Gilman, later chairman of the International Relations Committee; and Lee Hamilton, Gilman's predecessor in that chairmanship.

THE ARMS CONTROL AND POLITICAL RELATIONS TASK FORCES, MOSCOW, JANUARY 1989: CONVENTIONAL ARMS AND EUROPE

The months after Dartmouth XVI saw a rush to reform in the Soviet Union and the remainder of the presidential campaign in the United States. Gorbachev pushed the Soviet Union further down the road of political reform. The most important step, with consequences that he probably did not foresee, was to schedule contested elections the following spring. The rules established for the elections were carefully drawn up with the intent of preserving the dominance of the Communist Party. Gorbachev also moved resolutely to transform the Soviet Union's international relations, particularly with the United States. His speech to the United Nations given on December 7 was almost revolutionary in its implications. He drew on the themes of what had come to be called "the new political thinking" in the speech, presenting a picture of interdependence in the world. This, he asserted, required a different approach to international relations than had been adopted during the Cold War. These themes were familiar to those who had taken part in the Dartmouth meetings earlier in the year. Most specifically, he said that the Soviet Union would reduce its forces by 500,000 troops, unilaterally, over the next two years.[22] Particular attention would be paid to Eastern Europe in making the withdrawals. The Soviet Union would also withdraw tanks, artillery, and combat aircraft from its forces in Europe.

The victory of George Bush over Michael Dukakis in November ensured that there would be greater continuity in relations with the Soviet Union when the administration changed than there had been when Carter took over from Ford in 1977 or when Reagan succeeded Carter in 1981. But the new president was his own man. He and his new national security advisor, Dartmouth veteran Brent Scowcroft, had more doubts than their predecessors that the changes fostered by Gorbachev were good for the United States. The new administration, therefore, came into office with a more cautious approach to the Soviet Union than the Reagan administration had come to adopt.

In January two task force meetings convened back-to-back in Moscow. They met a month after Gorbachev surprised the United Nations and at the end of the transition to the new administration. The Arms Control Task Force met first, from January 16 to January 18, followed by the Political Relations Task Force.

The Americans' approach to the meeting was outlined in October.[23] Keeping in mind Gorbachev's evident readiness to make changes in the Soviet military posture in Europe and to contemplate changes in the countries of the Warsaw Pact, they intended to address questions arising from the new security system in Europe that seemed to be evolving. The intention was to have the task force meet six times over the next three years. It would discuss one of three issues each year—the political preconditions for a new security system, the conceptual framework for such a system, and, finally, the force posture the new system would require. It is not clear whether the Soviet side agreed to this agenda. It was, in any event, quickly overtaken by events. A year later, the Warsaw Pact was effectively dead.

Ten days before the Arms Control Task Force met in Moscow, members of the American delegation met with several senior officials from ACDA, the CIA, and the Department of Defense to discuss the topics expected to come up. Doty, as before, led the delegation that traveled to Moscow. Stewart, Chayes, Jones, and Les Aspin joined him.[24] All were veterans of the task force. There were also two new, distinguished members: General Edward Meyer, retired as the Army Chief of Staff, and Richard Burt. Burt was currently the American ambassador in Bonn and had been a *New York Times* reporter. As head of the State Department's Bureau of Political-Military Affairs, he was deeply involved in arms control matters early in the Reagan administration and then became assistant secretary for European affairs.[25]

The Soviet delegation was a remarkable conglomeration of military officers and defense intellectuals. Arbatov took part once again, but the Soviet cochairman was Sagdeev. Milstein was not there, but several other analysts from ISKAN were, a greater number than at any previous task force meeting. This reflected not only the institute's long-standing ties with Dartmouth, but, more important, the expertise in security issues that it had developed.[26] The analysts who attended included Valery Abarenkov, Yuri Davydov, Andrei Kokoshin, Alexander Konovalov, and Sergei Rogov. Also attending the meeting were several generals, active or retired. Two were on the staff of the Central Committee—General Lieutenant Viktor Starodubov and Major General Geli Batenin, who had also been at the meeting held in Moscow in 1984. Retired major general Konstantin Mikhailov was a first deputy chief of department in the Ministry of Foreign Affairs. Sergei Akhromeev had just retired as chief of the General Staff, possibly because he opposed the troop reduction announced by Gorbachev in New York.[27] Another three participants came from the Soviet policy apparatus—Ignat Danilenko, head of the Main Political Directorate for the Soviet Army and Military Marine; Andrei Grachev from the Central Committee's Ideology Department; and Vladimir Shustov of the Foreign Ministry. Other Soviet delegates came from other institutes. These included Stanislav Rodionov, one of Sagdeev's deputies at the Space Research Institute; Sergei Karaganov, Zhurkin's deputy at the Institute of Europe; and Sergei Kishilov, the sole representative of IMEMO. A contingent from the Soviet Peace Committee rounded out the delegation.

The discussions of the task force did not follow the agenda outlined by the Americans in October, but they did focus more than those of any previous task force meeting on the situation in Europe. This was, of course, not surprising, given what Gorbachev had said to the United Nations, but it also followed on the increased emphasis placed on conventional arms in recent meetings. Strategic arms, while not placed on the back burner, did not have pride of place.

The meeting tended to dwell on general issues rather than the technical issues involved. There was an extended discussion of trends in Eastern and Western Europe. Both sides saw centrifugal forces in the former and centripetal forces in the latter, where the 1992 initiative promised a Europe moving toward political integration. It need hardly be added that no one foresaw the imminent collapse of the Soviet bloc.

A change from the discussions held in Austin was a greater willingness by the Soviets to acknowledge the American argument that the complete elimination of nuclear weapons would be unwise. Elimination of these weapons remained a goal of Soviet policy, but the complications that that would bring were recognized. One Soviet speaker argued that it would be necessary to retain some nuclear weapons because the French, British, and Chinese were unlikely to give theirs up.

The last topic discussed, briefly, was verification. There was no significant disagreement among the participants. This was itself significant, showing, more than anything else, how far the discussions had come since the early 1960s, when on-site inspection was a great issue dividing the Soviets and the Americans. In fact, the Soviets had accepted, indeed they even proposed, on-site inspection as a part of the INF Treaty signed little more than a year before, in December 1987.

Another sign of change in the U.S.-Soviet relationship was the Soviet response to an American question about how the United States should respond to the unilateral reduction in Soviet troops. In the past, the Soviet participants would probably have made this a central topic of the meeting. They would have argued long and vociferously for significant concessions by the United States and would probably have spoken as if with one voice, with a precisely defined idea of what the American concessions should be. This time, however, there were several responses. And they ranged from a proposed withdrawal of neutron weapons to reaffirmation that the Soviet actions were purely and simply unilateral, made independently of any possible action by the United States.

Changes within the Soviet Union and in the Soviet Union's approach to the outside world had been topics of discussion in Dartmouth meetings for several years now. The theme of the Political Relations Task Force meeting that followed in January 1989 was change in a more general sense. That was not the way the agenda was written, but change had become so pervasive—not just in the U.S.-Soviet relationship—that participants were led time and again to discuss the meaning and question the extent of changes that they saw.

As before, there were few holdovers from the meeting of one task force to the next. Only Arbatov and Stewart were present at both task force meetings in Moscow. More delegates had been to previous meetings of the Political Relations Task Force, although neither it nor the Arms Control Task Force had the steady membership of the American side of the Regional Conflicts Task Force. Still, on the American side, Bialer, Lundeen, Mathews, Saunders, Stewart, and Zuckerman had been at the meeting the previous year in Moscow. Bialer, Saunders, and Stewart had been to all the meetings of the task force, as had Arbatov and Zhurkin on the Soviet side. Among their colleagues present in 1989, Bobrysheva, Bogdanov, and Shishlin had also been at the task force meeting the previous February.

The newcomers on the American side included two people who would become major figures in the Clinton administration. Madeleine Albright, then at Georgetown University, had been an advisor on foreign policy to Michael Dukakis in the campaign just past. She would become ambassador to the United Nations and then secretary of state under

President Clinton. Richard Holbrooke had a remarkable career that led him in and out of government for almost thirty years. In 1989 he was managing director of Shearson Lehman Hutton. Subsequently, as Clinton's assistant secretary of state for European and Canadian affairs, he would negotiate the Dayton Accords on Bosnia. Like Albright, he, too, would become ambassador to the United Nations in the Clinton administration. Another participant, Les Aspin, was Clinton's first secretary of defense, but in 1989 he was still chairman of the House Committee on the Armed Forces. The two remaining American members had close ties to the Kettering Foundation—Buchanan, who had played Jerry Falwell in Austin, and Robert Colby Nelson, a former correspondent for the *Christian Science Monitor.*

Members of the Soviet delegation who were new to the task force, though not to Dartmouth, included Plekhanov, the piano-playing deputy director of ISKAN who had been prominent at Dartmouth XVI, and Trofimenko, also at ISKAN, who had been at the first meeting of the task force. They were joined by S. N. Kondrashev, a diplomatic analyst for *Izvestiya,* and Ambassador A. V. Mendeleevich, chief of the Planning Department for the Ministry of Foreign Affairs.[28]

The meeting opened with an extensive discussion of the American presidential campaign just concluded and its implications for U.S.-Soviet relations. The Americans were divided on the meaning of the election and even over whether there was actually a debate on foreign policy.[29] There was a degree of consensus that the Bush administration had some room for maneuver in its relations with the Soviet Union.

A Soviet speaker who identified himself as a "representative of the Foreign Ministry" (which means that it was probably Mendeleevich) began a discussion of Soviet politics and foreign policy with a description of the new political thinking, the foreign policy counterpart to perestroika. Its essence, he said, was renunciation of "the peaceful coexistence approach," which he described "as a form of class struggle in the international arena [which] was the formula that was orthodox here for decades." He continued by saying, "The fundamental question at this point in history is whether humanity can survive," a statement that could have come from Cousins at Dartmouth I.

Most of the discussion that followed was about perestroika itself and the implications it held for Soviet society. Several Americans asked about the stability of the Soviet Union in the face of these changes. One speaker suggested that "it's historically been very hard to put controls on freedom without at some point people asking for more freedom than a central authority is willing to permit." Another asked what yardsticks the leadership used to measure stability. The increasingly evident ethnic tensions in the Soviet Union were also discussed.

The Soviets seemed to be less concerned with the problem of stability than with keeping perestroika moving. They emphasized the need to change people's mentality. The danger was not a social explosion; it was apathy and alienation. In answer to an American concern that the economic promises of perestroika would have to be fulfilled, one Soviet speaker answered that conditions had not become worse, and that as long as more people were being brought into the process of perestroika, there would be no significant social unrest.

This was followed by an extensive discussion of what was described as the approaching end of the Cold War.[30] There was some feeling both that the essence of the Cold War was in its military aspects and that, as one American put it, "the Cold War has to end where it began, which is in Eastern Europe." Partly by implication, the two delegations seemed to agree that the Cold War would end as a result of political changes in Eastern Europe. An American believed the end could come after "Soviet policy no longer insists on the continued primacy of the Communist Parties of Eastern Europe." A Soviet speaker saw the end of the postwar era coming "when Europe is truly a diverse collection of individual countries, united by common values, but not by bloc membership."

The discussion of change reached out to include the world at large, following a well-received presentation by Saunders of his ideas about the inadequacy of old ideas based on a model of the world centered on states. One American said:

> This year [after Austin], we have been challenged, first of all, to go beyond the original formulation of Dartmouth. The original purpose was very simple, although at the same time very difficult. The idea was to link the two nations in a conversation, which enabled us to share information, and to talk to one another.

The new purpose, participants said, would be to go beyond mutual communication to something else. A Soviet speaker echoed this thought, suggesting that whereas Dartmouth had previously run ahead of official thinking, it was now in danger of falling behind. Both sides wanted to explore where to go next.

With that, the Political Relations Task Force came to an end. It did not meet again. But this new purpose would be found in the Regional Conflicts Task Force.

REGIONAL CONFLICTS TASK FORCE, NOVEMBER 1988–APRIL 1990: NEW LEADERSHIP AND A NEW ERA?

In the aftermath of Dartmouth XVI and in light of the dramatic changes taking place in the Soviet Union and the increasingly evident changes in U.S.-Soviet relations, Saunders worked to move the discussions of the Regional Conflicts Task Force onto a new plane. He wrote to Primakov to propose that the overall relationship between the Soviet Union and the United States be made an explicit part of the discussions at the next meeting. By October 1988, when the American members of the task force met in Washington to prepare for the discussions to come, the meeting was set to take place in Dayton in late November after the American presidential election.

As it turned out, the meeting was held later, in early December, in New York rather than Dayton as had been planned. It was also held without Primakov, whose growing importance within the Soviet regime would take him out of Dartmouth. As late as October, plans were made for him to attend the conference, coming by way of Vancouver, British Columbia, and Seattle. Primakov was to come to New York with Gorbachev, so the venue of the Dartmouth meeting was changed to New York to make it possible for Primakov to attend part of it. At the last moment, however, he was sent to London instead to prepare for Gorbachev's planned visit to Britain (later canceled).

Primakov's place was taken by Gennadi Chufrin, who was named acting cochair. Chufrin was deputy director of the Institute of Oriental Studies, where Primakov had been director before going to IMEMO, and an expert on Southeast Asia. This was a region that Dartmouth had not discussed since the end of the Vietnam War, but the civil war in Cambodia had become an issue in the U.S.-Soviet relationship.

It had been suggested at the preparatory meeting in October that Cambodia be included in the discussions.

Chufrin was the only Soviet member of the task force new to Dartmouth and the Regional Conflicts Task Force. His colleagues at the New York meeting—Davidson, Markaryan, Sergo Mikoyan, and Moskalenko—had all been to at least two meetings before and to either Dartmouth XVI in Austin or the meeting in Moscow in February. The American side was once again made up of familiar faces: Saunders, Stewart, Gouttierre, Neumann, Purcell, and Stremlau. The only American new to the task force was Nelson, who had been at Austin in April, had been a member of the Political Relations Task Force in January, and had interviewed David Jones and Georgi Arbatov in 1986.

The meeting was in many respects similar to the task force meetings that had taken place before.[31] General discussions preceded and followed discussions of the problems in regions that had been sources of tension in U.S.-Soviet relations. Two sessions each were given to the Middle East, Afghanistan, and southern Africa. One session was devoted to Central America. On the last day, the delegates sat together to watch Gorbachev's speech to the United Nations. They later watched from the window of their meeting room as Gorbachev's motorcade passed below.

That speech, which included the proposal to unilaterally withdraw Soviet troops from Eastern Europe, marked a dramatic change in Soviet foreign policy. Similarly important, if less dramatic, changes were evident in the Soviet contributions to the task force discussions. There was an emphasis—also evident in Gorbachev's speech—on the use of multilateral mechanisms to resolve regional conflicts. These mechanisms would include the United Nations and regional organizations such as the Organization for African Unity. The Soviets were coming to a position similar to that advocated in the early Dartmouth conferences by Cousins, Grenville Clark, Louis Sohn, and Arthur Larson.

Other changes became evident in the discussion of southern Africa but were clearly relevant elsewhere as well. There was a new emphasis on ethnicity as a political reality. This partially replaced the Marxist reliance on class in analyzing the sources of conflict. The discussants found the Soviets more willing than before to condemn terrorism generally and to seek political solutions to conflict. This meant that the Soviets were less willing to defend the use of force by the African National Congress (ANC) in South Africa. The Soviets were also more in favor of fostering evolutionary change that could help preserve stability in a region.

The discussion of Afghanistan turned on the question of what would happen after the Soviet withdrawal. No one expressed much doubt that the withdrawal would be completed in February as scheduled. The Soviets continued to believe that the Najibullah regime would survive for several years (as it did in fact). They proposed that multilateral aid to reconstruct Afghanistan be extended through the United Nations, a proposal in line with the emphasis on multilateral means noted in the discussion on southern Africa. The Soviet participants also looked to regional organizations such as the Association of Southeast Asian Nations (ASEAN) and the Southern Asia Regional Council to "provide the answer to a lot of regional problems" where the two superpowers had little direct influence.

The most startling changes in the Soviet position were probably those seen in the discussion of Latin America. The Contras and the Sandinista government had agreed to a cease-fire the previous spring. American aid to the former had ended. Under the cease-fire agreement the Contras were guaranteed a place in the political system, but the Sandinistas had clamped down on opposition media, raising doubts about the future of democracy in a country that was in economic disrepair following a decade of conflict. But rather than defend the actions of the Sandinistas, as might have been expected, the Soviets assigned them part of the blame for problems in the region. They said that the Sandinistas should do more to bring the opposition into the political process. Moreover, one Soviet participant—remarkably—said that the United States was fighting for democracy in Nicaragua.

There were significant changes evident in the discussion of the Middle East as well. In particular, the Soviets did not see resolution of the conflict coming from an international conference along the lines described in the joint statement of 1977. Instead, in keeping with a new focus on the internal, evolutionary solutions to such conflicts, resolution had to come from agreement between Israel and the PLO, although at least one Soviet speaker favored discussions in the United

Nations. Both sides agreed that the two superpowers could facilitate such an agreement. The Soviets not only said that recognition of the PLO by the United States would be "a fundamental element" in the peace process; they also said that there were discussions in Moscow about whether the Soviet Union should restore relations with Israel. Some were skeptical, saying that reopening relations might strengthen the right-wing forces in Israel in the short run.

The month after the meeting, Saunders traveled to Moscow to take part in the meeting of the Political Relations Task Force. Primakov, cochair and Saunders' interlocutor on Middle Eastern issues since the Regional Conflicts Task Force was formed, told him that he could no longer continue to be a part of its work. He "passed the baton"—the cochairmanship—to Chufrin.[32] The recent Central Committee Plenum had approved of Primakov as one of the "Party Hundred" nominated to be elected by the Communist Party to the Congress of People's Deputies in the Soviet Union's first contested elections. He was elected before the next meeting of the task force and became chairman of one of the two houses of the Supreme Soviet soon after.

When the task force met again in May, its membership reflected the change in chairmen. The American delegation remained largely the same as at the previous few meetings. Alan Romberg, a senior fellow for Asia at the Council on Foreign Relations, was added to discuss Southeast Asia, as had been proposed after Dartmouth XVI. The Soviet delegation was quite different, however. Researchers from Chufrin's institute, the Institute of Oriental Studies, dominated it. Chufrin was joined by Irina Zviagelskaya, Anatoli Khazanov, Viktor Korgun, Vitali Naumkin, and Oleg Pleshov. The remaining two members of the task force were Sergo Mikoyan and Andrei Shumikin. Shumikin, a section head at ISKAN and an expert on the Middle East, had been an interpreter at several previous Dartmouth meetings. This was the first meeting he took part in outside the interpreter's booth.

The meeting was distinguished from its predecessors by a change in format. After Dartmouth XVI, Saunders wrote that he wanted the task force to address two sets of questions. He wanted it to continue to analyze conflicts in the Third World much as it had been doing for six years, but he also wanted the task force to examine how these conflicts affected the broader U.S.-Soviet relationship. This desire reflected his thinking about the nature of that relationship, expressed to the task force back in 1987. It also reflected the concern that the current improvement in relations between the superpowers could go bust, much as it had in the 1970s, because of "some damn thing" in the Middle East, southern Africa, or somewhere else. As he put it in his opening presentation to the task force meeting:

> Above all, the purpose of our discussion is to build a sounder relation-ship than was built in the 1970s and to prevent the disillusionment with our new relationship in the 1990s that gradually submerged détente at the end of the 1970s.[33]

To facilitate this dual agenda, Saunders proposed, and the Soviets agreed, to structure the meeting so that subgroups would meet to dis-cuss specific conflicts and the plenaries could focus on discussions of the influence of those conflicts on the overall relationship.

This new structure, reminiscent of the change in the structure of the main Dartmouth conferences made in the early 1970s, had several effects. It greatly expanded the time that could be given to discussions of the individual regions. In effect, it expanded the amount of discus-sion that could take place, allowing the participants to probe issues more deeply. The participants could also get to know one another bet-ter. Not only were the groups smaller—sometimes just two people—but they met in a less formal atmosphere than the task force as a whole, which usually carried out its discussions in conference rooms, across tables and microphones.[34]

Another new element at the May meeting of the task force was a discussion of Cambodia. Since the end of the Vietnam War, the Soviets had given strong support to Vietnam. Since about 1980 they had built their forces at Cam Ranh Bay, an important naval installation con-structed by the Americans. But the "new thinking" of Gorbachev was the principal factor in the slow but steady change in Soviet policy in Southeast Asia, a change that became evident as the conflict in Cambodia edged toward resolution.[35]

Chufrin and Romberg paired off for their discussions of the region. At the end of it they listed the points on which they agreed and dis-agreed.[36] They agreed on the general outline of a settlement, including the need for Vietnam to withdraw its troops from the country (Vietnam had announced such a withdrawal the previous month) and the undesirability of a return to power by the Khmer Rouge. As for disagreements, the Soviets—Romberg generalized in his summary of his meetings with Chufrin—were more suspicious of China and its motives in the region than was Romberg. In a continuing reflection of Cold War anxieties, they also suspected that the assistance that the United States was giving to Prince Sihanouk and his allies was proffered in the belief that the United States would benefit if a low-grade conflict continued. Romberg insisted that it was to improve the bargaining position of the noncommunist resistance in relation to the Khmer Rouge.

The discussions on Southeast Asia and the other regions were conducted under the guidance of a "checklist" of questions put together by Saunders that had been distributed before the task force met. These questions reflected his thinking but were readily adopted as a useful framework by the participants. They began by asking how interests were defined and ran through the creation of scenarios about how events might play out.

Sergo Mikoyan and Susan Purcell devised three scenarios each for Nicaragua and El Salvador. They concluded that the United States and the Soviet Union would be unable or unwilling to cooperate directly in Central America no matter where events led, but they could move in parallel on some issues. In any case, however, cooperation between the superpowers would have little influence on events in the region. The two seemed to agree that both countries would be satisfied with outcomes achieved through processes recognized as democratic, even if their ally should lose.

Stremlau and Khazanov agreed that the main problem in southern Africa in the wake of the settlement of the Namibian conflict and the withdrawal of the Cubans agreed to the previous December was apartheid in South Africa. But Khazanov was more willing to embrace the use of violence by the African National Congress than Stremlau or, it appears, than his predecessors at the task force meeting in New York five months earlier. They also disagreed on the amount of leverage available to the United States in South Africa. Stremlau argued that the United States had little. Therefore, he continued, sanctions were unlikely to have a strong effect. Khazanov criticized the United States for its continued support of Jonas Savimbi in Angola, a criticism that ran parallel to earlier Soviet criticisms of American support to the mujahideen in Afghanistan.

Korgun and Gouttierre continued their conversation on Afghanistan, now in the wake of the withdrawal of Soviet troops concluded in February. Pleshov and Randa Slim joined them. Slim was a member of the Kettering Foundation staff who served as rapporteur for the meeting. She would soon become a central member of the task force. Like Mikoyan and Purcell, the participants who addressed the conflict in Afghanistan organized their discussion around scenarios. They devised seven of them. The group concluded that Afghanistan was no longer a bone of contention in U.S.-Soviet relations but that the future was uncertain. The political dynamics were volatile; the form of government was unpredictable. Misunderstandings and suspicions could easily arise. The group made several suggestions for cooperation to minimize these. The suggestions largely amounted to ways to maintain and improve communications between the two, but the group also suggested that the two superpowers "[f]ollow paths of parallel or complementary action where an actual condominium cannot be achieved."[37] This seemed to contradict the concern expressed by other members of the task force about perceptions of superpower condominium elsewhere in the Third World. It also reflected divisions within the foreign policy establishments of the two countries over how close cooperation should be (the debate over this survived the collapse and continues still).

The discussion of the Middle East was carried out in light of the uprising by West Bank Palestinians against the Israeli authorities—the Intifada—and diminished activity by the United States in the search for a resolution of the Arab-Israeli conflict. Saunders and Neumann met with two new, dynamic Soviet counterparts—Zviagelskaya and Naumkin. The two sides found themselves close in what they wanted to see emerge from the conditions then current. The Soviets felt that the approaches of the two countries to a settlement—the Soviet approach based on an international conference; the American, on bilateral contacts—were converging. In a departure from earlier Soviet pronouncements, they also said that Soviet involvement in a settlement was probably not possible in the late 1970s when the Camp David agreement was reached, although the situation had now changed. The Soviet participants affirmed both that it was necessary to involve the Soviet Union in the process (this was certainly not new in Soviet foreign policy) and that the Soviet Union could contribute to a settlement by conferring legitimacy on it. This would make it possible to provide more serious guarantees of a settlement than either power could by operating alone.

The task force meeting included an extended conversation with a Soviet general, a representative of the General Staff. Much of this discussion was about Afghanistan. The general seemed to be a representative of Soviet conservatives who reluctantly accommodated themselves to the more revolutionary implications of Gorbachev's new thinking. He found the original intervention in 1979 to be justified, characterized the mujahideen as "people of Afghan origin who, following the April revolution, had to immigrate to Pakistan to gather some forces there and start the war to seize power in Afghanistan."[38] Such attitudes were in contrast to those of most of the Soviet participants in this task force meeting.

Shortly after the task force meeting, Stremlau, who had just moved from the Rockefeller Foundation to the World Bank, moved once again. He became deputy director of the Policy Planning Staff at the State Department and a vehicle for spreading the results of Dartmouth meetings in the United States government. Saunders and Neumann had lunch with him and two of his colleagues in August. They turned over to him a letter from Saunders to Secretary of State James Baker and reports on the May discussions on the Middle East, Afghanistan, Latin America, and Southeast Asia for Stremlau to distribute as he saw fit.

The next time the task force met, at the end of November 1989, the communist system in Eastern Europe was in the middle of being dismantled. Poland had held free elections in June; the communists were roundly defeated, and a noncommunist government took office in August. The Berlin Wall had been taken down earlier in November. The communist regime in Czechoslovakia surrendered its monopoly of power to Václav Havel soon after the task force meeting opened. Not surprisingly, the full import of these events—that they spelled the collapse of the Soviet empire and the end of the Cold War—was not perceived by the participants.

They did, however, have a sense, also evident in the task force meetings in January, that events and changes in official policy were leaving Dartmouth behind. It seemed, too, that the Third World had become a backwater of policy, where old thinking still ruled. Arbatov had raised this issue in an appearance at the National Press Club in Washington earlier in the month.[39] It was new thinking, it seemed, that was making possible the dramatic changes in Europe.

The people who came together in the Westfields Conference Center a few miles outside Washington included all but one of the American delegation that had gone to Moscow earlier in the year. The exception was Stremlau, now in government, who nonetheless found time to meet informally with the group the night before the meeting began. He also arranged a meeting at the State Department with colleagues from the Policy Planning Staff after the sessions had ended. His place was taken by Helen Kitchen, who had been the director of the Africa Studies Program at the Center for International and Strategic Studies since 1981.

The Soviet delegation changed little as well. Chufrin, Khazanov, Naumkin, Mikoyan, and Zviagelskaya all returned to the task force. Moskalenko, absent in May, was back again as well, taking the place of Korgun. The only participants completely new to Dartmouth were Aleksandr Popov, a researcher on Southeast Asia at the Institute of Oriental Studies, and Aleksandr Egorov, the representative of the Soviet Peace Committee.

The meeting was organized much like the meeting in May. It began and ended with plenary sessions but included a day and a half in which small groups met to discuss particular regions. Once again the small groups were spurred by a set of questions put together by Saunders to build on the work of the previous meeting and to identify current issues that cut across regions. The discussions of regional conflicts revealed much the same sets of agreement and disagreement that had been shown in the meetings in May.

But there were several new things seen at the meetings. For one, the Soviet participants showed a greater willingness to analyze the two superpowers in an even-handed fashion than they had shown before. By now, criticism of past Soviet positions by Soviet participants was no novelty; that had been a part of Dartmouth for several years. But the

Soviet participants had continued to be reluctant to criticize the current leadership. That reluctance was now gone. In its place were statements like the following:

> Another important factor is the definite incompetence in policymaking which appears in both the United States and the Soviet Union.
>
> I will allow myself to say that Gorbachev is a very good politician, but as an economist, he is probably not someone who should professionally deal with perestroika. He doesn't really have enough economic knowledge in this respect.[40]

Such statements suggested that the participants in the task force meeting were now truly able to approach issues "analytically," the ideal long subscribed to by Saunders. The Soviets had either gone outside the boundaries of ideology and political prudence or simply seen those boundaries dissolve. The Americans, in turn, were no longer compelled to respond defensively to Soviet charges or to pull their punches in suggesting changes in American policy. In neither case was the change from the preceding two or three meetings large. Nonetheless, the change became clear at this meeting and it was significant.

A related change could be seen in the way the Soviet participants discussed the influence of Soviet public opinion on foreign policy. This was particularly evident in the discussion of Cuba. No longer was Soviet policy toward Cuba described as the result of an objective determination of Soviet interests. Nor was Castro defended as the embodiment of the socialist aspirations of the Cuban people. Instead, the emotional attachment of segments of the Soviet population was held to account for Soviet policy toward Cuba:

> I think you should try to understand our emotional commitment to Cuba, our emotional investment there. It is not the KGB that is working its way there. I think Cuba's struggle deserves respect, and it has respect in our country, and we simply cannot abandon the Cubans.[41]

Similarly, emotions felt by some or all of the Soviet people were held to account for policies toward the Middle East and even Eastern Europe:

> [Y]ou must understand the sum total of our emotions and our values that are behind some of our policies—the fact that we are close to the Muslim world, the fact that Arab countries border our country, etc.
>
> Lately, perhaps within the past six months or so, isolationist

tendencies have come to the fore in the Soviet Union. To a large extent, the growth of these isolationist feelings also explains the Soviet reaction to the East European events. The Soviet Union's very calm reaction to events there otherwise would be hard to understand.[42]

The sense that Dartmouth was being left behind resulted in a set of proposals for extending the work of the Dartmouth Conference. Such proposals had not been seen since the conferences of the 1960s, when the participants were inspired by optimism about the work of the conference and a certain naïveté about what could be done. In 1989 the idea of sending a delegation from Dartmouth to Afghanistan to "look at the situation and make proposals as appropriate" was made by one Soviet speaker on the first day, seconded by another later, and referred to again on the last day of the meeting. A similar proposal was made in regard to Central America. Another proposal, made by a Soviet participant, was to have an exchange of scholars for a month or two at a time "within the framework of the Dartmouth Conference."

Participants also talked about what a model for resolving conflict in the Third World might look like and what role the two superpowers might play. The answer to the latter question was, in general, "It depends." In Angola, for example, the feeling was that the issue of Savimbi had become so politicized in the United States that resolution of the conflict should be left solely to the regional organizations involved. On the other hand, in South Africa itself, and Afghanistan as well, the participants seemed to conclude that joint action by the United States and the Soviet Union could usefully complement work done by others.

As often before, the participants in the task force were able to meet with others during and after the meeting. Several were able to meet for an hour and a half with the president of the interim government of the Afghan opposition, an important and rare point of contact between the opposition and the now-departed Soviets. The morning after the meeting ended, the entire task force met with Stremlau and his colleagues at the State Department. This meeting was followed by another with Undersecretary of State Robert Kimmett. In both these meetings the American officials raised the question of why changes in Soviet policy were less evident in the Third World than in Eastern Europe. The regional subgroups of the task force then had still another set of meetings with State Department officials with expertise on the regions.[43]

The next task force meeting took place just a month before Dartmouth XVII in the same city, Leningrad, where the plenary meeting would be held. The changes in Russia were, if anything, speeding up. Elections that spring heralded the creation of new legislatures in each of the sixteen republics that made up the Soviet Union.

But the bloom on perestroika was fading. The lack of progress in reinvigorating the economy was now evident. The 1990 elections marked the beginning of a "war of sovereignties" as the republics and regions within the Russian Federation began to contest the authority of the central government. The chief figure opposing Gorbachev, now the president of the USSR, was Boris Yeltsin, who was resurrected from political death by his election as speaker of the Supreme Soviet in Russia. No less important was Lithuania, which was leading the Baltic states in their drive for complete independence.

The American delegation was the same as the group that came to Washington in November, but sans Kitchen. The Soviet group included no one new to Dartmouth or the Regional Conflicts Task Force. Chufrin, Moskalenko, Popov, and Zviagelskaia returned. Davidson was back as well, having missed two meetings. Glinkin took the place of Mikoyan as the Soviets' expert on Latin America. The last member of the delegation was Kremenyuk, who had last come to the task force in 1985 but had been a part of the Arms Control Task Force meeting two months before (discussed later). A difference from Soviet practice in the past was that the Soviet delegation was not appreciably larger than the American, though the meeting was held in the Soviet Union.

The discussion differed in several respects from discussions at earlier meetings.[44] The main new element was the willingness of the participants to compare one conflict with another. The object of the comparison was to analyze what worked to move the conflicts toward resolution and to ask at least whether what worked in one conflict could work in another. This kind of discussion had been started in November, inspired by the success of Chester Crocker in negotiating the accords—with significant Soviet help—that gave independence to Namibia and removed the Cubans and the South Africans from Angola. The conclusion at that time was that much of what Crocker brought to the table—a long-term vision for the negotiations and the confidence of Secretary of State Shultz—was sui generis and unlikely to be readily duplicated.

The participants at the June meeting looked to Nicaragua as an example of a conflict resolved owing in part to cooperation between the United States and the Soviet Union. The Sandinistas, unexpectedly defeated in elections held in January, had voluntarily given up power to their enemies. The task force compared what had happened there with what was happening in Afghanistan and Cambodia. In the former, the PDPA and the mujahideen were still locked in battle despite the withdrawal of Soviet troops. In the latter, the withdrawal of Vietnamese troops left the Cambodian forces at loggerheads, unable to unite to form a government. In neither Afghanistan nor Cambodia was there an administrative structure regarded as legitimate enough to hold elections, even elections closely observed by outside forces. That was not the case in Nicaragua. The participants also saw differences in the roles of regional forces. President Arias of Costa Rica, among others, had fostered agreement in Nicaragua, but in Afghanistan, each country pushed for the victory of its chosen side. Also, agreement was encouraged by the cessation of aid from the superpowers to their allies in Nicaragua. But aid to both sides in Afghanistan continued.

The group looked at changes in Third World conflict now that the Cold War was ending. Once again, this was a conversation begun in November, when the southern Africa group suggested that its mandate be expanded to cover the Horn of Africa and other parts of the continent where conflicts were breaking out even as the conflicts in the south were moving toward resolution. In June the Asian group discussed the conflict in Korea for the first time, as well as Cambodia. The Central American group—Purcell and Glinkin—suggested that Panama and Cuba were likely to become more salient as the conflicts in Nicaragua and El Salvador approached an end.

Another new element was the growing perception that conflicts within the Soviet Union were subjects the task force should discuss. Earlier, the very existence of these conflicts would have been denied, but Soviet speakers now suggested that the task force address them. In addition, the Middle East group spent most of its time discussing the effects of Jewish emigration from the Soviet Union. The concern was with its influence on the Arab-Israeli conflict—the group concluded that emigration had made the Soviet Union "so intricately involved in the internal life of Israel through Jewish emigration, [that] there [was] an

intertwining of Israeli life with Soviet policy"—and with what had created the pressures that led to the emigration. The American who gave
the report in the plenary session on the discussion of the group said that
this "was the fullest discussion we've had on the interaction between
external and internal issues."

Summarizing the entire meeting, an American speaker said, "We
have moved to a new plane in our discussions of regional conflicts. We
are now talking about conflicts within countries, within regions, more
than the conflicts between the Soviet Union and the United States."
This was assuredly a reflection of the growing cooperation between the
United States and the Soviet Union as the Cold War came to an end
and the Soviet Union became increasingly preoccupied with the transformation that it was itself undergoing.

ARMS CONTROL TASK FORCE,
APRIL 1990: INTERREGNUM

The Arms Control Task Force met in late April 1990, just six months
after the Berlin Wall was demolished. The Soviet empire in Eastern
Europe had collapsed with astonishing speed, and the shape of the new
Europe was far from clear. Germany seemed to be moving toward
reunification, but it was not clear whether it would remain in NATO
as a whole, in part, or at all. Nor was it clear whether Germany would
continue to be attached to its Western partners or become an independent force working between East and West. The role the Soviet
Union would be able to play was very much in the air. How much
influence would it retain with the former satellites? How soon would
its troops withdraw? How would the continuing developments within
the Soviet Union affect its role outside?

This was an interregnum, a time between shocks, though that was
not evident at the time. The next several Dartmouth meetings reflected
what was in retrospect the contingent nature of a time when the United
States and the Soviet Union were not only trying to find their way to a
new relationship, but also entering a new time in history in which the
place of each country was uncertain. This was especially true for the
Soviet Union, where the changes that had aroused great hope from the
dawn of perestroika to the elections the previous year had turned into

the tremors—evident in Azerbaijan and Lithuania—that would make it collapse in the next. The participants in the Regional Conflicts Task Force meeting in Leningrad in June could feel these tremors; the Arms Control Task Force was confronted by their meaning.

Milstein headed the Soviet delegation; it was the first one that Arbatov had missed. General Batenin and Kokoshin were the only members of the Soviet delegation at the 1989 task force meeting to return. General Lebedev, who had made a difference to the arms control discussions at Dartmouth XV in Baku, would make a difference in these discussions as well. He had been on the USSR Armed Forces General Staff in 1986; he was now a political commentator for Novosti. Andrei Kortunov was back for the first time since Dartmouth XVI. As mentioned, Kremenyuk returned to Dartmouth for the first time in several years. He and Kokoshin, however, each attended only one of the meeting's four sessions; their compatriots were there for all.[45] Igor Malashenko, young and urbane, was an analyst serving on the staff of the Central Committee. He rose to prominence in the Russian media after the Soviet Union collapsed, becoming president of NTV, a privately owned television network that distinguished itself with its independent coverage of the war in Chechnya, and the first deputy chairman of Media-MOST, which owned NTV and other media outlets. He was also an important part of Yeltsin's 1996 presidential campaign team. The only member of the Soviet delegation completely new to Dartmouth was Peter Gladkov, an analyst at ISKAN.

The American delegation included several longtime members of the task force. Doty, again the chairman, was joined by Stewart, Chayes, Horelick, Jones, and Meyer. Ed Warner was back for the first time since 1987. New members included Phillip Karber, a vice president at BDM Corporation, a defense consulting firm, and General Harold Todd, a former commandant of the Air War College. Kurt Campbell had been the rapporteur for the 1984 meeting on southern Africa. A graduate student at that time, he joined the Arms Control Task Force while special assistant to the director of political-military affairs in the Pentagon. Congressman John Spratt, a Democrat from South Carolina with a strong interest in foreign affairs, spoke at the opening dinner the night before the meeting commenced and attended the first three sessions.[46] Congress was also represented by Robert Bell, a member of the staff of the Senate Committee on Arms Control.

By including Spratt, Campbell, and Bell, the task force gained unusual access to the U.S. government. This access was strengthened by a two-hour visit to the Office of the Joint Chiefs in the middle of the meeting. The group was received by General Harold Graves, special assistant to the chairman of the Joint Chiefs, and Stephen Hadley, assistant secretary for International Security Policy of the Department of Defense. According to Doty, there was "quite a good discussion where the Soviets put forward their concerns."[47] A few hours later, at their dinner that night, the group was joined and addressed by Arnold Kantor, senior director for arms control and policy at the National Security Council, a man on whom Scowcroft leaned heavily.[48] Steve Flanagan, a State Department official, opened a discussion the group held on future political arrangements in Europe. He heard the Soviet participants express their concern about the future of NATO and complaints about his own presentation, which, it seemed to the Soviets, left no place in a new Europe for the Soviet Union.[49]

The discussion during the task force meetings continued the trend of the past few meetings by focusing less on the strategic nuclear balance and more on security issues in Europe.[50] Participants also covered conventional arms, then the subject of the Conventional Forces in Europe (CFE) negotiations. They spent one session, but little more, discussing strategic arms, which had been the central topic for the Dartmouth discussions on arms control going back to Dartmouth I. Even these other sessions, however, drifted back to questions about the security structure that might be formed in the new, postcommunist Europe.

Curiously, the discussions of arms control agreements focused little on the agreements then being negotiated. The negotiations on CFE and START I, the participants seemed to believe, had gone too far for the task force discussions to be useful; the agreements were already fixed in outline. Instead, they discussed what CFE II and START II might look like.

In regard to the latter, they thought that the 6,000-warhead limits for each side expected to be in START I would be brought down to between 2,000 and 5,000. At these lower levels, they thought, the other nuclear powers might have to be brought into the talks—the lower numbers increased the significance of the smaller arsenals of France, Britain, and China. These lower numbers might, paradoxically, call for higher expenditures, as the two countries might have to restructure their forces to keep the balance of forces stable in the new strategic environment. They also discussed the implications for the proliferation of nuclear arms and what that meant for ballistic missile defense (BMD). Some Americans argued that BMD might be more necessary for both sides to defend against attacks by the likes of Iraq or Israel, prefiguring the debate that would run through the late 1990s into the new century.

The path the CFE Treaty would follow was less clear, and the recommendations given at the task force meeting reflected this. One was to have CFE II focus on qualitative restrictions, rather than the quantitative reductions that were expected to be in the agreement then being negotiated. An American proposal was to have the agreement put limits on reserve forces. A Soviet speaker suggested that the next agreement should simply formalize the changes taking place without trying to do more. It was also recognized that the format of new CFE negotiations would be different, owing to the collapse of the Soviet bloc. Rather than negotiations between two blocs, they would be negotiations among numerous countries. Hungary was already pushing the talks in that direction.

The participants examined the influence that different institutions might have in a new Europe. Several believed that the United Nations and the European Community would become more important. Some speakers found the Conference on Security and Cooperation in Europe (CSCE) weakened by its reliance on unanimity in making decisions. A Soviet speaker argued that

> [CSCE decision making] was much easier in the early 1970s when nations were divided into two blocs. There was a degree of discipline and hierarchy. . . . the CSCE framework will have more symbolic Pan-European meaning, rather than operational meaning.

They agreed that the Warsaw Pact would change, though it was not clear to all that it would disappear. One Soviet speaker, for example, argued, "its shell will continue, since nobody is really interested in publicly destroying existing structures, even if they are only symbolic." Another argued that the pact could offer the Eastern European states insurance to guarantee the "territorial status quo" against the revanchism that was bound to erupt in the wake of 1989. An American found that the most practical arrangement for the future would combine elements of the structures of the Warsaw Pact and NATO. Another Soviet speaker said bluntly that as "a practical matter, the Warsaw Pact has ceased to exist."

The future place of NATO in Europe was less clear to the participants. Several speakers believed that NATO would disappear, albeit more slowly than the Warsaw Pact, as its raison d'être—the Soviet threat—was fading away. There was little anxiety expressed by the Soviet participants about a threat to the Soviet Union, possibly because there seemed to be agreement on both sides that the military aspects of the alliance would become less important than the political. One Soviet speaker saw "NATO as the transitory mechanism to [a] new security system in Europe. In the context of balance of power," he continued, "NATO may be the best adapted mechanism for ensuring a stable transition."[51] A suggestion was made by a Soviet speaker that "joint organizations might emerge from NATO and the Warsaw Pact and carry out common action to avoid military conflicts."[52]

The idea of NATO expansion into Eastern Europe was brought up, though the danger from this was not thought significant. The Soviets showed little concern, although one looked on the inclusion of a united Germany—expansion of NATO "to the Oder"—as a provocation. An American said, "I think most East European countries, in their heart of hearts, have no interest in joining NATO." The entire discussion seemed predicated on the sense that the division of Europe into East and West would remain, with the Soviet Union continuing to have a strong influence on the East.

The most important unknown that lay behind the discussions, greater than the future of Eastern Europe and the place of Germany in the new system, a shadow not always discussed but, it seemed, always present, was the future of the Soviet Union. Participants spoke of the uncertainty of that future and of economic crisis. In one impressive presentation in the final session, a Soviet speaker foresaw, as few did at the time, what the future would hold.[53] Democratization, he said, was being tried as a source of legitimacy to replace the communist ideology and its party, but it could not hold the country together. Consequently, he concluded, "Those parts of the Soviet Union which were acquired as a result of imperial conquest and held together by force will inevitably separate from the Soviet Union."

It is a measure of how inconceivable were the changes that took place between 1989 and 1991 that, despite his perceptive analysis of the problems of the Soviet Union, this speaker then said, and no one disagreed, "I am sure that the core who will remain will be viable." Indeed, one reads the transcript of this meeting feeling that the Soviets especially, but the Americans, too, pulled the punches of their analysis. They seemed to believe that the complete collapse of the Soviet Union and the end of its influence in Eastern Europe were extreme outcomes, and so unlikely. They were not alone in this, and like the prescient Soviet speaker referred to above, they probably understood things better than most.

There was a brief but important discussion of the Soviet army. The Americans asked the Soviets what the condition of the Soviet army was, and the Soviets responded that it remained good. But the exchange was distinguished by the Soviet insistence that the army would have to become professional and cease relying solely on conscripts. This was a position held by Soviet military reformers but opposed stubbornly then and now by the Soviet military leadership.[54]

Now that the existence of Soviet public opinion was recognized, as it had been at least since the elections held the previous year, the Soviet participants referred to the influence of public opinion many times. These references were reminiscent of views expressed by American participants at Dartmouth meetings in the past. They cited no polls but gave their perceptions of how the Soviet public would react to changes in security policy. The public opinion they saw was conservative, suspicious of changes in the balance of forces between the United States and the Soviet Union, and reluctant to sanction changes of any kind in the strategic nuclear relationship.

DARTMOUTH XVII: THE TWILIGHT CONFERENCE

Dartmouth XVII was the last Dartmouth Conference plenary. It was fitting that Norman Cousins took part in it, four months before he died on November 30, 1990, a little more than thirty years after the first Dartmouth Conference convened in New Hampshire. Planning for the seventeenth conference began more than a year before, in

January 1989, when Stewart and Mathews exchanged letters with Arbatov discussing possible changes in the agenda, structure, and mission of the Dartmouth Conference. A meeting in New York with Arbatov and Plekhanov, discussions among the Americans, and communications with Soviets produced an agenda similar to older ones and a format that differed significantly from those used before. And so the conference began in July.

It opened in confusion. Many of the American delegates found their flight to Helsinki delayed by bad weather. Their connections lost, they took the train from Helsinki to Leningrad's Finland Station, arriving at the conference about thirty hours late. The twenty-five-person delegation was a mix of Dartmouth veterans and new faces. Besides Cousins, the former included Mathews and Stewart, Saunders and Neumann, Doty and Chayes. Flora Lewis took part in her first Dartmouth dialogue since Dartmouth XIV in 1984. The other Dartmouth veterans included John Buchanan, Robert Lundeen, Rob Nelson, and William Luers, president of the Metropolitan Museum of Art and former ambassador to Czechoslovakia and Venezuela. Among the veterans one can also include interpreters Sherry and Klebnikov.

The new faces included the granddaughter of President Eisenhower and the daughter of Robert Kennedy. Susan Eisenhower was president of the Eisenhower Group; Kathleen Kennedy Townsend was director of the Maryland Student Service Alliance. She has since been twice elected deputy governor of Maryland. Several people close to the Kettering Foundation also came: Katherine Fanning, a former editor of the *Christian Science Monitor;* Robert Lehman, who had become president of the Fetzer Institute; and Edwin Dorn, then with the Joint Center for Political and Economic Studies. Other newcomers especially worthy of note were S. Frederick Starr, a highly respected expert on Soviet affairs who was president of Oberlin College; Lawrence Korb of the Brookings Institution; and Larry D. Welch, who had recently retired as Air Force Chief of Staff.

The Soviet delegation included twenty-six participants. Arbatov was back to serve as the Soviet cochair. This was his first Dartmouth meeting in over a year, though he had met with people from the Kettering Foundation the previous November to plan Dartmouth XVII. He had, according to Susan Eisenhower, undergone "a process of radicalization," evident in the second Congress of People's Deputies, which had met the previous December. Roald Sagdeev, who had also been elected, told Eisenhower that "Arbatov acted like a kamikaze pilot," attacking the military during the discussion of the military budget.[55] His attacks continued in print after the Congress was over; the military responded in kind. Arbatov explained to Stewart why he became estranged from the Soviet military. Marshal Akhromeev, he said, lied to him directly about the real nature of the Bratsk ABM radar system, saying that it was used only for space exploration. Arbatov claimed that after his break with the military his reputation and even his life were threatened.[56]

In addition to Arbatov, the Dartmouth veterans included Zhurkin, Chufrin, Grachev, Kortunov, Mikhailov, Milstein, and Sagdeev. Also returning to Dartmouth were Lukin, who was now the chairman of the Foreign Affairs Committee of the Russian Supreme Soviet, and Shmelev, who, like Arbatov, was a deputy in the Soviet Congress of People's Deputies. Borovikh, president of the Peace Committee, was also a deputy. The newcomers included Otto Latsis, deputy editor in chief of *Kommunist*, the CPSU's main theoretical journal; Mikhail Berger and Stanislav Kondrashov, commentators for *Izvestiya;* and Yegor Gaidar, then a commentator for *Pravda,* but later prime minister and architect of Russian economic policy in the early years following the Soviet collapse. Andrei Kozyrev, a rising star at the Foreign Ministry who would become foreign minister of the Russian Republic later that year, was a late addition to the list of Soviet participants.[57]

Retired major general Valeri Larionov was prominent among military reformers and a collaborator with Kokoshin.[58] Nikolai Vorontsov was chairman of the USSR's State Committee for the Protection of Nature, responsible for environmental issues. Alberts Kauls, chairman of Latvia's Union of Peasants, was, like Shmelev, a deputy in the Congress of People's Deputies and a member of the USSR Presidential Council, formed by Gorbachev in the spring, after he was elected president of the USSR. He was the only representative of a non-Russian republic on the Soviet delegation. He had also taken part in Dartmouth XVI. Natalia Yeniseevna, a deputy of the Leningrad Oblast Soviet, stood out as one "who seemed to spout conventional CPSU ideology."[59] She was the only woman among the Soviet participants.[60]

The conference eventually took a form that purposely resembled the format adopted by the Regional Conflicts Task Force—plenary sessions surrounding a series of meetings of smaller groups. Unlike at Dartmouth XVI, which also had this format, the small groups were not the task forces that had been meeting between conferences. Instead, one group discussed security and global issues, another political relations and democracy. The third group, however, discussed regional conflicts and was, in effect, a version of the task force. Originally, a fourth group was to have discussed economics and trade, as at Austin, but it did not meet.

The meeting addressed the topics that had become usual to Dartmouth.[61] The summary of the conference lists five as paramount. Two could have appeared in some form on the agenda of any Dartmouth Conference—"international security and global issues" and "U.S.-Soviet cooperation in regional conflicts." A third topic, the future of the Dartmouth Conference, had been on the minds of participants since détente expanded the range of contacts between the United States and the Soviet Union. But the fourth and fifth topics, "domestic trends which shape the U.S.-Soviet relationship" and "the state of the Soviet economy and the potential for U.S.-Soviet economic relations" had an importance and foci that they could not have had before.

At earlier conferences, participants had talked about domestic politics, particularly in the United States, and the Americans had often made the point, not always heard, that domestic politics mattered. The state of the economies of the two countries was also a frequent topic of the discussions. But with the Soviet Union in turmoil, domestic politics and economics, particularly within the Soviet Union, had an importance that they never had before Dartmouth XVI. They now had an unprecedented urgency. Domestic conditions were discussed with candor and "a complete absence [of] ideological dogma and with a common effort to think together on the important issues facing both countries." The conference summary noted that

> [t]he remarkable level of communication, which was established between the U.S. and the Soviets in 1988, has now moved from the simple and forthright communication of each other's concerns for various bilateral and multilateral issues to a genuine commonality of

concern, with much greater attention to the increasingly multilateral nature of our future relations.

Such changes had been seen to some extent in the task forces, but the dialogue in the task forces had not focused as much on events inside the Soviet Union or the United States. Some aspects of the dialogue at Dartmouth XVII disturbed Kingston, who had come to the conference as an observer. He found that

> [t]he Soviets persistently refused to expose or explore the nature of and the reasons for their predicament, insisting, rather, on the immediacy of their interest in a solution. We, in turn, in our performance on the dais, in a precisely complementary fashion, insisted on our inability to share the concern that they had refused to articulate.

There was, he saw, an imbalance of concern. However severe the problems of the United States might have been, they were dwarfed by those that confronted the Soviets. This was a period in which many Soviets were willing, even eager, to listen to advice given by Americans, but they rarely had a model—an understanding—of their own circumstances into which they could mold the American suggestions comfortably and with confidence. Dorn described the approach of the Soviet participants to their ethnic conflicts:

> Our hosts were not eager to discuss the nationality movements and ethnic conflicts that have emerged in several of the republics. Their reticence seemed to spring less from a desire to conceal, than from a momentary speechlessness that immediately follows surprise.[62]

The discussions of even familiar topics took some twists from what might have been expected. The discussion of the Soviet economy seemed to focus on "the ruble overhang," regarded by many in 1990 as one of the most threatening problems facing the Soviet economy. It came about simply because Soviet consumers had too few goods to spend their wages on, and the inability of the Soviet price system to respond with a rise in prices meant that these rubles disappeared into savings, threatening to appear in an inflation-producing flood if the restraints on prices were lifted. The Soviet economists who addressed the issue in Leningrad proposed either that consumer goods be imported—this was the proposal Shmelev explained in Austin—or that state property be sold. In the end, eighteen months later, an inflationary flood washed the overhang away.

The discussions of both global security and domestic trends addressed environmental concerns. The place of environmental issues in U.S.-Soviet relations, and the recognition that they were a matter of mutual concern, had been a topic for discussion at the Dartmouth conferences of the mid-1970s, but not since (curiously, not even after Chernobyl). But the implications for democracy of a concern with the environment were discussed for the first time at Dartmouth XVII. Some commonalities were found between the two countries, such as the distrust environmental movements have of authorities. An American also suggested that democracy can provide ways to distribute environmental risk, citing a case in which workers in West Virginia voted to accept risk that others might consider too high. But they also concluded that the Soviet public was much less aware of environmental issues than the public in the West. The link in the Soviet Union between environmental and ethnic issues was also noted.[63]

As at earlier conferences, there was a lively exchange of information away from the official session. Doty's notes from the conference give a rare glimpse into the kinds of conversations that took place. His interlocutors gave him extensive insider views of people and positions. Doty wrote that Yeltsin has given "a few trusted people including Arbatov [authority to speak for him] . . . Yeltsin has just named a recent Ph.D. from ISKAN to a high economic position [this was Boris Fedorov—JV] . . . [Akhromeyev is now] his old conservative self . . . the Central Committee is losing power rapidly . . . Arbatov is happy to be off it; Zhurkin is apprehensive about being on it . . . some talk of rebuilding the Russian Academy of Science, but this is unlikely . . . rumors that Shevardnadze will be switched to domestic duties are false."[64] Several people also pressed on him their views about an issue of current importance in the U.S.-Soviet relationship, presumably with the hope or expectation that he would pass their arguments along to others in the United States. In this case, Soviet participants argued strongly that the United States should allow U.S. West to lay a fiber-optic cable across Russia. They said that the issue was a test of U.S.-Soviet relations, that the United States would gain little from not permitting the cable, and that it was a critical need for the Soviet Union from which the United States would benefit.

At his last Dartmouth conference, Norman Cousins made contributions that were notable both for the perspective he offered on Dartmouth's history and for his efforts to build bridges between the Americans and the Soviets. He told about the tensions that had gripped Dartmouth III. At a meeting with the mayor of Leningrad, Anatoli Sobchak, a prominent reformer at the time, Cousins, "so shy that he sits here in the back row," according to Mathews, spoke about the "committees of correspondence" of colonial times in America as a kind of joint venture that the two sides could engage in as a means of building democracy.[65] In the last plenary meeting he again drew on American history—the difficulties that the newborn United States faced after its revolution—to suggest a way of understanding the current travails of the Soviet Union and to show the need for patience.[66] Speaking earlier in the meeting, he echoed many other American participants in saying that the Soviet Union could not count on the United States for assistance; the problems the United States faced were such that many Americans thought their country could not give whatever support the Soviets believed they needed. But, he continued, "the nature of our society is such that there are always times when the citizens have to lead the government. I suspect that one of those times is now."[67]

For thirty years, the Dartmouth conferences and other exchanges with the Soviet Union were organized on the basis of a simple quid pro quo. The hosts made and paid for all arrangements for the visitors once they arrived in their country; the visitors returned the favor when they became hosts. This had long worked well for both sides. Arguably, the Americans often had the better end of the deal as they faced financial constraints for conferences in the United States that their Soviet partners did not on conferences in the Soviet Union. This was one reason why until Dartmouth XVI only one American plenary conference had been held away from the East Coast, but the Soviets, enjoying, in effect, full funding through the Soviet Peace Committee, treated the Americans to conferences in the Crimea and the Caucasus. It also explains why the Soviet delegations at Dartmouth I and III rode to the conference by bus rather than using more luxurious means of transportation.

By 1990, however, the economic reforms put into place by Gorbachev beginning in 1987 were having an effect on Soviet institutions of all kinds. The emphasis put on self-financing meant that institutions such as ISKAN and the Soviet Peace Committee had to begin to scramble for funds themselves. It also meant that the costs of transportation, hotels, and the like had begun to rise. Moreover, party-oriented institutions such as the Soviet Peace Committee were suffering from the exodus from the Communist Party that took place after March 1990, when the Soviet parliament took away the party's monopoly on power. That exodus deprived these organizations not only of members, but also of the dues the members paid.

These changes had their effect on Dartmouth XVII. On the night of July 24, in the middle of the conference, Kingston sat down and wrote in passionate disappointment at what he saw happening:

> At least for the time being, the Dartmouth Conferences as we have known them are finished. It is now apparent that Arbatov commands neither the people, nor the budget, nor the intellectual focus to sustain them.[68]

After the conference, in late August, Mathews sent a telex to Arbatov and Borovikh outlining some ideas about the future of Dartmouth. He suggested that the work of the Regional Conflicts Task Force continue and that two new task forces be formed. One would be the perennially discussed task force on economics; the other would work on issues of civil society. He suggested that a "Dartmouth plenary council" be formed and meet regularly. But, he wrote, "plenaries on the old scale" would not be appropriate.

REGIONAL CONFLICTS TASK FORCE, DECEMBER 1990–JULY 1991: STEPPING PAST THE COLD WAR

The Regional Conflicts Task Force met again at the beginning of December. It had become the most active of the Dartmouth dialogues, continuing to meet twice each year. The Arms Control Task Force met only once each year; the Political Relations Task Force was moribund. Efforts were being made to put together a task force to discuss problems of civil society in both the United States and the USSR, but these began only after the topic was discussed at Dartmouth XVII. Antonia Chayes, a long-standing member of the Arms Control Task Force, wrote after

Dartmouth XVII that the Regional Conflicts Task Force was clearly doing well and that it "had its own agenda and relationships."[69]

This was due both to the active intellectual leadership given to the group by Saunders and to the continuity of membership, which was particularly striking on the American side. Five Americans had been to every meeting going back to 1986, save the third meeting on Africa. Three—Saunders, Stewart, and Neumann, half the task force—had been to almost all the meetings held since 1983, and Purcell and Gouttierre had not missed a meeting in which their region was discussed since they joined. Stewart was not at the meeting in December 1990—it was the first he had missed—but the other four were, joined by Kitchen and Romberg, who were themselves becoming regular members of the group.[70]

The continuity was not as strong on the Soviet side, in part because much of the membership changed when Primakov left. But Moskalenko and Davidson had taken part in most of the meetings over the past four years, and Saunders had formed a sturdy relationship with Chufrin, one valued by both men. Popov had been at the two previous meetings and Zviagelskaya at the past three. Glinkin and Shumikhin, both of whom were also veterans, joined the other five at the December meeting. This continuity meant that at each meeting the dialogue could begin where the last one had left off. There was no need to build trust with a stranger or to discover the views and habits of thought of the new interlocutor. It was, therefore, easier to build the dialogue into a tool that could probe the issues in the U.S.-Soviet relationship more deeply.

At the time the task force met at Westfields that December the Soviet Union continued to be troubled, with several republics declaring their sovereignty (not to be confused with independence, but a menacing development to those who favored a strong central government). The CFE Treaty was signed and Germany was formally unified. Overshadowing these events, however, was the crisis brewing in the Persian Gulf. Iraq's invasion of Kuwait at the end of July was met with a military buildup along the Kuwaiti border in Saudi Arabia, led by the United States.

The format of the meeting was much the same as it had been in June. As before, the state of conflicts in the Middle East, southern Africa, Latin America, Southeast Asia, and Afghanistan was explored by subgroups that met after the opening plenary session and then by the task force as a whole after the subgroups reported back. The subgroups were charged, among other things, with discussing whether their dialogue and the discussions of the task force as a whole should be broadened in future meetings. Indeed, they thought it should, particularly given that the end of the Cold War and developments in particular regions had either changed the nature of the conflicts at issue or led to their resolution.

The conflict in Nicaragua was seen as largely solved, but Purcell and Glinkin thought other kinds of conflicts throughout Latin America were now more likely. New conflicts might arise over drug trafficking, for example, or over territorial claims where natural resources such as oil were at stake. They thought that their group might focus on El Salvador and Cuba as places where conflict continued and opportunities for cooperation might arise.[71] Kitchen and Davidson saw that the conflicts in South Africa and Angola had become primarily domestic in nature. They suggested that in the future it would be fruitful to focus on the Horn of Africa.[72] Gouttierre found a continuing stalemate in Afghanistan as the local parties, still receiving arms from outside, seemed disinclined to come to agreement with one another. He saw real danger of conflict between India and Pakistan. He also described instability in the countries of South Asia that stemmed from "issues of uncommon civil strife" from such things as differences in economic status, religion, and caste. He thought it time, therefore, to put the discussion of Afghanistan in its larger South Asian context.[73]

The central focus of the work of the task force, however, was the developing crisis in the Persian Gulf. The discussion provided one more example of how the nature of discussions between Americans and Soviets, particularly those taking part in this task force, had changed. It might have been expected that the Soviets would use the opportunity to complain about American actions against a state widely seen as a Soviet client or that the Americans would complain about Soviet actions that might have been seen as excusing a blatant act of aggression. But that did not happen. The positions of the participants in the task force mirrored the official positions of their countries, whose cooperation made it possible to use the United Nations against Iraq.

Instead of using the meeting as a forum for complaint, the task force approached the conflict "analytically." Participants discussed it in its context in the region, looking at its implications for the conflict between Israel and the Palestinians. Both Americans and Soviets found the two conflicts interrelated. They also discussed the charismatic appeal of Saddam Hussein through the Arab world and the influence he had on Arab nationalism.

The group discussed the use of force in the Gulf and other conflicts. All regarded force as a legitimate option, to be used when other options were exhausted. At least one American questioned whether the United States had paid enough attention to other options. The question of a Soviet contribution to the coalition produced a variety of answers. No Soviet speaker said the Soviet Union should not contribute; more than one said it could not. This was largely owing to constraints found within the Soviet Union, the nature of which was not entirely clear to the Americans.

The discussion on the United Nations was particularly timely, owing to that organization's role in efforts to turn back Iraq. Its potential role in conflicts in Europe was examined as well, covering ground touched on by the Arms Control Task Force in the spring. The speakers seemed to conclude that conflicts in Europe would be settled through actions by the CSCE or the United Nations, though the former was hampered by operating in the shadow of the more powerful NATO.

A central focus of the discussions was the lessons that could be learned from the past cooperation between the superpowers. This topic was discussed by the smaller groups as well as in the plenary sessions. Three lessons were found. The first was that the improvement in communications between the United States and the Soviet Union improved the prospects for settling a conflict. Afghanistan offered an important example of this. The second was that there was a relationship between domestic affairs within the superpowers and their ability to cooperate in regional conflicts. The third was that the United States and the Soviet Union tended to move a conflict toward resolution before putting it in the context of international diplomacy, a tendency that in fact made a stable resolution of the conflict more difficult to achieve.

At the next meeting, in July 1991 in Moscow, the cast of characters again changed but little. Purcell was not there, but her place was taken by Rob Nelson, the reporter for the *Christian Science Monitor* who had been at the conferences in Austin and Leningrad. He was now an anchor and executive producer with MONITORADIO. On the Soviet side, the delegation was somewhat larger than usual, as often happened when a meeting took place in Moscow. Shumikhin did not return, but Naumkin did, for his first meeting since November 1989. Also appearing were Rogov, Filin, for the Soviet Peace Committee, and G. A. Kuznetsov, a vice president of the Soviet Peace Committee.

By now the task force was beginning to deal with issues left by the end of the Cold War. The truth was that regional conflicts were no longer an important source of tension between the United States and the Soviet Union. Nor were they among the major issues in the relationship, to judge by the issues discussed at the summit meeting between Gorbachev and Bush that came two weeks after the task force meeting.[74] Cooperation between the two superpowers had been successful in fostering resolution of some conflicts, though cooperation in other conflicts had proved difficult to come by. This task force meeting looked at why and where cooperation might occur and what constraints it faced elsewhere.

The Middle East subgroup noted that in the Middle East, "the new aspects of the Soviet-American relationship are not comparable to the great achievements on the global level, such as those in Europe and in arms control. There have been no similar developments like this in the Middle East." Even cooperation during the Persian Gulf crisis was "somewhat troubled by the misunderstanding of some people in the United States" and apprehension in the Soviet Union about American actions. The task force also found elements of competition remaining in Afghanistan.

One characteristic of the discussions in the plenary meetings and the small groups was that they focused primarily on conditions within the regions and far less on the interests and policies of the United States and the Soviet Union. In general, the two superpowers were much less important to the conflicts than they had been a decade before. This was true even in Afghanistan. American and Soviet support for their allies in the conflict continued, but, as an American speaker noted, with decreasing interest on both sides. The question of cooperation, therefore, was less whether it was needed for the resolution of a conflict than whether it would be helpful. Kitchen and Davidson, in their discussions of southern Africa, thought "examples of coordinated US-Soviet encouragement of conflict resolution as well as separate but compatible initiatives in South Africa, are major contributions to Africa's future prospects." Yet the disengagement of the two superpowers following the end of their Cold War rivalry encouraged "Africans to take on greater responsibility in the area[s] of conflicts resolution and economic integration than at any previous time in the post-colonial era."

Several participants mentioned the influence of the past as a significant barrier to cooperation. This influence could be seen in continuing support for old allies, such as Cuba, who, it was felt, could not simply be turned aside. Another influence was residual fears and suspicions about the other side. These could be seen plainly during the Persian Gulf War in Soviet commentaries about American military actions so close to the Soviet border and the hostile reaction of many Americans to Soviet efforts to forestall the outbreak of war.

Another factor mentioned as a barrier to cooperation was the influence of interest groups in both countries, such as the Florida Cubans and the Israeli lobby in the United States. This led to a continuation of the discussion of the influence of public opinion on Soviet foreign policy. The Americans said they knew the mechanisms through which public opinion influenced American policy but had little understanding of how the public influenced Soviet foreign policy. Their interlocutors could not give a precise answer to the question but noted the importance of elements of civil society such as organizations of veterans of Afghanistan, who were effective in, among other things, making it difficult for the Soviet government to consider sending troops against Iraq.

Participants also discussed how to broaden the impact of the task force. They were told about requests from people in the Middle East and American ambassadors in South Asia for information about the potential of a Dartmouth-style dialogue in their regions. Chufrin and Saunders had agreed to write an article based on the deliberations of the task force. They asked for and got much advice about what the article might include. Other suggestions were given as well. The most notable was the idea of sending a group on something of a fact-finding tour of the Middle East, similar to the earlier idea of sending a group to Afghanistan. Most members of the task force favored this idea, although some questioned whether such a group would be able to learn much more than what had already been taken away from the task force discussions.

Midway through the meeting, several members of the task force spoke for an hour with Primakov, who was now a senior advisor to Gorbachev. He had been prominent in Soviet efforts to broker a resolution of the crisis in the Gulf before war broke out. These efforts had caused some consternation in Washington. He explained them to Saunders and the others. One of them reported to the task force that afternoon:

> [Primakov] recognized that Saddam Hussein was working from a variety of self-generated illusions about the situation, miscalculations which were wrong on almost every count—what the US would do, what the Soviets would do, what other Arabs would do, and what the consequences of going to war would be. Primakov was very aware of the kind of personality he was dealing with, but it's one of those cases where people working from different assumptions come to different conclusions.

Primakov also said that he did not believe that his efforts were being held against the Soviets by the American government as "the Soviet-US relationship is really dominated by larger considerations than a single episode."

ARMS CONTROL AND REGIONAL CONFLICTS TASK FORCES, OCTOBER AND DECEMBER 1991: "I DON'T KNOW WHAT COUNTRY IT IS NOW"

After July the Arms Control and Regional Conflicts Task Forces each met once more before the Soviet Union dissolved. They found the Soviet Union still alive but shrunken, with its survival in doubt. Looking back from the December meeting of the Regional Conflicts Task Force, Davidson remarked: "Never in the history of the Dartmouth Conference have there occurred such major events in the world as during the interval between last July and now."[75] In that time the August 1991 coup had shattered the Soviet Union. The independence of the Baltic states, declared shortly after the coup, had been recognized by the international community. Ukraine had voted in favor of its own independence days before the meeting opened. The monumental changes even included a decree that for a time outlawed the Soviet Communist Party. In Moscow

Doty found sullen crowds, fear of crime, a growing economic crisis that fueled rising inflation, and a drop in production that "already exceeds that in our Great Depression."[76] The end of the Cold War had long been recognized; the world, and Dartmouth, had to consider the prospect of a post-Soviet era.

Doty was in Moscow in October 1991 for the meeting of the Arms Control Task Force. His Soviet counterpart was not Arbatov this time, but Rogov. A brilliant analyst and, it turned out, influential in the Soviet and Russian governments at the time, Rogov had just been appointed deputy director of ISKAN. But he made a terrible impression on the Americans in his first turn as task force cochairman.[77] Nonetheless, participants found the meeting useful. It was both "unusually interesting" and appears to have had an exceptional influence on arms control negotiations.

The American delegation was largely made up of people who had taken part in the meeting in Washington the previous year—Doty, Campbell, Chayes, Horelick, Meyer, and Warner. Blackwill returned after his stint in government to add his expertise on conventional forces. Buchanan rounded out the delegation, joining the arms control task force for the first time.

The number of Soviet participants was much greater, although, as usual, few stayed through all the sessions. Only Kokoshin, Kremenyuk, and Milstein had been at the previous meeting, in April 1990. Aleksei Arbatov returned to the task force for the first time since 1985. Mikhailov and Konovalov had been at the meeting in 1989. Larionov had been at Dartmouth XVII. Aside from Rogov, the rest of the twenty-one Soviet participants were new to Dartmouth. They included two colleagues of Aleksei Arbatov at IMEMO, Gennadi K. Lednev and Yuri Pichukov; several officers from something called the Center for Operational Strategic Studies, including a deputy director, Vsevelod Medvedev; Grigori Berdennikov, a deputy head of the Department of Arms Control and Disarmament of the Soviet Foreign Ministry; Vitali V. Shlykov, deputy chairman of the Armed Services Committee of the Russian Federation; and several officers from the Soviet Ministry of Defense.

In some respects the dialogue resembled the discussions held in the task force two or three years before. The control of nuclear arms and ballistic missile defense was more prominent than the context for security policy in Europe or even the balance of conventional arms. But, of course, the context was different. The Soviet participants wanted to go beyond the 50 percent cut in nuclear weapons embodied in START I, signed in July. They spoke of demilitarization and wanted help to do it. According to Doty, even the generals wanted American help for this. They also wanted help in the destruction of nuclear weapons, insisting that it was critical to keep the costs minimal, with jointly monitored storage of the weapons as the fallback position if costs remained too high. There was also great concern expressed about Ukraine, which had scheduled a referendum on independence for December 1, just six weeks away. It was one of four republics where nuclear weapons were based. The Soviets faced the problem of extracting those weapons if the republics seceded. As the Soviet Union splintered, problems also arose in the implementation of the CFE Treaty.

After the meeting, the Americans met for an hour with Marshal Evgeni Shaposhnikov, Soviet minister of defense, appointed after the August coup, which he been instrumental in foiling. Doty found him charming, in contrast to his predecessor, Dmitri Yazov. Doty wrote that "[t]his [meeting] went very well and at the end he apparently told Rogov to discuss their plans for further arms reduction with some of us in order to convey their thinking to the US administration."[78] Rogov then met twice with Doty and told him "the post-START material was well developed, that Shaposhnikov had told him, 'This is the way I want to go.'" In their second meeting, Rogov read a brief that was to go to Gorbachev that day.

Doty wrote up his notes on the meetings with Rogov and sent them to Scowcroft. Scowcroft, in turn, himself had "an extended meeting" with Rogov.[79] Ideas that strongly resembled the ideas about strategic arms reductions in the memorandum that Doty sent to Scowcroft were included in the proposals President Bush made in January in the State of the Union address. Both the memorandum and the address proposed that MIRVed missiles be banned in exchange for limitations on nuclear weapons deployed on bombers and Trident submarines, two types of forces in which the United States had an advantage.[80] Yeltsin's response came shortly after. He proposed larger reductions, which may also have shown the influence of the ideas found in the memorandum to Scowcroft. These proposals became the basis for START II, signed by Yeltsin and Bush in January 1993.

No member of the Regional Conflicts Task Force who came to Westfields in December 1991 was new to it, and with only five Americans and seven Soviets, the group might be considered to be the core of the task force as of the end of the Soviet era. The Americans were Saunders, Neumann, Gouttierre, Kitchen, and Romberg; the Soviets, Chufrin, Davidson, Glinkin, Popov, Moskalenko, Naumkin, and Zviagelskaia. Unlike in July, however, they all now came from institutes of the Russian Academy of Sciences; the Soviet Academy was no more.

Saunders and Chufrin had met four times to draft the paper that had been discussed in July and to prepare for the December meeting, but events had put their agenda in a new context. This was made clear in the first meeting on the first day. Chufrin, summarizing events in the Soviet Union, declared: "The Soviet Union, as it has been known to the world, has completely and irrevocably ceased to exist."[81] Soon after, Davidson added: "What has come to an end is not only the Soviet Union, but the Russian empire created by Peter I at the beginning of the eighteenth century." Most seemed to believe that some form of union would be retained, but it was clear to no one what would take the place of the Soviet Union. That uncertainty pervaded the meeting.

Everyone understood that the ability of the Soviet Union to influence regional conflicts had fallen. So had interest in those conflicts in both the Soviet Union and the United States. A major question was what role could the Soviet Union still play. That role could still be significant in regions where the Soviet Union still had interests. Moreover, countries in the Middle East and South Asia would still want the Soviet Union to be active in their region. The Arabs wanted the Soviet Union involved because of lingering suspicions of the United States. Asian countries such as Sri Lanka and Thailand saw the Soviet Union "as playing the role of a counterweight, not against the United States per se, but as a broker between new players in the area," according to a Soviet speaker. The speaker had just visited Southeast Asia and was told many times that the situation was "evolving in such a way that the role of the Soviet Union as a balancing factor [was] more important now for those countries than for the Soviet Union itself."

All four groups examined what they thought the new structure of power in the world might mean for their region. For Africa, given the lack of importance of Africa to the Soviet Union, little had changed since July, but the other three groups, which dealt with regions close to the Soviet borders, had to wrestle with the implications of a diminished Soviet Union. The Middle Eastern and South Asian groups discussed the influence that countries in their regions might have on the "former underbelly of the Soviet Union," made up of the republics of the Caucasus and Central Asia that as they spoke still remained in the Soviet Union (they would leave it a week or two later). As one American speaker put it, "the issues surrounding ethnic groups within the Soviet Union [seem] to represent a stick of dynamite that is a little closer to the fire." A Soviet speaker saw that underbelly being "integrated into the Middle East." The Southeast Asian group barely touched on Cambodia but discussed the Korean peninsula at length, particularly problems arising from the potential for North Korea to create nuclear weapons. They concluded that a solution to the problem required "decisive, programmatic Soviet-American action."

More than one speaker referred to the rising tide of ethnic or national feeling and the growing importance of this factor in spawning conflict around the globe, in Africa, Yugoslavia, and elsewhere, including places in the Soviet Union. Several thought that the experience of the task force might prove useful in resolving such conflicts. The idea of dispatching parts of the group to Afghanistan or the Middle East was raised again. A new idea was to direct the attention of the task force to the growing conflict between Armenia and Azerbaijan.

While the meeting was coming to a close on Sunday, December 8, Boris Yeltsin was meeting with Leonid Kravchuk, the newly elected president of Ukraine, and Stanislav Shushkevich, chairman of the Belorussian Supreme Soviet, in the Belovezh Forest, near Minsk. Saunders wrote later:

> After most of you departed Westfields last December, those of us who spent Sunday evening with our colleagues will never forget the impact of the television report of the announcement of the new CIS early that evening. . . . Early the next morning, Gennady and I began talking only very speculatively about how we might reshape our agenda.[82]

What they had in mind was to build a new agenda to take advantage of the experience that they had built in the task force over one decade—and the Dartmouth conferences had build over three—with conflicts that seemed unbridgeable.

The end of the Soviet Union meant change for Dartmouth. It had been a product of the Cold War. More than that, it had been a product of the intense bilateral rivalry between two countries. Now, one of those countries had vanished. It was a shock to many who saw it happen. It was unimaginable to those who had gathered at Hanover in 1960. Thirty-one years later, those who kept the legacy of that first meeting had to ask whether the Dartmouth Conference had anything to offer the post-Soviet world.

6 | New Approaches from a Rich Tradition: The 1990s

by Harold H. Saunders and James Voorhees

ARMS CONTROL TASK FORCE

THE CIVIL SOCIETY TRACK

TASK FORCE ON THE OVERALL RELATIONSHIP

REGIONAL CONFLICTS TASK FORCE: TRANSITION, 1992

REGIONAL CONFLICTS: FOCUS ON THE NEW RELATIONSHIP, 1993–2001

THE INTER-TAJIK DIALOGUE

DIALOGUES INSPIRED BY DARTMOUTH

FORTIETH-ANNIVERSARY REUNION AND BEYOND

THE END OF THE SOVIET UNION INDEED MEANT CHANGE for the Dartmouth Conference—but not its demise. The large plenaries of the past, it was agreed after Dartmouth XVII, "would not be appropriate," in the words of David Mathews. They had become too costly and were less effective than the task forces. But the dangers, purposes, and opportunities that had motivated the people of Dartmouth for three decades would move them to face the challenges to the new Russian-U.S. relationship that they agreed remained critical to world peace.

The resilience of the Dartmouth tradition would be tested. Responses to the challenge would at times falter, and some initiatives would come to an end, but the first decade of this new era would also see some remarkable developments. The work of the 1990s—more intense and wide ranging than in any previous decade—would provide a springboard into the new century. The story of these efforts is one of new thinking, reshaping, and innovation—anything but an epitaph.

Perhaps the decision of the Regional Conflicts Task Force in 1992 captured the new decade's fundamental challenge: to conceptualize what participants had learned together in the "Dartmouth movement" so as to apply it to new relationships that would unfold. The inclination of Dartmouth veterans in each of the previous decades to reflect on their experience together and to rethink their future was possibly stronger than ever. Perhaps this book is only the latest manifestation of that tradition—part of a continuing struggle for new birth.

The challenge was not only, as Harold Saunders had repeatedly reminded colleagues, that the Cold War had ended or that the Soviet Union had dissolved—earthshaking as those developments were. The even greater challenge arose from the turbulence of a rapidly changing world—one whose transformation had largely been obscured under the frozen surface of the Cold War. To bring this new world into focus required changing our analytical lenses. "The lenses we use to understand events," he said, "will determine how we act."

The focus in world affairs for the last half of the twentieth century —if not also for the previous three centuries—had fallen on relations between states and their governments, he pointed out. This was perhaps more understandable than ever in an era when a miscalculation between two nuclear superpowers could destroy the world. It was perhaps understandable in a world arranged in significant ways around a profound ideological conflict; even those strong leaders who attempted to build a camp of the nonaligned were drawn toward one side or the other. The prevailing paradigm had focused on "power politics" as leaders of nation-states amassed economic and military power to pursue objectively defined interests against other such entities in zero-sum contests of power.

The formula that Saunders often repeated in meetings toward the end of the 1980s was: Relationships among countries are increasingly a political process of continuous interaction among significant elements of whole bodies politic across permeable borders. That view of the world was close to the view that Gorbachev expressed in his speech to the General Assembly of the United Nations in December 1988— a speech that members of the Regional Conflicts Task Force had watched together on television in their meeting room on an upper floor of a New York hotel not far from the United Nations building. Later in the day they had crowded together around a window to watch Gorbachev's motorcade pass along Broadway below.

No one can know the numberless sources that shaped Gorbachev's groundbreaking worldview, but many of the authors of the articles and speeches that came to embody "the new political thinking" in Moscow between 1985 and 1990 were longtime participants in the Dartmouth Conference or in one of the few other dialogues that had operated during the latter part of the Cold War. In part, Gorbachev said:

> And finally, since I am here on American soil, and also for other obvious reasons, I have to turn to the subject of our relations with this great country. . . .
>
> No one intends to underestimate the seriousness of our differences and the toughness of outstanding problems. We have, however, already graduated from the primary school of learning to understand each other and seek solutions in both our own and common interests. . . .
>
> We in Moscow are happy that an ever increasing number of statesmen, political party and public figures and—I want to emphasize this—scientists, cultural figures, representatives of mass movements and various churches, and activists of the so-called people's diplomacy are ready to shoulder the burden of universal responsibility.
>
> In this regard I believe that the idea of convening on a regular basis, under the auspices of the United Nations, an assembly of public organizations, deserves attention.[1]

The people of Dartmouth would spend the rest of the decade—and beyond—struggling through reflection and experience to develop their role in the interaction between these two "whole bodies politic." Governments had been their primary audience for three decades, but as a Russian participant said in a fortieth-anniversary Dartmouth Conference reunion in Moscow in September 2000: "We have lost our market."

STRUGGLING TO SHAPE THE FUTURE: FOUR ARENAS OF EXPLORATION

In that struggle to find a new role and new audiences, four thoughts crystallized with differing degrees of firmness through the explorations and experiments of the 1990s. At the beginning of the twenty-first century, they are still very much a work in progress, but the innovations and achievements of the 1990s had enlarged the foundations in significant ways.

First, from the time of Dartmouth XVI in 1988 on, American and Russian Dartmouth participants had discussed and explored the possibility of developing a range of interactions between the civil societies of the two countries. While they discussed this subject with intensity and frequency from 1990 to 1992 in a number of meetings, those meetings became less important. A steady flow of young Russians came to the Kettering Foundation for the equivalent of graduate-level study of democratic theory and practice. That cadre grew through the decade around two Russian nongovernmental organizations founded by former Kettering fellows. At the beginning of the new century those organizations in Russia and the National Issues Forums in the United States were framing for deliberation in more than a hundred public forums the issue of how citizens in each country see the relationship with the other. Experience will determine exactly how this energy will be channeled into the overall framework of the Dartmouth dialogue.

Second, and perhaps drawing from the first, is the continuing effort by Dartmouth veterans to find an appropriate way of replacing in modern format what the Dartmouth Conference had become—a mind at work at the heart of a relationship, continually taking its pulse, calling attention to its incipient cancers, providing early warning of new threats, and suggesting ways of making midcourse corrections in the unfolding new Russian-U.S. relationship.

Third, the Regional Conflicts Task Force decided to draw its focus closer to areas of the former Soviet Union. Participants decided that the new Russian-U.S. relationship could be threatened unless the two powers found mutually acceptable ways of interacting in the newly independent republics of the former Soviet Union—the area that Russians in the early 1990s were calling the "Near Abroad." In a dozen meetings through the decade they still pursued the original purpose of forming the task force in 1981—learning what could be learned from those interactions beyond our borders about each party's real interests, perception of the other's interests, and ways of conducting the core relationship.

Fourth, the Regional Conflicts Task Force made a reality out of a long-held aspiration of Dartmouth participants—actually working together in the larger interests of peace. In the 1990s, however, the design was not for cooperation between the two governments but rather for what may have become the first joint Russian-U.S. peacemaking project of citizens outside government from each country. In late 1992, after conceptualizing the process of dialogue they had learned together in the 1980s, they decided to try to start a sustained dialogue among individuals from opposing factions in the civil war in the former Soviet republic of Tajikistan. As that project went on, the Tajik colleagues came to call their group the "Inter-Tajik Dialogue within the Framework of the Dartmouth Conference." As two Russian members of the task force who recruited the Tajik participants explained: "They would not have accepted an invitation to a Russian meeting. They would not have accepted an invitation to an American meeting. They accepted the invitation because it came from an 'international movement'—the Dartmouth Conference." In this way, the mystique of the Dartmouth Conference illustrated its own convening power.

The eight-year experience of the Inter-Tajik Dialogue, as of this writing, has broken new ground in three ways. First, it expanded the field of conflict resolution by providing—along with the work of a few others in the field—an instrument of sustained dialogue for citizens whose conflicts are so deeply rooted in identity and grievance that they are not ready for formal mediation and negotiation. Second, it was the laboratory for refining that process of sustained dialogue for transfer to other conflicts. Third, in the opening years of the new century, it is exploring the possibility of using dialogue in various forms to build democratic elements into civil society and, in some instances, to do so in ways that help build the civic infrastructure—the social capital—essential to economic development.

By 2001 task force members were exploring further areas for work together. Meanwhile, Russian colleagues were applying sustained dialogue within Russia; U.S. members were doing so within North America.

This chapter is the story of the experiences that bring the Dartmouth tradition into the twenty-first century. Perhaps because they have been experimental and innovative, they may represent even more fully than pre-1991 Dartmouth the imaginative—though as yet not fully clear—potential of the Dartmouth Conference. But first we must deal with one traditional track that has not found its way into the future.

ARMS CONTROL TASK FORCE, MARCH–DECEMBER 1992: TWO MORE TIMES

The next meeting of the Arms Control Task Force, in March 1992, proved to be its next to last. The name of the task force had been changed to reflect changing realities. It was now the Task Force on Cooperation in Security. As at the previous meeting in October, some of the topics were familiar, but the context had changed yet again.

In the usual rotation, this meeting would have been held in the United States, but the cochairs had decided that the rush of events in Moscow made it more useful for the group to meet there. The Russian cochair's welcoming remarks reflected the tenuous context in which they met:

> We are still handing out the old business cards where the word "Soviet" appears. . . . You . . . have come here at an unstable time, if I am not to use a stronger word. . . . For decades Dartmouth meetings have been held . . . at times when we are again looking at world security anew. . . . I am very glad to see in this room people with whom we have become friends, and with whom we have had many fruitful talks. I would like to welcome our military participants to these meetings. In the last eighteen months, many interesting meetings have been held in this room linked to . . . the relationship with NATO. Ten years ago, it would have been impossible to think that generals from NATO would be sitting in this room to discuss these questions with our military people.

The U.S. cochair responded simply: "We look forward to coping with the multitude of problems which are facing you now. We are trying to be helpful, but we also want to begin to search for our directions in the long-term future, so that we are not always acting as though we were at the site of an accident, but were looking ahead, as difficult as that might be, to trace out our new relationships in the future."[2]

The American participants were largely the same as in October. Chayes and Campbell were gone, but Jones was back. And Saunders took part in the meeting, his second. On the Soviet side, most of the participants had changed. Rogov was cochair again, and both Arbatovs, *père et fils,* attended. But the rest included several representatives of the Federation of Peace and Conciliation—the new name for the Soviet Peace Committee—several people, staff and members, from the Committee for Defense and Security of the Russian Supreme Soviet, and several people from the Russian Ministry of Foreign Affairs. Colonel Vladimir N. Danilov, also present in October, was now at the Supreme Command of the CIS Unified Forces. He was one of two active-duty officers at the meeting, joined by Colonel General Petr S. Deinekin, the supreme commander of the CIS Unified Air Forces. He had been a deputy to Shaposhnikov during the August coup. No participant came from the newly created Russian Ministry of Defense.

A Russian speaker set the discussion of security issues in the larger context of a *Russian* security identity:

> The question of the new identity . . . is a crucial question. . . . While it is still very difficult for people to recognize what happened, the great empire which existed for many decades is gone. . . . Instead of the Soviet Union we are now in the process of the formation of nation states. The everyday life of the people of this country can change. They still live in the same houses—those who have houses— but they live in a different country. Probably this is the most difficult for Russians to understand. The Soviet Union, with all the internationalist ideology which was its foundation, was still the continuation of the Russian empire, and for most Russians, the notion of the Soviet Union and the notion of Russia was the same. . . . Only now, we understand that Russia is Russia and not the Soviet Union. So my first point is that while Russia exists today, the Russian Federation is really a brand new state which is in the process of formation into a nation state like Ukraine, like Uzbekistan, like all the others. And it is a new state because there never was a Russia within the present Russian boundaries. There never was a Russia with the present economic system . . . as far as the goal of our development is concerned—the market. And there was never a Russia under the present political system, and by that I mean the transition to democracy.
>
> This means that Russia has to reevaluate its identity, including its security identity. . . . the Russian security identity is going to be very different from the security identity of the USSR. . . . It is my conclusion . . . that the major priority security interest of Russia is survival and development as a democratic state. The threat is coming from inside. This is the threat of the fragmentation of Russia and the collapse of Russia as a society. Social ills, civil war—that is the

main danger to our survival. That . . . means that the problems of
security need political solutions, economic solutions. The military
solution to the problem of security is not valid. But it doesn't mean
that Russia doesn't have a security interest in "pure" military terms;
in terms of a possible emergence of an external threat to Russia.[3]

The Commonwealth of Independent States (CIS) would prove to
be weak and divided, but that was not clear in the spring of 1992. Its
future and the future of the CIS Armed Forces were hazy. The opinions
of the Russians reflected this. As one said, "The status of the CIS military
seems unclear at best." The status of the Russian armed forces was clearer but still confused. At the time of the meeting, the Russian Ministry of
Defense had just been formed, and such essential things as a budget and
a military doctrine to define things like potential opponents had yet to
be created. Several Russian speakers expressed concern about civilian control of the military. Disputes still raged with several republics—Ukraine
most of all—about the disposition of the forces on their territory, conventional and nuclear. There seemed to be general agreement that the
Russian armed forces would have to shrink from about 4 million men
under arms to about 1.5 million.

A major issue in regard to START was what would be done with the
nuclear weapons deployed in Ukraine, Belarus, and Kazakhstan. This
issue had been raised at the meeting in October, but the fate of these
weapons had not yet been decided. Ukraine had been the major source of
concern in the fall. That source was now Kazakhstan, which seemed to the
Russian participants to be inclined to hold on to its nuclear weapons.

The participants also discussed the proposals made by Bush and
Yeltsin for START II. The U.S. proposals, based as they were on the
composition of nuclear forces, were seen as having a pedigree that
extended back to proposals made by then secretary of state Cyrus Vance
in 1977. The Yeltsin counterproposal, based on equality of numbers,
was seen as more consonant with the usual Soviet approach. The
Russian participants believed that both proposals would make it easier
to get nuclear weapons out of Belarus, Ukraine, and Kazakhstan. But
the U.S. proposals, they believed, forced the Russians to concentrate
their nuclear forces at sea, where they felt vulnerable, and would require
modernization of their single-warhead land-based missile force, an
expense they were reluctant to make.

Ballistic missile defense was discussed again, but in the context of threats emanating from third countries rather than the balance of arms between the superpowers. The discussion centered on a proposal that Yeltsin had made at the United Nations for a global system. It would have a ground component created by Russia and a space component created by the United States that would use technology created for SDI and the GPALS (global protection against limited strikes) system described by President Bush the previous year. The idea was that such a global system would provide protection against small-scale nuclear attack from the likes of Iraq and North Korea. In the end, the participants dismissed the idea. As one Soviet speaker put it, if they cooperated in this, "in undermining the ABM treaty, we would get in exchange a very untrustworthy field against threats that do not exist today." The group felt that the goals of the two countries would be better met through cooperation in detecting and warning about potential threats.

After this meeting, Paul Doty bowed out of the work of the task force, after having led it since it was founded a decade before. His place was taken by Horelick, who would cochair for the American group what proved to be the final meeting of the task force.

When the task force met for the last time in December 1992 in Washington, in addition to Horelick, it included Chayes, Warner, Korb, Blackwill, Jones, and Saunders on the American side. On the Russian side, Rogov was again in the chair with the senior Arbatov, Colonel Zinovy Dvorkin of the Institute of the Ministry of Defense, Boris Ivanov of the Foreign Ministry, and Anton Surikov of ISKAN accompanying him. The overall agenda was framed in terms of examining "the legacy of the Cold War." It began with discussion of the underlying politics in each country that influenced what could be the next moves in arms control negotiations. There seemed to be agreement that, whatever the pace of negotiations might be, reductions could be accelerated by removing weapons from silos and warheads from weapons. Other practical steps that would play the role of further confidence-building measures included reducing alert status and cooperation in warning systems.

Although interest was expressed in discussing what a longer-term strategic relationship might include short of total denuclearization, participants recognized that it is not possible to "escape the logic of mutual deterrence" as long as more than one thousand warheads exist.

Participants expressed interest in such questions as: What kind of world would permit reliance on forces with nuclear weapons in the low hundreds? What do we really need for our respective defenses? Interest was also expressed in a larger dialogue on the international security environment to include issues such as Iran, the Arab-Israeli conflict, ethnic conflicts in Europe, religious fanaticism, Iraq, and limits on peacemaking and peacekeeping. An American participant pointed out that it would be difficult for the American side to move far beyond the general approach of the present until Americans were more confident that democratic reform in Russia was secure and not subject to reversal. In addition, it would be important to find practical ways to cooperate in dealing with some of these larger security challenges.

The group moved to issues of controlling nuclear proliferation and the transfer of high-tech weapons. The most immediate challenge was gaining control over nuclear weapons in the former Soviet Union and establishing practical systems for their removal or destruction. On the international scene, the group recognized the complexity of dealing with the new nuclear states. "What would we have done in the Gulf if Iraq had actually threatened use of a nuclear weapon?" asked one participant. As for limiting the transfer of high-tech weapons, the group heeded the caution of one member who described the problem as more difficult than nuclear proliferation and urged selecting a few problems that could be managed in practical ways and dealing with them rather than stating excessively ambitious goals. He cited the missile technology control regime as an example of one useful international effort.

Finally, discussing the problems of "peacemaking and peace enforcement" led participants to focus on respective attitudes toward United Nations missions for this purpose and the advisability of establishing a permanent UN force for this work. Russian participants noted that, first, while they were interested in participating over the long term, Russian forces were simply unavailable in the short term and that, second, Russia was obliged to play a role in the former Soviet Union, for instance, in Tajikistan. One Russian participant also noted that Russians were still suffering from the "Afghanistan withdrawal syndrome."

One American participant noted that the Regional Conflicts Task Force had addressed these problems in the broad context of UN secretary-general Boutros Boutros-Ghali's four-point agenda of crisis prevention (political processes), peacemaking (mediation, negotiation, and political efforts), peacekeeping (usually military involvement), and postconflict peacebuilding. He suggested that it is useful to separate the political and the military functions. Peace enforcement is largely an extension over time of the military component of peacemaking.

Ironically for what turned out to be the last meeting of this group, two Russian participants at different times stressed the importance of moving beyond even the frequency of semiannual meetings to establish "a permanent process," possibly with a research group working between meetings.

Even though the participants believed that the task force still had an important contribution to make—there were important issues left to work through and the task force had established trust within the group and attracted participants on both sides with broad access to the government and public—the task force lost momentum for several reasons. Horelick took on other responsibilities. Stewart, who had been the key organizer for Kettering, took a job out of the country. Also, arms control played less to the strengths and interests of the Kettering Foundation than did political methods of resolving conflict such as sustained dialogue and exploration of interaction between the two civil societies. This left a void in leadership on the American side, and the Russians were suddenly preoccupied with the challenges of their new situation. Moreover, the American side lacked the additional funding needed because of the inability of the Russian side to continue the old arrangements for organizing and funding meetings on a fifty-fifty basis.

The discussions on arms control thus came to an end. These discussions had been a central part of Dartmouth since its beginning, but the world had changed. The threat of a nuclear Armageddon had receded. Serious threats remained, but they were in many ways different from the old, which had its base in the era of superpowers.

CIVIL SOCIETY TASK FORCE, 1990–92: BUILDING BLOCKS FOR A NEW DEPARTURE

A result of the broad Russian representation and the involvement of American citizens at Dartmouth XVI in 1988 and the lengthy preparation for Dartmouth XVII was the 1990 creation in Leningrad of a Civil Society Task Force. This had been an issue central to the work of the Kettering Foundation in the United States. Now, as the Soviet Union sought democracy, strengthening civil society was becoming an important issue among those inside and outside the Soviet Union who were concerned with how communist states could make a transition to democracy. During much of 1991 and 1992 a plethora of conversations probed this subject in depth to determine whether a civil society task force would be added to the Dartmouth Conference complex over the long term—as David Mathews suggested—or whether there would be other ways of enhancing interactions between the two civil societies.

At the same time, the Kettering Foundation established a program of international fellows at the foundation—first for twelve months and later for six—to study democratic theory and practice, focusing particularly on the process of deliberative dialogue. This stream of Russian fellows continued steadily through the 1990s and into the twenty-first century. It became the most enduring product of these early explorations.

In early June 1991 a small Kettering group met with Russian counterparts gathered at the offices of ISKAN in Moscow to exchange ideas, and particularly to talk about the role of media in civil society. In October a Kettering group that had gone to Moscow for other purposes continued these conversations.

Illustrative of thinking together about the nature of civil societies and their potential interactions was the idea of a "task force without walls." The thought was to create a conceptual framework for these interactions but not confine the interactions themselves within the boundaries of a structured task force. There might need to be a mind at work that would keep the totality of these interactions in view in order to understand how they might complement one another and what they might add up to. With the possible exception of a little steering group, no one would come together to talk about the interactions but would simply make them happen. This idea returned from time to time but without any more formal expression.

The most concrete outcome of these first explorations was agreement to meet in Moscow in March 1992 on the subject of civil society. The planning group was still very much in an exploratory mode. One of its problems was the breadth and diversity of interest in this subject and the concern that it might be impossible to produce anything but a fragmented program of unrelated contacts to start with. One of the unplanned products of the March meeting was that it enabled Russians participating from a number of different organizations to become more aware of their possibilities of working together in informal networks.

Described as a turning point in this exchange was the question articulated by one Russian who had explained his personal motivation for participating in the meeting and then asked: "What is the motivation of members of the American group, both on a personal level and as part of a continuing project?" "At this point," according to American participants, "the discussions moved to a deeper level as we each explained both our personal concepts of politics and democracy and then reflected on why we, individually, thought interaction with like-minded Russians was important."[4] In the concluding session, Saunders outlined the possibility of a Russian delegation coming to the Kettering Foundation's Summer Public Policy Institute in Ohio in July to acquaint itself with the National Issues Forums in the United States and the experience of deliberative forums in other countries. A strong Russian delegation came.

Meanwhile, in late May and early June, two further meetings took place in Moscow. The first included both a group meeting and meetings with individual Russians to explore particularly the role of journalism in civil society. The two principal American participants were Robert Nelson of the *Christian Science Monitor* and Jay Rosen of the New York University School of Journalism, who later became the principal American academic expositor of the philosophy that came to be called "public journalism." At the same time, Georgi Arbatov was in the process of making arrangements to open a new center for the press at his institute in collaboration with the New York University School of Journalism.

By this time several Russian colleagues had spent periods of about two months each at the Kettering Foundation familiarizing themselves with the concepts and practice of deliberative democracy. The first full-time fellow, Igor Nagdasev, a young student of philosophy at Moscow State University, had completed his tour and returned to Moscow to establish the Russian Center for Citizenship Education, which began work in the winter of 1992–93. With the support of Georgi Arbatov, the center was formally registered on September 13, 1993, and was housed for a time at ISKAN in the office of Boris Mikhailov. Mikhailov and a colleague, Viktor Borisyuk, had become principal thinkers in deliberative democracy at the institute. This complex of people was also responsible for the publication in Russian of several Kettering Foundation books laying out the philosophy of deliberative democracy. Nagdasev's center extended this, doing its own work to frame Russian issues and using these books to bring the experience of deliberative democracy to the Moscow body politic.

After one more meeting in Moscow, in October 1992, following the Russian group's visit to the United States in July, the number of such meetings faded, but Russian participation in the fellows program at Kettering continued steadily. A later fellow, Denis Makarov, a young professor at the Moscow State Pedagogical University, returned from his fellowship to establish the Foundation for Development of Civic Culture, which was formally registered in 1996. Materials on deliberative democracy entered the university's curriculum. After Nagdasev moved his operation to St. Petersburg, this foundation became the umbrella under which most of the former Kettering fellows in Moscow operated. In addition, the Library of Foreign Literature, where former fellow Anastasia Kornienko worked, became interested in working through the library network to hold public forums around the country.

Both Nagdasev's center and Makarov's foundation regularly held training institutes in other Russian cities—reaching as far as Siberia—to enable people in communities to frame their own issues for deliberative forums. Out of the fortieth-anniversary Dartmouth Conference reunion in Moscow in September 2000 came a decision that it could be a solid contribution to the exchange between the two bodies politic if citizens in both countries were to hold deliberative forums on how each regarded the other country and the Russian-U.S. relationship. Nagdasev and Makarov teamed up to frame the issue for forums across Russia in 2001, while a team from the U.S. National Issues Forums prepared to hold mirror-image forums in the United States. A decade of work has opened the door for citizens outside the walls of any named task force to deepen their own perceptions of one another and perhaps eventually to come together in some way. This, too, remains very much a work in progress.

A TASK FORCE ON THE OVERALL RELATIONSHIP, 1994–PRESENT: THE ELUSIVE CORE

From the early years of the decade, Mathews and Saunders repeatedly expressed concern about the absence of a group focusing on the overall Russian-U.S. relationship, which they were convinced would again become critical for world peace, hopefully in a constructive mode. Periodically through the decade and beyond, Kettering drew Dartmouth veterans together for the purpose of exploring what kind of configuration might fill this vacuum.

In October 1994, as the "honeymoon" in the immediate post–Cold War Russian-U.S. relationship began to fade, Kettering drew together in the Washington suburbs a collection of Dartmouth veterans and a few new faces, including journalists and businesspeople. Following that meeting, Andrei Kortunov, one of the younger Russian participants who had played a role in the Dartmouth process since 1984 and felt a strong commitment to it, was invited to the Kettering Foundation in Dayton to share his reflections on that kind of Dartmouth meeting and what might lie in the future. His conclusion was that "the dialogue in its present form and its present composition can no longer be sustained." Among the reasons for this, he reflected, were the following:

First, whereas Dartmouth during the Cold War provided one of the few forums for high-level elite interaction between Moscow and Washington, now there are many opportunities for politicians, businesspeople, military, journalists, and academics to discuss issues of common interest.

Second was the change in the social and professional setting— mainly in Russia but also in the United States. The old institutes of the Academy of Sciences in Russia no longer had the stature and influence they had enjoyed in Soviet days—partly because the academy could not pay competitive salaries and young people had to look for other ways of earning a living in order to support their families or had to work two jobs in order to do so.

Third, and a further reason for the second, whereas Dartmouth during the Cold War was an exchange oriented to the "political mainstream," the just-concluded meeting had included "predominantly people who have turned into very consistent, rigid, and even radical Yeltsin critics." Dartmouth has not been able to involve the current mainstream.

Fourth, the Cold War agenda of arms control, regional conflicts, economic cooperation, domestic politics—even though these issues remain important—does not reflect the broad range of post–Cold War interactions.

Fifth, it was also clear that a generational shift was essential, for the most part, to capture new ways of looking at the world. In today's world, dominated heavily by technology and business, drawing participants in their forties into such a dialogue is extremely difficult because "just talking" does not fit into their lifestyle, in which "time is money."

Sixth, the traditional conference-style format was not flexible enough to spark new ideas, and the lack of interaction between conferences limited the productivity of the meetings.

Seventh, new sources of funding were essential, especially on the Russian side.

In March 1996 Kettering pulled together in Washington another small group of Dartmouth veterans and others to review the situation, and in September, in a visit to Moscow headed by David Mathews, Kettering experimented with its own version of a "dialogue without a table." Although there was a common meeting in the style of the old Dartmouth plenary, members of the U.S. group went in pairs to talk with a variety of Russian colleagues in their different fields and then came back together to share insights.

Why did these proposals not take root? Like Kortunov's analysis, the answer is a subtle one and has several elements. There was no readiness on either side to devote the nearly full-time attention of one individual committed to making this kind of Russian-U.S. dialogue an ongoing reality. Phil Stewart's shoes were not filled. Although the Kettering Foundation on the American side was an early and continuing supporter of Dartmouth, its interest as an organization lay perhaps more in the political processes involved in the dialogue than in analytical or scholarly attention to the substance of the relationship itself. In the mid-1980s, for instance, Kettering wrote of its interest in the process of what it then called "supplemental diplomacy"—a process through which citizens outside government could explore the quality of the relationship between two countries. While Kettering was describing Dartmouth as a whole that way, Saunders and his colleagues in the Regional Conflicts Task Force were developing a process that came to be called in the 1990s "sustained dialogue" to transform conflictual relationships. Also in the 1990s, the exploration of the civil society track reflected Kettering's strong interest in the role of citizens outside government in sustaining viable democracy as contrasted to the traditional governmental agendas of the Cold War.

Perhaps supporting this reflection are the characteristics of the two tracks in Dartmouth that became consistently stronger in the 1990s and seemed to provide the springboard into the next century. First were the activities of the Regional Conflicts Task Force described in the next section. The task force explored the nature of the new Russian-U.S. relationship as seen through the familiar prism of the countries' interactions abroad—now the Near Abroad. This built from the process of sustained dialogue developed with Saunders' involvement in the task force over the previous decade. Then it established the joint project of the task force—the Inter-Tajik Dialogue and its Public Committee for Democratic Processes. It was a practical application of sustained dialogue. The other track, born in the year 2000 out of a decade of work on civil society and deliberative democracy, was the potential in the conduct of public forums in the two countries—particularly the possibility of bringing together a new generation of citizens from diverse areas of the two countries. The proposal played directly to the strengths of citizens in both countries trained in the work of deliberative democracy.

By the end of 2001, work was well under way for the launch of a new task force focusing on the overall relationship. It would go well beyond the traditional exchanges between elites around the intergovernmental agenda, engaging a wider range of citizens outside government—leaders in policy-influencing communities who are attuned to how publics think about the relationship between whole bodies politic. This time the effort seemed likely to take off because it was rooted in the strengths, interests, and philosophies of key organizations on both sides.

REGIONAL CONFLICTS TASK FORCE, 1992: A MOMENT OF TRANSITION AND DECISION

When participants sat down in Moscow, in May 1992, at the tenth-anniversary meeting, they were acutely aware of the magnitude of the changes that had taken place—just as they were aware that they could not fully comprehend their implications. Former ambassador Robert Neumann, who had grown up in Austria and fled the Nazis, captured the moment in this reflection:

> I would like to make a very personal comment. . . . I think I have a feeling of how you must feel now. I remember two periods where a social order totally changed. As historians, of course, we've known of many such periods. But a personal experience is always different. One of the periods was Austria. After the end of the Hapsburg empire, there was a serious question as to whether there could indeed be such a thing as Austria. This question ultimately worked itself out. A second period was Germany, toward the end of the Second World War. The war was still going on, but it was coming to an end. As an American army officer, I called together a group of students and professors from the University of Marburgh. Without asking their names or what their political leanings were, I asked: "What is the future of Germany?" There was total agreement that Germany was finished, that it had no future. I reminded them that fifty million people couldn't simply go away, but they proceeded to disagree.
>
> I mention this only because I would imagine that similar questions exist in the minds of our Russian colleagues. But I would like to leap into the future, although it's a future that I will certainly not see. Russia is a very large country, it is composed of great people, and it will be a very great country with a significant role to play. I think that we need to leap ahead and envisage such a period especially today, when we don't know what role it will play or what Russian foreign policy interests will be. Second, I believe that the types of conflicts that we see now, especially in Yugoslavia, will be the norm for some time to come, perhaps over the next thirty or forty years. Moreover, I believe that the traditional methods of peacekeeping, mediation, and negotiation are no longer sufficient to rise to the challenge.

Naumkin immediately picked up the last point: "I'd like to endorse the American speaker's thinking. Today, traditional methods of conflict resolution, and even our traditional views on the sources of conflict and how to address conflict, clamor for review. The fear of conflict is expanding, and changes are occurring in the classification of conflicts and their sources."[5]

This thinking would mature in the two meetings of 1992 to set the task force on two paths for the rest of the decade and beyond. One was to probe the nature of the conflicts that now seized attention in the early post–Cold War era and to understand the new Russian-U.S. relationship as revealed in the interaction of the two countries in those conflicts in the former Soviet Union. The other was the very concrete Inter-Tajik Dialogue.

Saunders responded to Chufrin early in the May 1992 meeting with words that set the tone for this meeting and the next:

> As you have already said, this is a transitional meeting because of global factors, but also because of events in your country and in ours. Transitions can be positive. What we are trying to do here is to re-shape our agenda so that we can build on what we have learned in the last ten years, and take that experience into the period ahead. Our task is to re-shape our agenda on the basis of a well-established foundation. My colleague has referred to a methodology that has come to characterize our group. I think we ought to stop for a moment and characterize what this approach is.[6]

He went on to lay out his thoughts about elements of that approach. He suggested that the approach the task force had learned together had helped to enlarge the professional and academic field of conflict resolution by focusing on dialogue rather than on diplomacy or formal mediation and negotiation. His points were summarized as follows in the record of the meeting:

> First, we sat down together in 1982 as "rivals" or "enemies" when there was virtually no serious dialogue occurring between our two governments. It was one of the lowest points of the Cold War. We focused on the state of the relationship between our two countries. We dared to hope that our work might make some contribution toward improving the Soviet-U.S. relationship. By focusing on the relationship itself, we shaped a non-traditional agenda. To be sure, we talked about regional conflicts in depth, but our overriding purpose was to use those discussions to discover how our interactions in those areas revealed and affected the central relationship between our two countries.
>
> Second, we have not talked about those conflicts as disputes over technically defined issues. Rather, we have talked about them as deep-rooted human and political conflicts. More important, we have talked about the resolution of these conflicts not simply in the diplomatic terms of mediation and negotiation, but also in human and political terms.

Third, we have created a "microcosm" of the Soviet-U.S. relationship. In talking about these conflicts and their resolution, we
almost embodied our two countries and their efforts to deal with
strengthening the overall relationship, as opposed to undermining it.[7]

From the exchange that followed emerged the first decision in
reshaping the focus of the task force for the new era—conceptualizing
the process of dialogue that had come to be known as "the Dartmouth
process" so that it could be transferred to other conflicts. As Gouttierre
put it at the end of this task force meeting, "This process, the Dartmouth process, is exportable; not in the role of third party mediators,
but perhaps as tutors of a process which conflicting parties could lead
and sustain."[8] After this tenth-anniversary meeting, Chufrin and
Saunders distilled the experience of the task force in an article published in April 1993 titled "A Public Peace Process."[9]

In their joint article, published in the Harvard-based *Negotiation
Journal* and subsequently translated by Chufrin into Russian, Chufrin
and Saunders laid out the process of dialogue sustained over time as
unfolding through a series of stages. First is a period in which individuals
in conflict make the difficult decision to reach out in dialogue to the
adversary. Next is a period in which participants in the dialogue sit down
for the first time together and pour out their grievances, their anger, their
pictures of who has been responsible for the conflict—a time in which
moderators of the dialogue are able to map the dynamics of the interactions among the parties. This second stage ends when the group agrees
that they should focus their energies on a particularly important part of
the problem. Third, they go on to probe that problem in detail until they
reach some judgment about how the problem they identified might be
dealt with. Fourth, they begin to think together about steps that might
enable adversaries to begin changing their relationship, ending violence,
and beginning to rebuild their community. Finally, participants place
their design in the hands of broader elements of the community in an
effort to engage them in resolution of the conflict and gradual transformation of the relationship.

The second decision the task force tackled—on which conflicts to
focus their attention—led to a wide-ranging discussion of the nature of
conflict. Participants sought to understand more fully the role of conflict not so much between their two countries but among regional

actors that had emerged from the former Soviet Union and were already intensely affected by waves of ethnic and nationalistic fervor. In a new departure, they also talked about conflicts within the United States. In this regard, Russian participants showed great interest in the sources of the riots in Los Angeles that had occurred in April 1992. These discussions also inspired comments on the relationships among minority rights, democratization, and civil society.

The task force focused on two additional subjects. First was the role of Islam and Islamic fundamentalism in Central Asia (especially in the former republics of the Soviet Union). The rise of Islamic fundamentalism was discussed in conjunction with the probable foreign policy tendencies of the Central Asian states and the degree to which Islam could represent a destabilizing influence in Central and South Asia. Second, the task force spent an entire day discussing the conflict in Moldova. This discussion was particularly insightful as representatives of the Russian Federation for Peace and Conciliation provided detailed accounts of their recent efforts to establish a dialogue between those who favored unification with Romania and the Russian-speaking minority who opposed this.

Toward the end of this meeting a participant raised "the possibility of having a few of us go to another area of conflict and talk with people to see if there are people on two sides of a conflict willing to talk with each other. Could we find six people who would sit down with us and explore the idea of creating a dialogue on the deeper roots of their conflict? This would not be a one-time dialogue, but would last several days, and would be repeated a few months later. The participants might then return to their own communities and conduct dialogues of their own." This statement reflected the discussion of Moldova and seemed to foreshadow two future steps by the task force.[10]

First, the discussion seemed to lean toward a focus on regions "contiguous to Russia in the new Commonwealth" on the theory that interaction between Russia and the United States in Russia's new backyard—the Near Abroad—could create tension in the evolving relationship between the new Russia and the remaining superpower.[11] This meant that the task force would eventually leave behind discussions of the Middle East, South Asia and Afghanistan, Northeast Asia, Latin America, and Africa. Ethnic conflict in the former Soviet republics gradually evolved into the primary focus of the task force.

Second, it also foreshadowed a major step that would be crystallized in the meeting of the task force the following December. This was to apply the process of systematic dialogue over time to one of the conflicts that had broken out on the territory of the former Soviet Union. In May, however, that idea was still a glint on the horizon. In retrospect the idea returned the task force to the theme of cooperation between the two countries in practical projects that had been discussed over the years by Dartmouth steering groups.

The task force met in Washington in December 1992 against the background of interim work and discussion that had emerged from the May meeting. On the Russian side, that work continued in the form of a research paper, "The Situation in Central Asia: Internal and External Aspects." An October visit to Moscow by Saunders and Slim to attend one of the civil society meetings offered an opportunity for them to meet at the Institute of Oriental Studies with Russian task force colleagues to talk about the conflict in Tajikistan. That discussion covered both the internal and the external causes of the conflict and Russian and U.S. interests in it. They also noted that "there is inside Tajikistan a group of citizens who strive for political stability, have the political connections with the different conflicting factions to work out a compromise, and have the power, mostly economic, to bring about such a compromise." On the American side, questions were raised about whether Russia was too intimately involved in Tajikistan to permit Russian colleagues in the task force to be part of a neutral team convening a dialogue, but that question was soon put to rest.

In preparation for the Washington meeting, the American team invited to the task force meeting a guest from the Joint Center for Political and Economic Studies, an institute that had been established in the late 1960s to reflect on issues affecting the black community and other minority communities in such a way as to improve their abilities to represent their own interests in the democratic process. It had come into being as a result of the accelerated representation of the black community after 1970 in the electoral process. This session was intended to continue the May discussion of the Los Angeles riots to broaden understanding of internal racial and ethnic conflict in the

United States. What emerged from this meeting was a consolidation of two decisions that had been under discussion for much of the previous year.

The first half of the meeting was devoted to an extensive discussion of the nature of the conflict that had broken out in the newly independent republic of Tajikistan. The discussion produced a picture of a complex mix of economic, ethnic, cultural, regional, tribal, religious, ideological, and clan-based factors with the focus sharpening on a combination of regional and clan contests to fill the power vacuum left by the dissolution of the Soviet Union.

Americans raised questions about whether any sense or definition of Tajik statehood existed. Several Russian participants noted that the issue of Tajik national identity was compounded by the disintegration of the Soviet Union and the fact that the Tajiks had never experienced a state of their own. At the same time, however, there seemed to be a consensus that for many Tajiks the notion of Tajikistan has real import, especially in cases where the other party involved is also a state, such as Uzbekistan. Neumann pressed hard on whether focusing on Tajikistan was a good choice for the task force: "We know where we are coming from—a superbly successful Dartmouth process. . . . I think this process is ripe for application to Central Asia, but the choice of Tajikistan puzzles me. . . . Why Tajikistan, and where do we go from here?"[12]

In the end, Tajikistan was chosen for three reasons. First, it was an area of interest to Russia, with Russian troops stationed there and a Russian minority in the population. Second, the conflict could affect American interests because it could spill over into neighboring countries, undermining regional stability. A third reason, related to the second, was that the conflict involved several regional powers, spread geographically from Turkey to China.[13] In addition, Naumkin and Zviagelskaya had extensive contacts there. Six members of the task force—Chufrin, Naumkin, Zviagelskaya, Saunders, Gouttierre, and Slim—were designated to form the dialogue. They were the "management team" for the project. The Inter-Tajik Dialogue began in March 1993. It continued through the rest of the decade and into the new century, becoming deeper as the meetings continued.[14]

The story of the Inter-Tajik Dialogue is told later in this chapter, but it is worth noting at this point that the decision of the task force to mount a collaborative project of its own for the first time made a reality of an aspiration voiced by participants in the Dartmouth Conference since the 1970s—designing and carrying out a cooperative project that would bring the Soviet Union and the United States closer. The difference is that earlier conversations focused primarily on designing projects for cooperation between the two governments, while the Inter-Tajik Dialogue was a project of citizens outside government. In fact, some have called it "perhaps the first joint American-Russian citizens' peacemaking mission." This fact cannot be overlooked if we are to understand the Dartmouth Conference reshaping itself as a movement by citizens working with much less reference to their governments.

This line of thinking—linked to the focus of the Kettering Foundation on civil society—only crystallized as time went on. It was captured much later as part of the strategy toward Tajikistan in a joint article by Saunders and Slim.[15]

The second half of the meeting focused more tightly on the second decision on the future of the task force—the ways in which these new conflicts could affect the new Russian-U.S. relationship. This was, in effect, a continuation of the purpose of the Regional Conflicts Task Force since its beginning in 1982—now with a focus on a new collection of regional conflicts closer to the borders of Russia that could affect the new Russian-U.S. relationship. The rapporteur noted: "While the last several meetings of the Task Force have built the newly emerging cooperative dimensions of the US-Russian relationship, this session indicated that, like the past, there could be issues which could test certain limits of cooperation."[16]

The core participants in the task force remained largely the same through much of the 1990s. Two new members were brought onto the American side for the May 1992 meeting and remained members of the group for years thereafter. They were Wallace Warfield, director of Clinical Programs at the Institute for Conflict Analysis and Resolution at George Mason University, and Randa Slim, a program officer at the Kettering Foundation who had attended several previous Dartmouth meetings as a member of the Kettering staff. Together they contributed expertise in the growing academic field of conflict resolution and experience in working with different kinds of conflict—Warfield in American communities, Slim in Lebanon.

New members were added from time to time as the task force explored new subjects. Depending on the focus, the Americans included Ed Luck, who had been an important figure in the Soviet dialogues with the UN Association of the United States; Jack Matlock, the former U.S. ambassador to the Soviet Union; Robert Oakley, who had been ambassador to Somalia and Pakistan; and S. Frederick Starr, who was now a founder of the Central Asia Institute at Johns Hopkins University's Nitze School of Advanced International Studies. In the latter half of the decade, Martha Olcott, a longtime scholar of Central Asia, principally at the Carnegie Endowment for International Peace, became a regular member of the group.

The core members on the Soviet side came to be Chufrin, Naumkin, and Zviagelskaya. Though Africa was no longer on the agenda, Davidson came to several meetings, his good sense valued highly. Moskalenko was also a regular and, as secretary for the Federation for Peace and Conciliation, Yuri Drozdov made several appearances. So did Popov. Others were drawn in for one or several meetings. Andrannik Migranian, an astute writer on Russian affairs, was a part of the 1994 discussion in Moscow, which also included Aleksandr Ignatenko of the Gorbachev Foundation.

The influence of the task force did not diminish. Meetings continued to be held with State Department and Foreign Ministry officials. For example, meetings at the State Department in 1995 attracted the director of the Policy Planning Staff; Sheila Heslin, who was the official responsible for Russian affairs on the National Security Council staff; the director of the Office of Russian Affairs at the State Department; several desk officers; and a number of other State Department officials as well as the national intelligence officer for Russia on the National Intelligence Council.[17] Another official present was Alan Romberg, who, like John Stremlau before him, had become deputy director of the Policy Planning Staff.

In addition to the path-breaking common work in Tajikistan, the probing of the new Russian-U.S. relationship in the task force itself may have been the most systematic and insightful anywhere. Rarely has a group met repeatedly over more than a decade to focus on the core relationship between two great countries. That struggle—an exploration of sensitivities, opportunities for collaboration, and slowly deepening understanding—is the story of the Regional Conflicts Task Force through the 1990s and into the twenty-first century.

THE REGIONAL CONFLICTS TASK FORCE, 1993–2001: FOCUS ON THE NEW RELATIONSHIP

Between the December 1992 meeting and the next meeting in Moscow in early June 1993, six members of the task force had held what they called an "exploratory" meeting with seven Tajiks. That meeting had been followed quickly by a second, which seemed to establish the new Inter-Tajik Dialogue as a viable process. With that venture launched—its story will be recounted in the next section of this chapter—the full task force turned to the challenge of probing Russian-U.S. interactions in the Near Abroad to learn more deeply what interests that revealed and how the interactions affected their central relationship. What follows is the story of a group struggling to understand a relationship that had never existed before. It has been a mind at work at the heart of a new relationship.

They began this meeting against the background of a new Russian foreign policy document titled "The Basic Concepts of Russian Foreign Policy," which had been signed by President Yeltsin the previous month, having been commissioned by the Russian National Security Council.[18] As elaborated by several Russian speakers, Russian interests could almost be seen as encompassing a set of concentric circles beginning with the states composing the Commonwealth of Independent States, extending to the countries of Eastern Europe, Asia and Japan, Western Europe and the United States, and finally to the Third World. In this picture, regional conflicts were generally seen as a lower priority for Russian policy commitments, except for those—as in the CIS and South Asia—that could potentially threaten "the integrity of Russia and the integration processes within the CIS."

After hearing a report on progress in the Inter-Tajik Dialogue, participants went back one more time to their familiar agenda in an effort to begin understanding the new elements in the post–Cold War international setting. While setting aside Latin America, subgroups continued their exchanges on South Asia, the Middle East, and Africa, addressing three questions: (1) How might the conflicts in these areas unfold in the future? (2) What are the new dimensions of conflict in these areas given the dissolution of the Soviet Union? (3) How might these dimensions suggest new definitions of the region as more southern states of the former Soviet Union begin to interact directly with China, South Asia, Iran, and Turkey? Specific issues that were more broadly applicable to conflicts in the former Soviet Union included Islam, growth of the drug and weapons trades, the appearance of potential regional powers such as Saudi Arabia, Iran, and Pakistan in South Asia and China in East Asia, and causes of instability. In one departure from the familiar agenda, they discussed challenges posed by the conflict in the former Yugoslavia. Several Russian participants provided perspective on Russia's cultural and historic ties to the Serbs.

When the group next sat down together, in January 1994—for the first time at the Kettering Foundation's headquarters in Dayton, Ohio—participants were ready to leave the traditional agenda behind. From this point on, they focused largely on the Russian-U.S. interaction in the former Soviet Union. From their dialogue a deepening sense of the elements of the relationship gradually emerged—where real interests lie and where acceptance of asymmetries of interests is necessary. This meeting necessarily began with a discussion of internal Russian developments, since President Yeltsin had shelled the Russian Parliament the previous fall. Following this discussion, participants concentrated primarily on the conflict in the former Soviet republic of Georgia.

The discussion brightly illuminated Russian interests in the Georgian conflicts. The instability there, Russian participants underscored, had serious potential impact on the integrity of Russia. The present Russian government, they said, had an interest in playing a significant role in the resolution of the conflict, but that government claimed to have no interest—or possibility—of reestablishing control there. Moderate Russians expressed an interest in a Georgia that would remain unified but would allow greater self-expression and self-government for units within the state. Russians expressed an interest in gaining international endorsement for the use of Russian troops as peacekeepers in Georgia. American participants expressed the thought that Russia ought to have an interest in a process of moving toward a resolution of these conflicts in a way that strengthens the views of Americans and

Europeans that Russia and the West now share common views of
Georgian independence, human rights, democratization, and market
economy.

American participants felt that their country's interests were subject to increasing debate within the American body politic. They did
not believe the U.S. government would conclude that national interests required significant involvement in the Georgian conflict, but
they did point out that the United States recognized an important
interest in the Russian-U.S. relationship, which will be affected by
how the two powers deal with such conflicts. The United States has a
strong interest that Russia not fragment. To the extent it judges that
there is a danger that the conflicts in Georgia will spread like a virus
into Russia, the United States has an interest in minimizing turmoil in
this area in a way that increases chances for long-term stability. For all
of these interests, it is unlikely that the American people would support a highly visible or costly U.S. involvement. At the same time,
those who choose to see minimal U.S. interest would need to be willing to live with the fact that Russia will be playing a central role, for
better or for worse. That is a critical choice in defining U.S. interests
and the U.S. relationship with Russia.

In the next two meetings—September 1994 and September
1995—participants stepped back again to discuss larger issues. They
returned again and again to what they called "the politics of the
Russian-U.S. relationship." They spent hours on questions such as:
What is the Russian identity now that the Soviet identity is no more?
How are Russians debating and refining Russian interests in the Near
Abroad? How did these issues become embroiled in Moscow's emerging democratic politics? How did internal U.S. political exchanges on
these issues play into political debate in Moscow? How did political
statements in each capital affect perceptions in the other?

From these wide-ranging exchanges, Chufrin and Saunders crystallized insights in another joint article—eventually published in
1997—that captured the feelings of task force participants in its opening sentences: "Nowhere is the politics of the unfolding Russian-US
relationship more clearly and broadly revealed than in the 'Near
Abroad.' . . . Nowhere else can one see more sharply what each side
really wants and fears in the Russian-US interaction on the world

stage."[19] They described the Near Abroad—with appropriate caution
but still perhaps with some excess of optimism—as "the one region
where the two powers are beginning to define the key elements of a
sound working relationship." In any case that conviction led participants to pursue their inquiry in the task force while continuing to support the ongoing work of the Inter-Tajik Dialogue.

Their exchanges probed the intricate nuances of the full spectrum
of views in Moscow politics, but at the center of the picture they produced was a relatively clear scene, albeit sometimes clouded in contra-
diction and ambiguity. These former republics—minus the three Baltic
states—had until recently been parts of a tightly integrated nation-
state, the USSR; they were not just marginal units in a far-flung
empire. Russia and they had become highly interdependent. It was
impossible for Russians not to see these now independent republics as
part of their world picture. They had economic and security interests
there, and ethnic Russians still lived there. It was natural that Russia
would continue to meet important needs there and to regard with deep
suspicion any activity by the United States that looked like an effort to
establish a challenging position there. For all of that, the stark reality
was that Russia had suddenly lost the apparatus of control and—given
the overwhelming challenges of its own internal transition—both the
will and the resources to play a role as significant as the one it had once
played. That neither stopped politicians from bold talk that reasserted
the Soviet position nor discouraged serious leaders from trying to fashion mutually useful ties of necessary cooperation.

Americans were not without their own dilemmas, although those
could not compare with what the Russians faced; Americans faced their
new situation without the crushing sense of material and psychological
loss that Russians suffered. The former Soviet republics, apart from the
Baltic states, were areas where most Americans could see no vital interest
that would justify direct intervention—or indeed even intensive diplomatic involvement. At the same time, many Americans recognized that
the end of the Cold War offered an unexpected and almost heaven-sent
opportunity to replace a hostile and frighteningly dangerous relationship
with one of at least modest cooperation. Yet, as time passed, those Americans would put the relationship on the back burner. Despite that attitude, Americans' attitudes would be adversely affected by any signs

(1) that Russia was acting to reestablish control in some form over its former "empire" or (2) that Russia was dealing with those republics in ways that showed disdain for human rights or the right of self-government reflected in the newfound independence of those countries. Some of the diehard Cold Warriors in the U.S. body politic argued for adaptation of the Cold War strategy of containment to prevent Russia from recapturing significant positions in the former Soviet Union; a few even argued for pressing on to encourage the breakup of the Russian Federation. These voices were heard clearly in Moscow.

This was the new interaction between these two bodies politic that members of the task force probed, but they reached well beyond that in two important ways. First, in their September 1995 meeting—again at the Kettering Foundation—they began trying to define "red lines"—points beyond which the actions of one side would be seen by the other as touching its important interests in unacceptable ways. Second, they tried to identify situations and mechanisms for coordinated action that could strengthen the Russian-U.S. relationship.

The discussion of "red lines" outlined a range of definable interests on both sides that should not be transgressed, but it also identified ambiguous areas in which perception of intent played a major role. For instance, participants understood that "upsetting the military balance" in areas adjacent to the other country would touch raw nerves. Other areas could be far more difficult. For instance, it is difficult to deal with a story, once spread widely, that U.S. intelligence services are working to undercut Russian positions in states of the former Soviet Union or to counter a perception that U.S. businesses in a potentially oil-rich country like Azerbaijan are deliberately trying to exclude Russian interests rather than simply competing for commercial gain.

This complexity and ambiguity led participants to two conclusions: (1) issues like these could be worked through only in persistent dialogue and (2), in the words of an American participant, we should "worry less about 'red lines' and more about opportunities for collaboration." Seeking mechanisms to ensure such dialogue, one participant suggested two steps: first, that the Russian foreign minister and the U.S. secretary of state name a small group of officials and nongovernmental experts to stay in virtually continuous dialogue on these questions both in face-to-face meetings and by other modes of communication, at least to provide early warning of hot issues; and second, that a nongovernmental dialogue be funded and staffed for the same purpose. Only through such deliberate efforts at dialogue could major misunderstandings be headed off and important opportunities for collaboration be identified.

It is worth interrupting this account at this point to note that the former task force cochairman, Evgeni Primakov, was appointed foreign minister of Russia on January 9, 1996. Saunders sent him a personal note saying, in paraphrase: "I know from our work together that you will be a dedicated and fair defender of your country's interests. At the same time, I hope that you will know from our time together that there are Americans who are deeply committed to a sound working relationship between our countries." After leaving office—he later became prime minister—Primakov was always strongly positive in stating his respect for his American counterpart, the U.S. secretary of state, and the way the two dealt with each other.

After the 1995 meeting, the task force settled into a succession of six meetings between June 1996 and February 2001 in which they focused on interactions in specific regions.[20] Several times they experimented with different formats.

In 1996 the task force turned to a pair of successive meetings to focus on Afghanistan, where Russia and the United States now shared significant interests, where opportunities for collaboration seemed ripe, but where new circumstances raised questions in Moscow about U.S. intentions.[21]

Despite mutual suspicions about intent, participants had little difficulty in agreeing that Russia and the United States share many interests there, albeit, as one Russian participant said, "of a different order." Both had an interest in isolating extremist Islamic forces; in curbing the flow of drugs, weapons, and terrorism; in strengthening the role of the United Nations; in humanitarian concerns; in limiting external interference in the conflict; in not working at cross-purposes in the ultimate reconstruction in Afghanistan. At the same time, some Russian interests were more intense because of the potential spillover of negative influences into nearby areas where developments directly threatened stability in Russia. This asymmetry of interests and capabilities was a constant thread in the dialogue. Nevertheless, they saw an interest in cooperation in Afghanistan that had never existed before, although they acknowledged that neither the Russian nor the U.S. government seemed able or willing to mount a priority effort beyond possibly complementary support for a United Nations attempt to produce a cease-fire.

Following the meeting some participants produced a "working draft" of a framework that Russia and the United States might use as a basis for continuing dialogue. When the task force met again in December, building on the previous meeting, the Taliban had captured Kabul. Participants again agreed that the most important development could be Russian and U.S. support for negotiations under UN auspices. The presence in the task force of several participants who knew Afghanistan intimately enabled the group to analyze possible approaches to negotiation in detail. In the end, it was difficult to see a solution; the group fell back on discussing interim measures.

These two meetings demonstrated that an intense dialogue between the two sides on cooperative—if halfway—measures was possible. They concluded, however, that a solution in Afghanistan could be worked out only by Afghans themselves. Russian and U.S. influence, at best, could affect how outsiders, including the United Nations and the Central and South Asian states, played their roles in relation to Afghanistan. Of the dialogue itself, one relatively new Russian participant at the end of the meeting marveled at the quality of the exchange: "Here we worked as a unanimous team."

Having exhausted this subject in light of the limited abilities of the two governments to influence it, the task force in its next meeting—in Washington in October 1997—turned back to "the impact of the evolution of Russian-CIS relations on the Russian-U.S. relationship." The intent was expressed in an early statement by a Russian participant: "It is desirable to begin dialogue before the stage of government decision-making—as was not the case with NATO expansion. . . . We want time to determine to what extent are Russian and US asymmetrical interests compatible and to what extent they are divergent. . . . It would also be welcome if we could get rid of myths." He concluded by echoing the call in the Chufrin-Saunders article on the Near Abroad for "an on-going international dialogue to which governments paid attention."

Enough time had now passed since the dissolution of the Soviet Union for one American participant to articulate the principle that

Russian relationships with other CIS states should be judged in terms of whether they are based on the "principle of mutuality." A Russian participant asked a critical question: "Can the United States today concede that Russia can be right in treating members of the CIS differently from other independent states?" A former senior U.S. diplomat said candidly that it is difficult to respond in official language because a direct positive response would imply "conceding formal spheres of influence," but "those who make U.S. policy clearly understand that Russia has a greater interest in events closer to its borders." An American participant, also with long government experience, suggested that alongside the principle of "mutuality" it might be pragmatic to recognize the practical effect of proximity on the intensity of a nation's interests. Another American participant put the point in terms of recognizing the facts of "natural interdependence." Russian participants spoke with feeling about a "common culture" or a "uniformity of mentality" that had developed from the close association among some of the CIS states "long before the Soviet era." Another Russian participant said, "Post-Soviet space is not unified, but culturally it is highly integrated."

An American participant lamented the problems created by misperceptions. "There's simply something wrong in the way we look at each other." On the American side are some citizens who will regularly interpret Russian moves as "attempts to reconstruct the USSR." On the Russian side, said one American participant, it seems impossible to dislodge the perception spread by some Russian intelligence officers at the highest levels that the United States is hard at work to undermine the Russian presence.

Looking beyond this exchange, S. Frederick Starr, a newcomer to the task force—though neither to Central Asian affairs nor to Dartmouth—observed: "This is the right agenda, but maybe we are reaching the end of the period when this should be an exclusively Russian-US discussion. It is a binary discussion. It ignores two parties—the other CIS nations and the nations outside the region for whom this is also their 'near abroad.'" We must recognize, he continued, that "the southern regions of the USSR were isolated from neighbors and are now exploring natural relationships with geographic neighbors." "New market relations," another said, "may determine new networks." Another way of thinking about the "new economic geography" that is developing, said

Martha Olcott, is to recognize that "states can belong to several neighborhoods simultaneously." At the same time, she said, "we shouldn't abandon the concept of post-Soviet space."

Participants turned for the first time in detail to one of the more sensitive intra-CIS relationships—that between Russia and Ukraine. Russian participants pointed to the long, especially close historical relationship and then to the contradictions that had emerged as Ukraine sought its own separate identity, a preoccupied Russia ignored Ukraine, and Ukraine suffered internal instability. In the light of long interdependence, Russians found it deeply objectionable when Americans declared Ukraine "a zone of special U.S. interest."

As the task force wrapped up this meeting, participants responded to Chufrin's question: "What has been useful about this meeting?" Olcott observed, "There is now much less difference of views." Starr suggested that both sides were moving toward a greater understanding of "how plural forces can work together in the area for Russian security. . . . Stability and security in this region are essential to many parties. The practical question is how we engage."

Following the meeting, the group again met with State Department officials just as it had done with Foreign Ministry officials in Moscow. One of the senior officials responded to the concern expressed by Russian participants during this and previous dialogues: "We fully understand that Russia has close historical, cultural, economic, and political interests in the CIS states. We don't see these as exclusive." At the same time, some said they could not get a clear idea of what the CIS as an organization was or did.

This was to be Robert Neumann's last meeting. Declining health kept him away thereafter; he died in 1999. His wisdom, rooted in broad experience, and a sharp analytical mind, coupled with subtle humor, a wry turn of phrase, and generous respect for human differences and for others' strengths, had made him a beloved colleague and mainstay for more than a decade.

The next two task force meetings— in October 1998 and March 1999—experimented with a new format that reflected a suggestion in the previous meeting that some CIS members should be drawn into the dialogue. Chufrin had accepted an invitation to lead a research project on Russian-Asian security relationships at the Stockholm

International Peace Research Institute (SIPRI). Taking advantage of connections developed in that project, he and Saunders agreed that it would add a dimension to the work of the task force if core Russian and U.S. groups could interact with a group composed of one participant from each of the five Central Asian countries.

This group yielded important results in terms of the interactions among Central Asian participants themselves and their candid view of the main security threat they faced. Most were quick to say that the primary threats to the security and integrity of their states were more internal than external. They seemed to take for granted a range of economic and security relationships with Russia that had roots in the past, but they also seemed to value the broader spectrum of relationships that they were developing. Some of them needed the guarantees that some Russian presence provides, but most were diversifying the base of their independence.

Their most pressing concerns emanated from uncertainties about whether their political systems could evolve in a stable way and from recognition that governments and societies were falling seriously short in addressing the economic causes of popular dissatisfaction. Political systems, they recognized, were not providing adequate constructive channels for opposition.

They talked at length about growing Islamic movements. While respectful of Islam as a religion, many saw a threat in any movement that would not participate with respect for honest differences in a pluralist system. This led some of them to recognize that governments invited trouble when they sought responses to radical Islam through the "power to control" rather than by addressing the causes of dissatisfaction.

In February 2001 the task force—again in collaboration with SIPRI—turned to the Caspian region, defined not only as the states bordering the Caspian Sea but also as including those neighboring in Central Asia and the Caucasus. The dialogue returned to the bilateral Russian-U.S. format. While a session was devoted to oil and gas regions, the dialogue ranged across the full spectrum of Russian-U.S. interactions in the region.

As had seemed to be the trend steadily since 1996, exchanges in this meeting led to two conclusions. First, the development and export of oil and gas—which in the early 1990s seemed a likely cause of geopolitical competition or even confrontation—would increasingly be dealt with on their commercial merits. Second, both Americans and Russians seemed ready to acknowledge each other's interests within the context of U.S. recognition that historical ties and geographic proximity made it inevitable that Russia would have special interests in the area that need not necessarily exclude U.S. interests.

In October 2001 the task force held an exploratory meeting on one of the intractable conflicts in the CIS—the conflict between Armenia and Azerbaijan regarding the status of Nagorno-Karabakh. It was another experiment in seeing whether the process of sustained dialogue could play a role in such a conflict. Whereas the conflict in Tajikistan was relatively fluid when the Inter-Tajik Dialogue began, in this conflict positions had become ever more fixed after more than a decade.

Thus the Regional Conflicts Task Force approached the second decade of the post-Soviet era having explored with persistent thoroughness the evolving Russian-U.S. relationship in former Soviet space. Although causes of potential friction remained, most participants felt they had developed a broad picture of the interests involved and of the points of legitimate sensitivity to be respected. Although they had maintained their exchanges with the governments on both sides, they were disturbed that governments above the level of the senior professionals who listened carefully seemed less inclined than in the past to invest care in shaping and tending the new relationship.

THE INTER-TAJIK DIALOGUE WITHIN THE FRAMEWORK OF THE DARTMOUTH CONFERENCE, 1993–PRESENT

In the three months following the December 1992 meeting of the Regional Conflicts Task Force, Naumkin and Zviagelskaya went to Tajikistan to talk with potential participants in the dialogue that the task force had decided to try to form. Through their work at the Institute of Oriental Studies, they had developed numerous contacts that could help them start their exploration. They were, in effect, doing the work of the first of the five stages that Chufrin and Saunders in their joint article had laid out as describing how a process of sustained dialogue unfolds. That first stage is a period in which participants decide to risk engaging in dialogue and organizers establish the essential framework for the dialogue.

Naumkin and Zviagelskaya went to Tajikistan with essentially five criteria in mind. Although these criteria were not set down in a list before Naumkin and Zviagelskaya departed, their importance had been made clear in the joint article and in conversation within the management team.

First, they were seeking individuals who wanted to end the violence and were ready and willing to risk reaching out to the enemy. It was potentially dangerous to do this. In fact, two participants eventually came to a meeting of the dialogue and were told that they were on a "hit list." One did not return to the country for two years. Another came to the airport but at the last moment decided not to get on the plane for the first meeting.

Second, Naumkin and Zviagelskaya sought individuals with the capacity to listen to the concerns of others. Sustained dialogue is sometimes criticized because it does not include extremists, but it is in the very essence of dialogue that participants must listen and interact. That tends to rule out extremists, who are usually so sure of their own position that they can only press others to accept it. As a dialogue evolves, experience tells us that it becomes possible to reach across the political spectrum and include a wider and wider band of participants.

Third, participants must be able to speak from the heart as well as from the mind. Sustained dialogue cannot be another academic seminar. Participants must be willing—whether explicitly or implicitly—to come to terms with their relationships. This requires a willingness to show emotions ranging from anger to compassion. Dialogue is among citizens outside government who may be academics or may have occupied official positions, but in the dialogue they leave those positions at the door. In the dialogue they represent only themselves, while necessarily reflecting the life experience—the identity—that brought them there.

Fourth, they sought participants at the second and third levels of their institutions—the vice chairman, the vice chancellor, the deputy director. The purpose was to avoid highly visible political figures who would understandably feel the need to defend hard positions and even to posture. The purpose was to find individuals who felt free to listen to new ideas and to explore them with others.

Fifth, participants had to be individuals who can reflect with authenticity the views of the groups with which they identify and individuals who will speak with credible authority to people in their own group in describing the views that emerge from the dialogue.

After speaking with more than a hundred Tajikistanis, they selected a group that seemed to meet their informal criteria. Their choices proved to be remarkably sound. The membership of the group evolved slowly as circumstances evolved, with older members stepping aside for various reasons and new participants joining to add necessary new voices. Nevertheless, the group has shown remarkable continuity. One participant attended some twenty-five of thirty-two meetings, and most present participants have attended at least ten to fifteen.

Asked later why the Tajiks seemed willing to come to a meeting sponsored by a group of Russians and Americans, Naumkin and Zviagelskaya reflected: "First, although we believe they respect us as individuals, we do not think they would have come to a meeting unless you Americans were present. Second, we are not sure they would have come to a Russian-U.S. meeting, but they were willing to accept an invitation from what they see as an international movement—the Dartmouth Conference." As noted earlier, they came to call themselves the "Inter-Tajik Dialogue within the Framework of the Dartmouth Conference." Even more important, they absorbed the way of talking in dialogue that had come to characterize the "Dartmouth process." Sometimes, when new participants joined the dialogue and began delivering lectures as if they were in a traditional academic seminar, it was not the co-moderators of the dialogue but the participants who said, "That is not the way we talk in this dialogue." The "Dartmouth process" seemed to have acquired a character of its own that, in some part, may account for the continuity of participation and the commitment of the participants.

While Naumkin and Zviagelskaya were in Tajikistan building the human foundations for the dialogue, Saunders and Slim were seeking funding. The Kettering Foundation budget continued to support the Regional Conflicts Task Force, but this would be a costly enough project to require grants from other foundations. (As a research and operating rather than a grant-making foundation, Kettering enjoys the same tax status under U.S. law as a university and is therefore in a position to receive grants, despite a substantial endowment of its own.) Their approach to funders revealed three significant points in the philosophy that would guide the dialogue—all points learned partly in the Dartmouth experience and all points that were central to the work of shaping the Dartmouth Conference in the 1990s and beyond to respond to the needs of the new Russian-U.S. relationship.

First, their approach focused on generating the capacity among citizens to resolve their own conflict and to prevent its recurrence. It went beyond the traditional approach of many practitioners in the field of conflict resolution in the United States. Whereas many approached the new "ethnic conflicts" with a view to mediating agreements between opponents, Saunders and Slim had a different goal. As they wrote in a memo to a potential funder, their objective was "to *see whether* a group can be formed from within an intra-state conflict that can design a peace process for *their own* country." The experience of Dartmouth had not been to come together under the auspices of a third party. Saunders was once asked in an international conference by a practitioner of conflict resolution, "Who was the third party in the Dartmouth Conference?" His reply was that the cochairs of the conference and of the task forces were the "stewards of the process," shaping the cumulative agenda for meeting after meeting and moderating the meetings so as to get the most possible out of the dialogue. Although the management team opened the space for the Inter-Tajik Dialogue, the hope in this new project was to see whether a group could be formed that would, first, play roles as individuals in their country's peace process and, second, ultimately take over the dialogue process itself. That hope was gradually becoming reality through the collaboration of Americans, Russians, and Tajiks as the new century began.

Second, the vehicle for this effort would be the first application of a now systematized process of sustained dialogue. The joint Chufrin-Saunders article was published as the Inter-Tajik Dialogue began, and in the next few months it would be translated into Russian so that participants could begin reflecting on the process itself as they lived it.

Members of the management team would be continuously conscious that one aspect of the project was to test the five-stage process of sustained dialogue to refine and develop it so that it could be transferred to still other conflicts. As the dialogue proceeded, Saunders was writing his book, *A Public Peace Process.*[22] Each meeting of the dialogue produced further refinement in the manuscript, which was published in 1999.

The president of one of the two funding organizations, the Charles Stewart Mott Foundation, fixed on the importance of the "transferability" of the process. After initially rejecting a proposal, he read accounts of the first two meetings of the dialogue and recognized the importance of the process itself. Indeed, the process later became the framework for a dialogue between native Estonians and Russian-speakers in Estonia left behind by the withdrawal of Soviet troops. It has also been used in a handful of North American communities to deal with relationships involving whites, blacks, Hispanics, Asians, and native populations and within Russia itself.

Third, in recognizing that the process of sustained dialogue differs from formal mediation and negotiation, participants focused on transforming conflictual relationships in addition to focusing on ending violent conflict with an agreement mediated by some official body. After formal negotiations started—partly as a result of their efforts—participants in the dialogue restated their objective as "designing a process of national reconciliation for our country."

Three years later, the senior staff of the Kettering Foundation would articulate an insight into the nature of intrastate conflict that came to be central in the convergence of the efforts through dialogue to resolve conflict and parallel efforts to strengthen democratic civil society. Mathews and Saunders wrote a joint letter to the cochairs of the Carnegie Commission on Preventing Deadly Conflict—former secretary of state Cyrus Vance and David Hamburg, president of the Carnegie Corporation of New York. They stated that the world would not have an adequate theory of conflict prevention or conflict resolution until scholars and practitioners recognized what happens to a society during internal conflict. As violence increases, the institutions and practices that normally permit citizens to reach across the lines of division within any society to work together are torn apart as citizens retreat into groups of like-minded people to fight each other. Usually, mediators arrive on the scene to help the combatant groups agree to a cease-fire, perhaps to new ways of dealing with each other, or to some division of contested political power or material resources. More often than not, the mediator then goes home. No one stays around to help rebuild the sinews of a functioning society in which people of different views must work together despite having recently been enemies. It was this insight that led them to see the importance of bringing together the work of conflict resolution with the work of building healthy civil societies.[23]

The Kettering Foundation paid for the first meeting of the dialogue. Then the first of three grants from the William and Flora Hewlett Foundation began. Later in the year, so did the first of two grants from the Mott Foundation. These two foundations—in an unusual act of perseverance—funded the Inter-Tajik Dialogue through the remainder of the decade. Kettering, of course, nourished the conceptual framework and supported the work of Saunders and Slim. The University of Nebraska at Omaha (UNO) supported Gouttierre's participation. It also developed its own collaborative relationship with the Technological University of Tajikistan and hosted Tajik groups and students on its campus. The Russian Center for Strategic Research and International Studies (later renamed the International Center for Strategic and Political Studies), led by Naumkin and Zviagelskaya, became the Russian partner.

Participants in the dialogue came together for their first meeting in March 1993. When they first sat down around a conference table at the Institute of Oriental Studies in Moscow, they could barely look at one another. This was the beginning of the second stage in the sustained dialogue process—one in which participants voiced their grievances, their analyses, their hopes, their fears, often in a random manner, "downloading" or "dumping" all of their concerns and grievances on the table almost simultaneously. This was an essential period in which participants experienced others' perceptions, feelings, identity while moderators "mapped" the dynamics of the relationships in conflict. Chufrin and Saunders co-moderated the meetings.

Participants recognized at the outset that they were unprepared for independence when the Soviet Union dissolved. The last few years of glasnost and perestroika in the Soviet Union had opened the door in Tajikistan to different points of view about what the country should be.

A new democratic party was formed, and a movement called Rastokhez sought to resurrect the thousand-year Tajik heritage as a model for life in a country freer to be itself. They had been unable to manage that diversity. The first postindependence president—a survivor of the communist period, although elected—was forced to resign at gunpoint, and the country slid into internal conflict. There was, participants acknowledged, little sense of a Tajik identity; the country had never existed as an independent entity within present boundaries. Nor, as they would discuss at length in later meetings, was there a "political culture"—a way of dealing with fundamental differences among citizens. Fighting began. Citizens were driven from their homes into exile until at least one out of every seven Tajiks had fled his or her home. The fighting in many instances was vicious. No one knows how many people actually died, but the most common estimates range from around 50,000 upward.

Dialogue participants remained in Stage Two for three meetings—a second in June and a third in August. It should be noted that, to the best of the management team's knowledge, this was the only systematic channel of communication at that time between pro-government and pro-opposition Tajiks. Whereas the first two meetings took place in Moscow, the third meeting took place in an old fortress and convent in Rostov-Veliki, one of the old Russian cities in what is called the Golden Ring. This meeting was the first time the group had met under the same roof, with participants meeting, eating, and walking together. Toward the end of the second day, as participants continued to pour out their recriminations about the parties' interactions during the civil war, someone said: "What we really have to work on is how to start a negotiation between the government and the opposition about creating conditions so refugees can go home. We can do nothing in our country until people are back in their homes." At that meeting, they could take this thought no further. It was obviously too frightening for each side to think about how their warring groups could reach out to each other. But the seed had been planted. With that identification of a shared subject to work on together, the group was poised to move from Stage Two to Stage Three.

In Stage Three, participants stop talking *at* one another and begin talking *with* one another about the subject that they have identified together as affecting the interests of all parties. The style of moderating also changes as Stage Three begins. Whereas in Stage Two moderators encourage a scatter-shot range of comments to get all thoughts and analyses on the table, in Stage Three the moderators serve more as disciplinarians to keep the group focused on the subject they have agreed to talk about.

Participants came back to their November meeting ready to talk in depth about how to start a negotiation. A deteriorating situation in their country and the drama of Russian president Yeltsin's shelling of the Russian Parliament the week before set a somber mood for these discussions, which again took place outside Moscow—this time in Vladimir, another city in the Golden Ring. Participants engaged in a serious discussion of how a negotiation could begin between the government, on the one hand, and opposition forces that were ideologically diffuse and geographically dispersed from Afghanistan through CIS states to Moscow. Pro-government participants asked: "If we wanted to invite members of the opposition, whom would we invite? Where would we find those people?" And not so facetiously: "What are your phone numbers? What are your addresses?" They also dealt with the question of whether people "with blood on their hands" could participate in the negotiation. Participants left with a new working relationship established among them, having aired at some length the problems involved in starting a negotiation.

Less than two months after that meeting, leaders of the main opposition factions gathered in Tehran, Iran. They drafted a common platform, which two participants in the dialogue signed, and they formed an opposition coordinating center in Moscow. Five members of the dialogue served on its steering committee.

In early January, the group came together for its fifth meeting and heard the opposition members present the platform of the new United Tajik Opposition. The main points that opposition participants made in explaining the platform were written down. Pro-government participants grilled pro-opposition members for two days. Opposition members responded with candor, realism, and tact to serious questions such as whether and how the demilitarization of armed forces would take place. At the end of the meeting, pro-government participants expressed the view that the "basis for negotiation existed," and they promised to report to the government.

During this period, an emissary of the United Nations secretary-general had been attempting to bring government and opposition together in a mediated negotiation. Within a month after the dialogue meeting, the government accepted that invitation.

This was the first of a number of examples of how difficult it is to assess the influence of a group such as the Inter-Tajik Dialogue. In complex political situations, there are many inputs into a decision, and no participant in decision making can know exactly how any of those inputs influenced a particular decision. Participants in the dialogue feel that their report to the government played a significant role in its decision making. A senior Tajik official who participated in that decision making later told members of the management team that the work of the dialogue had made it impossible for opponents of negotiation to argue any longer that it was impossible to deal with the opposition. Did the dialogue play a role? Yes, almost certainly. Can it claim credit for the government's decision? No, but it can claim to have helped shape the environment in which that decision was made.

In March, when the dialogue met for the sixth time, participants produced their first joint memorandum, "Memorandum on a Negotiating Process for Tajikistan."[24] They had talked about this subject for a day, and overnight some members of the management team wrote what they had said and translated the paper into Russian and Tajiki. Participants in the dialogue then met without moderators to discuss the document. Thereafter, the participants and management team met to make changes.

One of the most significant ideas in this joint memorandum was that four working groups should be created under the negotiating teams so as to draw elements of Tajik society and government together to solve such important problems as the demilitarization of armed elements, economic rehabilitation, political reform, and refugee return. In other words, they proposed that the negotiating process itself become the center of a larger political process for stitching the war-torn country back together. These were certainly "ideas in the air" at that time, but the dialogue established for itself—and for others with whom participants talked and who read their memorandum—a conceptualization of a negotiating process that would go beyond just what happened in the negotiating room. The idea of a political process growing out of and extending the reach of negotiations became an accepted part of the conceptualization of their peace process.

When the group came together again in May, the first meetings of the UN-mediated negotiation had taken place in April. Three participants in the dialogue were delegates in the negotiation—one on the government side and two on the opposition team. (They had asked the management team to organize a two-day workshop on negotiation for them.) Dialogue members asked themselves whether they should disband now that negotiations had begun. Their answer: "We helped to start the negotiations, and we should continue to work to help assure their success." Having set for themselves in their third meeting the objective of "helping to start a negotiation," they now reformulated their objective as "designing a political process of national reconciliation for the country."

Between that meeting and the next, members of the management team paid a visit to Tajikistan. During that visit, they not only spent time with participants in the dialogue, but they visited important institutions in the capital city of Dushanbe. Most important perhaps, some members of the management team met with the foreign minister to discuss the dialogue. Naumkin and Zviagelskaya had explained the process to him on their exploratory visit to Tajikistan in early 1993, and pro-government participants in the dialogue had reported to him, among others, as the dialogue proceeded. During this meeting, Saunders assured him that the dialogue did not intend to second-guess the negotiators. "We are citizens outside government. We know we have no authority to negotiate anything. Participants in the dialogue believe they can play a useful role in helping to develop a process of national reconciliation that would help prepare the country for whatever agreements come out of the negotiations. We will not interfere with the negotiations."[25]

That is the way the dialogue proceeded. At times, participants did address issues that had brought the negotiations to impasse, but they dealt with those issues not as negotiating issues but rather as options for dealing with issues in the relationship between government and opposition forces.

Shortly after that visit, dialogue participants made their own visit to the United States for the only meeting that would be held outside the Commonwealth of Independent States. They began their visit with a four-hour public appearance before an invited audience at the United

States Institute of Peace. One purpose was to demonstrate the process of dialogue; the other, in that context, was to engage in discussion on one of the principal issues facing Tajikistan. Dialogue participants chose to talk about how Tajikistan could develop a political culture of power sharing that would reflect the various interests of regions, political parties and movements, and nationalities in Tajikistan. Underlying this discussion was the fact that the very concept of power sharing had not been experienced, as Americans understand it, in Tajik culture. The phrase used there denoted the allocation of power positions among parties rather than the actual sharing of power, as would happen between a principal officer and a deputy in the United States or as would happen in the federal system of the United States.

Following that appearance, the group went to a conference center near Princeton University for the eighth meeting of the dialogue. Although they attempted to write another joint memorandum, the fact that the meeting took place on the verge of the next round of formal negotiations made participants wary of being seen to agree on anything with the adversary. They wrote several papers but agreed to leave them as working papers of the dialogue.

During the next year, Tajikistan underwent a round of elections, and participants in the dialogue, while meeting in September and November 1994, produced nothing in writing. They spent most of their time together talking about obstacles to national reconciliation—top among them, "the lack of political culture"—and analyzing the electoral process. When they came together for their eleventh meeting in March 1995, the elections were over. Several international organizations declared that they did not meet international standards. Opposition members of the dialogue had to consider how they would react. Their choices were either to say that they rejected the elections and would urge opposition forces to work to overturn the results of the elections or to declare the period ahead "a period of transition to a more inclusive political system." They chose the latter. The idea of a transitional period in negotiating processes is certainly not an original one, but they did at least make this concept an instrument in their own picture of the situation.

The dialogue next met in June 1995 shortly after the formal negotiations had failed the previous month to agree on a mechanism for national reconciliation. In reaction, participants in this twelfth meeting completed the "Memorandum on National Reconciliation in Tajikistan." It urged confidence-building measures that would help create "conditions for agreement on a mechanism for national reconciliation." It urged creation of two kinds of bodies. The first was a coordinating Council for National Reconciliation to be created *under* the authority of the Inter-Tajik negotiations, including representatives of principal regions, political parties and movements, and national communities to implement the decisions of the negotiations through commissions on internal security and disarmament, refugees and temporarily displaced persons, democratic law and practice, and national economic development. The important aspect of the coordinating council as the participants in the twelfth meeting presented it was that they placed it under the authority of the negotiating teams rather than, as the United Tajik Opposition in the negotiations had proposed, making it a supra-governmental organization. They felt this would relieve the government's suspicion of a necessary mechanism. The second was a public body—a political consultative committee or a congress of the peoples of Tajikistan— "to bring together citizens from all regions, political parties and movements, and national communities to consider and solve important questions facing the people of Tajikistan."

As with all other such assessments, it is not possible to attribute later developments to any particular source, such as this joint memorandum. The fact is that the National Reconciliation Commission established in the General Agreement on Peace in June 1997 created that commission with four subcommissions as a space where, in effect, negotiation of details of the relationship between government and opposition would continue, even following the signing of a peace agreement. Dialogue participants felt they were the originators of this idea, but again no one can know exactly how such an idea becomes a reality.

Later that summer, the president of Tajikistan, Emomali Rakhmonov, and the leader of the United Tajik Opposition, Said Abdullo Nuri, signed an agreement that included creation of a Consultative Forum of the Peoples of Tajikistan. This idea had been "in the air" for some time; the dialogue put it into context in its memorandum along with other options. A participant in the dialogue, who actually wrote the agreement between the two leaders in his own hand, attributes influence to the dialogue's memorandum, but again no one could claim exclusive responsibility. In a series of joint memoranda beginning with the thirteenth meeting, in September 1995, the dialogue appealed for early establishment of the Consultative Forum.

By this time the dialogue was falling into the practice of producing a joint memorandum during every meeting. It is worth noting at this point that a well-established dialogue group may go through at least Stages Three and Four in each meeting and Stage Five following a meeting. The Inter-Tajik Dialogue had spent the fourth and fifth meetings in Stage Three, probing the question of how to begin negotiations. In writing the first joint memorandum in March 1994, participants entered Stage Four—designing a course of action. In distributing that memorandum to government and opposition leaders as well as to the headquarters of the United Nations, they took action by putting it in the hands of those in a position to act. In subsequent meetings—as is natural in such dialogues—they moved back and forth among the last three stages. A pattern for their meetings evolved in which they would talk up until lunch the first day about the situation in the country since their last meeting. From that discussion, they would select one or two subjects they thought deserved particular attention. Then they would talk about each subject in depth and write a joint memorandum about it.

Up until mid-1998 the method employed to produce the first joint memorandum continued with the co-moderators reducing the main points in dialogue to writing for revision and ultimate agreement by the whole group. This, in essence, was the procedure employed at the 1978 Camp David meetings with U.S. president Jimmy Carter, Egyptian president Anwar Sadat, and Israeli prime minister Menachem Begin, where Saunders was a principal drafter. Beginning in June 1998, members of the dialogue themselves began drafting elements of the joint memoranda. Since their twenty-second meeting they have taken responsibility for the entire process.

Meeting for the first time in Tajikistan in May 1996, the dialogue produced its most sober memo up to that time. Participants expressed the belief that "the territorial integrity and even the sovereignty of Tajikistan comes under serious threat." They returned to their conviction that a primary element in that threat was the lack of a full understanding of how

power might be effectively shared among the various elements in Tajikistan. They urged both parties to the conflict to broaden participation in
the negotiating process. In dialogue seventeen, meeting near Moscow in
October 1996, the joint memorandum the group wrote emphasized the
importance of a "multilevel peace process." One participant had been a
member of a commission that negotiated a significant cease-fire between
government and opposition forces who had cut an important road
between east and west. At the dialogue meeting he recounted how the
agreement had been worked out among local field commanders and
authorities of local government. When he had finished his account,
another dialogue participant said: "What we really need in Tajikistan is a
multilevel peace process in which the official negotiators are connected
with the combatants on the ground with their own local interests and with
their guns." In articulating this concept, they had established for themselves a framework within which they would work in the postconflict
phase.

In dialogues eighteen and nineteen, in February and May 1997,
they continued to analyze what they regarded as the increasing fragmentation in the country and the importance of a political system that would
include a broad range of Tajiks. Dialogue twenty, in November 1997,
was the first meeting to be held in the wake of the peace agreement that
had been signed in June. Four participants in the dialogue became members of the National Reconciliation Commission established by the peace
agreement. The closer collaboration between government and opposition
in that context opened the door to bringing into the dialogue individuals with even closer relationships to the leaders on both sides.

For the next three years, meetings usually began with a report from a
member who participated in the work of the National Reconciliation
Commission. Members continued to address in their joint memoranda the
principal issues raised by the important developments in the country. Space
in this volume does not permit a meeting-by-meeting account, nor do
readers need that to consolidate their understanding of the role the dialogue
was now playing. It is worth noting that one of the mainstay participants
was appointed during this period to be a deputy foreign minister of Tajikistan, and members of the president's office and political party as well as representatives of other political parties were participants as the elections

of 1999–2000 unfolded. Several additional members of the National Reconciliation Commission joined the dialogue.

The formal transitional period established for the work of the National Reconciliation Commission ended in February 2000 with the completion of that series of elections. Three participants in the dialogue had attempted to become candidates in those elections and, they felt, had been thwarted by government obstruction of their registration or of their parties' registration. They had every reason to be bitter, but the assessment of those elections in the dialogue was threefold: (1) Yes, the government had set up the election machinery to favor the cause of the president's party. (2) At the same time, opposition parties needed to recognize that they themselves had not adequately organized; nor had they presented coherent platforms and programs. They needed to look within themselves, said one participant in a losing party, for causes of the government's substantial victory. (3) With all of these deficiencies, Tajikistan had just held the "first genuinely contested elections in Central Asia."

With the beginning of a new phase under a new constitution, dialogue members reached out to prominent individuals outside the dialogue to form and legally register their own nongovernmental organization—the Public Committee for Promoting Democratic Processes. Having long recognized the importance of nongovernmental organizations and citizens' participation in the political process, they adopted a four-track program for strengthening the capacities of citizens to play their role in the civil society and in the political process. One member of the dialogue had early in the dialogue's history established the Tajikistan Center for Civic Education. She and other Tajiks had attended workshops in deliberative democracy at the Kettering Foundation, and three had been international fellows for six months each at the foundation. Now building on their experience, the Public Committee—with the help of Randa Slim, working with them on behalf of the dialogue—established the following four tracks for their work.

First, they would establish a second dialogue—with the long-standing dialogue continuing its work—with younger people inside Tajikistan. They began a dialogue group in Dushanbe. They have focused on significant problems facing the country such as the role of religion in politics and the role of regionalism. These initial dialogues are chaired by veteran members of the senior dialogue. In 2001 they started dialogues in four other cities. They planned to bring all moderators together in early 2002 to train more moderators to launch an "all-national dialogue."

Second, they have embarked on a series of public forums in different regions of Tajikistan on such broad issues as poverty, drugs, and education. The purpose is to give Tajik citizens an experience in deliberative dialogue. To help train moderators in these forums, Igor Nagdasev, former Kettering international fellow and director of the Russian Center for Citizenship Education, went to Tajikistan to work with two dozen potential moderators and to train a smaller number of Tajiks to frame their own issues in ways that would permit the public to engage in deliberation about them.

Third, the Public Committee worked with citizens in three communities that had been seriously torn apart by the civil strife to establish Economic Development Committees to help those communities come together around the challenge of rebuilding their economic base. As one former Kettering international fellow said: "The government does not have the resources or the ability to help every community get on its feet economically. If anybody is going to do this work, it is the citizens of those communities." As those committees proceeded, it became increasingly apparent that their work could bring together the experience of sustained dialogue to address relational issues and deliberative dialogue to engage larger numbers of the community in deciding on economic courses of action. Placed in a global perspective, those committees became small laboratories for learning how communities can start building the civic infrastructure—now widely called social capital—that economists are increasingly recognizing as the long-missing ingredient in theories of economic development.

Fourth, the Public Committee signed an agreement with the Ministry of Education to work together with professors from nine Tajik universities to develop courses and programs in conflict resolution. The Kettering Foundation with the support of its grant from the Hewlett Foundation agreed to make available one or two Western scholars to work with these professors. The professors began their work by doing their own research on traditional Tajik approaches to resolving conflict. Their hope is that the interaction between that research and Western methods of conflict resolution can produce something that reflects the best of both traditions.

At this writing, work on these four tracks seems likely to proceed for some time. The hope of the management team and their Tajik colleagues is that this work can be embedded in the Tajik political, social, academic, and economic landscape, but, just as was the case at the beginning of the dialogue, it is unlikely that anyone is sufficiently wise or farsighted to know what the impact of this process will be. As with the larger Dartmouth Conference, the people who have participated have played significant roles as individuals in helping to make peace and to begin building a peaceful society. No one would claim exclusive credit for promoting peace, but no one can ignore the role that the Inter-Tajik Dialogue within the Framework of the Dartmouth Conference has played.[26]

FORTIETH-ANNIVERSARY REUNION OF THE DARTMOUTH CONFERENCE

Two dozen Dartmouth veterans gathered in late September 2000 at the Institute of Europe in Moscow to mark the fortieth anniversary of the first Dartmouth Conference meeting. It was just a month shy of forty years since that first group had sat down together in Hanover, New Hampshire.

The principal Russian hosts for the meeting were Zhurkin, formerly of ISKAN, then founding director of the Institute of Europe, at this time recently retired. His cohost was Nikolai Shmelev, analyst of the Soviet and now Russian economy, a former Dartmouth participant, and then Zhurkin's successor as director of the institute. A. Arbatov, Davidson, Grushin, Karaganov, Kislov, Kondrashov, Kortunov, Kremenyuk, Yuri Legeev, Lukin, Naumkin, Primakov, Rogov, Nodari Simonia, Sokolov, Vorontsov, and Zviagelskaya were present for all or parts of the meeting. Georgi Arbatov was away from Moscow. Dobrynin was ill. Chufrin was at his post in Stockholm. Alice Bobrysheva joined the delegation as she had since the beginning. In preparation for the meeting, Zhurkin had interviewed a dozen Russian Dartmouth veterans at length about the current state of the Russian-U.S. relationship and their reflections on the Dartmouth process.

Kettering president Mathews led the American delegation, and Saunders, since 1991 Kettering's director of international affairs, shared chairing responsibilities. Dartmouth veterans Doty, Gouttierre, Horelick, Slim, and Stewart also attended. They were joined by Robert Kaiser of the *Washington Post*, who had had extensive journalistic experience in the Soviet Union and Russia, and Allen Lynch of the University of Virginia, a scholar of Soviet and Russian foreign policy and politics. Patricia Coggins came out of retirement to shepherd the American delegation.

It was significant—in both symbolic and practical terms—that the American delegation embraced two groups. One was the group just described, which sat down to mark the Dartmouth anniversary. The other was a smaller group that conducted parallel meetings with former Kettering international fellows and their colleagues working to introduce deliberative democracy into Russia. Among those were senior librarians at the Library of Foreign Literature who had sent a delegation to Kettering workshops and for visits with libraries around the United States that had made themselves centers for public deliberation. The librarians were developing a comparable network in Russia. Out of this combination of meetings came the project already mentioned for these Russian colleagues to frame for public forums in Russia the question of how Russians see America. A comparable group in the United States, which would include some who participated in this visit to Moscow, would frame the issue and organize mirror-image forums for Americans.

Zhurkin began the anniversary meeting with a moment of silence remembering those who had passed away since the last formal Dartmouth plenary in 1990—Cousins, Milstein, Shishlin, Klebnikov, and Neumann. All of them had been mainstays of the Dartmouth process. Their passing was not only important in its own right but symptomatic of the feeling that many had at the end of the meeting—that the people of Dartmouth not only had to adjust to the loss of a country and to the loss of an enemy but also to the gradual passing of a generation that had lived the Cold War and the Dartmouth Conference response to it. Numerous comments during the meeting noted that, while the Dartmouth process would be much needed in the new century, it had to find new ways to attract succeeding generations.

Although the meeting was billed as a reunion, participants typically spent most of their time assessing the state of the Russian-U.S. relationship and the state of the world that influenced it before they talked about the state of the dialogue itself. One American participant perhaps captured the contradictions and ambiguities in the relationship when he spoke of the "in-betweenness" of the relationship. He spoke of the "asymmetrical" character of the relationship that made it difficult to manage. Later he reflected to Primakov, who sat with the group one afternoon, that the asymmetry had its roots partly in the fact that the 1990s had been a successful decade for the United States and a difficult one for Russia.

Underlying much of the discussion of the relationship was the feeling that the proverbial glass was half-empty and half-full at the same time. Later in the meeting, one Russian participant said: "The relationship is the same today as during the Cold War. It is largely government-to-government. It seems able to withstand even the worst of shocks although the relationship has not been good in this decade." Another Russian participant said that, in his view also, the relationship seems "quite sustainable, despite its crises and stresses."

Participants focused heavily on the problems that Russia faced, but a prominent Russian economist noted in the same statement both the "miracles of initiative in the shadow economy" and the difficulty of distinguishing between "what is shadow and what is criminal." There was significant discussion on the state of the economy, in which the principal Russian economist said that Russians were clearer about their goals than was often recognized. "We have achieved a preliminary national consensus on economic goals," even though the need for further change and the lack of achievement were recognized.

Sharp Russian sensitivity to perceived affronts by the United States threaded its way through the conversation, while at the same time Russians acknowledged that "some Russians have lost their identity" or perhaps were suffering from centuries-old uncertainty about their identity.

Several American participants made clear that all of the weaknesses in the relationship do not lie on the Russian side. One

acknowledged that an important issue is "whether Russia can establish economic and political conditions for a natural, normal, mutual
dependency." Then he turned to the American side to note that
"Americans have had a difficult time adjusting to the end of the Cold
War. As a society we have done a poor job of adjusting to the loss of
this organizing principle. Americans are having trouble deciding
what Russia is now, but they are also having trouble articulating their
own goals in the world." Another American participant noted that
Americans "like being called the only remaining superpower, but we
are quite ambivalent about how we should use that power."

One participant noted that perhaps the most important factor in
how the relationship will develop is how well Russia does in consolidat-
ing democracy and its market economy. Since Americans still harbor
residual suspicions born in the depths of the Cold War, what Russia does
will shape U.S. perceptions of what kind of relationship is possible. The
war in Chechnya was symptomatic of the events that have reinforced
questions in American minds about what Russia's long-term character
and intent may be.

Participants noted with deep concern that, in the arms control
field, the two countries had "failed to finish their job. We failed to
establish the basis for a non-competitive relationship. This is not stable
ground." There is a need for new thinking in depth about the role of
nuclear weapons in the world, and "we have lost a decade in that thinking, although it is possible to note small areas in which steps could be
taken that would help enhance the stability of the present situation."

Throughout this discussion, despite the ambiguities, there was little disagreement that the relationship is poor—not in comparison with
the low points in the Cold War relationship but in the sense that a relationship with much positive potential is not being realized. There was
a general feeling that the "relationship is moving in the wrong direction." Another Russian participant said: "The relationship is fragile.
There is very little partnership." One Russian participant noted that
"ten years ago everyone in Russia wanted to cooperate with the United
States, but now seventy percent say no." One American participant—
a scholar of Soviet and Russian foreign policy—introduced some
perspective into the exchange when he said: "We all know what kind
of relationship we want. We want a relationship in which each country

can protect vital interests and pursue lesser but important interests without transgressing the interests of others. The challenge is how to move from sluggishness to constructive collaboration." He noted that there are "no ideologically driven interests" and that there are "no conflicting vital material interests. At the same time there are many common interests, including the mutual interest of the two countries in Russian economic recovery. Perhaps most important but often unstated is the recognition that neither country opposes the other as a matter of principle. The challenge before citizens of both countries, especially those in the room, is to define where are the boundaries of this new relationship."

In statements that echoed comments made in the last two Dartmouth plenaries and the work on civil society that had increased in the 1990s, participants from both countries noted one important new ingredient in the post–Cold War relationship. It was a Russian participant who first recalled that, while the primary focus in the Dartmouth exchanges had been on governments, "in 1988, Arbatov mentioned for the first time public opinion in Russia. We have to include this dimension in our discussion." Just as a footnote, Yankelovich's impressive review of American public opinion in 1984 had stimulated an interest in the later 1980s on both sides to understand the role of public opinion in the relationship more fully.

An American participant responded to the Russian comment by noting that the Dartmouth Conference before 1990 had largely been a series of exchanges among elites. After 1990 the two countries entered a "popular phase" with mushrooming exchanges at all levels between "whole bodies politic." He recalled the strong Russian delegation to Dartmouth XVI that was composed in order to demonstrate the important broadening of the interaction between the two peoples.

As the discussion turned to the state of dialogue between the two countries a younger Russian participant picked up this theme: "The market for our product is no longer there. In the past, we concentrated on the intellectual product. The market during the Cold War included the foreign relations, defense, and intelligence departments of governments. Now we have to shape a new market for our ideas. We not only have to pay more attention to economic trends; we also have to concentrate on the social base. We need to give attention to the general educational base which shapes the social base for the relationship. Most groups still concentrate on top political leadership," he concluded. "We need to cultivate the social and popular political levels."

Throughout the dialogue, participants repeatedly noted that the Russian-U.S. relationship has been and will be heavily influenced by the larger changes on the world scene—globalization, wider financial flows, transnational corporations, regional integration, disintegration of nation-states that causes weakening of government control. At the same time, participants noted the danger spots in that changing world that argued all the more strongly for continuation of a strong Dartmouth-like exchange. Certainly the handling of nuclear relationships remains at the top of the list—from the threat of proliferation of nuclear devices to the impulses to create nuclear missile defenses against that threat. All seemed to agree that the move of the United States toward a system of national missile defense would undermine the infrastructure of efforts to achieve a stable security system. An American participant, joined by some Russian colleagues, pointed to South and Central Asia as an area of great potential danger but at the same time an area of great opportunity for Russian-U.S. collaboration. He acknowledged with regret that the opportunity for collaboration would be negatively affected as much by the apparent inability to move U.S. policymakers to focus on this area as by Russian policies.

Perhaps an American participant best summed up the foundations that exist for building a strong Russian-U.S. relationship for the future: "We have had an extraordinary experience together, living on the brink of world destruction. It is our extraordinary experience. We must not ignore that experience. We have a lot to build on." Another participant agreed: "Yes, the relationship is in trouble, but our capacity to address that trouble is far greater than it was at the beginning of Dartmouth." Looking to the future, an American participant noted: "During the Cold War, Dartmouth was all that was possible. Now, the real potential for interaction lies in the bodies politic of both sides." Several Russian participants noted that there is a large Russian community in the United States now. Most young people in Russia "take for granted that they will go to the United States or Europe at some point in their early lives. Businessmen look to the potential of the Russian economy once there is a genuine rule of law." In short, they agreed that the work that the Dartmouth Conference had done must in some way continue.

In sum, journalist Stanislav Kondrashov, a Dartmouth veteran, captured the essence of the meeting in an article in one of Moscow's prominent papers:

> Last week in Moscow one very significant meeting took place generally unnoticed by mass media and broad public. The working language was English. The organizers defined the meeting as a reunion or to say it in Russian the restoration of the union. Which one?
>
> The Dartmouth conference (or meetings), Dartmouth process, Dartmouth movement have their own long history, their source and, as it seemed before the Moscow reunion, their end. But no. After the reunion maybe the revival will take place.
>
> Sunrays of golden autumn looked into the assembly hall of the building on the old territory of the Moscow State University. They increased the feeling of nostalgia as if it was not simply a reunion but a family reunion, the reunion of the Dartmouth family. This family wants to somehow pave the abyss, which is widening, because if to total up the last decade Russia and the USA are against all expectations drifting away from each other. The former nuclear-missile, life-and-death bond is, thank God, broken. But another one which should be organizing and disciplining is not yet found. And it creates a state of uncertainty. Both powers are looking for their new positions.
>
> The American and the Russian Dartmouthers tried through different prisms to look through and to solve the geopolitical situation of the new time.
>
> Where will Russia and America be then—together or apart? A strong and concerned Russia will be important for America as a partner. . . . The Dartmouth meetings, as one American defined them, were a kind of a system of early warning. Objectively, life again calls for that.[27]

Little could the group gathered in that room foresee how events would once again produce an environment for change in the Russian-U.S. relationship following the terrorist attacks on the United States on September 11, 2001. Nor could they know that just a year later a smaller group would meet in Moscow after several months of preparatory talks to shape concrete plans for launching a new Dartmouth task force on the Russian-U.S. relationship. It would be deliberately designed to capture the relationship between the whole bodies politic in both its composition and its agenda. As they had periodically in the past, the people of Dartmouth were redesigning their work to meet the challenges of a changing world.

7 | The Influence of the Dartmouth Conference on Policymakers and Policy

AT THE FIRST SESSION OF THE DARTMOUTH CONFERENCE, in Hanover, it was said, "Governments pay attention to citizens of good will." The truth of that statement, or, more precisely, the question of whether Dartmouth had influence in the United States and the Soviet Union, bedeviled a number of those who took part in Dartmouth, notably Harold Saunders and Philip Stewart. Their claims were modest, and they were well aware that their discussions were unlikely to have much effect on policy in the short term. Their hopes, like those of Mosely earlier, were for longer-term, incremental, indirect influence.

As suggested in chapter 1, the influence of transnational communities such as the Dartmouth Conference on policymaking communities can be assessed by examining either the direct influence by such communities on state policy or their indirect influence, that is, their ability to influence the climate of opinion in which policy is made. This chapter will use these two approaches to analyze the influence of Dartmouth on policymakers.

DIRECT INFLUENCE

In the early years of the conference, the organizers eschewed any declaration that they intended to directly influence policy at all, preferring to speak in more general terms of increasing understanding among those who took part. As Philip Mosely put it in 1970, a decade after the first conference was convened:

> The immediate purpose of the conferences is to educate the partici-
> pants themselves, not to influence the policy of either government.
> This purpose seems to have been achieved. Members of both sides
> have come to a better understanding of views on the other side, and
> why, and have learned to communicate better with participants on
> the other side. Beyond this, there may be some influence on govern-
> ment policies, but this is very indirect.[1]

In truth, the American participants in the early Dartmouth conferences came with different sets of hopes for the amount and the manner of influence that the conference would have.

There was a genuine reluctance to advance recommendations for
policy under the aegis of Dartmouth. In part, this reflected the absence
of a consensus among participants about what specific changes in policy should be sought. Some came to the conference with the general
goal of preventing nuclear holocaust. All may have shared a vague sense
that this uncontroversial goal could best be achieved if the relationship
between the two countries improved. They would not have agreed on
much else.

Unlike groups in the advocacy networks described by Keck and
Sikkink, Dartmouth was not made up of like-minded advocates of a
principled idea drawn together by a similar set of values. Indeed, the
organizers of Dartmouth on the American side sought a variety of views
on the issues they expected to be discussed. On the Soviet side, a similarity of ideas and values was assumed for most of the history of the dialogue, and preservation of that similarity was a matter of state policy.
Consequently, Dartmouth did not choose to adopt the tactics of persua-
sion and socialization that advocacy networks use, which "involve not
just reasoning with opponents, but also bringing pressure, arm-twisting,
encouraging sanctions, and shaming."[2] Instead, the people of Dartmouth exerted their influence quietly—Dartmouth never strove to make
headlines—and often did so as individuals rather than as representatives
of the Dartmouth Conference, so that the lines of influence are not easily drawn.

This ambivalence about exerting influence and the lack of consensus about policy meant that, unlike Pugwash and the advocacy networks,

Dartmouth did little to gain publicity. Editorials by Cousins and writings by other participants gave it some, but Pugwash did more, and most advocacy networks rely on publicity to make their issues known, mobilize opinion, and gain leverage over their targets. They address audiences broader than Dartmouth's. The public statements of Dartmouth, in contrast, said little, at least in the early years. Press releases issued at the end of each conference, for example, were limited to lists of the people who attended and a general description of the topics discussed. Manifestos were strictly avoided, and when joint statements were proposed, as during Dartmouth III, which took place in the middle of the Cuban missile crisis, they were never issued.

This reduced the ability of Dartmouth to exert indirect influence—to affect the climate of opinion. But the advantage for Dartmouth was that the conference itself was not associated with a single position; it was not perceived as an advocate for a particular point of view, though some of the participants were. This gained it credibility among policymakers. It was an important element in Dartmouth's ability to exert direct influence.

ACCESS OF AMERICANS TO AMERICAN POLICYMAKERS

From the beginning, the Dartmouth Conference took place with the encouragement and cooperation of the governments of the United States and the Soviet Union. In the Soviet case, this was probably because it was seen as having propaganda value, reflecting the Soviet history of transnational relations. On the American side, however, according to Norman Cousins, the Dartmouth Conference came about at the behest of President Eisenhower and took place with the directly expressed approval of the State Department. This helped to ensure that policymakers would take the results of the early conferences seriously. The approval of the government, which the participants sought and maintained, was another element that distinguished Dartmouth from the Pugwash Conference and from the advocacy networks described by Keck and Sikkink.

The most important source of the credibility of the conference, and the primary source of the access to policymakers that it achieved in the early years, was the reputation of participants and their personal acquaintance with policymakers. Many participants had worked in government or, like David Rockefeller, had easy access to policymakers. Mosely worked in the State Department during World War II and got to know many of the senior Soviet experts who still worked in the government in the 1960s. These participants were able to speak or write to senior officials and communicate the results of the Dartmouth dialogues directly. Cousins met with and influenced both President Eisenhower and President Kennedy, moving them toward the value-changing ideas that he sought to foster through the Dartmouth Conference. David Rockefeller gained access to Soviet leaders by virtue of his name and reputation. He was also able to speak directly to President Johnson after the Dartmouth Conference in 1964.

The president, of course, is the ultimate decision maker within the U.S. government. But Dartmouth participants gained access to other decision makers as well. Cousins had lunch with Secretary of State Dean Rusk in 1963 to discuss a possible meeting between Cousins and Khrushchev.[3] Several Dartmouth participants met with Secretary of State Alexander Haig early in 1981, shortly before going to the Soviet Union for the first Dartmouth Conference of the Reagan era.

A number of Dartmouth participants gained access to highly placed bureaucrats within the U.S. government. Indeed, the ability to exert influence was one criterion used to invite people to take part. Philip Mosely developed personal relationships with senior diplomats such as Charles Bohlen and Llewelyn Thompson when serving with them in the State Department during World War II. Philip Stewart maintained contacts that included William Hyland and Brent Scowcroft (themselves participants in at least one Dartmouth Conference), former colleagues and students in the Defense Department, and "a close friend who works as an analyst" in the Central Intelligence Agency. He was also able to "consistently [discuss] Dartmouth meetings with the National Intelligence Officer for Soviet Affairs—the highest official specifically responsible for the Soviet Union within the Agency." Other Dartmouth participants had similar contacts through whom they spread the word about what had been said at the conferences.

A number of congressmen, who can also be regarded as decision makers in the American political system, actually took part in conferences and task force meetings themselves, beginning with Dartmouth VI in Kiev. Members of Congress took part in several later conferences as well and then in task force meetings during the 1980s. They came from both the House and the Senate, were both junior and senior members, and were both Republicans and Democrats. Among them were Senators Mark Hatfield, Frank Church, who was prominent in the debates over policy toward the Soviet Union during the 1970s, Charles Mathias, Edward Kennedy, and Paul Tsongas, who became a contender for the presidential nomination in 1992, and Representatives Morris K. Udall and Les Aspin, chairman of the House Armed Services Committee and later secretary of defense. Former vice president Al Gore took part in a meeting of the Political Relations Task Force in 1986.

Attendance at a conference did not guarantee that legislators' actions would reflect the dialogue they took part in. Nonetheless, their participation in Dartmouth meetings created the potential for direct influence on individual legislators and indirect influence on the Congress and the public as they communicated what they had learned at Dartmouth to their colleagues, staff, and constituents. Specific instances in which influence was shown are difficult to find. Each conference was, after all, but one of many sources of information available to members and staff in Congress. Moreover, the Dartmouth traditions that minimized publicity made it less likely that the influence of Dartmouth would become known. Senator Scott, however, had a report on the Tbilisi conference printed by the Committee on Foreign Relations and made two statements about the conference that appeared in the *Congressional Record.*

From the beginning of the conferences, the American participants made a point of consulting with policymakers in the U.S. government. Indeed, the conferences came about after a long meeting with State Department officials in charge of exchanges with the Soviet Union, plus Charles Bohlen. It became standard practice for the American participants to be briefed by administration officials before conferences and to brief the State Department after. The preparations for Dartmouth VI, in 1971, included discussions by the new chairman of the American delegation, General James Gavin, with Henry Kissinger, then the national security advisor, and State Department officials not only about the agenda, but also about which members of Congress to invite. After that same conference Gavin and David Rockefeller met with Secretary of Commerce Peter Peterson, Secretary of State William

Rogers, Undersecretary of State John Irwin, three assistant secretaries of state and, perhaps most important, Kissinger.

The policymakers who took part in these briefings included, in the Carter administration, Shulman, Brzezinski, and Philip Habib, undersecretary of state for political affairs; in the Reagan administration, Scowcroft, General Jones, Stoessel, and Stoessel's successor as undersecretary of state, Michael Armacost; Joseph Twinam, deputy assistant secretary of state for Near Eastern and South Asian affairs; Chester Crocker, assistant secretary of state for African affairs; Lawrence Eagleburger, undersecretary of state; Thomas Simons, who was then head of the Soviet desk and later a senior official in the Reagan, Bush, and Clinton administrations; and Matlock, who at that time worked on the staff of the National Security Council. This pattern of meeting with senior officials did not stop in the 1990s and continues even today.

Access to the Reagan administration posed a special problem for the group organizing the Dartmouth Conference. President Reagan had proclaimed the need for a tougher approach toward the Soviets during his campaign, and the organizers of Dartmouth feared that dialogues like Dartmouth would be anathema to the new administration. Moreover, they had developed strong contacts among the crowd of policymakers— Republicans as well as Democrats—who were now being supplanted. Yet the reputation of Dartmouth, stemming from its unwillingness to put forward a "Dartmouth position" on the issues addressed in the conferences, the reputation of the American participants, and the willingness of the organizers to bring in people respected by the new crowd in Washington, such as Scowcroft, Neumann, and Horelick, raised the credibility of the conference in the eyes of the new administration. They came to consider Dartmouth as a tool for communication as well as a source of information. The American delegates who met with Secretary of State Haig and then other administration officials before Dartmouth XIII, in 1981, were given a number of specific points and an overall message to pass on to the Soviets. The Reagan administration took advantage of the opportunity for communication that Dartmouth afforded when Reagan sent a message to Chernenko three years later.

The access that Dartmouth Conference participants had to Soviet policymakers increased their access to American policymakers (the reverse was true as well). In early 1963, learning that Cousins was to meet with Khrushchev, a meeting that came about as a result of a Dartmouth Conference, President Kennedy and other senior officials in the administration met with Cousins. More than two decades later, in 1984, President Reagan took advantage of Scowcroft's participation in a Dartmouth task force meeting in Moscow to send a personal message to the Soviet Union. Thus the access that Dartmouth afforded to policymakers in both capitals, and the trust placed by the policymakers in the Dartmouth participants, made Dartmouth a potentially valuable conduit for information. This supplement to official channels of communication between two sides to a conflict is a significant contribution that a trusted unofficial transnational dialogue can make.

An analysis of the access of the Dartmouth participants to policymakers must also note that many American participants in the conferences became policymakers themselves. The conferences in effect served as training grounds for officials on both sides of the Iron Curtain. The American participants-turned-policymakers could use the understanding of Soviet thinking and attitudes gained from Dartmouth in their own approach to policy. Several of them entered government after taking part in one or more Dartmouth conferences. They include Brzezinski; his predecessor at the National Security Council, Scowcroft; Herbert York, who became the chief negotiator in the talks on a comprehensive test ban after going to Latvia for a Dartmouth Conference in 1977; Paul Warnke, a former assistant secretary of defense, who attended a Dartmouth Conference in Arizona in 1976 shortly before becoming a lead negotiator in the SALT talks; and Walt Rostow, who joined the Kennedy administration months after he took part in Dartmouth I. More recent examples of Dartmouth participants who became policymakers after their Dartmouth experience include Stremlau, who became deputy director of policy planning at the State Department in the first Bush administration, and Romberg, who was appointed to the same position in the Clinton administration.

ACCESS OF SOVIETS
TO AMERICAN POLICYMAKERS

Soviet participants gained access to American policymakers as well because of the conferences. This was often simply because half the conferences brought them to the United States. The American organizers fit time into the schedule after each conference ended for the Soviet participants to schedule meetings with Americans in New York or Washington and used their good offices to help these meetings take place.

During the 1980s it became common for the American organizers to arrange to have American policymakers meet with assorted members of the Soviet delegation. Thus, after Dartmouth XVI, most of the Soviet participants continued on to Washington for conversations with members and staff from Congress (including Aspin), and with experts from the CIA, the State Department, universities and think tanks, Robert Oakley and Dennis Ross of the National Security Council, and Edward Djerejian, deputy assistant secretary of state. Another example came in 1990, when both the American and Soviet participants in the Arms Control Task Force went to the Office of the Joint Chiefs in the Pentagon and spoke with senior officials.

The Soviets also benefited from the ease with which the Americans moved into and out of government. During the first conference, for example, Korneichuk spoke to Harriman and Rostow, two advisors to Kennedy, and tried to get a feeling for the approach of Kennedy and the people around him toward the Soviet Union and to send a message to the new administration. Harriman, at least, passed a summary of the conversation along to the man who became president a short time later.

ACCESS OF SOVIETS TO SOVIET POLICYMAKERS

Determining the amount of access Soviet participants had to their own policymakers is both simpler, owing to the structure of Soviet decision making, and more difficult, owing to Soviet secrecy. Though the number of decision makers and the paths through which information and ideas could reach them were both limited, there were still ways through which Soviet decision makers could be influenced. As with so much in the Soviet Union, the access of Dartmouth participants to policymakers depended on personal relationships. Many of the Soviet participants, like their American counterparts, had worked among policymakers or had easy access to them. Mendelson notes that "scholars and party functionaries studying different issues had regular contact with one another through conferences and written reports (*zapiski*)."[4]

Several of those who took part in Dartmouth had relationships with the general secretaries of the time. Korneichuk had been a protégé of Khrushchev's since the 1930s. His wife, writer Wanda Lvovna Wassilewska, often visited Khrushchev at home.[5]

Fedorov, who served as cochair in Korneichuk's absence, also had access to senior policymakers. In 1971 Kosygin told a group of American participants in Dartmouth that he had spoken to Fedorov the week before about environmental issues.[6] This was, indeed, one of the subjects addressed at the Dartmouth Conference that had just been held.

Arbatov, of course, had a significant amount of influence in the higher circles of the Soviet regime, particularly under Andropov and Gorbachev. If Arbatov can be considered to have been influential, his institute was probably less so. The analysts at ISKAN, many of whom attended Dartmouth conferences, certainly had contacts with party bureaucrats in the Central Committee apparatus, though probably little direct contact with the highest-ranking officials in the Soviet system. Their influence was probably mostly indirect, largely through their contribution to the set of ideas that formed the climate of opinion within which foreign policy was made.[7]

Primakov was appointed head of IMEMO in 1985, replacing Aleksandr Yakovlev, regarded by many as the architect of perestroika. He rose further as the Gorbachev years wore on. After the collapse of the Soviet Union, he became head of the Foreign Intelligence Service and then foreign minister and prime minister. In 1985 he was, with Arbatov, one of the "Gang of Four" who accompanied Gorbachev to the Geneva summit with President Reagan.[8] By his estimation, he was able to exert some influence on Soviet policy toward the Middle East before the Gorbachev era, though the mechanism through which he did so is not clear. But the evidence is strong that he was able to influence the thinking of Gorbachev about the nature of contemporary capitalism and other matters.[9] It is reasonable to expect that his thinking, transmitted to Gorbachev, reflected lessons learned from his Dartmouth experience.[10]

In addition to direct access to policymakers, there seem to have been two other routes of access to senior policymakers. As recounted in chapter 2, the Soviet leadership received two reports from Soviet participants in the

Dartmouth Conference at Oreanda.[11] One came through the Foreign Ministry apparatus and was seen by Khrushchev himself. The other source, not surprisingly, was the KGB. The report from the Crimea conference described a conversation by several American participants about the new administration in front of an unnamed KGB informant, who reported on what McGeorge Bundy and Rostow had told a group of American participants about Kennedy's intentions at the upcoming summit in Vienna. The head of the KGB, Aleksandr Shelepin, saw the informant's report. It is possible that Khrushchev saw it and that it influenced how he approached the new U.S. president. There is also evidence that Arbatov met regularly with the head of the KGB in the United Nations in New York.[12] It is more than likely that the *rezident* sent reports to Moscow about what Arbatov had told him about the Dartmouth meetings he attended in the United States.

It has long been known that Soviet citizens with foreign contacts filed reports about their experiences and the people they met. It was a part of the quid pro quo for being allowed to have the contact in the first place. The documents from the Crimea conference suggest that some of them did come to the attention of senior policymakers in the Soviet bureaucracy and that they may have had an effect on policy.

Whereas the Americans were able easily to slide between policy-making positions and the private sector, the Soviets were rarely able to make that jump until perestroika was well under way. York, the chief negotiator at the Comprehensive Test Ban talks in the late 1970s, noted that the official Soviet delegations he encountered rarely included Soviets he had met at Pugwash or Dartmouth, but that Americans who had been a part of one of the unofficial dialogues "in one era" were officials in another. Moreover, they and the current participants in the unofficial dialogues knew one another.[13]

There were exceptions on the Soviet side. Fedorov was a significant figure in the early Soviet arms efforts. In 1958 he took part in the Conference of Experts in Geneva, and in 1959 he led the Soviet delegation in the discussions of Technical Working Group II, convened by the Conference of Experts to examine the matter of on-site inspections.[14] But it was not until perestroika began to loosen up Soviet society that Dartmouth participants began to find their way into the senior ranks of policymakers. Significant examples of this were Primakov, of course, who became both foreign minister and prime minister; Kozyrev, post-Soviet Russia's first foreign minister; Vladimir Lukin, former Russian ambassador to the United States and chairman of the Committee on International Affairs of the Russian Duma; and Andrei Kokoshin, one of the few civilians to hold senior posts in the Russian defense establishment, including first deputy minister of defense and secretary of the Defense Council. These four, and other Dartmouth alumni, remain active in Russian politics.

Just as doors were opened in Washington by the knowledge among American policymakers that Dartmouth participants had access to Soviet policymakers, so doors were opened in Moscow by the knowledge that Dartmouth participants—the Americans—had access to policymakers in Washington. For Soviet policymakers as well as American officials, the Dartmouth Conference had value as a conduit for communication. This was shown by Primakov's use of Saunders and Neumann, his colleagues on the Regional Conflicts Task Force, to deliver messages about the situation in Syria in 1983 and 1984. Primakov suggested later that U.S. policy toward Syria changed in December 1983, perhaps after his colleagues had passed the first message along. When he passed his second message he prefaced it with the remark that it was obvious that the first message had been transmitted, another indication both that trust was important and that the Americans had gained the trust of an important Soviet counterpart.

ACCESS OF AMERICANS
TO SOVIET POLICYMAKERS

As the Soviet participants had access to American policymakers when they came to the United States, so American participants had access to Soviet policymakers when they came to Moscow. As with the Soviets, this access stemmed from the position and reputation of the Americans and the opportunity the conference created simply to be in Moscow and available. The American participants were sometimes able to speak to the decision makers at the top of the Soviet system. Cousins met with Khrushchev twice early in 1963, with significant consequences for U.S.-Soviet relations. He was to have met with him a third time, but David Rockefeller saw Khrushchev again after Dartmouth IV, in 1964, going in place of Cousins, bearing a message from McGeorge Bundy.

There is no evidence that this meeting directly influenced U.S. policy, but it did improve the understanding of Khrushchev's thinking and, by extension, Soviet thinking about trade and other issues at the highest levels of the U.S. government. Also, while we do not know what advice Rockefeller gave Johnson about writing Khrushchev, the opportunity for direct communication between the U.S. president and the Soviet general secretary was opened by the meeting with Rockefeller. Bundy's suggestion that Rockefeller write Khrushchev is an indication of how important such informal contacts can be to policymakers. In the event, no letter seems to have been written, and the removal of Khrushchev the following month rendered any possible consequences moot. In this instance Dartmouth might have shown significant influence had Khrushchev stayed in power.

In 1971 a delegation of Dartmouth participants also met with Kosygin, who made a proposal for a pilot project to increase trade with the United States. Soviet ambassador Dobrynin told Gavin that Kosygin had used the Dartmouth group to respond to a request from the Commerce Department. Gavin then met with Kissinger and Secretary of Commerce Peterson, had dinner with Secretary of State Rogers, and held meetings with senior officials from both Commerce and State. All these conversations addressed Kosygin's proposal. That proposal was not followed up, but these meetings took place on the eve of the dramatic increase in U.S.-Soviet trade that accompanied détente, and the conversation with Kosygin might have helped open the doors that made that increase possible.

David Rockefeller met with Prime Minister Kosygin after Dartmouth VIII. Kosygin again made a suggestion for a project of U.S.-Soviet cooperation. As with the pilot project proposed in 1971, nothing came of this. Kosygin got what he probably regarded as authoritative information about financial conditions in the American and world economies from this conversation.

The American participants did not meet Brezhnev or his successors as general secretary,[15] but they did gain access to other senior Soviet policymakers, including Minister of Defense Shaposhnikov in October 1991, two heads of regional departments of the Ministry of Foreign Affairs in 1985, a deputy minister (the day before he was to meet with the secretary of state), and Dobrynin and his staff after he became head of the International Department of the Central Committee. It was common for American members of the Regional Conflicts Task Force to meet with senior staff of the International Department in the late 1980s, and uniformed Soviet and Russian military officers met regularly with and even joined the Arms Control Task Force beginning in the mid-1980s.

INSTANCES OF DIRECT INFLUENCE

There were a few instances in which the direct influence of Dartmouth alone seems reasonably clear. The cases described are the achievement of a partial nuclear test ban treaty in 1963, the Soviet reappraisal of the American position on intermediate-range nuclear weapons in 1981, the reopening of U.S.-Soviet talks in 1983, and changes in the Soviet position on conflicts in the Middle East. They were described fully in the preceding chapters.

THE LIMITED NUCLEAR TEST BAN TREATY

The Dartmouth Conference played a significant part in the achievement of the limited nuclear test ban treaty signed in Moscow in August 1963. The discussions of the conference themselves did not lead to this role, though the question of the test ban came up often at the three conferences held before the treaty was signed.

It may be that the early efforts of the Kennedy administration toward an arms control agreement were influenced by the signals given to Rostow by Korneichuk at Dartmouth and at the Pugwash meetings in Moscow in October and November 1960 that the Soviet Union was ready for agreement on arms control.[16] But the influence of Dartmouth in the events that led to the partial nuclear test ban treaty stems from the second of two conversations held by Cousins with Khrushchev at Sochi, where Cousins could transmit a message from President Kennedy about the negotiations over the treaty. This made it possible to clear away a major stumbling block, the disagreement over on-site inspections.[17] The conversation came about simply because of Dartmouth and Father Morlion's conversations with the Soviets and Cousins at Dartmouth III, during the Cuban missile crisis. Khrushchev told Cousins that several of the participants in the Andover conference had suggested that Cousins be invited to speak to him. It seems to have been their knowledge of Cousins, gained over the course of a week of discussion, rather than Cousins' reputation, established over two decades of writing and activism, that gained Cousins his audience. In other words, it was through discussions at Dartmouth that the Soviet delegates, some of whom were known to and trusted by Khrushchev, learned that Cousins could be an acceptable intermediary.

The influence of Dartmouth on U.S.-Soviet relations in this instance stemmed not from the ideas of the participants, but from their availability. The meetings provided useful means of communication, even if unofficial, that supplemented the official means available.

U.S.-Soviet Negotiations in the Early 1980s

There were several specific instances in which Dartmouth's influence on relations between the superpowers in the early Reagan administration was apparent. One was at Dartmouth XIII, when the American participants delivered messages given to them by Secretary of State Haig and other officials. Dartmouth XIII ended the day after President Reagan proposed what he called the "zero option" for theater nuclear weapons, the complete elimination of the weapons in Europe. The Americans emphasized that the president had created an opportunity and had diverged sharply from past rhetoric on the issue. According to Stewart, "These exchanges appear to have directly influenced the subsequent Soviet reappraisal of the US position."[18] As it turned out, this influence was fleeting; it took six years and the ascendancy of Gorbachev before the zero option was made manifest in a treaty.

Two years later, however, the Dartmouth Conference became a small but significant factor in the reopening of talks after the freeze in U.S.-Soviet relations that followed the destruction of Korean airliner 007 and the deployment of the Pershing missiles in Germany. Scowcroft's mission at the time of the March 1984 meeting of the Arms Control Task Force backfired, with the Soviets interpreting it as an effort to go around Gromyko. Nonetheless, the Dartmouth Conference seems to have made the counterproductive Scowcroft mission possible. That, too, is influence, undesirable though it may be.

Later in 1984 signs came to Shultz that conditions were changing in Moscow, making an improvement in relations and even the resumption of arms control talks possible. He was preparing for a meeting with Foreign Minister Gromyko and seeking as much information as he could. Shultz later wrote:

> I got a readout from [Lt. Gen.] Jack Chain [assistant secretary of state for political-military affairs] about the Dartmouth Group's encounter with Soviet officials. Former Chairman of the Joint Chiefs of Staff USAF General David Jones reported that the Soviet attitude had changed 100 percent. They now wanted a political atmosphere under which arms control negotiations could make progress. They seriously feared that the US modernization program, along with SDI, meant that we were building a first-strike capability. Gromyko was a powerful figure on the current Kremlin scene, the "Dartmouth" people felt.[19]

Shultz met with Gromyko in Geneva in early January. Armed with the information about Soviet desires and the power of Gromyko from Dartmouth, he discussed his instructions with President Reagan before going and was able to get an agreement to begin arms control negotiations anew. Shultz considered this a turning point. He received his information about the change in Soviet intentions from a number of sources, as he says, but judging by what he wrote, the information from Dartmouth had special credibility, probably largely because of credibility that Shultz and Chain attached to the people involved— General Jones in particular.

THE SOVIETS AND THE MIDDLE EAST

The informal Dartmouth task force on the Middle East that met at the St. Regis Hotel is another specific instance where Dartmouth's influence seems to have been felt. At Dartmouth X and later, the Soviet participants noted that the task force discussions had influenced a rethinking of official Soviet policy on the Middle East. Primakov later told Saunders that these conversations had significant influence on the Soviet government and added that they had contributed, at least on the Soviet side, to the joint statement issued by Secretary of State Vance and Foreign Minister Gromyko at the United Nations in October 1977.[20]

This is an example of how the work of policy communities outside government may contribute to official thinking. Details about the meeting and how it may have been influential were given in chapter 3. Primakov has suggested that the meeting may have directly influenced

Soviet policy, though it is not clear how. There is no doubt, however, that those who took part in the St. Regis talks contributed to the climate of opinion that surrounded Middle Eastern policy. Members reinforced one another in generating "ideas in the air." The ideas discussed in New York reflected those in the Brookings report a week later. People who took part in the St. Regis meeting or picked up the ideas at Brookings later discussed the same issues with policymakers in the Carter administration.

INDIRECT INFLUENCE

The influence of Dartmouth stretched beyond what can be attributed to it through direct contacts with policymakers. Ideas discussed at Dartmouth—both about the specific issues of the day and broader social and political practices and concerns—were not held tightly within the circle of those who took part but were shared broadly beyond it. They joined the host of other ideas that circulated among those who cared about the issues at stake. Saunders reflected on his own experience in government when he wrote: "Anyone who has participated in the policymaking process will affirm that the 'ideas in the air' do influence the way public officials approach a problem. . . . These 'ideas in the air' often come first from the private sector, especially when they reflect changes in viewpoint."[21]

The direct influence of Dartmouth contributed to its indirect influence. The direct contacts that came about because participants and officials knew one another helped put these ideas into the air that surrounded officials. So did transmittal of the results of the conferences to government officials orally and in writing. In addition, many participants wrote about the issues discussed at the Dartmouth conferences in newspapers, journals, and books that helped form the climate of opinion. Cousins did this through his editorials in the *Saturday Review* in the early years and through articles elsewhere later. Other participants also wrote about their Dartmouth experiences. They included Senator Benton, Shepard Stone, Pisar, Bolling, Stewart, and Saunders. Indeed, Flora Lewis was chosen to attend in part because the organizers knew that as a journalist she would write about what she learned at Dartmouth.

Much of the indirect influence of Dartmouth came about through its effects on the participants. Through the first decade, the Dartmouth experience was unique for many, if only because there were few opportunities to talk to people on the other side. The accounts given by Galbraith, Pisar, and others speak to the power of the experience. Later, as the dialogue came to be sustained and people participated in it consistently for several years, those who took part in effect joined a community. They came to share experiences with one another and were able to take the measure of their interlocutors, having seen them on occasions formal and informal time and time again. Participants may have liked one another. Or not. But they came to know one another and to understand what to expect. They carried these expectations and their experiences at Dartmouth with them as they interacted with colleagues and friends.

Many of the Americans came to Dartmouth expecting to leave with an improved understanding of the people on the other side. As Bolling put it: "Certainly, the Dartmouth Conference experience was immensely helpful in shaping my understanding of the attitudes and values, hopes and fears, and personality structures and psychology of the peoples of the then Soviet Union."[22]

Importantly, the Dartmouth Conference and other dialogues between citizens of the two countries, such as the Pugwash Conferences and the dialogues of the United Nations Association of the United States, exposed the participants to the thinking of the other side about the issues affecting the relationship between the United States and the Soviet Union. For Soviet analysts, many of whom, particularly in the early years, had only limited exposure to Western ideas and societies, this was especially important. But it was also important to the American participants, even those well acquainted with the pages of *Pravda* and *Izvestiya*. In the first two decades in particular, before the Soviet Union began to open up under the influence of Gorbachev's glasnost, the direct contact that the conferences made possible gave the Americans an opportunity to gain an understanding of official Soviet policy that was broader and deeper than could be obtained by any other means.

These dialogues were important in helping the vocabularies and concepts of American and Soviet analysts converge.[23] This was not an achievement of Dartmouth alone, but an achievement of the transnational dialogues with the Soviets as a whole. For example, the idea that an antiballistic missile (ABM) system could upset the strategic balance was inconceivable to Premier Aleksei Kosygin when he met with President Johnson at Glassboro College in New Jersey in 1967. Within a few years, however, owing at least in part to dialogues such as those of Pugwash and Dartmouth, the idea was accepted by an important part of the Soviet establishment, making possible the limitations set by the ABM Treaty in 1972.[24]

INFLUENCE ON THE SOVIET CLIMATE OF OPINION

The indirect influence of Dartmouth was important on the American side, but it was almost assuredly more profound on the Soviet side. This was not obvious during the Cold War. It was, in fact, hidden from the Americans, though some sensed it. Some of the Soviets, while uttering the propagandistic statements in compliance with the rules of the game, were gathering information that became essential to the changes that began in the Gorbachev era. Some of this found its way into articles without attribution to Dartmouth or other dialogues. One Soviet participant pointed this out with a rhetorical question at a meeting of the Regional Conflicts Task Force in July 1991: "Why is it that we don't refer to the fact that some of the ideas which appear in our various articles are generated in this Dartmouth Task Force?" The answer, of course, has much to do with the nature of the Soviet system. But ideas that would have been dangerous or at least controversial in a Soviet context were discussed at length when the Soviet participants were away from their American colleagues. Yankelovich told a Soviet participant, a prominent exponent of new thinking, that

> we tend to be very self-critical and it really is disturbing that none of you seem to be willing to stand back a little bit and to be objective about your own. He said, "Well, don't let that fool you. We may be the most self-critical people in the world, but . . . we just don't do it in public."[25]

One of the American participants tried to explain the Soviet view this way:

> We know what we have to say [is] strained; pay no attention to it unless there is something there that may become of occasional value;

but it is also said because we have to say it; but your criticisms [of] our policies are terribly important to us for two reasons: 1) They help us to understand the reality. 2) We can quote what you say against us in our own [policy] discussions. They are your ideas even though we can never say them ourselves.[26]

The Soviet participants would leave the discussions with the Americans and then talk among themselves—with other participants whom they could trust. Saunders told an interviewer in 1988:

I ask some of the Soviets now, [it's] one thing for them to be open now that they have a leader who says be open; what were they doing . . . five years ago? I've asked that question of a number of different people. They say that they talked among themselves. They did have these talks . . . I think I remember Seweryn [Bialer] saying at one point that he talked privately to some of the economists. I didn't know who, but that they had plans in their drawer for the time when the door might open.[27]

Marshall Shulman, a participant in Dartmouth, once said, "The transfer of ideas had a 'residual educational effect that you cannot always measure but which may be terribly important. There is a kind of diffusion of conceptions that goes on, there is an educational process.'"[28] It is indeed difficult to measure the "educational effect" of Dartmouth, and it may be impossible to measure it accurately. But the recent work by English and Evangelista supports the evidence given here that Dartmouth, Pugwash, and their kin, by affecting the climate of opinion within which Arbatov, Sagdeev, and their colleagues within the ranks of new thinkers developed their ideas, in the end had a profound influence on the Soviet Union.

DIALOGUES INSPIRED BY THE ORIGINAL DARTMOUTH DIALOGUES

Apart from having an influence on policymaking communities, Dartmouth became an inspiration—if not an exact model—for other dialogues. The Inter-Tajik Dialogue might be included here though it was a direct extension of the original Dartmouth dialogues. Beginning in the middle of the 1980s, the Kettering Foundation explored the potential that a Dartmouth-type dialogue might have in other contexts. It launched two additional dialogues with the Dartmouth Conference experience explicitly in mind. Both deepened in the 1990s. By the turn of the century, both had broken new ground.

A MODEL AND THE INTER-TAJIK DIALOGUE

The Inter-Tajik Dialogue was built on a model developed by Chufrin and Saunders in the Regional Conflicts Task Force. That model is another legacy of Dartmouth. Chapter 6 addressed it in detail, but a few comments are pertinent here. First, the Inter-Tajik Dialogue began with a relationship to government and the opposition that was similar to the relationship that Dartmouth had to the governments of the two superpowers—participants were close to both sides but remained independent of them. As with the Dartmouth conferences, this gave participants the flexibility of speech and formal position that policymakers do not have. And, again as with Dartmouth, by avoiding positions that would have brought the dialogue into open conflict with either side, this relationship made it possible for both the opposition and the government to hear what those in the dialogue had to say. As a result, indications are that the dialogue influenced in some ways—at least indirectly—both the initiation of negotiations between the government and the opposition and the course they took. It may also have influenced the mechanism for bringing government and opposition together to govern the country. As chapter 6 says in several instances, it is impossible to know exactly what the degree of that influence was or its nature, but the participants most directly involved believe that the joint memoranda from the dialogue affected in some measure the immediate environment in which negotiations took place.

But the Inter-Tajik Dialogue differed from the older Dartmouth dialogue in two ways. First, the dialogue was conducted with a third party. That third party—Chufrin, Saunders, and their colleagues—went to some length, however, to ensure that the Tajik participants owned the dialogue themselves. The job of the "management team" was to facilitate, not to teach. This is one important difference that the Inter-Tajik Dialogue had not just with Dartmouth in general but also with the "seminar diplomacy" used by the OSCE.[29] As described by Adler, seminar diplomacy resembles the Dartmouth process in many respects, but the OSCE approach is designed to teach "the would-be members of a community [of states] the principles on which the community should be based."[30] The Dartmouth process is designed instead to facilitate dialogue, to foster learning by all who take part. There can be a fine line between teaching and facilitating, in this sense, but the Dartmouth process does not begin with a set agenda of points that must be conveyed. Moreover, it can count itself successful only after participants have taken their dialogue wherever they wish.

Second, the Inter-Tajik Dialogue eventually came to reach out to a broader audience. Whereas the traditional Russian-U.S. Dartmouth Conference was focused almost entirely on an elite made up of those in the higher reaches of government or close to them, the Inter-Tajik Dialogue has begun to reach out further into Tajik society. It has been with this dialogue that the idea of a multilevel peace process has come into full flower. The dialogue itself, it appears, has contributed to—and participants have taken part in—the official peace process. The dialogue itself has been a public peace process. Participants in the dialogue have done significant work to strengthen civil society in Tajikistan. This gives the dialogue the potential to have greater influence than the Russian-U.S. Dartmouth meetings were able to muster in their forty years. The Russian-U.S. forums project, now beginning, may also prove influential in the civil society arena in Russia.

Both of these differences—the use of a third party and the desire to reach more broadly into a society—will remain characteristic of the Dartmouth process as it continues to develop.

THE U.S.-CHINA DIALOGUE

In 1985 Kettering president David Mathews took two staff members to China to explore the possibility of a Dartmouth-style dialogue. With help from former U.S. president Gerald Ford, Kettering was assigned to the American Studies Institute of the Chinese Academy of Social Sciences as its partner.

The first meeting took place in the fall of 1986. This was an extraordinary nine-day meeting that began at the Wingspread Conference Center in Racine, Wisconsin, and then moved to Washington, D.C., and New York. The meeting was distinguished by the participation, at the Chinese chair's suggestion, of a second delegation from the "successor generation." Li Shenzhi, director of the institute, chaired the Chinese delegation. He was an eminent Chinese philosopher whose life reflected the turbulence of political life in the People's Republic of China since it was founded in 1949. The U.S. delegation was chaired by Saunders, whom Kettering selected in light of his experience in developing the Dartmouth Regional Conflicts Task Force.

The Chinese asked the dialogue to address the issue of Taiwan. Both the State Department and an important American scholar on China urged the foundation not to deal with this subject. The State Department's policy was that the United States should not put itself between the People's Republic and the Republic of China on Taiwan. The scholar's argument was that the issue was so sensitive that Kettering risked killing the dialogue before it began. The foundation took the position that a potential partner in dialogue had proposed the agenda because it regarded the subject as critical to the U.S.-China relationship. It seemed proper to respect that interest.

Li and Saunders agreed to frame the agenda in a way that would avoid setting the dialogue up as a confrontation between the positions of the two governments. Instead, they began with the premise that both sides in the dialogue place great value on the relationship between their countries. The discussions would then focus on how developments on Taiwan might affect that relationship and how the two countries could avoid damaging it. The purpose of this approach was to avoid an alternative way of framing the dialogue that would have explored the policies of the Chinese and U.S. governments toward Taiwan. With the framing chosen, the cochairs proposed talking together about a situation that could harm something of value to both—the U.S.-China relationship. The purpose of the visits to Washington and New York was to expose the Chinese delegation to how the Taiwan issue figured in U.S. politics.

When Li informed Saunders that his delegation had come with the permission of Chinese leader Deng Xiaoping and that he hoped to return to Beijing with a written statement, the two recognized that trying to develop a common document would be unproductive. Saunders proposed that he write his personal reflections on the meeting and then clear them with U.S. colleagues and—quite informally—with Li. That report, Li later said, went to Deng.

Our purpose here is not to recount the ups and downs of this dialogue but simply to establish that it took a series of experimental steps to explore new approaches. The first setback in the U.S.-China Dialogue was the death of a senior patron in Beijing. The second was the Chinese government crackdown on dissidents in Tiananmen Square in Beijing in June 1989. The third, probably reflecting the second, was an increasingly rigid adherence on the Chinese side to government policies. Kettering decided to try to find new ground by inviting participants from a range of Chinese organizations to a meeting in the United States. That produced a far more open exchange that continued through the decade.

In 1999 the foundation and the institute decided to embark on a research project together. It had been frequently stated by Chinese participants that the U.S.-China relationship would be better if the American media did not present a negative image of China to its audience. The two organizers of the dialogue decided that each side would conduct research to learn more about how citizens in each country form their images of the other. The Chinese pursued a series of focus groups and surveys. The American side, after reviewing survey material and conducting focus groups, asked members of the National Issues Forums network to frame the issue for deliberation among citizens in public forums. Twenty-five forums with more than 500 participants were conducted in the summer of 2000. They addressed the question "How should the United States conduct its relationship with China?" Each side reported on its research in a meeting of work groups in the spring of 2000 and to a full meeting of the dialogue in the fall. The two produced a joint publication in 2001. They agreed to continue their research, focusing on why each side held the perceptions it held and what steps might be taken to change those perceptions.

In an example of how moving out of Dartmouth into another arena produced a new experience that could return to enrich Dartmouth, Kettering's experience with the public forums on China inspired a proposal made to young Russians who had been Kettering international fellows to have networks in each country conduct forums on the U.S.-Russia relationship. That project began in both countries in 2001.

CIVIL SOCIETY CONSORTIUM

The second course of dialogue inspired by the Dartmouth Conference experience began as the Western Hemisphere Exchange in 1989. Encouraged by the active work of the Dartmouth Conference task forces and by the exciting plenary in 1988, Kettering began exploring ways to develop a dialogue in the Western Hemisphere.

The challenge was to avoid having the dialogue become merely an opportunity for the Latin American countries to unload their grievances on the United States. Rodrigo Botero, former finance minister of Colombia, suggested that the dialogue be about developing civil society. The starting premise was that most countries in the hemisphere were working to develop more vibrant civil societies. The agenda could be built around the challenges each faced. One of the rules of the dialogue was that each participant would address those challenges but could speak only of what her or his country was doing. It would not be appropriate to criticize other countries' efforts. The response to the challenge was to talk and then to work on a common problem over time rather than to focus first on the relationship.

After five years of meetings among a growing network—paralleled by a flow of young Latin Americans as international fellows at Kettering—participants in the exchange agreed to broaden the meetings to include colleagues from Europe, Africa, and Asia. Thus was born the International Civil Society Exchange. In a meeting in Barbados, participants constituted themselves informally as the International Civil Society Consortium for Public Deliberation. Acknowledging that there are numerous ways to strengthen democratic practice, they stated that they shared the use of public deliberation as their vehicle for doing so. As the exchange grew, smaller numbers began meeting as a research group to examine subjects such as what makes civil society democratic and how efforts to build civic infrastructure—often called "social capital"—could enhance economic performance. This thinking lay behind the project of the Inter-Tajik Dialogue's Public Committee for Democratic Processes to establish the three economic development committees described in chapter 6.

Thus the experience of a dialogue process inspired by the Dartmouth Conference has returned to a child of Dartmouth—the Inter-Tajik Dialogue—as conceptual nourishment. In turn, the Economic Development Committees in Tajikistan will be principal laboratories for bringing the deliberative and sustained dialogue processes into a "citizens' political process" for economic development that can be transferred to other parts of the Civil Society Consortium. This work has begun in Latin America.

WHAT MADE DARTMOUTH EFFECTIVE?

As the work of Robert English, Matthew Evangelista, Jeffrey Checkel, and others makes clear, the influence of Dartmouth during the Cold War was commingled with the influence of other transnational groups, such as Pugwash, the Palme Commission, and the National Academy of Sciences Committee on International Security and Arms Control.[31] This distinction is, in a sense, artificial. Many participants in Dartmouth also took part in other dialogues. On the American side, people such as Paul Doty and Marshall Shulman took part in the efforts of several groups, including Dartmouth. On the Soviet side, there were a limited number of people to whom the Soviet party and government gave permission to have contact with Westerners. The influence of Dartmouth, therefore, must be included in the influence of all these groups on Soviet and American policy.[32] To the extent that Dartmouth can be analyzed separately, however, it can be said that several things, combined, account for its success. These were the access it had to officials, the related matter of the trust those officials had in Dartmouth, the longevity of the dialogues, and the social structures of the two countries. No one of these was unique to Dartmouth. But together they made the Dartmouth model of sustained dialogue an effective approach to two countries at odds with each other.

As this chapter argues, participants in the Dartmouth conferences had clear access to policymakers—both decision makers and bureaucrats—in both capitals during the Cold War. At times they had access to the highest decision makers, the U.S. president and the Soviet general secretary. It may be tautological to point out—it is certainly obvious—that this access is what brought Dartmouth much of its influence, which came about not so much because of a general influence on public opinion as because of Dartmouth's specific influence, direct and indirect, on those who made policy. Dartmouth sought access to them and got it.

Trust was an important element in the ability of Dartmouth to gain this access to policymakers on both sides of the Iron Curtain. Dartmouth was formed by people who identified with those in power. It cultivated its relationships with those people, both in the choice of participants and the contacts, written and oral, with officials in both Moscow and Washington that it tried to make as the dialogues continued.

Trust was not only important in extending the influence of the dialogues beyond the conference rooms; trust—or its absence—was essential to understanding what happened between the participants in those rooms. The silence of Dartmouth on the public stage, the norm of nonattribution that Mosely criticized Senator Benton for violating, and the unwillingness of the American participants to join with their Soviet colleagues in joint statements were all part of an effort to build trust either among participants, or between participants and their governments, or both. The difference in tone between the formal plenary sessions and the informal, personal dialogues that took place after is attributable to efforts on both sides to build trust.[33]

Emanuel Adler and Michael Barnett find trust an essential element in fostering security communities, organizations of states that, like transnational organizations, show the limitations of the realist paradigm as developed by Hans Morgenthau or Kenneth Waltz. They note that trust "always involves an element of risk because of the inability to monitor others' behavior or to have complete knowledge about other people's motivations."[34] They go on to say:

> Trust does not develop overnight but rather is accomplished after a lifetime of common experiences and through sustained interactions and reciprocal exchanges, leaps of faith that are braced by . . . verification . . . trial and error, and a historical legacy of actions and encounters that deposit an environment of certitude notwithstanding the uncertainty that accompanies social life.

This is to suggest that trust comes about not merely through experiences with others that are pleasant. Trust comes about through shared experiences that produce expectations that are reinforced by subsequent experiences. Dartmouth came to foster trust by making such experiences and reinforcement possible. The traditions that grew up around Dartmouth made it easier for experiences at conferences to reinforce trust. The American side at Dartmouth took no formal position on any issue; it was impartial in its views and independent of both the Soviets and any American political movement. What participants said remained confidential.

Another element in Dartmouth's success was simply its longevity. Dartmouth began with the sense that the conference would not meet just once, but that there would be a continuing series of conferences.

It was to be—it became—a sustained dialogue, in which one meeting began where the previous one left off. The element most essential to such a dialogue is the continuity of participants. While some participants— Mosely (through the 1960s), Rockefeller, Cousins, and Stewart, for example, on the American side; Korneichuk, Arbatov, and Zhukov on the Soviet—gave some degree of continuity, greater continuity was developed by the task forces that began to meet in the 1980s. They, more than the earlier plenaries, relied on sets of participants who attended virtually every meeting. About the time Landrum Bolling left Dartmouth, he spoke to a Soviet delegate about the need for those long involved with Dartmouth to step aside and allow others to have the benefit of the Dartmouth experience. His interlocutor brought him up short, saying firmly: "But it is essential that we have a considerable amount of continuity. It takes time to get to know one another, and to get past the inevitable suspicions, and beyond the formal politeness, and begin to build up some real sense of open communication and trust."[35]

The process of sustained dialogue also takes discussions that are honest, open, and, to use Saunders' term, analytical, rather than vitriolic or given to the regurgitation of propaganda. With such people and such circumstances, participants who sit down together as enemies often, over time, change their perceptions of one another. They may not come to like one another—that is not necessary—but they can begin to accept the others as human beings who deserve serious attention. This opens the possibility for the development of a common set of knowledge and common action. This makes possible achievements like those of the Inter-Tajik Dialogue. Saunders and Zhurkin examine this possibility more fully in the next chapter.

Like the continuity of participants, this open dialogue was not achieved at first but only developed over time. No doubt attitudes common to Americans during the Cold War contributed to the difficult nature of the dialogue in the early years, but the need for the Soviet participants to hew to the party line was a constant source of frustration for the American side. It undoubtedly made Dartmouth less effective than many of its participants hoped. Dartmouth shared this limitation with other dialogues with the Soviets. As Bolling described it:

> At some point, I became frustrated with the endless polemics and empty rhetoric we had to put up with as the Soviet delegates, one by

one, always had to establish in plenary sessions their political correctness among themselves.[36]

Lundeen, speaking about Dartmouth XIV in 1984, said that though he was warned, he was not prepared for the vitriol.[37] His experience, with vitriol in 1984 and candor in 1988, suggests that the Soviet part of the dialogue stayed within the parameters allowed by official policy. As Arbatov wrote, this was a part of the rules of the game for the Soviet participants.[38] Yet candor on the Soviet side could sometimes be heard before the breakthrough fostered by Gorbachev with glasnost. Zhurkin's concurrence in 1984 with American assertions about Third World policy, for example, suggests that the barriers were beginning to break down even before Gorbachev came to power.[39] Over time, the rules changed. Partly because open dialogue became a matter of state policy under Gorbachev, but also partly because of experience gained on both sides and because of changes made in the way the dialogues were conducted, the analytical discussions that Saunders sought became the norm. The longevity of the dialogue made this possible by giving participants the time necessary to form relationships of understanding and trust with one another.

The analysis here supports the work of Thomas Risse-Kappen, Evangelista, and others who have argued that the structure of a society affects how much influence transnational actors such as Dartmouth can have; both the mobility of people in a society and the amount and kind of communication between citizens inside and outside government can be important in considering to what extent and in what ways a community such as Dartmouth influences policy. On the one hand, the mobility between the private sector and government in American society augmented the influence of Dartmouth on American policy as former Dartmouth participants took what they had learned into policy positions in government. Also (as the case of Scowcroft suggests), this helped make the U.S. government conscious of Dartmouth as a possible conduit of communication to the Soviet Union. The reverse seems not to have been true on the Soviet side until the late 1980s, when the Gorbachev reforms turned Dartmouth participants, such as Primakov, into policymakers. Despite that difference of degree, Primakov twice in the 1980s conveyed messages on behalf of his government. On the other hand, both governing systems on occasion made use of communities outside government—or were recipients of their perspectives—to augment their knowledge or to shape or reexamine their assumptions. In the Soviet Union, the Academy of Sciences peopled those communities. In the United States, they were more broadly based.

FINAL WORDS

Today, Russia and the United States are closer than the superpowers were forty years ago. They are no longer seemingly irreconcilable antagonists—particularly now that, in the wake of the attacks of September 11, 2001, they seem to have found a common foe. Troubles in the relationship have at times obscured this convergence. To be sure, important issues remain unresolved and misunderstandings persist. We can expect that the relationship between Russia and the United States will have its seasons, cooling, then warming, then cooling again. Nonetheless, the relationship has changed profoundly—and for the better since 1960. Communications have improved enormously. Opportunities for contact, formal and informal, between officials and among citizens, have grown beyond what most would have imagined possible. Most important, perhaps, the threat of a nuclear holocaust, though it has not disappeared entirely, long ago lost its prominence among our concerns. Did Dartmouth play a part in that? Did the ideas exchanged and the community of people who grew up around the conferences help change the U.S.-Soviet relationship? There can be little doubt that they did. The continuing access that they had to policymakers on both sides of the Iron Curtain ensured that the ideas expressed at Dartmouth would be heard. They were not always heeded, as Gouttierre found when he suggested at the State Department that Soviet withdrawal from Afghanistan was imminent. But the response of Secretary Shultz and the involvement of former officials who had heard Dartmouth's voice while serving in government—people such as Jones, Scowcroft, and Matlock—suggest that the voice was an important one. Primakov echoed this recently when asked about the usefulness of a group such as Dartmouth that exchanged views in parallel to formal diplomatic exchanges:

> The whole history of the Dartmouth meetings demonstrates the usefulness of such non-official group[s]. . . . [E]ven the present formal

contacts between the Foreign Ministry and the State Department—
not to speak about summits—do not exclude the necessity of nonofficial exchange of opinions in particular between those people who
have the capability to report their impressions and conclusions after
such exchanges to the highest state officials.[40]

Governments do, indeed, pay attention to citizens of goodwill.

8 | The Conduct of Sustained Dialogue: What Have We Learned? What Next?

by Harold H. Saunders and Vitali Zhurkin

CHAPTER 7 EXAMINED HOW ONE UNDERSTANDS AND JUDGES the influence of nonofficial dialogues on the relationship between the Soviet Union and the United States. This chapter reflects on what we have learned about the conduct of such systematic, sustained dialogue by citizens outside government—dialogue that amounts to a citizens' counterpart to the formal mediation, negotiation, and diplomacy that have been the instruments of statecraft.

The Dartmouth Conference began when relations between the Soviet Union and the United States were conducted almost exclusively by the two governments. Citizens on both sides were unable or reluctant to engage in dialogue. The need to find ways to broaden the scope of communication and mutual understanding between the nuclear superpowers was compelling. It was in this context that the Dartmouth Conference began, its aim being to deepen interactions between the two peoples. Although the Dartmouth Conference was launched with the encouragement of President Eisenhower and the support of Chairman Khrushchev, it has always been steered by citizens outside government.

As pioneers who introduced and developed a citizens' dimension in the overall relationship between the two superpowers, the men and women of the Dartmouth Conference have lived the ups and downs of this increasingly complex great power relationship for forty years.

At first, it was novel and challenging just to have a meeting. In the 1970s participants began working together in smaller groups focused on specific problems and on enhancing their influence with governments. In the 1980s the conference established two task forces to engage in disciplined, sustained dialogue that built cumulative agendas, common bodies of knowledge, and the ability to seek solutions to common problems and to influence governments.

Since the dissolution of the Soviet Union, participants, focusing on the new Russian-U.S. relationship, have worked principally on two tracks. First, the Regional Conflicts Task Force systematized and refined the process of sustained dialogue the participants had developed together, principally through the Inter-Tajik Dialogue within the Framework of the Dartmouth Conference. Second, starting from a sharp focus at Dartmouth XVI, in 1988, on civil society as the Soviet system began opening up, participants have looked to broaden interaction between the two bodies politic. In 2001 American and Russian citizens held as many as one hundred public forums in the two countries focusing on the Russian-U.S. relationship.

All of this the Dartmouth Conference has accomplished visibly, but less visible are the dozens of participants who have gone from the Dartmouth exchanges where minds were stretched and perceptions modified—each to her or his respective walk of life, often in high office or other influential positions. The question before Dartmouth veterans through the 1990s and into the new century has been how to provide spaces for follow-on generations of citizens outside government to experience, to reflect on, and to shape the evolving Russian-U.S. relationship.

As the new century dawned after a decade of drift and growing suspicion in the Russian-U.S. relationship, Dartmouth veterans were attempting to organize and consolidate new ventures in providing a citizens' "mind at work" in the center of this critical relationship. The reflective analysis in this chapter builds from the entire forty years of the Dartmouth Conference experience—in plenaries, in task forces, in the Inter-Tajik Dialogue within the Framework of the Dartmouth Conference, and in the new work on deliberative democracy. It concludes by looking to the future with the conviction that the tradition of Dartmouth has contributed, and has much still to contribute, to a relationship between two great powers that will always be critical to world peace and development.

WHAT WE HAVE LEARNED ABOUT CONDUCTING CITIZENS' DIALOGUE

This book, as its title indicates, is a study in the evolution of sustained dialogue among citizens outside government as part of a multilevel peace process. It tells the story of a pioneering experience in such dialogue. That story is a unique part of a larger experience in which a few scholar-practitioners began experimenting to discover what roles citizens outside government can and cannot play in a world in which relationships among groups and countries are—with some exceptions—increasingly a political process of continuous interaction among significant elements of whole bodies politic across permeable borders. Much of this experience has focused—deliberately and by trial and error—on how to conduct dialogue among informed citizens in ways that would enhance its usefulness to participants and to the groups from which they come. This chapter distills what we have learned about that subject.

The Dartmouth Conference started from the assumption that nonofficial, informal dialogue among citizens outside government has some advantages that official exchanges do not have. Of course, there are some things that only duly constituted governments can do, but there are some things that only human beings outside government can do—such as changing conflictual human relationships. Dartmouth has played an important part—not always intentionally in the earliest years—in developing a systematic process for citizens to use in playing their role.

These forty years of often intensive experience began when systematic unofficial dialogue among citizens was relatively new. Most organized communication between states took place through formal diplomatic exchanges. While these often led to broad-gauged analytical discussions, diplomats had to stay within the limits of government positions. The idea of citizens addressing issues on governmental agendas was not common. The idea of citizens interpreting whole bodies politic to each other was perhaps even more remote. Academic exchanges addressed research agendas.

Individual conversations could cover the full range of human issues, and this was the purpose of student and people-to-people exchanges. Ecumenical dialogues between religious groups had begun in the 1920s, but they were limited exchanges between institutions. The idea of a group formally constituted to talk about the relationship and problems between two countries broke new ground. Only in the mid-1960s did scholar-practitioners devote serious attention to ways of organizing productive dialogue—as contrasted to negotiation—between groups that reflected the experience of different countries, nationalities, or cultures.

Through these four decades when efforts at systematic dialogue in other areas—between Arabs and Israelis or Indians and Pakistanis, for instance—were also developing, the Dartmouth Conference introduced new approaches and ideas. Two innovations stand out: the practice of groups coming together repeatedly through an extended period of years, and the conceptualization of sustained dialogue as a political process. The Dartmouth experience also offers one of the most elaborate laboratories from which to draw or affirm lessons from a broad complex of interrelated dialogue experiences.

The reflections reported here are drawn from the coauthors' extensive experience in the Dartmouth Conference and from interviews with more than two dozen Dartmouth veterans from both countries and from all four decades.[1] The interviews were collected from transcribed face-to-face talks and from written responses to questions. Zhurkin began participating in Dartmouth in 1971, Saunders in 1981. Both attended all task forces at one time or another. Saunders cochaired the Regional Conflicts Task Force and the Inter-Tajik Dialogue from their beginnings. It has normally been a Dartmouth rule that statements are not attributed to anyone outside the dialogue room, but an exception has been made in this book; and interviewees have agreed to be cited here. The coauthors can document each quotation.

As a preface to these reflections, it is important to note that participants in such dialogues come from deeply differing cultural, ideological, ethnic, historical, religious, or national backgrounds. It is a purpose of dialogue to provide a context for participants to learn to communicate despite these differences. However, as Arnold Horelick recalled, in the Dartmouth Conference the American participants faced an "enormous challenge ... in dealing with the very serious asymmetrical constraints on unfettered dialogue imposed by the very character of the political and social system to which our Soviet colleagues belonged." This challenge, which took a particularly tenacious form from the outset, often led to statements and interpretations that U.S. participants regarded as Soviet propaganda—not analysis. Soviet participants seemed unable to depart from these statements in meetings, even though in many private conversations they expressed different views. This often made analytical work in the meetings very difficult. The situation changed progressively in the task forces in the early 1980s and markedly after 1985.

In response, Vitali Zhurkin expressed thoughts along the same lines: "Unfortunately in the first years of the dialogue both sides or at least some participants made propagandistic statements. Maybe with some difference: Soviets did so more often, and Americans did so in a more sophisticated form. Maybe some understood this unfortunate practice as a promotion of national interests. Anyhow, what was much more important was the dynamics: the situation was changing, and the change started rather early. The attempts to understand the other side and an inclination to compromises and cooperation grew and finally prevailed."

With that introduction, our reflections follow.

FIRST: *Citizens outside government can talk productively even in the context of a hostile and intensely competitive relationship between their governments or political authorities. They can enlarge the picture of the overall relationship between whole groups or countries.*

Despite the risks, individuals can be found who understand the value of unofficial dialogue—sometimes, as initially in the U.S.-Soviet case, with political permission and, later or in other cases, sometimes without. Americans learned only in the 1990s that the first Soviet team came to New Hampshire with the permission of Nikita Khrushchev. It is interesting that both governments encouraged the two delegations to continue meeting during the Cuban missile crisis; this seems to suggest that even hostile governments can value such dialogue. In the 1980s it seemed that Soviet cochairs of the new task forces came with considerable latitude to select their teams and to speak their own views.

Whatever the requirement to deliver or defend a formal party position, those individuals gradually learned—not without difficulty—

to talk and think together and, ultimately, to engage in common analytical and policy-relevant work. One of the early examples in the Dartmouth Conference was a small meeting in New York in 1975 of three participants from each side particularly concerned about the Arab-Israeli conflict. The task forces of the 1980s provided regular instances of this capacity to work together, even though the governments remained locked in the rigid standoff of the Cold War.

Personal relationships can form in enough cases to justify the effort—not necessarily in any sentimental sense but in the sense that some individuals, with repeated testing over time, can come to value one another's insights and perspectives as authentic.

In 1984, for instance, exchanges in the Regional Conflicts Task Force called into question the conventional U.S. government view that Soviet policy in the Middle East was directed primarily at undermining the U.S. diplomatic role in the Arab-Israeli peace process. The exchanges revealed serious concerns among the Soviet participants that U.S. policy was directed at excluding and humiliating the USSR. The U.S. participants said they could understand why their Soviet colleagues might feel this way, given some U.S. actions. The Soviets' statement that "we are your nuclear equal and should be treated as your political equal" led to a serious discussion of what a relationship between "political equals" would require of each side in the Arab-Israeli context. This conversation differed from the usual intergovernmental jockeying for position—a conversation that in no way compromised a serious U.S. approach to the peace process and left open the possibility for Soviets to think more fully about what a realistic role in this highly flexible diplomatic process would require of their more conventional diplomacy. An honest statement of feelings on both sides opened the door to analytical talk.

The other task forces had similar experiences, in their own particular ways. In arms control, for example, the early stages of the Dartmouth process had coincided in a way with the beginning of determined arms control negotiations between the two governments. Special attention had been devoted to conceptual aspects of arms control and international security. During U.S.-Soviet détente in the 1970s, the idea of reinforcing political détente by military détente was strongly advanced at Kiev (1971) and in several subsequent meetings. Other fundamental concepts of easing international tensions and promoting international cooperation that were novel and unusual at that time were worked out, developed, and advanced by the Dartmouth movement.

When they began negotiating the most sensitive problems of national security, both governments strictly limited the availability of information. A substantive public dialogue was initially difficult. As the arms control negotiating process matured and information on the results of the talks and positions of both sides was published, however, detailed discussions started. Their distinctive feature was that both American and Soviet participants were often disappointed that the positions of their respective governments were too cautious, timid, and limited. Both Soviets and Americans believed that a more radical reduction of arms—and of strategic arms in particular—had to be envisaged than the reductions their respective governments were proposing. They also believed that the equality of reductions could be preserved and carried out without prejudice to either party.

During the Dartmouth dialogues, an extensive consensus developed on the desirability of further cooperation in the field of ballistic missile defense. Some officially debatable positions were carefully discussed. For instance, American participants during the 1980s produced a number of convincing points against Soviet deployment of the Krasnoyarsk phased-array radar. A number of Soviet participants themselves considered this radar within the national territory to be a violation of the SALT I Treaty in spite of vigorous denials by the Soviet officials, especially some military figures. As we know from the later decision of the Russian government, the radar was finally dismantled, and thus history solved this political controversy that spoiled Soviet-American relations over several years. Many Russians recall this historical episode now when half a dozen such radars are planned in the United States as the first stage of national ballistic missile defense.

There were also significant examples of approaches by participants in the Economic Relations Task Force that ran against narrow official stances. At least some American participants were persuaded by the Soviet participants that denial of most-favored-nation treatment to Moscow was an injustice, particularly when large-scale Jewish emigration started in 1970s. That was just one example of many exchanges in which participants on each side took positions closer to the other side's than to the positions of their own governments.

The deeper picture of the overall relationship between two bodies politic that can emerge in dialogue enlarges, deepens, and complements the picture formed in official diplomacy and negotiation. In the Dartmouth Conference, participants on both sides changed perceptions that had been initially shaped by their governments. For instance, each gradually began to understand better the dynamics of policymaking on the other side, including the role of public reactions in the United States and the debate within Soviet governing circles. Pictures of the other side as monolithic gave way as views acquired human faces. Each side recognized that the other could make mistakes and acknowledge them.

The evidence from the Dartmouth Conference itself was augmented in the 1990s by the experience of the Inter-Tajik Dialogue within the Framework of the Dartmouth Conference. Individuals sat down together in March 1993 after a particularly intense phase of a vicious civil war; though they could hardly look at one another, they felt it was important to be there. After six three-day meetings spread out over a year, they had played a role in the creation of a united opposition that helped make negotiations possible and had contributed to the government's decision to negotiate. They produced their first joint memorandum, "Memorandum on a Negotiating Process in Tajikistan." Their twenty subsequent joint memoranda constitute probably the most coherent body of political philosophy in the country.

SECOND: *The Dartmouth Conference exchanges provided a context for understanding the extent to which participants did and did not change their mind-sets in dialogue.*

As noted, Americans in the Regional Conflicts Task Force in 1984 discovered that, in the eyes of the Soviets, U.S. policy, at least in the Arab-Israeli arena, seemed bent on humiliating them. Some Americans could acknowledge that those feelings were not entirely unjustified. At the same time, Americans could argue that mediation in the peace process required a degree of flexibility not always exhibited in Soviet diplomacy. But acknowledging Soviet feelings permitted participants to change the terms of reference for the exchange—profitably for both sides.

There seems little question that a number of Soviet participants eagerly embraced new concepts of security and politics, which they published during the period of the "new political thinking" from 1985 to 1990 in Moscow. Dartmouth XVI in 1988 provided the stage on which Soviet cochair Georgi Arbatov placed a panoply of stars of the new Soviet "civil society," as defined then. Arbatov himself embraced and preached the idea of "common security," and others proposed the concepts of "equal security" and "reasonable sufficiency." Some of these ideas originated on the Soviet side. Of course, there were limits: "If you think democracy in the Soviet Union will mean multiparty elections," said one participant, "you are wrong." This position was not completely monolithic; some Russians expressed the opinion that with time a multiparty system might emerge in their country. Americans were impressed not only by Soviet openness but also by references to Alexis de Tocqueville's description of the fundamentals of democracy as one possible example for Russia's endeavors.

In the Regional Conflicts Task Force in 1989, participants together devised a mechanism for moving beyond traditional modes of analysis. In each of the conflicts the task force focused on, participants together designed a scenario of interactive steps that could be taken by both sides to deal with the conflicts in question. Through this innovative process of analysis, Soviet participants came to understand more fully the interactive political process that is the essence of a peace process.

At the same time, despite these changes in perception, deeply ingrained feelings and suspicions remained through the 1990s on both sides, even in the minds of longtime veterans: Russians resented what they saw as the U.S. tendency to try to impose its way of life—democratic machinery and market mechanisms most prominently; Americans suspected that Russia would reassert control in the former Soviet republics to any degree possible.

Numerous statements by participants over the years attest to how exchanges erased stereotypes, enhanced respect, changed perceptions, deepened understanding, and even generated empathy for others' positions or analyses. Here are some opinions of Dartmouth veterans who were asked how their participation had influenced their views and opinions.

OLEG BYKOV, who rose to be deputy director of IMEMO: "The interaction with [the American participants] brought about the strongest impression on me. I saw that these people, while being unquestionably patriots of their country like my colleagues, at the same time nevertheless had a special view of problems of our bilateral relations. In spite of a very severe Cold War, nevertheless they approached these problems not only from the point of view of the interests of their country but from the point of view of our common interests as well. In other words, they were thinking to what extent we could help avoid extremely sharp, critical situations after which an uncontrolled escalation could start. Some of them looked even further; their outlook was even wider. They saw that after some, evidently quite long time the period will start when it will be possible to speak not only about limiting our contradictions, but about what we can do together for our countries, for the whole world. It may sound rather abstract. But I accepted it very concretely because it was connected with very concrete people like the late Norman Cousins and Philip Mosely, like David Rockefeller and others, both Democrats and Republicans—which was also quite significant."

NIKOLAI SHMELEV, economist and now director of the Institute of Europe, who joined the Dartmouth process at its later stages: "My participation in the Dartmouth conferences strengthened in me a trust in the American society, in the goodwill of Americans and their sincere interest and desire that Russia will transform itself out of the scarecrow, by whom the whole world was accustomed to be scared, into a normal, reasonable democratic and quiet country. And I do hope that, though in a Russian variant with all our torments and all our griefs, still we have turned to this road and it is our road into the future. To the extent that the public plays a certain role (and it really does play such a role) and because of the participation in the meetings of very authoritative people, American society had become accustomed to listening to them and later our society had become accustomed to listening to them. As a result these conferences played a very serious role."

VLADIMIR LUKIN, former Russian ambassador to the United States, now vice speaker of the State Duma: "Dartmouth from my point of view brought up a whole generation of people both in Russian and American elites who were interested in the other country, visited this country, were understanding and personally came to know the circle of people on whom political decisions depend. Of utmost importance was the fact that an extensive group, a whole layer of political forces emerged which had interest—an ear so to say—in relation to one another. Then there existed the factor of secondary influence, because the people who were activists in Dartmouth came with new ideas, new approaches, and a new type of personal relations with participants of the Dartmouth conferences. They influenced their colleagues. That's why the influence of the Dartmouth conferences on that generation, which plays now an active role in Russian affairs, was very big and direct as well as indirect. There exist people who were brought up by Dartmouth. There exist people who were brought up by those people who were brought up by Dartmouth. Similar processes could be observed in the United States."

ARNOLD HORELICK: "The problem was to try to rationalize and humanize the relationship without succumbing to the fallacy that 'they are just like us,' which our Soviet colleagues most assuredly were not and could not be in pre-perestroika years. Dartmouth made an important contribution in that direction. The Dartmouth experience had a significant impact, I believe, on the evolving understanding of American and Soviet participants of each other's systems and of each other as individuals. This paid off especially when some participants subsequently assumed leading positions in their polities and societies, some with direct responsibilities in U.S.-Soviet and U.S.-Russian relations. . . .

"Dartmouth helped greatly in . . . deepening contacts as a function of the Dartmouth methodology. Under Soviet circumstances, in many cases a remarkably high degree of mutual trust and confidence developed between some Russian and American participants, especially among those who understood and appreciated the constraints under which the relationship had to operate and factored knowledge of those constraints into what they took away from the interactions."

DAVID JONES, a former chairman of the U.S. Joint Chiefs of Staff: "I always had a suspicion that we were probably overrating the Soviet Union from a military standpoint. I think this was borne out in my discussions with many people in the Soviet military. . . .

"I would go out jogging with . . . we would gain confidence in each other, and we were very candid. . . . He trusted me, and I trusted him to be careful about the use of information."

Perhaps this point is best captured in the reflection of a U.S. participant who played a key role for almost two decades: "It is really the changed mind-sets on each side that are important. These are the capital that can be used to resolve political issues more constructively and to work together more constructively on common problems. In the U.S.-Soviet case, opportunities for long-term interactions among citizens were very few. Those who could shape policy over the long term had only very limited personal experience of those on the other side. This was where Dartmouth found its special role. It could provide a place where participants could feel they were 'doing their work' in the short term by focusing on critical issues on their professional agendas, but through the frequency of their interaction . . . the participants did come to play a role—for the most part unintended—in fundamentally changing the relationship through the long-term impact of changed mind-sets."

THIRD: *The Dartmouth Conference experience demonstrated the value of repeated meetings over one-time meetings—a point relevant to the entire field of unofficial dialogue.*

The credentials of the Dartmouth Conference to make this point lie in its unmatched experience of seventeen plenary meetings over thirty years, more than fifty task force meetings over twenty years, and thirty-two meetings of the Inter-Tajik Dialogue between 1993 and late 2001. Saunders recalls the question that became more and more pressing as one task force meeting followed another in the early 1980s: "We are spending a lot of energy and money. We have good conversations and enjoy meeting. But how can we get more out of the next meeting than from the last?"

At the simplest level, only repeated meetings could allow relationships to develop that provided the context for a deepening exchange of insights and analyses. This point may seem self-evident in general terms, but it is possible to be specific in terms of how a relationship evolves. Interacting in meetings, over meals, and on bus rides; walking through Piskariovskoye Cemetery in Leningrad with a Soviet colleague who has relatives buried there; talking about the death of a spouse or a child; sharing stories of grandchildren—all take time; all help to replace the stereotype of communist or capitalist with the reality of a fellow human being; all reveal the essence of identity in the context of a particular national tradition. Brunch at home with just a son and a Soviet colleague produces memories that can be recalled twenty years later. Conversation at the dinner table presents opportunities to explain how citizens in our very different polities form their ideas of such concepts as the national interest. Time, honest dialogue, working together on problems of common concern, and sharing knowledge can all change patterns of interaction—and all take time.

Time and repeated meetings also allowed for the evolution of format, agenda, and participants in light of unfolding experience and changing circumstances. Task forces were introduced. Agendas moved from arms control and foreign policy to the role of domestic affairs and public perceptions in the relationship. As one U.S. participant, Randa Slim, commented: "The ownership of a developing agenda over time by the same core group enabled a level of trust and confidence to develop despite the misperceptions and fears that initially divided them. It is partly because of this trust and familiarity that Russian members of the Regional Conflicts Task Force were willing in the 1990s to suggest a joint Russian-U.S.-managed sustained dialogue in Tajikistan—a country that was then part of the Russian 'Near Abroad,' where Russians were extremely sensitive to U.S. efforts to establish a presence."

The evolution of such relationships was gradual but constant and matured over the years. Even so, one unique feature of the Dartmouth process should not be overlooked: such relationships began to emerge (albeit, in rather simple forms originally) at very early stages. It is instructive to remember the third conference, which started on the eve of the Cuban missile crisis. When the crisis erupted, some of the participants— both Americans and Soviets—proposed to terminate the conference and quickly return home. But the majority (again both Americans and Soviets) persuaded the skeptics to continue.

As the chairman of the Soviet group, Evgeni Fedorov, formerly a famous Arctic explorer and one of the first Russian environmentalists, later remembered: "We together decided to continue aiming at preserving the contacts and testing how we shall be able to discuss the critical questions in such a difficult and crucial situation. This decision proved to be the only right solution: in spite of sharp disagreements in analyzing the situation that had developed, both Soviet and American participants in the meeting were in complete accord in their desire to help solve the crisis by peaceful means."[2] Naturally the degree of mutual trust at that time was small compared with the trust that came to exist with the passage of time. But the first roots of the Dartmouth-type relationships were pointing in a promising direction. Participants in the first meetings found individuals on the other side for whom they gained respect and with whom they could hold frank private conversations.

As knowledge of one another's strengths and interests developed and recognition of shared concerns gradually emerged, smaller working meetings were arranged, either in conjunction with the plenaries or, in the case of the Middle East group in 1975, separate from regular meetings. One U.S. participant with extensive experience in Afghanistan even had side meetings with specialists in both the Soviet and the U.S. foreign ministries—an outcome that could have happened only when enough time had passed for him to prove his knowledge and to allay initial suspicions that he was a CIA agent.

Formation of the task forces in 1981–82 permitted a series of small meetings to be held at shorter intervals—normally semiannually—than was the case with the plenaries, which met every two years on average. This frequency produced six major gains.

First, frequency allowed participants to develop a cumulative agenda, to be carried forward from one meeting to the next. This practice was articulated by Evgeni Primakov when he said to Hal Saunders: "Let's begin the next meeting where this one ended."

Second, frequency allowed a common body of knowledge to develop so that differences of interpretation could be narrowed over time as those differences were discussed repeatedly in changing circumstances. Frequency also allowed time for participants in their separate travels between meetings to test new information, interpretations, or insights that colleagues had presented in one meeting and to deepen their exchange in the next.

Third, frequency gradually reduced—but did not initially eliminate—the temptation to make set-piece speeches on familiar positions, because anyone engaging in such practice risked loss of respect from colleagues. Participants made allowances for politically necessary responses to new developments, and though they could not avoid reflecting established positions, the level of polemic certainly declined.

Fourth, frequency created—slowly but steadily—a feeling of trust toward one another, a belief in the genuineness of not only positive impulses but also grievances. This mutual trust forced both sides to look again and again into the motives and logic of the other side's positions that first looked unacceptable.

Fifth, frequency educated all the participants in the art of compromise. A give-and-take approach to the dialogue was extremely important, particularly in areas where differences looked at first completely irreconcilable. Little by little, participants grew to understand that it is more important to forge a common platform than to adhere rigidly to one's original position. This understanding guided their search for solutions to shared problems and taught them to focus on their similarities as well as on their differences.

Sixth, and perhaps most important, repeated meetings at relatively regular and short intervals made genuine dialogue possible, thereby establishing a different way of talking. This different way of talking set these exchanges apart from the familiar policy-style or academic-style exchanges often heard at larger meetings between adversaries. The difference resulted from the fact that a small dialogue group over time establishes relationships that permit participants to move from talking at one another to talking analytically together, defining shared problems together, and even talking about common efforts for dealing with problems.

FOURTH: *Working together between task force meetings can begin to transform a series of meetings into a political process.*

This experience evolved only gradually through a range of experiments over a period of time. In the mid-1970s participants aspired to move from a series of meetings to a more continuous process of communication and interaction.

In the 1970s each side began to prepare papers on agenda items to share with the other side before meetings. This work required participants to sharpen their own analysis before meetings and enabled them to begin engaging one another. It encouraged each side to think in terms of the other's anticipated analysis between meetings.

With the beginning of the task forces after 1981, cochairs developed agendas and, in a few instances, refined and developed points made in one meeting for discussion in the next. The Regional Conflicts Task Force in the later 1980s began the practice in meetings of developing analytical scenarios to project different ways that conflicts might evolve. These provided a vehicle for monitoring developments between meetings.

The epitome of this experience was reached in 1993 and after with the "common work" of the Regional Conflicts Task Force in overseeing the Inter-Tajik Dialogue, which met almost every two months in the first three years. The Inter-Tajik Dialogue itself followed suit after the dialogue created its Public Committee for Democratic Processes. Without Americans or Russians participating, dialogue members interacted regularly around the four program areas covered by the committee, as well as engaging compatriots outside the dialogue.

One of the proposals in the mid-1990s for forming a task force on the overall Russian-U.S. relationship involved engaging a staff member on each side to host a continuing electronic conversation around well-crafted analytical questions. That proposal remains on the agenda as the new century begins.

The American and Russian public forums project begun in early 2001 provide another example of parallel work. The two projects will be brought together in some form in 2002 and beyond.

FIFTH: *The Dartmouth Conference from its outset dramatized the possibility and the importance of focusing on the overall relationship between the two superpowers rather than isolating for separate consideration the individual issues on the governmental agendas.*

The initial Dartmouth Conference participants from the United States were prominent citizens from the worlds of arts, letters, and politics. They included few specialists, but they were eminently equipped to interpret their society, economy, and polity to the other side; to explain broad public perceptions and fears; to embody the essence of U.S. national identity; and to explain the underlying workings and human elements of their system.

The Soviet and later Russian participants did not constitute a monolithic group. Some were rigid and conservative; others, more liberal and reformist. Most were constructive, and all supported détente and the improvement of the international atmosphere.

Many of them were the people whom Evgeni Primakov later called dissidents within the system. They were advocates of reform though they usually underestimated how deep, radical, and fundamental the necessary transformations would have to be. They proclaimed the need for arms control and the limitation and reduction of armaments. Most of them considered the intervention of Soviet troops in Afghanistan to be a gross mistake. They were presumably selected to participate because they could think creatively and analytically about problems their own country, the United States, and the world faced.

At the same time they were citizens of their country and parts of their society and their nation. They tried to protect and defend the interests of their society and their nation and were themselves not immune to mistakes. They consequently worked faithfully within their political system to improve it—not to overthrow or undermine it. It is not accidental that later, during the time of perestroika and reforms, a sizable number of them occupied important positions in the government, parliament, and political and public life. Although they learned to keep their more radical thoughts to themselves in earlier times, they were able to interpret their country to American participants with a human voice.

When the Regional Conflicts and Arms Control Task Forces were created in 1981, their purpose was to probe Soviet-U.S. interactions in these critical areas to discover what could be learned about the overall relationship. The issue before the 1981 plenary that prompted creation of the task forces was: What happened to détente? The task forces were formed for the explicit purpose of probing for answers in the arenas of interaction where bottom-line interests were often directly revealed. The task forces became laboratories for analyzing the overall relationship.

Later in the 1980s a Political Relations Task Force was formed to focus on the overall relationship, but despite its highly experienced participants, it never really found a niche, perhaps because of the difficulty in reaching far beyond the concrete work of the other two task forces. Another reason probably was that this task force was created at the beginning of the end of the thirty years of what may be called "the classical Dartmouth period" and never had time to establish its own agenda.

Since the early 1990s a feeling has persisted that a serious gap exists at the heart of the Russian-U.S. relationship because no one—in the Dartmouth Conference, at least—is focusing on the overall relationship. As the cochairs of the Regional Conflicts Task Force, Gennadi Chufrin and Hal Saunders, wrote in 1997 in the *Washington Quarterly:* "The mutual work of defining the new relationship requires new mechanisms for genuine discussion between the two governments and renewed processes of sustained dialogue between the citizens of the two countries. . . . A more constructive relationship is essential."[3]

At the beginning of the new century two new attempts to focus on the overall relationship between the Russian and U.S. bodies politic are in exploratory stages: (1) a new effort is under way to form a small task force on the overall relationship built primarily around participants from Dartmouth's "middle generation" to work alongside the continuing Regional Conflicts Task Force and the Inter-Tajik Dialogue and (2) the Kettering Foundation in the United States, the Russian Center for Citizenship Education in St. Petersburg, and the Foundation for Development of Civic Culture in Moscow have agreed to engage American and Russian citizens outside government in parallel deliberative forums on how they think each country should conduct its relationship toward the other. The purposes of this latter project are to broaden citizen engagement in the relationship to the extent possible and to understand public perceptions of the relationship and what public interests in the relationship are.

SIXTH: *The process for changing conflictual relationships called "sustained dialogue" has its deepest roots in the work of the Regional Conflicts Task Force.*

This process was first presented in print in a Dartmouth Conference context in an article by the task force cochairs entitled "A Public Peace Process." The article was an explicit conceptualization of the process of dialogue that had evolved in the task force over more than twenty meetings. Harold Saunders amplified and placed the process in a larger context in his book *A Public Peace Process: Sustained Dialogue to Transform Racial and Ethnic Conflicts.*[4]

This five-stage process provided the operational framework for the Inter-Tajik Dialogue from the outset. Indeed, that was the second laboratory for refining the process. It is now being applied more widely.

Sustained dialogue—the "public peace process" as we called it—was a conceptualization of ten years of experience in the Regional Conflicts Task Force and, for Saunders, of extensive dialogues between Arabs and Israelis.[5] It was simply an effort to capture the stages through which experience unfolds when adversaries or enemies begin talking with one another to change a conflictual relationship.

Stage One is a period when adversaries agonize over whether to reach out to the enemy and eventually decide to engage in dialogue. That can be a painful decision. During the Cold War, anyone who seemed to engage in some kind of positive relationship with the enemy could be accused of naïveté or even disloyalty to his or her country.

Stage Two is the period when two groups sit down together for the first time. Normally, the two sides spend a lot of time "unloading" their grievances with each other. This venting is essential. Participants begin to learn how the other side feels, and moderators begin to "map" the dynamics of the interactions between them. Stage Two usually ends when the two sides feel that the venting has reached a point of diminishing returns and decide to focus on one or two specific problems.

Stage Three is a period in which the quality of the talk changes as the two parties begin talking more analytically about a problem they have decided affects them both. They probe the nature of the problem and how it affects each of them. They weigh different approaches to the problem and perhaps begin to see some direction in which they might move to deal with it. They make a judgment about whether they want to try to move in that direction. If so, they move on to the next stage.

In *Stage Four,* they ask four questions: (1) What are the obstacles to moving in the direction they have selected? (2) What steps could overcome those obstacles? (3) Who could take those steps? (4) How could those steps be arranged in an interactive sequence so that a succession of mutually reinforcing steps would generate momentum?

Stage Five is a period when they put their action plan into the hands of the groups that have the capacity to carry it out.

These stages are not rigid. Groups move back and forth among them or spend long periods in one. They are useful as a guide to moderators and participants to help them preserve some discipline in their talk as well as a sense of purpose and destination. The purpose is to change relationships in the dialogue room; the destination is to change the relationship between groups in the larger body politic.

From 1994 to 1999 this conceptualization provided the framework for a series of psycho-political dialogues among Estonians, Russian-speaking residents of Estonia, and Russians from Moscow conducted by the Center for the Study of Mind and Human Interaction at the University of Virginia with Saunders' participation. Since 1995 the process has been applied to racial and ethnic conflicts first in one and then in five more North American communities. As in the Dartmouth Conference itself, this is a work in progress. Following the terrorist attacks on September 11, 2001, in New York and Washington, D.C., the Kettering Foundation redoubled its efforts to teach sustained dialogue more broadly. Experimental projects are in the early stages for using a modified version of sustained dialogue in a political process for building social capital—the civic infrastructure essential to effective economic performance. The first of these projects began in 2000 in Tajikistan, organized by the Inter-Tajik Dialogue's Public Committee for Democratic Processes. That experience led to refined conceptualization of the process for use at sites in Central and South America.

SEVENTH: *We have learned from these forty years of experience how to think in our own way as citizens outside government about realistic criteria for judging the success of such dialogues.*

Because of the centrality of the superpower relationship in world affairs, there was a strong tendency to see the importance of the Dartmouth Conference in terms of its influence on government policies. Indeed, there were important instances of exchanges that were valuable to government negotiators. This was particularly true in the decade of the task forces—both on particular arms control issues and on Afghanistan. In several instances over two decades, it seems that economic discussions with high-level U.S. businessmen attracted by David Rockefeller fed significant ideas into Soviet debate on economic cooperation. There were also instances when particular relationships grew out of Dartmouth Conference interactions that were useful in dealing with specific problems (e.g., Norman Cousins' role as intermediary between Nikita Khrushchev and the Vatican).

However, the Dartmouth Conference experience suggests that it would be a serious mistake to judge such unofficial dialogues only or even primarily in terms of their influence on governments. That experience demonstrated a far more important perspective on such dialogues that is difficult for conventional evaluators, funders, and congressional committees to grasp. In a historical perspective—a forty-year perspective—it may be that the most valuable product was citizens with an alternative view of the world and of the relationship and the abilities to articulate those views in ways that changed interactions between the two countries. Those citizens' views in many instances may have been sharpened by exposure to different perspectives from the other side. Instincts were reinforced.

The citizens' dimension of the Dartmouth process on the one hand was envisaged from the very beginning by its founders and above all by Norman Cousins. His ideas met a welcome response from his counterparts. On the eve of departure to the first conference, the head of the Soviet delegation, Aleksandr Korneichuk, a parliamentarian and writer, stated in an interview with the TASS news agency: "In the present tense international situation, the public of the USSR and the USA can play a particularly important role in strengthening peaceful international cooperation. We hope that representatives of the U.S. public deeply believe as we do, that any disputable problems between states may be solved in only one possible reasonable way—in a way of peaceful negotiations."[6] It should be recognized, however, that behavior in the first conferences often fell far short of this ideal and that there were many heated statements and sharp political exchanges. In the beginning the citizens' dimension was more of an intention than the norm.

Still, as the years passed, so these intentions gradually became realities. The Dartmouth process steadily evolved into a dialogue of citizens, of the public. That evolution was connected in part with broader geographic exposure. In the Soviet Union the conferences were intentionally held in Kiev, Tbilisi, Baku, Leningrad, and other places outside the constraining official atmosphere of Moscow, places where interaction among citizens was wider, freer, and growing. A similar widening was happening in the United States. The culmination of this process occurred at the second part of Dartmouth XVI, near Los Angeles, where the citizens' participation and interaction were significant.

Soviet Dartmouth Conference participants absorbed a perspective on our increasingly interdependent world quite different from the then traditional view. These views were expressed between 1985 and 1990 in the articles that came to be called the "new political thinking" in Moscow. The preeminent statement was Mikhail Gorbachev's speech to the United Nations General Assembly in December 1988. It is virtually impossible to know, to measure, or to prove exactly how the Dartmouth experience shaped individuals' views or what difference that body of thought made, but there is little doubt that it played some role in ending the Cold War. The conceptual lenses people use to give meaning to the world around them determine how they act.

There is also little doubt among Americans who participated in Dartmouth XVI in 1988 in Austin, Texas, that their interaction with Soviet colleagues explaining glasnost and perestroika was a defining moment in judging whether changes in the Soviet Union were "for real."

As of late 2001, eight years' experience and thirty-two meetings of the Inter-Tajik Dialogue within the Framework of the Dartmouth Conference have offered further insights into what constitute the important products of such dialogues. To be sure, one can point to concrete examples of the Inter-Tajik Dialogue's influence on the General Agreement on Peace of June 1997 and to the personal roles played by dialogue participants in the peace negotiations and in the implementing mechanism, the National Reconciliation Commission. But the products of the dialogue that will probably have much more significance over the long term are the participants with experience in the dialogue, the political philosophy expressed in twenty-one joint memoranda, and the approach to postconflict peacebuilding expressed in the founding of the dialogue's Public Committee for Democratic Processes.

Reflecting on the accomplishments of the Dartmouth Conference, one longtime U.S. participant focused on the development of basic human capacity to conduct a relationship—"the ability developed through the dialogue process itself to address complex, politically highly charged issues of great consequence in a calm professional manner where facts and analysis could and did dominate the exchange."

He also felt that the exchanges caused participants on one side or the other to recognize problems they had closed their eyes to because participants on the other side "whose views carried growing credibility" held those problems up in bold relief. "For me, the rapid growth in the 1980s of readiness by our Soviet partners to expose their own 'superiors' in the Central Committee apparatus and in the Foreign Ministry to U.S. participants in the dialogue provided evidence of the importance of this process." He continued: "I am not saying we created a new view on the Soviet side. I am saying that, against the background of events, our dialogue created a 'safe haven' in which these issues could be addressed with the resulting opportunity for rethinking basic assumptions."

These reflections suggest that citizens should conduct their dialogues in ways that help citizens develop capacities and change perspectives. They should not necessarily aim, in the first instance, at having an impact on governments.

EIGHTH: *We have learned that sustaining a complex of dialogues such as those that made the Dartmouth Conference what it was requires (1) a core group of individuals with commitment to the process and concern for the fundamental issues at stake and (2) some minimal organizational structure to provide continuity through staff and funding.*

The preceding chapters of this book have clearly shown how important it is to have one "mind at work" in the middle of a project such as Dartmouth, a mind that embraces the totality of the relationship between two large and complex bodies politic and that can keep the dialogues going in ways that meet the changing needs in the relationship. Beyond that one person, a few others—such as the task force chairs in the 1980s—can amplify the conceptual and operational framework. These "stewards of the process" must believe deeply in its importance, invest their capacities in moving it forward, and recognize that sustaining the process over time is essential to nourishing new perspectives.

From 1960 to 1990 Dartmouth benefited in varying configurations from a combination of six strong continuing sources of support. On the U.S. side were Norman Cousins, David Rockefeller, and, after 1969, the Kettering Foundation. On the Soviet side were the Soviet Peace Committee and, after 1970, the Institute for the Study of the USA and Canada (ISKAN), with Georgi Arbatov as the leading figure. On both sides in the 1980s were the task force cochairs.

Norman Cousins, of course, was the source of the founding concept and, with Philip Mosely, the prime mover in the 1960s and the inspirational father until his death in 1990. David Rockefeller's commitment and perseverance were unique, as was his capacity to draw in very senior figures from the business and financial worlds. After 1969 the Kettering Foundation provided strong institutional support through more than three decades. As part of the Kettering team, Phil Stewart played a central role, promoting continuity, discipline, and creativity on the U.S. side of Dartmouth in the 1970s and 1980s. On the logistical side, Patricia Coggins at Kettering provided institutional memory, grace, and first-rate support for twenty-five years.

The Russian side benefited first from the support of the Soviet Peace Committee and then from an organization—ISKAN—the main mission of which was to understand the United States. Georgi Arbatov and his deputies, particularly Vitali Zhurkin and, later, Andrei Kokoshin, Viktor Kremenyuk, and Sergei Rogov, were the "mind at work" in Moscow. Alice Bobrysheva of the institute provided organizational support along with the Peace Committee staff. As in the United States, a lot of the substantive work was carried out in the 1980s by task force chairs.

Actors like this are essential. No one could pull together in the 1990s, despite some effort, a comparable combination of capacities. After the end of the Cold War, it may be that no individual or group could have persuaded Americans or Russians of the compelling importance of the Russian-U.S. relationship. But for analytical purposes, it is important to recognize that—second to the structural change in the relationship—changes in the "management team" partly explain the Dartmouth Conference experience in the 1990s.

On the U.S. side, those elements of Dartmouth that continued to be strong in the 1990s—the Regional Conflicts Task Force and the civil society work—remained strong because they built on substantive interests and strengths of the Kettering Foundation staff. During the Cold War, Kettering had supplemented its own in-house strengths by contracting for a substantial part of Phil Stewart's time. He was a tenured professor at Ohio State University. Russian culture, language, history, and the Soviet experience were his personal passion and academic focus. He added a substantive Soviet dimension to Kettering's capacity. In the

1980s the task force chairmen added their own substantive depth, but it was Stewart with strong Kettering support and input who provided the continuity, framework, and cumulative agenda on the overall Russian-U.S. relationship.

During the 1990s, on the U.S. side the new approaches of the Regional Conflicts Task Force and its new venture—the Inter-Tajik Dialogue—built on Saunders' experience and continuing work, which reflected a view of the relationship between conflict prevention and resolution and civil society deeply rooted in the Kettering Foundation's citizen-focused view of politics. In 1991, after a decade of service as a part-time associate, Saunders became full-time director of international affairs at the foundation. The civil society track played from Kettering's strongest suit—the study of democratic practices in the lives of citizens as political actors, largely stimulated by the thinking and writing of its president, David Mathews. The Arms Control Task Force, however, lost its chairman and potential chairman, and Kettering regarded the Task Force's agenda as more appropriate to governments than to citizens. That task force and, more particularly, the work on the overall relationship suffered from the loss of Stewart's leadership. In short, any nonofficial dialogue will reflect the interests and capacities of its management team.

On the Russian side, the two leading institutions—ISKAN and the Soviet Peace Committee—suffered major blows with the loss of government financial support and political influence after the dissolution of the Soviet Union. The Russian side could no longer finance its traditional share of the exchange. By 1994—as a young Russian Dartmouth veteran pointed out—many key Dartmouth veterans had become critics of the regime.

While it is important in looking to the future to recognize the key role that important people and organizations have played, it is also essential to recognize the challenge that those people face as they work in a larger—sometimes limiting—political environment. Central to that environment in the 1990s has been the general perception in both countries that the relationship has lost its dominating importance. During the Cold War, the goal of avoiding nuclear holocaust was paramount. In the immediate and traumatic aftermath of the Cold War's end, other factors preoccupied the citizens of both countries. In the absence of a dramatic reason for interest in the Russian-U.S. relationship over the long term, it did not seem

possible on either side to draw participants from the follow-on generations into dialogue. The dangers seemed diffuse; people in both
countries—each for very different reasons—were unclear about their
identities, partly because they could not define themselves in terms of
a clear enemy. Russia necessarily turned inward to focus on devastating
economic, social, and political problems. The United States had
unmatched power, but most Americans were confused about how the
United States should use that power in the world—or did not care.
They were less and less interested in Russia.

In the Dartmouth fortieth-anniversary reunion held in September
2000, one Russian participant stated: "We have lost our audience. The
government isn't interested, and besides our institutes have lost their
influence." The U.S. team can still muster participants at the senior professional level with access to the second and third levels of government,
but without David Rockefeller's stature, it has not been able to draw from
the business community—partly because business leaders now have their
own access and partly because they see little opportunity in Russia.
Beyond that, it has been extremely difficult to interest new participants
from wider backgrounds—partly because the existing management team
has not been able to devote the necessary time and person-power to the
task and partly because it is still struggling to hit on a format appropriate
to the new relationship and the new level of citizen interest.

BEYOND THESE FORTY YEARS: WHERE NEXT?

As the new century began, the Russian-U.S. relationship had fallen far
short of the hopes that citizens in both nations had held in 1992. It was
characterized by disillusionment, resentment, anger, and even suspicion among Russian citizens that the United States was actively trying
to keep Russia from resuming its role as a major power or even to
encourage fragmentation of the Russian Federation.

It is instructive to examine the moods, psychology, and mentality
of contemporary Russians, to look into the roots of their present attitude toward Americans, the United States, and the West as a whole. It
should be noted first that the Russian mind-set at the turn of the century is shaped by many factors, trends, and influences. This mind-set
consists of many layers of political psychology, layers that partly con-

tradict one another, partly coincide, and partly exist independently.

Among the most notable elements in this mind-set are a widespread nostalgia for what many Russians refer to as their country's "greatness" and a longing to see it reacquire a leading role in the contemporary and future world. These sentiments are generally based not on affection for the Soviet past but on pride in Russia's history, cultural-civilizational heritage, enormous natural resources, and the special "spirituality" of its people.

This nostalgia is interwoven with and fed by an inferiority complex that has deepened and widened in the past decade. It has many roots, among them faulty economic and other reforms; political instability and uncertainty; spreading poverty, corruption, and crime; and, not the least important, Russia's diminishing economic output and its shrinking place and role in the world.

Like any country, Russia has its own extremists on both flanks of its society. In a highly politicized and unstable society like Russia, however, extreme groups compound the level of societal uncertainty and foster what some have called an "atomization" of society.

Very mixed attitudes toward the Russian-U.S. relationship emerge from this state of affairs. Envy toward the prosperous West and in particular the United States is mixed now and then with a respect toward Americans and Westerners as a whole for their hard work, which created their wealth and prosperity. On the one hand, Russian suspicion deepens about U.S. intentions toward a weakened Russia; on the other hand, Americans' lack of interest in Russia itself deepens Russian humiliation. Russians want to establish themselves as a strong, stable partner of the United States, but they fear that Russian interests may be harmed in such a relationship. Above all, Russians have an overwhelming desire to stand up and construct a strong democratic society that will stay equal to other major powers of the world.

On the U.S. side of the relationship, Americans by default have been left as the "only superpower," with unmatched ability to project military power and with the world's largest economy. The 1990s were an extremely successful decade for the United States—and a humiliatingly disastrous one for Russia. The lack of a reliable rule of law in Russia has led potential U.S. investors to look elsewhere for opportunity.

At the same time, Americans have little sense of what kind of country they want the United States to be in a world that is changing rapidly for reasons entirely apart from the end of the Cold War. As one U.S. participant said at the fortieth-anniversary Dartmouth Conference reunion, Americans are not dealing well with their loss of the Cold War as an organizing principle for their role in the world. Americans enjoy being the only superpower, but they have no clear ideas about how the United States should use its power—economic or military.

While some Americans recognize that Russia has the potential to act the role of a great power again and that a constructive Russian-U.S. relationship will be critical to world peace and progress in the twenty-first century, they do not assign a high priority to the promotion of such a relationship at present. Just as Russians have turned inward to deal with dramatic economic deterioration, Americans have turned inward to build on unprecedented economic growth and, in 2001, to attend first to their own economic retreat and then to the shock of the terrorist attacks on September 11. The challenge is to find individuals in each country who are far-seeing enough to recognize the need to sustain a sound relationship.

Phillips Ruopp, an American who was deeply involved with Dartmouth from the early 1970s through the later 1980s as a senior member of the Kettering Foundation staff, reflected on the importance of such dialogue beyond the Russian-U.S. relationship:

> I find myself uneasy about what seems to be the inability or disinclination of Americans and others to talk about reinvigorating larger goals in the relationships of states and peoples. In particular, a short-sighted U.S. foreign policy in the name of realism and narrowly defined national interests will fail to come to grips with economic, environmental, and political problems that demand imaginative international action.
>
> It's understandable that the idealistic rhetoric that animated many of us after the Second World War has lost its old persuasiveness. It got tongue-tied in the face of harsh events and the consequences of myopic nationalism. But we need to find a new articulation of what needs to be done for the sake of a decent human future.
>
> Where will that come from? One source would certainly be ongoing international dialogues that tap what has been learned

about productive communication on difficult questions, and the diversification of the leadership groups who participate in it.

What do the multifaceted experiences of the Dartmouth Conference suggest for that future? How may the people of Dartmouth inspire rising generations to meet the challenges of an unfolding relationship?

The basic requirement is to find individuals who feel that the relationship is important—not an easy task in an era when young Americans are absorbed in the excitement of high-tech ventures and a globalizing economy and young Russians, although they have similar interests, live in an atmosphere that forces them to focus on earning a basic living and gives them little incentive to see Americans as likely partners. Perhaps the conduct of public forums, like those held in the two countries in 2001, will provide an opportunity to identify interested individuals from a larger range of regional backgrounds. Those who live and work outside the traditional policymaking and policy-influencing communities—if they are interested in world affairs—might find this an exciting opportunity. As a U.S. participant of the middle generation said: "Gone are the days when Moscow could speak for all of Russia. The same has always been true of the United States. The more regional representation we can get on both sides, the deeper we will get into our respective understanding of the ever-changing spirit and soul of each country." And of the relationship, we would add.

The next requirement is to find a vehicle for dialogue that the middle and younger generations will find attractive, challenging, and rewarding enough to cause them to commit time and energy. Perhaps the best approach would be to work out in a dialogue between them and Dartmouth veterans in both Russia and the United States a format that meets their needs and suits their ways of communicating, including their predilection for electronic exchange.

Even more complicated in the light of the first two challenges is the fact that two large and complex countries such as Russia and the United States really need (1) a complex of dialogues on particular aspects of the relationship and (2) a context in which to bring insights from those individual dialogues together in reflection on the overall relationship. Both countries will continue to gain insight into their overall relationship by probing their interactions in particular arenas that generate friction, but there is also a need to discover the underlying dynamics of the overall relationship. One group—perhaps with a continuing staff—needs to focus on the relationship itself, drawing together insights from a range of other sources. As the new century begins, that is the most glaring need.

The relationship will also be strengthened to the extent that citizens of the two countries can find important opportunities for engaging in common work. Our rapidly changing world in which there is still so much instability, poverty, and illness offers ample opportunities for such work. The Inter-Tajik Dialogue within the Framework of the Dartmouth Conference will continue to provide a model for such joint efforts. It is an experience that, with adaptive ingenuity, could well be applied in other situations.

REFLECTIONS ON PAST AND FUTURE: THE MULTILEVEL PEACE PROCESS

The Dartmouth Conference reinvented itself several times to make itself more effective. It is now in the process—a very complex process—of doing so again.

The dialogue over the conflict in Tajikistan has been in a sense a distillation of the forty-year experience of the Dartmouth Conference. It became a laboratory for developing and refining what Saunders came to call "sustained dialogue"—a process designed for addressing the deep-rooted human conflicts that increasingly divide haves and have-nots, liberals and fundamentalists, the included and the excluded, and proponents of different ideologies. As a vehicle for designing interactions in the multilevel peace process, it can be applied more widely by those who have experienced it. The Public Committee for Democratic Processes in Tajikistan and the project by citizens in Russia and the United States to conduct some one hundred forums on the Russian-U.S. relationship may together foreshadow the most important new breakthrough in the Dartmouth process. They may be the first significant efforts—along with the Regional Conflicts Task Force—to develop other levels of what the Tajiks call the multilevel peace process.

Despite these striking achievements, Dartmouth veterans remain concerned above all about the absence of a group at the heart of the overall Russian-U.S. relationship. The tensions between the two countries over many issues, including NATO expansion, intervention in Serbia/Kosovo, and Chechnya have steadily eroded the relationship. Trust seems to be decreasing, and the opportunities for misunderstanding are increasing. A future in which the relationship between the two countries steadies and is recognized in both as critical to both seems distant as each country struggles to find its way in a very different world from the one that gave birth to the Dartmouth Conference in 1960.

Yet the men and women who took part in the Dartmouth conferences during the forty years that have passed since the first meeting was convened in Hanover can take pride in the efforts they made to shape a future that was dangerous and uncertain. This was not their job—they were not officials. But for many it was nonetheless their duty, and they proved that citizens can help shape relationships between countries. In ways that seem as certain as they are impossible to measure, participants played their individual and collective roles in shaping the environment in which the Cold War ended and the threat of nuclear holocaust was reduced.

That they know their job is not over is clear from their redoubled efforts in the 1990s. The resilience, imagination, and energy they have brought to the task reflect the courage, perseverance, and experience that began with Cousins and Korneichuk in the Wren Room at Dartmouth College in 1960.

Notes

Except where otherwise noted, unpublished letters, reports, memoranda, and similar materials are held in the archives of the Kettering Foundation in the Philip Mosely papers at the University of Illinois at Urbana-Champaign or are in the author's personal files.

1. Sustained Dialogue in Perspective

1. These examples are given in Glenn T. Seaborg, *Kennedy, Khrushchev, and the Test Ban* (Berkeley: University of California Press, 1981), 202, 206.

2. Ibid., 205.

3. Kenneth N. Waltz, *Theory of International Politics* (New York: Random House, 1979); and Hans J. Morgenthau, *Politics among Nations*, 5th ed. (New York: Alfred A. Knopf, 1973).

4. According to Waltz, "To be politically pertinent, power has to be defined in terms of the distribution of capabilities." Waltz, *Theory of International Politics*, 191.

5. William Curtis Wohlforth, *The Elusive Balance: Power and Perceptions during the Cold War* (Ithaca, N.Y.: Cornell University Press, 1993), 6–7.

6. Thomas Risse-Kappen, "Bringing Transnational Relations Back In: Introduction," in *Bringing Transnational Relations Back In: Non-State Actors, Domestic Structures, and International Institutions*, ed. Thomas Risse-Kappen (Cambridge: Cambridge University Press, 1995), 10.

7. Ann M. Florini and P. J. Simmons, "What the World Needs Now," in *The Third Force: The Rise of Transnational Civil Society*, ed. Ann M. Florini

(Tokyo and Washington, D.C.: Japan Center for International Exchange and the Carnegie Endowment for International Peace, 2000), 9.

8. For the role of technology in fostering transnational networks, see Ann M. Florini, "Lessons Learned," in *The Third Force,* ed. Florini, 220–224.

9. Krasner makes an argument for how transnational relations can fit into the realist paradigm. See Stephen D. Krasner, "Power Politics, Institutions, and Transnational Relations," in *Bringing Transnational Relations Back In,* ed. Risse-Kappen, 257–279.

10. This is to say that they were not an epistemic community as defined by either Ernst Haas or Peter Haas. See Ernst B. Haas, *When Knowledge Is Power: Three Models of Change in International Organization* (Berkeley: University of California Press, 1990), 40–46; and Peter M. Haas, "Introduction: Epistemic Communities and International Policy Coordination," in *Knowledge, Power, and International Policy Coordination,* ed. Peter M. Haas (Columbia: University of South Carolina Press, 1997), 3.

11. Joseph V. Montville, "Transnationalism and the Role of Track-Two Diplomacy," in *Approaches to Peace: An Intellectual Map,* ed. W. Scott Thompson and Kenneth M. Jensen with Richard N. Smith and Kimber M. Schraub (Washington, D.C.: United States Institute of Peace Press, 1991), 262. The quoted material comes from Montville's definition of track-two diplomacy. John McDonald and Louise Diamond expanded the idea into multitrack diplomacy in *Multi-Track Diplomacy: A Systems Approach to Peace,* rev. ed. (West Hartford, Conn.: Kumarian, 1996). See also the Web site of the Institute for Multi-Track Diplomacy: www.imtd.org. This definition gives the essence of that broader concept. For an overview of interactive conflict resolution and the approaches of those who practice it, see Ronald J. Fisher, *Interactive Conflict Resolution* (Syracuse, N.Y.: Syracuse University Press, 1997).

12. Harold H. Saunders, *A Public Peace Process: Sustained Dialogue to Transform Racial and Ethnic Conflicts* (New York: St. Martin's Press, 1999), 24–28, 165. See also Harold H. Saunders, "The Multilevel Peace Process in Tajikistan," in *Herding Cats: Multiparty Mediation in a Complex World,* ed. Chester A. Crocker, Fen Osler Hampson, and Pamela Aall (Washington, D.C.: United States Institute of Peace Press, 1999), esp. 161–164.

13. McDonald and Diamond, *Multi-Track Diplomacy,* 7.

14. This arena may become increasingly common as the importance of nongovernmental organizations grows. Their role in the multilateral negotiations that led to the Comprehensive Test Ban Treaty is but one example.

15. The concepts behind sustained dialogue are laid out in Saunders, *A Public Peace Process.* See also chapter 6 in this volume.

16. Risse-Kappen, ed., *Bringing Transnational Relations Back In,* 5, 287.

17. For a discussion of such a conception of power, see Robert A. Dahl, *Modern Political Analysis,* 5th ed. (Englewood Cliffs, N.J.: Prentice-Hall, 1991). Wohlforth points out its limitations (*The Elusive Balance,* 4–5). So does Waltz (*Theory of International Politics,* 191–192). The definition suggested comes from Peter Morriss, *Power: A Philosophical Analysis* (New York: St. Martin's Press, 1987).

18. Dahl, *Modern Political Analysis,* 4.

19. See Margaret Keck and Kathryn Sikkink, *Activists beyond Borders: Advocacy Networks in International Politics* (Ithaca, N.Y.: Cornell University Press, 1998).

20. See David D. Newsom, ed., *Private Diplomacy with the Soviet Union* (Lanham, Md.: University Press of America, 1987); Maureen R. Berman and Joseph E. Johnson, eds., *Unofficial Diplomats* (New York: Columbia University Press, 1977); and John W. MacDonald, Jr., and Diane B. Bendahmane, eds., *Conflict Resolution: Track-Two Diplomacy* (Washington, D.C.: Foreign Service Institute, U.S. Department of State, 1987). See also the forthcoming work by Yale Richmond on U.S.-Soviet exchanges.

21. Principled beliefs are "normative ideas that specify criteria for distinguishing right from wrong and just from unjust." Judith Goldstein and Robert O. Keohane, "Ideas and Foreign Policy: An Analytical Framework," in *Ideas and Foreign Policy: Beliefs, Institutions, and Political Change,* ed. Judith Goldstein and Robert O. Keohane (Ithaca, N.Y.: Cornell University Press, 1993), 9.

22. As Weber put it: "In general, we understand by 'power' the chance of a man or a number of men to realize their own will in a communal action even against the resistance of others who are participating in the action." H. H. Gerth and C. Wright Mills, eds., *From Max Weber: Essays in Sociology* (New York: Oxford University Press, 1958), 180.

23. This definition is based on the definition of power given in Morriss, *Power.* See James Voorhees, "Soviet Policy toward the Conflict between South Africa and Angola in the 1980s" (Ph.D. diss., Johns Hopkins University, 1992), 28–32.

24. This formulation appears in many places in Saunders' work. See, for example, Harold H. Saunders et al., "Interactive Conflict Resolution: A View for Policy Makers on Making and Building Peace," in *International Conflict Resolution after the Cold War,* ed. Paul C. Stern and Daniel Druckman, published under the auspices of the Committee on International Conflict Resolution, Commission on Behavior and Social Sciences and Education, National Research Council (Washington, D.C.: National Academy Press, 2000), 251.

25. As Keck and Sikkink put it: "The ability to generate and use information strategically is the main asset of transnational advocacy networks" (*Activists beyond Borders,* 147).

26. George Kenney, "The Bosnia Calculation," *New York Times Magazine,* April 23, 1995; and George Kenney, "Steering Clear of Balkan Shoals," *Nation,* January 8–15, 1996.

27. The idea of policy windows is taken from John W. Kingdon, *Agendas, Alternatives, and Public Policies,* 2d ed. (New York: HarperCollins College Publishers, 1995). An earlier version of the same argument, derived independently from his own experience in government, can be found in Harold H. Saunders, "The Dartmouth Conference and the Middle East," in *Private Diplomacy with the Soviet Union,* ed. David D. Newsom (Lanham, Md.: University Press of America, 1987), 29–38.

28. See Anatoli Dobrynin, *In Confidence: Moscow's Ambassador to America's Six Cold War Presidents (1962–1986)* (New York: Times Books, 1995), 229–231. His description of the relationship between Nixon and Kissinger also sheds light on the distinctions being made here.

29. Ibid.

30. Evgeni Primakov, former foreign minister and prime minister of Russia, was asked whether there were differences in how he talked at Dartmouth and later as an official. He replied that although his convictions did not change, "as far as my statements and actions connected with the Middle East conflict were concerned, they were naturally to a large extent conditioned, at least in form, by the official position which I occupied." Evgeni Primakov, "Answers by Academician Evgeniy Primakov to Questions Posed by Dr. Harold H. Saunders for the Book on the History of the Dartmouth Conferences," trans. Vitali Zhurkin, June 29, 2001.

31. In this respect, it is instructive to look at the relationship between Anatoli Dobrynin and officials in the Kennedy administration. The ambassador met regularly with Secretary of State Dean Rusk at the latter's home, on a yacht, or at Dobrynin's residence to drink whiskey and discuss issues, such as Berlin, that were on the bilateral agenda (Dobrynin, *In Confidence,* 63). Later on, the back-channel relationship with Henry Kissinger may have been even more important, even though they both pressed the positions and strategy of their governments.

32. "Dartmouth VIII Conference Report: An Analytic Summary of Conference Discussions Held in Tbilisi, Georgia, U.S.S.R., April 22–26, 1974," prepared for the Charles F. Kettering Foundation by Philip D. Stewart, conference rapporteur, n.p., n.d., 65.

33. Dobrynin, *In Confidence,* 229–231.

34. Robert English, *Russia Views the West: Intellectual and Political Origins of Soviet New Thinking* (New York: Columbia University Press, 2000), 226.

35. Sarah E. Mendelson, *Changing Course: Ideas, Politics, and the Soviet Withdrawal from Afghanistan* (Princeton, N.J.: Princeton University Press, 1998), 55.

36. Aleksandr G. Savelyev and Nikolai N. Detinov, *The Big Five: Arms Control Decision-Making in the Soviet Union,* trans. Dimitri Trenin (Westport, Conn.: Praeger, 1995).

37. John Newhouse, *Cold Dawn: The Story of SALT* (New York: Holt, Rinehart, and Winston, 1973), 56. English gives further examples of the limited access civilians had to Soviet information about Soviet forces, noting their "humiliation" at being dependent on Western sources. English, *Russia and the Idea of the West,* 149–150.

38. Arkadi N. Shevchenko, *Breaking with Moscow* (New York: Alfred A. Knopf, 1985).

39. Anatoli Adamishin, "The White Sun of Angola," *International Affairs* 46, no. 3 (2000): 231.

40. Documents from the Central Committee archives show that permission for Soviet scientists to go abroad sometimes came from as high in the Soviet bureaucracy as the Politburo. Matthew Evangelista, "The Paradox of State Strength: Transnational Relations, Domestic Structures, and Security Policy in Russia and the Soviet Union," *International Organization* 49 (winter 1995): 12–13.

2. The Early Years

1. Norman Cousins, *Albert Schweitzer's Mission: Healing and Peace* (New York: W. W. Norton, 1985), 133.

2. For Cousins' role in SANE and the nuclear disarmament movement, see Milton S. Katz, *Ban the Bomb: A History of SANE, the Committee for a Sane Nuclear Policy, 1957–1985* (New York: Greenwood Press, 1986); and Lawrence S. Wittner, *Resisting the Bomb: A History of the World Disarmament Movement, 1954–1970* (Stanford, Calif.: Stanford University Press, 1997).

3. Norman Cousins, *Anatomy of an Illness as Perceived by the Patient: Reflections on Healing and Regeneration* (New York: W. W. Norton, 1979).

4. Norman Cousins, "An Address in Moscow," in *Present Tense: An American Editor's Odyssey* (New York: McGraw-Hill, 1967), 295. This was his speech to the Presidium of the Soviet Peace Committee. See Alice Bobrysheva, "Thanks for the Memories: My Years with the Dartmouth Conference" (Dayton, Ohio: Charles F. Kettering Foundation, n.d.), 9–10.

5. Arkadi N. Shevchenko, *Breaking with Moscow* (New York: Alfred A. Knopf, 1985), 89.

6. My thanks to Yale Richmond for pointing this out (e-mail to author, June 17, 1999).

7. Charles E. Bohlen, *Witness to History, 1929–1969* (New York: W. W. Norton, 1973), 390–391. Charles Bohlen was the U.S. ambassador to Moscow from 1953 to 1957.

8. Matthew Evangelista, *Unarmed Forces: The Transnational Movement to End the Cold War* (Ithaca, N.Y.: Cornell University Press, 1999).

9. The connection between the Geneva conferences on a test ban and "a vast amount of extra-governmental activity" was evident by 1961. See Bernhard G. Bechhoefer, *Postwar Negotiations for Arms Control* (Washington, D.C.: Brookings Institution, 1961), 488. Bechhoefer's account of the conferences is illuminating and detailed.

10. The letter is reproduced in *The Papers of Dwight David Eisenhower, NATO and the Campaign of 1952: XII,* ed. Louis Galambos (Baltimore, Md.: Johns Hopkins University Press, 1989), 148–149. Cousins gives his fullest account of his relationship with Eisenhower in Norman Cousins, *The Pathology of Power* (New York: W. W. Norton, 1987), 74–82.

11. The relationship had its ups and downs while Eisenhower was president. See Wittner, *Resisting the Bomb,* 142–143, 368–369.

12. Arthur Larson, *Eisenhower: The President Nobody Knew* (New York: Charles Scribner's Sons, 1968), 172–173.

13. Stephen Ambrose, *Eisenhower: Soldier and President* (New York: Touchstone Books, 1991), 535–536.

14. Norman Cousins, *The Improbable Triumvirate: John F. Kennedy, Pope John, Nikita Khrushchev* (New York: W. W. Norton, 1972), 162–164; and Wittner, *Resisting the Bomb,* 369.

15. Cousins, *Present Tense,* 402. The phrase is from an editorial that first appeared on June 24, 1961.

16. See Bobrysheva, "Thanks for the Memories," 9–10. Bobrysheva was there. The *New York Times* (July 20, 1959) reported that he "was given a polite hearing."

17. Cousins, *Present Tense,* 302.

18. Ibid., 400.

19. "A Proposal for an American-Soviet Non-Governmental Conference on Key Questions Related to the Peace," n.p., n.d.

20. Robert Colby Nelson, "Notes Prepared at the Files of Norman Cousins in Beverly Hills, California, on Thursday, October 28, 1993."

21. John S. D. Eisenhower, "Memorandum of Conference with the President, August 6, 1959—8:49 AM," Eisenhower Papers as President, DDE Diary Series, Box 43, Staff Notes August 1959 (1). Many thanks to Herb Pankratz at the Eisenhower Presidential Library for making this document available.

22. Nelson, "Notes Prepared at the Files of Norman Cousins in Beverly Hills, California, on Thursday, October 28, 1993." Yale Richmond also found Cousins to be modest. He recalled that at a meeting at the Kennan Institute in Washington in the 1980s, Cousins gave Richmond credit for starting the Soviet-American Writers' Conferences. But, Richmond writes, "I helped him, but the credit, and the idea, were really his." E-mail to author, June 17, 1999. His characterization of Cousins, with whom he worked to set up the Writers' Conferences, is worth noting: "An idealist, a doer, a pragmatist—a rare combination." E-mail to author, November 13, 1998.

23. Gale Warner, "Proving the Experts Wrong: A Profile of Norman Cousins," *Kettering Review* (fall 1986): 53.

24. W. Phillips Davison, "Notes on a Conversation with Professor Philip E. Mosely, Director, European Institute, Columbia University, June 29, 1970."

25. Particularly after the first Dartmouth Conference, there was some dissatisfaction with Norman Cousins' leadership. George Fischer, in particular, threatened not to return if Cousins was still in charge. See George Fischer, letter to Philip Mosely, November 6, 1960; in his response, sent on November 10, Mosely expresses understanding of the "Cousins problem." With Mosely named cochairman, Fischer stayed. It seems likely that without Mosely's influence, the character of the Dartmouth Conference would have been significantly different.

26. Mary Kersey Harvey, letter to Philip Mosely, August 7, 1961.

27. Robert Colby Nelson, interview with George Klebnikov, April 26, 1988.

28. Arthur Larson, Philip Mosely, A. William Loos, and Norman Cousins, "A Proposal for an American-Soviet Non-Governmental Conference on Key Questions Related to the Peace," n.p., n.d. The senior officials included Charles Bohlen; Robert H. Thayer, special assistant to the secretary for the Coordination of International Educational and Cultural Relations; Ambassador William S. B. Lacy, special assistant to the secretary for East-West Exchanges; and Frederick T. Merrill, director, East-West Contacts Staff.

29. Bobrysheva, "Thanks for the Memories," 22.

30. George Kennan wrote that Benton was one of only three in the Senate "who, to their everlasting credit, would muster the courage to challenge McCarthy head-on and to oppose him uncompromisingly for what he was." George F. Kennan, *Memoirs, 1950–1963* (Boston: Little, Brown, 1972), 226.

31. Sidney Hyman, *The Lives of William Benton* (Chicago: University of Chicago Press, 1969), 519.

32. Ibid., 551.

33. See Lazar Pistrach, *Khrushchev's Rise to Power* (New York: Praeger, 1961), 177–179, 183–184.

34. Sergei Khrushchev, *Khrushchev on Khrushchev: An Inside Account of the Man and His Era,* ed. and trans. William Taubman (Boston: Little, Brown, 1990), 23.

35. A. D. Shveitser, *An Interpreter Remembers . . . Japan USA Pugwash— Dartmouth* (Moscow: Stella, 1996). Found at www.prodigy.com/casanova/memoir.htm, October 16, 1997.

36. I. Koshelivets, "Oleksander Korniichuk," in *Encyclopedia of Ukraine,* vol. 2, ed. Volodymyr Kubijovyc (Toronto: University of Toronto Press, 1988), 611–612.

37. George Fischer, "Conversations with Korneichuk (U.S.-Soviet meeting at Dartmouth College)," typescript, November 16, 1960.

38. Bobrysheva, "Thanks for the Memories," 20.

39. L. Larry Leonard, "Rapporteur's Notes on Discussion at First Meeting."

40. Walter Rostow, *The Stages of Economic Growth: A Non-Communist Manifesto* (Cambridge: Cambridge University Press, 1996).

41. Walt Rostow, "The Role of the United States and the Soviet Union in the Economic Development of the Emerging Nations," typescript, October 29, 1960. Rostow was also prescient: "In my view, [Eastern Europe, North Korea, and Vietnam], too, in time, will resume their own history and recapture their own sovereignty; and as a matter of simple faith, I believe that Russians—of the next generation if not of this—will come to understand that this release is in the Russian interest."

42. For more on Grenville Clark, see the recollections of his associates, including Norman Cousins, in Norman Cousins and J. Garry Clifford, eds., *Memoirs of a Man, Grenville Clark* (New York: W. W. Norton, 1975); and his biography, Gerald T. Dunne, *Grenville Clark: Public Citizen* (New York: Farrar, Straus, and Giroux, 1986).

43. Norman Cousins, "Grenville Clark: A Man for All Seasons," in *Memoirs of a Man,* 5–6. This chapter had been published as an editorial in the *Saturday Review,* November 26, 1966; see Cousins, *Present Tense,* 627–628. Korneichuk's account of the incident in an interview in *Literaturnaya gazeta,* February 4, 1961, is similar.

44. Daniel Yankelovich, *The Magic of Dialogue: Transforming Conflict into Cooperation* (New York: Simon and Schuster, 1999), 77–86.

45. Fischer, "Conversations with Korneichuk (U.S.-Soviet Meeting at Dartmouth College)."

46. Philip E. Mosely, letter to George Fischer, November 16, 1960.

47. Michael R. Beschloss, *The Crisis Years: Kennedy and Khrushchev, 1960–1963* (New York: Edward R. Burlingame Books, 1991), 41.

48. Ibid., 40.

49. *New York Times,* December 15, 1960.

50. "Report of Talks Given in Moscow on December 14, 1960." This appears to be a wire service report, but no author is given. It can be found among the Philip Mosely papers. This tendentiousness was also noted in a letter to Cousins by Leslie Brady, the counselor for cultural affairs in Moscow, and in a report to the State Department on the meeting, which was attended by Brady and three colleagues. See Robert Colby Nelson, "Notes Prepared at the Files of Norman Cousins in Beverly Hills, California, on Thursday, October 28, 1993."

51. Bobrysheva, "Thanks for the Memories," 48–50.

52. Cousins, "Dialogue with the Russians," in *Present Tense,* 404. This editorial was originally published in the *Saturday Review,* June 24, 1961.

53. Bobrysheva, "Thanks for the Memories," 57–58.

54. Margaret Mead, *Soviet Attitudes toward Authority: An Interdisciplinary Approach to Problems of Soviet Character* (New York: Shocken Books, 1966). The study was originally published in 1951. Philip Mosely served as a consultant to the group that conducted it. In the introduction to the 1966 edition, Mead speaks about how important the Dartmouth conferences at Oreanda and Andover were to her understanding of Soviet attitudes.

55. Most of this biographical information comes from U.S. Senate Committee on Foreign Relations, *Détente* (Washington, D.C.: U.S. Government Printing Office, 1975), 181–184.

56. Ved Mehta wrote a profile of George Sherry that appears in *John Is Easy to Please: Encounters with the Written and the Spoken Word* (New York: Farrar, Straus, and Giroux, 1971), 3–25.

57. "George Klebnikov, 73, Innovative UN Translator," *New York Times,* November 13, 1996.

58. Harold Karan Jacobson and Eric Stein, *Diplomats, Scientists, and Politicians: The United States and the Nuclear Test Ban Negotiations* (Ann Arbor: University of Michigan Press, 1966), 214; and Christer Jonsson, *Soviet Bargaining Behavior: The Nuclear Test Ban Case* (New York: Columbia University Press, 1979), 149.

59. Jacobson and Stein, *Diplomats, Scientists, and Politicians,* 229.

60. Thomas M. Nichols, *The Sacred Cause: Civil-Military Conflict over Soviet National Security, 1917–1992* (Ithaca, N.Y.: Cornell University Press, 1993); and Harriet Fast Scott and William F. Scott, *Soviet Military Doctrine: Continuity, Formulation, and Dissemination* (Boulder, Colo.: Westview Press, 1988), 136–137.

61. William Zimmerman, *Soviet Perspectives on International Relations, 1956–67* (New York: Columbia University Press, 1969); Scott and Scott, *Soviet Military Doctrine,* 58–59.

62. Bobrysheva, "Thanks for the Memories," 57.

63. Erwin N. Griswold, "Diary and Report of a Trip to Russia, May 13–31, 1961," manuscript, 15. Griswold also includes a seating chart (p. 47).

64. Peter Juviler, "Memoranda," in Griswold, "Diary and Report of a Trip to Russia," 122.

65. Bobrysheva, "Thanks for the Memories," 50.

66. Ibid., 51–56.

67. Griswold, "Diary and Report of a Trip to Russia," 24.

68. I. I. Artobolevsky, letter to Philip Mosely, September 27, 1961 (received October 25, 1961, probably translated by Mosely). As Mosely wrote Stone a year later, this paragraph "says a great deal more than most Soviet scholars would dare say, and is an interesting, though unpublishable document about the efforts we made during our meetings at the Crimea." Philip E. Mosely, letter to Shepard Stone, August 1, 1962.

69. Bobrysheva, "Thanks for the Memories," 57.

70. Griswold, "Diary and Report of a Trip to Russia," 67.

71. Robert Colby Nelson, interview with Alice Bobrysheva, April 26, 1988.

72. Boris Polevoi, however, appears to have said, "We should take steps now, however small, toward disarmament." This suggests the arms control argument made by Doty.

73. Griswold, "Diary and Report of a Trip to Russia," 15. Copies of the statement in English and Russian are on pages 44 and 45 of Griswold's report. Cousins had urged Clark to prepare the statement. Mary K. Harvey, memo to Philip Mosely, May 17, 1961.

74. Grenville Clark and Louis B. Sohn, *World Peace through World Law* (Cambridge, Mass.: Harvard University Press, 1958). A second edition, slightly revised, was published in 1960.

75. Cousins, "Notes from the Crimea," in *Present Tense,* 408–410. This editorial was originally published in the *Saturday Review,* July 6, 1961.

76. Philip Stewart made this observation in his comments on an earlier version of this manuscript.

77. The first joint Soviet-American production was *The Blue Bird,* made in 1976. It was directed by George Cukor; its cast included Jane Fonda, Ava Gardner, Elizabeth Taylor, and Cicely Tyson.

78. The description of Soviet reports on the conference comes from Aleksandr Fursenko and Timothy Naftali, *"One Hell of a Gamble": Khrushchev, Castro, and Kennedy, 1958–1964* (New York: W. W. Norton, 1997), 126–128. Their information comes from the archives of the Foreign Ministry and the Russian Foreign Intelligence Service.

79. Griswold, "Diary and Report of a Trip to Russia," 27–28.

80. The determination to have the communiqués express nothing but basic facts about the conference was made clear before the conference to people whom the American organizers hoped to attract. For example, in a letter to Charles Percy, then president of Bell and Howell, later elected senator from Illinois, Mosely wrote: "We will not issue any common declaration or manifesto, except for an agreed general communiqué stating that we have met and discussed certain broad issues" (March 30, 1961).

81. William Benton, letter to Edward R. Murrow, dictated in Moscow, May 27, 1961, dated June 1, 1961; and William Benton, letter to Chester Bowles, June 1, 1961. Benton sent the letters after he left the Soviet Union.

82. Benton, letter to Bowles.

83. "Stuart Chase Reports on Crimea Conference," *Bridgeport Sunday Post,* July 2, 1961.

84. William Loos, "Semi-Annual Report of the Executive Director," June 14, 1961.

85. Thomas J. Dodd, letter to Philip E. Mosely, August 21, 1961. Dodd referred specifically to a recent Pugwash conference: "I believe that the Pugwash Conferences represented a loss for our side because the Western participants come to those meetings totally unprepared." He allowed that it seemed that the participants at Oreanda may have done better.

86. Osgood Caruthers, *New York Times,* June 1, 1961; editorial praising the conference, *New York Times,* June 16, 1961; *Pravda,* June 1, 1961.

87. "Benton Describes Parley in Soviet," *New York Times,* June 18, 1961, 20.

88. William Benton, letter to Philip E. Mosely, August 8, 1961.

89. Glenn T. Seaborg, *Kennedy, Khrushchev, and the Test Ban* (Berkeley: University of California Press, 1981), 85–90.

90. Bobrysheva, "Thanks for the Memories," 61–62.

91. Raymond L. Garthoff, *Reflections on the Cuban Missile Crisis,* rev. ed. (Washington, D.C.: Brookings Institution, 1989), 12.

92. Philip Mosely and Norman Cousins, telegram to Akademik A. Korneichuk, December 1, 1961.

93. Aleksandr Korneichuk, telegram to Philip Mosely and Norman Cousins, March 14, 1962.

94. Philip E. Mosely, letter to Frank G. Siscoe, director, Soviet and East European Exchanges Staff, March 22, 1962; and Philip E. Mosely, letter to John J. McCloy, April 5, 1962.

95. Darrell Hammer, rapporteur's notes for Dartmouth III, "Third session, 9:30 a.m.—October 22, 1962," 12.

96. This account of the discussion within the Soviet delegation comes from Shveitser, *An Interpreter Remembers*. Shveitser was there.

97. Darrell Hammer, rapporteur's notes for Dartmouth III, "Fifth session, 8:30 p.m.—October 22, 1962," 3. In Cousins' own account in the *Saturday Review*, his role was more modest; the Americans needed no prompting.

98. Cousins, "Experiment at Andover," in *Present Tense*, 413. This editorial was originally published in the *Saturday Review*, November, 10, 1962.

99. Philip E. Mosely, letter to Shepard Stone, January 18, 1963.

100. Ibid.

101. Norman Cousins, "First American Draft," October 24, 1962.

102. This account taken from the rapporteur's notes by Darrell Hammer and the report on the conference to the Ford Foundation is contained in Mosely, letter to Stone, January 18, 1963.

103. This account of the origin of the papal appeal comes from Cousins, *The Improbable Triumvirate*, 17–18. The text of the appeal can be found in the *New York Times*, October 26, 1962.

104. According to Cousins, Morlion "felt individual citizens had the responsibility to undertake initiatives which might not always be feasible or possible for officials. If the initiatives worked out well, the officials could appraise the results and follow through. If the initiatives were unproductive or unworkable, they could be dropped. In any case, the leaders could remain uncommitted." Cousins, *The Improbable Triumvirate*, 20–21.

105. Dunne, *Grenville Clark*, 212–213.

106. Sergei Beglov wrote about this for *Izvestiya;* a translation is included in the papers on Dartmouth made available by David Rockefeller.

107. Cousins, *The Improbable Triumvirate*, 18.

108. This was Philip Mosely, *The Soviet Union since Khrushchev* (New York: Foreign Policy Association, 1966).

109. Philip E. Mosely, letter to Academician A. E. Korneichuk, July 20, 1964.

110. McGeorge Bundy, memo to President Lyndon Johnson, September 11, 1964, LBJ Library; and Joseph Finder, *Red Carpet: The Connection between the Kremlin and America's Most Powerful Businessmen (Hammer, Harriman, Eaton, Rockefeller)* (New York: Holt, Rinehart, and Winston, 1983), 181.

111. Cousins, *Present Tense,* 66. Cousins also found Simon energetic, totally focused on the work before him, and invariably prepared, never one to be "caught without doing his homework" (p. 73).

112. In their evaluation of the Dartmouth conferences written for David Rockefeller, Dana S. Creel and James M. Hyde make it clear that this role was important. Dana S. Creel and James M. Hyde, memo to David Rockefeller, May 21, 1964.

113. H. W. Brands, *Inside the Cold War: Loy Henderson and the Rise of the American Empire, 1918–1961* (Oxford: Oxford University Press, 1991), 308.

114. William Benton, memo to Philip Mosely and Norman Cousins, March 21, 1961.

115. In 1999, more than a decade after he left the Dartmouth Conference, Evgeni Primakov described Rockefeller and his role in Dartmouth in glowing terms, writing more about him than any other figure he met in almost twenty years of Dartmouth meetings. Evgeni M. Primakov, *Istoriya odnogo sgovora* (Moscow: Izdatel'stvo Politicheskoi Literaturi, 1985), 39–40.

116. The description of David Rockefeller here relies heavily on E. J. Kahn, Jr., "Profiles: Resources and Responsibilities," *New Yorker,* January 9 and 16, 1965; and Finder, *Red Carpet.* chap. 11.

117. Kahn, "Profiles: Resources and Responsibilities," January 9, 1965.

118. Nathan M. Pusey, quoted in ibid.

119. "Arrangements for Second 'Dartmouth' Conference," February 22, 1961 (mimeograph); and Philip E. Mosely, letter to David Rockefeller, March 6, 1961.

120. Creel and Hyde, memo to Rockefeller, May 21, 1964. A sign of the carefulness with which Rockefeller approached the matter was that Creel had been an aide for more than twenty years and was director of the Rockefeller Brothers Fund.

121. The description of the discussions at Dartmouth IV is taken from George Feifer, "Rapporteur's Notes, Fourth Dartmouth Conference, Leningrad U.S.S.R., July 25–31, 1964"; and Marshall D. Shulman, "Dartmouth Conference, Leningrad, Private, Unofficial Notes," 1964.

122. But Fedorov did acknowledge the artistic quality of *One Day in the Life of Ivan Denisovich.* Feifer, "Rapporteur's Notes, Fourth Dartmouth Conference, Leningrad U.S.S.R., July 25–31, 1964," 87.

123. Yale Richmond, e-mail to author, June 16, 1999.

124. Frank G. Siscoe, director, Soviet and Eastern European Exchanges Staff, letter to Norman Cousins, September 21, 1964.

125. Marshall D. Shulman, "Dartmouth Conference, Leningrad, Private, Unofficial Notes," 1964, 46.

126. Paul Dudley White, with the assistance of Margaret Parton, *My Life and Medicine: An Autobiographical Memoir* (Boston: Gambit, 1971), 242.

127. Writing more than a decade after the events, Fuller has this exchange of views taking place all day Saturday. Shulman's notes, taken at the time, place them on Friday evening. R. Buckminster Fuller, *Critical Path* (New York: St. Martin's Press, 1981), 189–190.

128. Ibid., 189.

129. John Kenneth Galbraith, *A View from the Stands: Of People, Politics, Military Power, and the Arts* (Boston: Houghton Mifflin, 1986), 267.

130. Shveitser, *An Interpreter Remembers.*

131. Finder says that the invitation was originally to Cousins, who declined but suggested that Rockefeller go in his stead. Finder, *Red Carpet,* 181.

132. Ibid., 182.

133. Kahn, "Profiles: Resources and Responsibilities," January 9, 1965, 37.

134. Neva Rockefeller, "A Summary of the Conversation between Chairman Khrushchev and David Rockefeller in Moscow, Thursday, July 29, 1964, between 3:30 and 5:15 p.m.—Submitted by Neva Rockefeller, Daughter of David Rockefeller, Who Was Also Present," typescript.

135. Bundy, memo to Johnson, September 11, 1964. This memo is also described in Finder, *Red Carpet,* 187.

136. Ibid.

137. Ibid.

138. Ibid.

139. Cousins, *Anatomy of an Illness as Perceived by the Patient,* 31–34.

140. Seaborg, *Kennedy, Khrushchev, and the Test Ban,* 180–181.

141. Ibid., 180; Cousins, *The Improbable Triumvirate,* 93–94.

142. Cousins, *The Improbable Triumvirate,* 24–25.

143. Ibid., 78–79.

144. Seaborg, *Kennedy, Khrushchev, and the Test Ban,* 207.

145. Cousins, *The Improbable Triumvirate,* 116, 122. Cousins' role in the American University speech is suggested by Seaborg in *Kennedy, Khrushchev, and the Test Ban,* 212, and, more significantly, by Sorenson himself. See Theodore C. Sorenson, *Kennedy* (New York: Bantam Books, 1966), 822.

3. The Rise and Fall of Détente

1. Oleg Bykov, letter to Norman Cousins, October 14, 1965; Aleksandr Korneichuk, letter to Norman Cousins, October 20, 1965; "Extract from a letter from Robert Legvold [to Marshall Shulman], dated January 28, 1966, from Moscow"; Ralph Thomson, Fletcher Ph.D. candidate, excerpt from letter to Marshall D. Shulman, October 11, 1965, from Moscow. Bykov asked Thomson to ask Cousins and Mosely not to confuse the personal and official positions of Bykov and his colleagues, clearly implying some difference between the two, suggesting that the postponement of the conference occurred on orders from above.

2. Norman Cousins, "Dialogue with the Russians," in *Present Tense: An American Editor's Odyssey* (New York: McGraw-Hill, 1967), 404. This editorial was originally published in the *Saturday Review,* June 24, 1961.

3. W. Phillips Davison, "Notes on a Conversation with Professor Philip E. Mosely, Director, European Institute, Columbia University, June 29, 1970." These notes include corrections by Mosely.

4. See, for example, James M. Gavin, letter to Estelle Linzer, August 16, 1971, in which Gavin describes meetings with officials in Washington: "I have long been of the conviction that the importance of the Dartmouth Conference will ultimately rest upon what we do after the meeting."

5. This account of Kettering's entry into the Dartmouth picture comes from Phillips Ruopp, letter to Harold Saunders, March 20, 2001.

6. Cousins, *Present Tense,* 43.

7. Norman Cousins, "The Fifth Dartmouth Conference," *Saturday Review,* February 8, 1969, 16.

8. Georgi Arbatov, *The System: An Insider's Life in Soviet Politics* (New York: Times Books, 1992), 37.

9. Robert Colby Nelson, interview with Robert Lundeen, May 4, 1988.

10. Arkadi Shevchenko thought that Arbatov had little influence in the Brezhnev period. See Arkadi Shevchenko, *Breaking with Moscow* (New York: Alfred A. Knopf, 1985), 209–210. Oded Eran, on the other hand, writing in 1979, speaks of the "evident closeness of Arbatov to Brezhnev's staff," in *Mezhdunarodniki: An Assessment of Professional Expertise in the Making of Soviet Foreign Policy* (Ramat Gan, Israel: Turtledove Publishing, 1979), 251. See also Matthew Evangelista's references to Arbatov in *Unarmed Forces: The Transnational Movement to End the Cold War* (Ithaca, N.Y.: Cornell University Press, 1999). And, of course, see Arbatov's memoirs, in English, *The System;* and, in Russian, Georgi A. Arbatov, *Zatyanuvsheesya vyzdorovleniye (1953–1985 gg.): Svidetel'stvo sovremennika* (Moscow: Mezhdunarodnye Otnosheniya, 1991).

11. A. S. Chernyaev, *Shest' let c Gorbachevym: Po dnevnukovym zapiskyam* (Moscow: Izdatel'skaya gruppa "Progress," 1993), 23–24; Roald Z. Sagdeev, *The Making of a Soviet Scientist: My Adventures in Nuclear Fusion and Space from Stalin to Star Wars* (New York: John Wiley and Sons, 1994), 266–271.

12. This is a tale ably told in Robert D. English, *Russia and the Idea of the West: Gorbachev, Intellectuals, and the End of the Cold War* (New York: Columbia University Press, 2000).

13. Arbatov, *The System*, 23.

14. A. D. Shveitser, *An Interpreter Remembers . . . Japan—USA—Pugwash —Dartmouth* (Moscow: Stella, 1996). Found at www.prodigy.com/casanova/memoir.htm, October 16, 1997.

15. "Dartmouth V, Rye, N.Y., January 13–18, 1969," Chase Manhattan Archives, n.d.

16. Arbatov expressed similar suspicions the next day as well. "Rapporteur's Notes, Fifth Dartmouth Conference, Rye, New York, U.S.A. January 13–19, 1969," 5. Emphasis in the original.

17. Evangelista, *Unarmed Forces*, 133–136.

18. "In our country also generals are used to dealing with muscles rather than brain, but we all know the fate of the dinosaur." Arbatov expressed a similar sentiment the next day in a discussion of the Middle East: "Certain forces, in our country as well as abroad, fear a solution in the Middle East more than they fear conflict, and wish discord between us." "Rapporteur's Notes, Fifth Dartmouth Conference, Rye, New York, U.S.A. January 13–19, 1969."

19. Harry Schwartz, "The Washington-Moscow-Peking Triangle in the Nixon Era," *New York Times,* January 27, 1969.

20. R. Buckminster Fuller, *Critical Path* (New York: St. Martin's Press, 1981), 190.

21. Shveitser, *An Interpreter Remembers.*

22. Philip E. Mosely, letter to Yuri Zhukov, March 4, 1970.

23. Yuri Zhukov, letter to Philip E. Mosely, March 16, 1970.

24. James M. Read, letter to Gen. James M. Gavin, December 15, 1970.

25. "To Paraphrase Arthur Larson's Comments, Made Immediately Following the Fifth Dartmouth Conference," February 26, 1971.

26. James M. Gavin, memo to File, March 8, 1971; and James Read, "Summary of Bob Chollar's visit to Washington with General Gavin to see Henry Kissinger on March 5, 1971, telephoned to James Read from Florida."

27. Robert G. Chollar, "A Report on Some Russian and American Dialogue," *Journal-Herald* (Dayton, Ohio), August 11, 1971.

28. For more information about his career, see Charles W. Yost, *History and Memory* (New York: W. W. Norton, 1980).

29. "Evaluation of Dartmouth Conference VI, Kiev, USSR, July 12–16, 1971," 1.

30. Mark J. Kasoff, in "Evaluation of Dartmouth Conference VI, Kiev, USSR, July 12–16, 1971," 10.

31. This information comes from a set of notes on the expected Soviet participants in Dartmouth VIII, probably prepared by Philip Stewart.

32. Michael MacGwire, *Perestroika and Soviet National Security* (Washington, D.C.: Brookings Institution, 1991), 139. Their book was Vitali V. Zhurkin and Evgeni M. Primakov, *Mezhdunarodnye konflikti* (Moscow: Mezhdunarodnye Otnosheniya, 1972).

33. Samuel Pisar, *Of Blood and Hope* (New York: Macmillan, 1979), 196.

34. The description of the conference comes from C. Grant Pendill, Jr., "Summary Record, Dartmouth Conference VI, Kiev, July 12–16, 1971"; and the "Evaluation of Dartmouth Conference VI, Kiev, USSR, July 12–16, 1971." Pendill put the former on tape during the sessions; the Kettering Foundation commissioned the latter. It is not clear who put most of it together, but the evaluation contains content analysis by Mark J. Kasoff, the chairman of the Department of Economics at Antioch College.

35. Pendill, "Summary Record, Dartmouth Conference VI, Kiev, July 12–16, 1971," II-7, II-8.

36. Murray Feshbach and Alfred Friendly, Jr., *Ecocide in the USSR: Health and Nature under Siege* (New York: Basic Books, 1992).

37. Pendill, "Summary Record, Dartmouth Conference VI, Kiev, July 12–16, 1971," IV-3. Pendill put Fedorov's remarks in quotation marks, suggesting that they came straight from Fedorov's paper.

38. "Evaluation of Dartmouth Conference VI, Kiev, USSR, July 12–16, 1971," 25.

39. Interestingly, the rapporteur wrote, citing Arbatov, that "[o]ver the past several years, [I have] taken part in many informal discussions on disarmament and many of the ideas have become part of Soviet proposals. Among the many examples is that of halting nuclear testing, which can be monitored by national means of detection." Pendill, "Summary Record, Dartmouth Conference VI, Kiev, July 12–16, 1971," V-6.

40. Pisar, *Of Blood and Hope,* 199–200.

41. Pendill, "Summary Record, Dartmouth Conference VI, Kiev, July 12–16, 1971," V-15. Pendill's account of Pisar's remarks and Pisar's account in *Of Blood and Hope* are close.

42. Ibid., V-17.

43. James M. Gavin, "Notes on the Meetings with Prime Minister Kosygin in His Office in Moscow on July 16, 1971"; "Memorandum of Conversation with Kosygin in Moscow at the Time of the Dartmouth Conference in the USSR—July

1971," Chase Manhattan Archives; and Kettering Foundation, *Dartmouth Conference VI: Searching for New Methods of International Communication,* n.p., n.d. The last source includes the impressions of the conference and the conversation with Kosygin of Senator Frank Church as published in an October 1971 report to the Senate Committee on Foreign Relations.

44. James M. Gavin, "Meeting with Ambassador Dobrynin, U.S.S.R., August 23, 1971," August 24, 1971, Chase Manhattan Archives. Gavin found Dobrynin less eager to foster trade than Kosygin had been.

45. "Dartmouth VI Miscellany," Chase Manhattan Archives, n.d.; Gavin, letter to Linzer, August 16, 1971.

46. Gavin, letter to Linzer, August 16, 1971.

47. "Dartmouth VI Miscellany." See also James Gavin, letter to David Rockefeller, October 12, 1971.

48. G. B. Kistiakowsky, letter to R. G. Chollar, August 10, 1971.

49. Zbigniew Brzezinski, *Between Two Ages: America's Role in the Technetronic Era* (New York: Viking Press, 1970); and Zbigniew Brzezinski, *The Fragile Blossom: Crisis and Change in Japan* (New York: Harper and Row, 1972).

50. For the early years of the Trilateral Commission, see Jeremiah Novak, "The Trilateral Connection," *Atlantic Monthly,* July 1977, 57–59; and Stephen Gill, *American Hegemony and the Trilateral Commission* (Cambridge: Cambridge University Press, 1990).

51. Howard Raiffa, *The Art and Science of Negotiation* (Cambridge, Mass.: Belknap Press, 1982), 1–3.

52. Shevchenko, *Breaking with Moscow,* 74.

53. Ibid., 120–122. According to Yale Richmond, Federenko was "the guy Adlai Stevenson told that he would wait for his reply 'until hell freezes over.'" Yale Richmond, e-mail to the author, June 17, 1999.

54. Philip D. Stewart, "Dartmouth VII Conference Report: An Analysis of Dartmouth VII: Structure, Process, Outcome, Impact."

55. Ibid., 2–3.

56. For Rathjens' role in the arms control debates, which included a very public dispute over Safeguard with Albert Wohlstetter conducted in the *New York Times* and elsewhere, see Gregg Herken, *Counsels of War* (New York: Alfred A. Knopf, 1985), 211, 235–237, 238–239, 253–255.

57. Philip D. Stewart, "Dartmouth VII Conference Report: An Analysis of Work Group Discussions," 11.

58. Hertha W. Heiss, Allen J. Lenz, and Jack Brougher, "U.S.-Soviet Commercial Relations since 1972," in *The Soviet Economy: Continuity and Change,* ed. Morris Bornstein (Boulder, Colo.: Westview Press, 1981), 237–238.

59. Marshall I. Goldman, *Détente and Dollars: Doing Business with the Soviets* (New York: Basic Books, 1975), 193–224.

60. J. H. Billington, "Memorandum on Items of Potential CMB Interest from Conference—Dartmouth VII, December 2–7, 1972."

61. Stewart, "Dartmouth VII Conference Report," 70.

62. Ibid., 13–14.

63. This description is based on the summary of the work group discussion prepared by Stewart in "Dartmouth VII Conference Report: An Analysis of Work Group Discussions," 91–129.

64. Donella H. Meadows et al., *The Limits to Growth: A Report for the Club of Rome's Project on the Predicament of Mankind* (New York: Signet Books/New American Library, 1975). The report was first issued in 1972 and mentioned by the participants in Dartmouth VII.

65. This description of preparations for the conference is based on Philip D. Stewart, "The Evolution of an Idea: An Analysis of Dartmouth VIII: Dartmouth VIII Conference Report," n.d. Stewart based the report on questionnaires filled out by eleven of the American participants.

66. The Kettering Foundation published both texts in a booklet after the conference. See *Dartmouth Conference VIII: An American-Soviet Examination of the Problems of Détente in the Next Five Years* (Dayton, Ohio: Charles F. Kettering Foundation, n.d.).

67. Philip D. Stewart, "The Evolution of an Idea: An Analysis of Dartmouth VIII: Dartmouth VIII Conference Report," n.d.

68. Norman Cousins, "From Hanover to Tbilisi," *Saturday Review/World,* June 15, 1974, 5.

69. Landrum Bolling, abstract of interview by Andrea Hamilton, July 11, 1984, Kettering Foundation. Landrum Bolling, "Strengths and Weaknesses of Track II: A Personal Account," in *Conflict Resolution: Track-Two Diplomacy,* ed. John W. MacDonald, Jr., and Diane B. Bendahmane (Washington, D.C.: Foreign Service Institute, U.S. Department of State, 1987), 53–64.

70. U.S. Senate Committee on Foreign Relations, *Détente* (Washington, D.C.: U.S. Government Printing Office, 1975), 184. For more on SADS and the important role it played in U.S.-Soviet discussions on arms control, see Evangelista, *Unarmed Forces.*

71. U.S. Senate Committee on Foreign Relations, *Détente and the Further Development of U.S. and U.S.S.R. Relations: Report by Senator Hugh Scott to the Committee on Foreign Relations, United States Senate on the Dartmouth VIII Conference in Tbilisi, Georgia SSR, April 20–27, 1974* (Washington, D.C.: U.S. Government Printing Office, 1974).

72. Stewart, "The Evolution of an Idea."

73. Later, Zakhmatov spent a year at Chase Manhattan studying finance, probably at David Rockefeller's invitation. Philip Stewart, note, November 1999.

74. The ambassador also briefed the delegation before the conference using the "clean room" above the Chancery. Stewart, note, November 1999.

75. The descriptions of the discussions in the three work groups come mainly from U.S. Senate Committee on Foreign Relations, *Détente and the Further Development of U.S. and U.S.S.R. Relations;* Stewart, "The Evolution of an Idea"; and Cousins, "From Hanover to Tbilisi."

76. Philip Stewart, e-mail to the author, February 17, 2000.

77. U.S. Senate Committee on Foreign Relations, *Détente and the Further Development of U.S. and U.S.S.R. Relations,* 9.

78. Stewart also pointed out that the equality in global affairs the Soviets were seeking to make real was the realization of a goal set by Stalin in 1945. Stewart, note, November 1999.

79. Pisar, *Of Blood and Hope,* 238–239.

80. Stewart, "The Evolution of an Idea," 16–17.

81. Cousins, "From Hanover to Tbilisi," 4.

82. Evgeni Primakov, *Gody v bolshoi politike* (Moscow: Kollektsia Sovershenno Sekretno, 1999), 40.

83. Alfred R. Wentworth, "Notes Covering a 1½ Hour Conversation between Prime Minister Kosygin and David Rockefeller, Chairman of the Board, The Chase Manhattan Bank, at the Kremlin on April 25, 1974."

84. According to Pisar, Kosygin suggested that a high-level group be composed to discuss the proposal he had made at Tbilisi. Kissinger endorsed the proposal, and Rockefeller suggested that Pisar head it. The Soviets, however, vetoed Pisar's appointment, and a "docile American business executive" led the group instead. Pisar, *Of Blood and Hope,* 239.

85. The preparations for Dartmouth IX are described in Philip D. Stewart, "Towards Greater Understanding: An Analysis of Dartmouth IX," Kettering Foundation, Dayton, Ohio, n.d.

86. Two others, Yost and Paul Warnke, were listed in David Rockefeller's notes of the conference but attended either infrequently or not at all.

87. Stewart, "Towards Greater Understanding," 10.

88. Stewart also said that there was a similar problem in finding opportunities for informal contacts at Dartmouth VI and Dartmouth VIII. Ibid., 11.

89. Philip D. Stewart, "Dartmouth X: Soviet-American Relations in an Era of Détente: Conference Evaluation," November 1, 1976, 28.

90. Norman Cousins, "Dartmouth IX," *Saturday Review,* July 12, 1975, 4–5.

91. According to Robert Chollar, speaking at the last session. See "Agenda and Format for Future Dartmouth Meetings," an excerpt from the stenographic report of Dartmouth IX, 130.

92. Lawrence Brainard, memo to Joseph Reed, vice president, et al., June 12, 1975.

93. Ibid.

94. Stewart, note, November 1999.

95. Stewart, "Towards Greater Understanding," 48.

96. This account of the meeting comes from Landrum R. Bolling, "The Dartmouth Conference Process: Subjective Reflections," in *Private Diplomacy with the Soviet Union,* ed. David D. Newsom (Lanham, Md.: University Press of America, 1987), 48–51.

97. Harold H. Saunders, telephone conversation with author, April 21, 1997.

98. Hugh P. Callahan, Jr., *Dartmouth Conference XVI, Stenographic Record of a New Basis for the U.S.-Soviet Relationship, Austin, Texas, April 25–29, 1988, Lyndon Baines Johnson Memorial Library* (Dayton, Ohio: Charles F. Kettering Foundation, 1988), 351–352. Kislov was the Soviet cochairman for the discussions of the Regional Conflicts Task Force at Dartmouth XVI.

Three years earlier, before glasnost, and writing for a Soviet audience, Primakov described the importance of the Brookings paper in terms of its influence on American policy (Primakov, *Istoriya odnogo sgovora,* 137–138). He also cited Brzezinski at Dartmouth X, saying that he saw the need for a general settlement in the Middle East with both the United States and the Soviet Union taking part in making it.

99. Zbigniew Brzezinski, *Power and Principle: Memoirs of a National Security Adviser, 1977–1981* (New York: Farrar, Straus, and Giroux, 1983), 107–108. See also Cyrus Vance, *Hard Choices: Critical Years in America's Foreign Policy* (New York: Simon and Schuster, 1983), 191–193.

100. Harold H. Saunders, interview by Rob Nelson, May 5, 1988.

101. Ibid.

102. "On Improving the Effectiveness of the Dartmouth Conference (Report Adopted by Dartmouth Conference X)."

103. Stewart, "Dartmouth X: Soviet-American Relations in an Era of Détente: Conference Evaluation."

104. On Gardner's relationships with Brzezinski and Carter, see Brzezinski, *Power and Principle.* See also Vance, *Hard Choices,* 29–30; and Gill, *American Hegemony and the Trilateral Commission.*

105. This information on Runov comes from a short biography prepared for Dartmouth VIII, dated October 30, 1973.

106. John Newhouse, *Cold Dawn: The Story of SALT* (New York: Holt, Rinehart, and Winston, 1973).

107. This description of the work of Dartmouth X comes largely from Philip D. Stewart, "Dartmouth X: Soviet-American Relations in an Era of Détente: Conference Evaluation"; and Norman Cousins, "Dartmouth X," *Saturday Review,* June 12, 1976.

108. Bolling, "The Dartmouth Conference Process," 50.

109. Yale Richmond pointed out that both Arbatov and Zhurkin are part Jewish, which may be why they were chosen to speak before this audience. Yale Richmond, e-mail to author, June 17, 1999.

110. Cousins, "Dartmouth X."

111. This account of the April 7 meeting is from James M. Read, "Notes of Meetings of James Read and Phil Stewart," April 19, 1977.

112. Several of these conferences were held. They were encouraged by Yale Richmond, who then worked at the State Department, and received some State Department funding. Yale Richmond, e-mail to author, June 17, 1999.

113. Most of this account of efforts to convene a food task force comes from Michelle Bender, memo to B. Chollar et al., June 6, 1977, on the Dartmouth Task Force on Food Research and Policy.

114. Gill, *American Hegemony and the Trilateral Commission,* 151.

115. Jeffrey T. Checkel, *Ideas and International Political Change: Soviet/Russian Behavior and the End of the Cold War* (New Haven, Conn.: Yale University Press, 1997), 100.

116. Herbert F. York, *Making Weapons, Talking Peace: A Physicist's Odyssey from Hiroshima to Geneva* (New York: Basic Books, 1987), 256.

117. Norman Cousins, "Dartmouth at Jurmala," *Saturday Review,* September 3, 1977, 6.

118. John Wilson, "Comments on Dartmouth XI Conference, Jurmala, Latvia, U.S.S.R., July 9–13, 1977," August 1, 1977, Chase Manhattan Archives.

119. Shveitser, *An Interpreter Remembers.*

120. Philip Stewart, "The Future of Dartmouth" (1977).

121. Ibid. *U.S. News and World Report* (July 25, 1977, 27), reporting on Dartmouth XI, said that Brzezinski was called "a devil in the White House."

122. York, *Making Weapons, Talking Peace,* 256.

123. Shveitser, *An Interpreter Remembers.*

124. Wilson, "Comments on Dartmouth XI Conference, Jurmala, Latvia, U.S.S.R." Their superiors shared their bewilderment. Dobrynin tells of a conversation between Gromyko and Carter in September 1977 in which Carter brought up the Sharansky matter. Dobrynin thought to himself about the great skill the foreign minister had shown in feigning ignorance of the dissident, then was amazed to find that Gromyko's ignorance was real. Anatoli Dobrynin, *In Confidence: Moscow's Ambassador to America's Six Cold War Presidents (1962–1986)* (New York: Times Books, 1995), 399–400.

125. Bolling, "The Dartmouth Conference Process," 50–51.

126. Norman Cousins, "Editorial: Dartmouth XII," *Saturday Review,* July 21, 1979, 7.

127. Wilson, "Comments on Dartmouth XI Conference, Jurmala, Latvia, U.S.S.R."

128. Ibid.

129. Ibid.

130. Robert G. Chollar, letter to Georgi Zhukov, March 14, 1978.

131. Cousins described his move to UCLA and his career there in Norman Cousins, *The Healing Heart: Antidotes to Panic and Helplessness* (New York: W. W. Norton, 1983); and Norman Cousins, *Head First: The Biology of Hope* (New York: E. P. Dutton, 1989).

132. A measure of the extent of Bolling's contacts in the Middle East and the Carter administration is his use as President Carter's personal representative to the Palestine Liberation Front in late 1977. Following a meeting with Brzezinski, he delivered a message from Carter to Arafat, with whom he met twice. Janice Gross Stein, "Prenegotiation in the Arab-Israeli Conflict: The Paradoxes of Success and Failure," in *Getting to the Table: The Processes of International Prenegotiation,* ed. Janice Gross Stein (Baltimore, Md.: Johns Hopkins University Press, 1989), 184.

133. *Rice News,* November 6, 1997; and Thomas W. Wolfe, *The SALT Experience* (Cambridge, Mass.: Ballinger, 1979), 31.

134. Strobe Talbott, *Endgame: The Inside Story of SALT II* (New York: Harper and Row, 1979).

135. Royal B. Allison, letter to Norman Cousins, August 2, 1979. Allison wrote this letter to correct certain errors in Cousins' account of these meetings in "Editorial: Dartmouth XII," *Saturday Review,* 8–9.

136. Allison, letter to Cousins, August 2, 1979.

137. Cousins was a part of the Middle East group, so his impressions had to come from discussions with members of the Political Relations Work Group.

138. Allison, letter to Cousins, August 2, 1979.

139. John J. Stremlau, *The International Politics of the Nigerian Civil War, 1967–1970* (Princeton, N.J.: Princeton University Press, 1977).

140. Phil Stewart, memo to David Mathews, December 5, 1985.

141. Robert Legvold, *Soviet Policy in West Africa* (Cambridge, Mass.: Harvard University Press, 1970).

142. John Stremlau, memo to Harold H. Saunders, August 4, 1982.

143. Philip Stewart, memo to R. G. Chollar, February 26, 1979.

144. Ibid.

145. Cousins, "Editorial: Dartmouth XII," *Saturday Review,* 9.

146. Ibid., 8.

147. Stewart, note, November 1999.

148. Shulman's response is given in Phil Stewart, memo to Phillips Ruopp, January 14, 1980; Brzezinski's is in Philip D. Stewart, memo for the record, February 14, 1980.

149. See Green's obituary, written by Herbert Levine, *Johnson's Russia List,* no. 2259, July 1998.

150. Arbatov, *The System,* 197. It was in the hospital that he—and Anatoli Dobrynin, the Soviet ambassador to the United States—heard about the invasion of Afghanistan.

151. For Falin's career through 1980, see Alexander G. Rahr, *A Biographical Directory of One Hundred Leading Soviet Officials,* trans. Stelianos Scarlis (Munich: RFE/RL, 1981), 54–55.

152. This summary comes from Philip Stewart, "Dartmouth Leadership Consultation, Rockefeller Study and Conference Center, May 22–26, 1980: Summary Report," n.d.; and Philip Stewart, "Continuation of Memorandum for the Record, October 20, 1980," transcribed by Sandy Servais.

153. Ibid.

154. John J. Stremlau, "Talking with the Soviets," Bellagio, Italy, n.d.

155. This description of the conversation comes from Paul Doty, memo for the record, June 2, 1980.

156. Leonard A. Cole, *The Eleventh Plague: The Politics of Biological and Chemical Warfare* (New York: W. H. Freeman, 1996), 178–180.

157. Arbatov, *The System,* 200; and *Zatyanuvsheesya vyzdorovleniye,* 231.

158. Stewart, "Continuation of Memorandum for the Record, October 20, 1980"; and Philip D. Stewart, memo to Phillips Ruopp, October 20, 1980.

4. A New Cold War and the Beginnings of Perestroika

1. Phillips Ruopp and Philip Stewart, memo to Dartmouth Advisory Group, December 31, 1980.

2. Paul Doty, memo to Phillips Ruopp, December 29, 1980.

3. Information on the Soviet-American Parallel Studies Program and other exchanges can be found in *U.S.-Soviet Exchanges: A Conference Report* (Washington, D.C.: Kennan Institute for Advanced Russian Studies, 1984); and Yale Richmond, *U.S.-Soviet Cultural Exchanges, 1958–1986: Who Wins?* (Boulder, Colo.: Westview Press, 1987).

4. On CISAC and other transnational efforts to discuss arms control begun during the late 1970s and early 1980s, see Matthew Evangelista, *Unarmed Forces: The Transnational Movement to End the Cold War* (Ithaca, N.Y.: Cornell University Press, 1999), 144–160. Paul Doty was offered the chairmanship of CISAC but refused it, perhaps because of his continuing activity in Dartmouth.

5. Landrum R. Bolling, memo to Phillips Ruopp, May 11, 1981.

6. The previous December, Milstein had also told Doty that the Soviets "preferred continuity with people that they knew." Doty, memo to Ruopp, December 29, 1980.

7. Bolling, memo to Ruopp, May 11, 1981.

8. Georgi Arbatov, "Charles Woodruff Yost, R.I.P. (1907–1981)." The obituary was published in the July 1981 issue of *USA: Economy, Politics, Ideology.* The copy the author has seen is a typescript given to Paul Doty in June 1981.

9. Charles Yost, letter to David Rockefeller, April 9, 1981.

10. Phillips Ruopp, memo to David Mathews, May 28, 1981.

11. Phillips Ruopp, letter to Norman Cousins, February 2, 1981.

12. "Dartmouth XIII, Moscow, November 16–19, 1981," Chase Manhattan Archives, n.d.

13. See Harold H. Saunders, *A Public Peace Process: Sustained Dialogue to Transform Racial and Ethnic Conflicts* (New York: St. Martin's Press, 1999).

14. David Mathews, "Memo to Colleagues in Dartmouth XIII," November 4, 1981.

15. Leslie M. Vanderzee, memo to David Rockefeller, December 11, 1981.

16. Ibid.

17. Philip D. Stewart, *Dartmouth XIII: A Soviet-American Dialogue, Moscow, U.S.S.R, November 16–19, 1981* (Dayton, Ohio: Charles F. Kettering Foundation, 1982), 3; and "Dartmouth XIII, Moscow, November 16–19, 1981," Chase Manhattan Archives, n.d.

18. Stewart, *Dartmouth XIII,* 8.

19. Leslie M. Vanderzee, memo to David Rockefeller, December 11, 1981.

20. General David C. Jones, letter to David Mathews, March 11, 1982.

21. Philip Stewart, memo to David Mathews and Phillips Ruopp, February 18, 1982.

22. Philip D. Stewart, memo to Harold Saunders, April 21, 1982; Philip D. Stewart, memo to Seweryn Bialer, April 21, 1982.

23. Robert Colby Nelson, interview with Harold Saunders, May 5, 1988.

24. Ibid.

25. Philip Stewart, e-mail to Harold Saunders, April 2, 2001.

26. Robert A. Pastor, *Condemned to Repetition: The United States and Nicaragua* (Princeton, N.J.: Princeton University Press, 1987), 38–39, 91–92, and 362–363 n. 19.

27. James Voorhees, notes, Dartmouth Conference Regional Conflicts Task Force, December 8, 1991.

28. Harold H. Saunders, letter to David Mathews, September 13, 1982.

29. Philip D. Stewart, "The Prevention and Settlement of International Conflict: Transcript of a Dartmouth Conference Task Force Dialogue, Amelia Island, Florida, February 1–4, 1983," Charles F. Kettering Foundation, Dayton, Ohio, 1983, 1.

30. Harold Saunders and Philip Stewart, memo to David Mathews, n.d.

31. For a description of the agreement and its origins, see Alexander L. George, "The Basic Principles Agreement of 1972: Origins and Expectations," in *Managing U.S.-Soviet Rivalry: Problems of Crisis Prevention,* ed. Alexander L. George (Boulder, Colo.: Westview Press, 1983), 107–118.

32. See George, "The Basic Principles Agreement of 1972," 107–118. His observations are supported by two senior Soviet officials in their memoirs written after the collapse of the Soviet Union. See A. M. Aleksandrov-Agentov, *Ot Kollontai do Gorbacheva* (Moscow: Mezhdunarodnye Otnosheniya, 1994), 226–227; and G. M. Kornienko, *Kholodnaya Voina: Svidetel'stvo yeyo uchastnika* (Moscow: Mezhdunarodnye Otnosheniya, 1995), 144–145.

33. Writing in 2001 about the positions he took while a part of Dartmouth, Primakov said that "both then and now I think that the Middle East conflict should in no way be looked [at] through the prism of the rivalry between great powers. We lost a lot already and we shall lose even more if any state carries on a line aimed at monopolization of the mediatory mission in the settlement of the Middle East conflict. . . . [Dialogue between two governments should be] the cooperation of . . . equals. This is exactly what is necessary for the successful settlement of the Middle Eastern conflict." Evgeni Primakov, "Answers by Academician Evgeniy Primakov to Questions Posed by Dr. Harold H. Saunders for the Book on the History of the Dartmouth Conferences," trans. Vitali Zhurkin, June 29, 2001.

34. Harold Saunders and Philip Stewart, memo to David Mathews, n.d.

35. Harold H. Saunders, letter to David Mathews, July 18, 1983.

36. Harold H. Saunders, draft letter to David Mathews. The date given, handwritten, is "After Moscow 1985." In the letter Saunders largely repeats what he told the April 1985 meeting of the task force (remarks attached to a letter from Philip D. Stewart, September 19, 1985).

37. Saunders and Stewart, memo to Mathews, n.d.

38. David Mathews, cable to Yuri Zhukov, July 29, 1983.

39. Phil Stewart, memo to David Mathews, December 5, 1985.

40. Raymond L. Garthoff describes this group in *The Great Transition: American-Soviet Relations and the End of the Cold War* (Washington, D.C.: Brookings Institution, 1994), 90.

41. Raymond L. Garthoff, *Détente and Confrontation: American-Soviet Relations from Nixon to Reagan,* rev. ed. (Washington, D.C.: Brookings Institution, 1994), 850. The characterization of Bovin comes from Georgi Arbatov, *The System: An Insider's Life in Soviet Politics* (New York: Times Books, 1992), 87–88.

42. In fact, one Soviet participant spoke of the "deideologicalization of policy." See Philip D. Stewart, "Dartmouth Conference Regional Conflicts Task Force, Evaluating the International Situation and Soviet-American Relations, Moscow, U.S.S.R., November 29–December 1, 1983," Charles F. Kettering Foundation, Dayton, Ohio, n.d., 13.

43. Ibid., 87.

44. Saunders, draft letter to Mathews.

45. Harold H. Saunders, "Informal Soviet Points," December 1984.

46. Harold H. Saunders, "Regulating Soviet-U.S. Competition and Cooperation in the Arab-Israeli Arena, 1967–86," in *U.S.-Soviet Security Cooperation: Achievements, Failures, Lessons,* ed. Alexander L. George, Philip J. Farley, and Alexander Dallin (New York: Oxford University Press, 1988), 572.

47. Evgeni M. Primakov, *Istoriya odnogo sgovora* (Moscow: Izdatel'stvo Politicheskoi Literaturi, 1985), 300.

48. Stewart, memo to Mathews, December 5, 1985.

49. William Hyland recounts his experience at the National Security Council and the State Department in *Mortal Rivals: Superpower Relations from Nixon to Reagan* (New York: Random House, 1987).

50. Stewart, memo to Mathews, December 5, 1985.

51. Robert M. Gates, *From the Shadows: The Ultimate Insider's Story of Five Presidents and How They Won the Cold War* (New York: Touchstone, 1996), 457–458.

52. George Bush and Brent Scowcroft, *A World Transformed* (New York: Alfred A. Knopf, 1998), 11–12.

53. Strobe Talbott, *Deadly Gambits: The Reagan Administration and the Stalemate in Arms Control* (New York: Alfred A. Knopf, 1984), 303–304; and Garthoff, *The Great Transition,* 40, 101.

54. Arnold Horelick expressed this opinion in a handwritten note to Philip Stewart, sometime after the meeting.

55. Philip D. Stewart, letter to Pat Coggins, June 3, 1983. The document sent was Philip D. Stewart, "Rapporteur's Notes on the Concluding Session Dartmouth Task Force Meeting on Arms Control, Denver, Colo., April 27–30, 1983."

56. This account of the Scowcroft mission comes from George P. Shultz, *Turmoil and Triumph: My Years as Secretary of State* (New York: Charles Scribner's Sons, 1993), 473–474; Garthoff, *The Great Transition,* 148; and Don Oberdorfer, *The Turn: From the Cold War to a New Era: The United States and the Soviet Union, 1983–1990* (New York: Poseidon Press, 1991), 81–82.

57. Georgi Kornienko, who was first deputy foreign minister at the time, told Don Oberdorfer that the correspondence from Chernenko to Reagan was in fact prepared in the Foreign Ministry; Chernenko had little or nothing to do with it (Oberdorfer, *The Turn,* 83).

58. Philip D. Stewart, "Summary of Dartmouth Conference Task Force Preparatory Meeting, Washington, D.C., April 11–12, 1984"; and Philip D. Stewart, "Dartmouth Conference XIV: A Soviet-American Dialogue," Kettering Foundation, Dayton, Ohio, n.d.

59. Evangelista, *Unarmed Forces,* 234–245; and Matthew Evangelista, "The Paradox of State Strength: Transnational Relations, Domestic Structures, and Security Policy in Russia and the Soviet Union," *International Organization* 49 (winter 1995): 14–17.

60. The information on Velikhov comes from Roald Z. Sagdeev, *The Making of a Soviet Scientist: My Adventures in Nuclear Fusion and Space from Stalin to Star Wars* (New York: John Wiley and Sons, 1994); Evangelista, *Unarmed Forces,* 156-160; and Evangelista, "The Paradox of State Strength."

61. Sagdeev, *The Making of a Soviet Scientist,* 261.

62. The picture can be found in Susan Eisenhower, *Breaking Free: A Memoir of Love and Revolution* (New York: Farrar, Straus, and Giroux, 1995), the story of the romance between Eisenhower and Dr. Sagdeev. See also his memoirs, *The Making of a Soviet Scientist.*

63. This account of the April meeting is from Stewart, "Summary of Dartmouth Conference Task Force Preparatory Meeting"; and Meg Krause, memo to David Rockefeller, April 18, 1984. Krause says the meeting took place on April 12 and 13.

64. Eagleburger's views—though he is not named—are given in an addendum to Stewart, "Summary of Dartmouth Conference Task Force Preparatory Meeting." See also Krause's memo to Rockefeller.

65. This account of the conference comes from Stewart, "Dartmouth Conference XIV."

66. Stewart, "Dartmouth Conference XIV," 8.

67. This is an important element behind the traditional perspective described in Bruce Parrott, *Politics and Technology in the Soviet Union* (Cambridge, Mass.: MIT Press, 1983), 193–194.

68. Bruce Parrott, *The Soviet Union and Ballistic Missile Defense*, SAIS Papers in International Affairs, no. 14 (Boulder, Colo.: Westview Press, 1987), 15–16, 31–32, 53.

69. Shultz, *Turmoil and Triumph*, 487.

70. The description of the meeting is based on Philip M. Klutznick, "Confidential Memorandum of Philip M. Klutznick as Member of Dartmouth Task Force Meeting with Soviet Counterparts under Aegis of Soviet Peace Committee, Leningrad—November 1984"; and Philip D. Stewart, *Dartmouth Conference Task Force on Prevention and Settlement of Regional Conflicts, Leningrad, U.S.S.R., November 1–18, 1984: Stenographic Record* (Dayton, Ohio: Charles F. Kettering Foundation, n.d.).

71. Harold H. Saunders, "Informal Talking Points," attached to a letter from Harold H. Saunders to David Mathews, December 20, 1984.

72. This evaluation was given in Robert Leiken, Susan Purcell, William Rogers, Harold Saunders, and Philip Stewart, memo to David Mathews, n.d.

73. Abraham F. Lowenthal, letter to Philip Stewart and Harold Saunders, May 8, 1985.

74. Leiken et al., memo to Mathews, n.d.

75. This account of the task force meeting is based on Philip D. Stewart, *Dartmouth Conference Arms Control Task Force, Washington, D.C., December 3–4, 1984* (Dayton, Ohio: Charles F. Kettering Foundation, n.d.).

76. Interestingly, one of the Soviet speakers said that SDI would not be deployed "until energy is cheaper," suggesting a concern about the cost of SDI rather than its technology. Stewart, *Dartmouth Conference Arms Control Task Force, Washington, D.C., December 3-4, 1984*, 26.

77. George Klebnikov and George L. Sherry, letter to Phillips Ruopp, February 14, 1985.

78. Strobe Talbott, *Endgame: The Inside Story of SALT II* (New York: Harper and Row, 1979), 40–41.

79. Raymond L. Garthoff, *Deterrence and the Revolution in Soviet Military Doctrine* (Washington, D.C.: Brookings Institution, 1990), 133–134.

80. Sagdeev, *The Making of a Soviet Scientist*, 269. The four also had a chance to give Gorbachev, Shevardnadze, and the chief of the general staff,

Marshal Akhromeev, their assessment of the summit. See also Primakov's account in Evgeni Primakov, *Gody v bolshoi politike* (Moscow: Kollektsia Sovershenno Sekretno, 1999), 47–48.

81. The account of the meeting is taken from Philip Stewart, "The Dartmouth Conference, Arms Control Task Force (Fourth Session), Near-Verbatim Summary of Discussion on S.D.I., Moscow, U.S.S.R., November 28–30, 1985" (Dayton, Ohio: Charles F. Kettering Foundation, n.d.); and Phil Stewart, memo to David Mathews, December 5, 1985.

82. Stewart, "The Dartmouth Conference, Arms Control Task Force (Fourth Session)."

83. Philip D. Stewart, "Dartmouth Task Force on Political Relations, Discussion Summary, Moscow, USSR, January 30–February 2, 1986," Charles F. Kettering Foundation, Dayton, Ohio, n.d.

84. Alexander G. Rahr, *A Biographical Directory of 100 Leading Soviet Officials,* 4th ed., revised with some additions, January 1989 (Munich: Radio Liberty Research, RFE/RL, 1989), 158–159.

85. Stewart, "Dartmouth Task Force on Political Relations, Discussion Summary."

86. Ibid., 21.

87. "Conceptual Agenda for Dartmouth XV," n.p., n.d.

88. "We did not come here to compliment one another" was said by Harrison Salisbury, quoted in *Baku Vechernaya,* May 17, 1986.

89. This account of the December meeting comes from Phillips Ruopp, "International Planning Group Meeting, December 10, 1985," December 11, 1985. Many of the issues discussed in December were also the subject of an earlier meeting between Mathews, Lehman, and Ruopp. See "Meeting of Mathews, Lehman and Ruopp 10/29/85, Opening observati[o]ns of Phil Ruopp."

90. Philip Stewart, note, November 1999.

91. For changes in policy toward Angola, see James Voorhees, "Soviet Policy toward the Conflict between South Africa and Angola in the 1980s" (Ph.D. diss., Johns Hopkins University, 1992).

92. Gates, *From the Shadows,* 387; and a quotation from Michael Armacost in Diego Cordovez and Selig S. Harrison, *Out of Afghanistan: The Inside Story of the Soviet Withdrawal* (New York: Oxford University Press, 1995), 229–230. In truth, the move seems to have been made to facilitate a Soviet withdrawal, but that was far from obvious outside Moscow. See Cordovez and Harrison, *Out of Afghanistan,* 204–205.

93. For more about GosAgroprom, see Penelope Doolittle and Margaret Hughes, "Gorbachev's Agricultural Policy: Building on the Brezhnev Food

Program," in U.S. Congress, Joint Economic Committee, *Gorbachev's Economic Plans* (Washington, D.C.: U.S. Government Printing Office, 1987), 2:33–36.

94. Philip D. Stewart, "Dartmouth Conference XV, Baku, Azerbaijan, May 13–17, 1986, Stenographic Report," Charles F. Kettering Foundation, Dayton, Ohio, September 16, 1986, 5.

95. Ibid., 313.

96. Ibid., 314.

97. Philip D. Stewart, "Supplemental Diplomacy at Dartmouth XV," *Connections* (spring 1987).

98. Thomas E. Gouttierre, "Regional Conflicts Task Force Working Paper: Afghanistan," faxed December 3, 1990.

99. Philip D. Stewart, *Dartmouth Conference XV, Work Group on Prevention and Settlement of Regional Conflicts, Baku, Azerbaijan, May 13–17, 1986* (Dayton, Ohio: Charles F. Kettering Foundation, n.d.), 217.

100. Ibid., 251.

101. Stewart, "Dartmouth Conference XV, Stenographic Report," 273.

102. Stewart, "Supplemental Diplomacy at Dartmouth XV."

103. Primakov, *Gody v bolshoi politike,* 49.

104. Most of this information comes from Gouttierre's biography on the University of Omaha Web site (www.unomaha.edu/ipd/tombio.html, accessed January 10, 2000).

105. Harold H. Saunders, letter to Patricia Coggins and Robert F. Lehman, August 26, 1986.

106. Ibid.

107. Harold Saunders, memo to Thomas Gouttierre, Robert Neumann, Robert Lehman, Susan Purcell, Philip Stewart, and John Stremlau, September 24, 1986. This document contains penciled notations presumably made after the meetings.

108. *Christian Science Monitor,* December 1, 1986. Sarah E. Mendelson described Gankovsky as "perhaps the preeminent Afghan specialist in the Soviet Union." Sarah E. Mendelson, *Changing Course: Ideas, Politics, and the Soviet Withdrawal from Afghanistan* (Princeton, N.J.: Princeton University Press, 1998), 116.

109. "Memo for the Record: Comments of Yuri Gankovsky."

110. "Memo for the Record: Comments of Viktor Korgun."

111. Cordovez and Harrison, *Out of Afghanistan,* 208.

112. Thomas Gouttierre, "Sessions on Afghanistan," n.p., n.d.

113. This discussion is summarized in a document entitled "12 November 86 Lunchtime."

114. On both Zagladin and Brutents, see David E. Albright, "The CPSU International Department and the Third World in the Gorbachev Era," *The International Department of the CC CPSU under Dobrynin* (Washington, D.C.: U.S. Department of State, Foreign Service Institute, 1989), 143–153.

115. Dobrynin had been named head of the International Department in February. Until then he had been the Soviet ambassador in Washington. Neumann characterized this meeting as one that "settled nothing and excluded nothing as Dobrynin obviously wanted to avoid being pinned down." Robert Neumann, handwritten memo to Harold Saunders.

116. The International Department had focused its attention on the international communist movement and its leftist and radical allies. Dobrynin, with Gorbachev's approval, broadened its mandate in May 1986. See Anatoli Dobrynin, *In Confidence: Moscow's Ambassador to America's Six Cold War Presidents (1962–1986)* (New York: Times Books, 1995), 619–620.

117. Hal Saunders and Phil Stewart, handwritten memo to David Mathews and Rob Lehman.

118. U.S. Foreign Broadcast Information Service (FBIS), "Moscow TV Roundtable on Regional Conflicts," *Daily Report: Soviet Union,* November 19, 1986, CC1–CC12.

119. Harold H. Saunders, letter to Evgeni M. Primakov, December 3, 1986.

120. The account of the meeting of the Arms Control Task Force is taken from Philip Stewart, *The Dartmouth Conference, Arms Control Task Force Arms Control after Reykjavik, Washington, D.C., December 3–4, 1986* (Dayton, Ohio: Charles F. Kettering Foundation, n.d.).

121. Accounts of the negotiations can be found in Paul H. Nitze, *From Hiroshima to Glasnost: At the Center of Decision—a Memoir* (New York: Grove Wiedenfeld, 1989), 429–432; Shultz, *Turmoil and Triumph,* 751–780; and Garthoff, *The Great Transition,* 285–291.

122. Philip Stewart, note, November 1999.

123. This account of the Political Relations Task Force meeting is based on the stenographic record as given in Janusz Makawiecki and Philip D. Stewart, *Dartmouth Conference Task Force on Political Relations: From Deterrence to Mutual Security? Washington, D.C., December 5–6, 1986* (Dayton, Ohio: Charles F. Kettering Foundation, n.d.).

124. In the stenographic record of this meeting, as in the record of all Dartmouth meetings from the early 1970s on, the speakers are not named. Many thanks to former vice president Gore for confirming that he was the one who spoke and giving permission to cite him.

125. Max M. Kampelman, letter to Robert F. Lehman, February 20, 1987.

126. Michael H. Mobbs, letter to Robert F. Lehman, February 20, 1987.

127. My thanks to Yale Richmond for giving me Borovik's background (e-mail to author, June 17, 1999).

128. This summary is based on Hugh P. Callahan, Jr., and Philip Stewart, "The Dartmouth Conference Task Force on Arms Control (Seventh Session), Stenographic Record of On the Brink of Agreement? Moscow, USSR, July 6–8, 1987," Charles F. Kettering Foundation, Dayton, Ohio, n.d.

129. Philip Stewart, memo to Rob Lehman, September 11, 1987.

130. See Hugh P. Callahan, Jr., "Dartmouth Conference: Task Force on Arms Control, Seminar on Conventional Arms Control, Washington D.C., November 21, 1987; Summary of Discussions," Charles F. Kettering Foundation, Dayton, Ohio, n.d.

131. This account of the meeting is taken from Brendan Kiernan and Philip D. Stewart, *The Dartmouth Conference: Task Force on Prevention and Settlement (Tenth Session), Stenographic Record: Washington, D.C., USA, May 4–8, 1987; Graylyn Center, Winston-Salem, North Carolina, May 5–7, 1987* (Dayton, Ohio: Charles F. Kettering Foundation, June 26, 1987).

132. The description of the three exchanges comes from Thomas Gouttierre, e-mail to Harold Saunders, December 18, 2000.

133. Harold H. Saunders, memo to Michael Armacost, May 7, 1987.

134. Allison Stanger, *Dartmouth Conference Task Force on Regional Conflicts, New Thinking on Southern Africa, Institute for African Studies, USSR Academy of Sciences, Moscow, USSR, September 1–3, 1987: Stenographic Record* (Dayton, Ohio: Charles F. Kettering Foundation, n.d.), 68.

135. Gouttierre, e-mail to Saunders, December 18, 2000.

136. John Stremlau, letter to Rob Lehman, September 11, 1987.

137. This account of the 1984 discussions comes from Kurt M. Campbell, "Soviet-American Discussions on Southern Africa, Moscow, U.S.S.R., April 21–April 23, 1984: Final Report."

138. Phil Stewart, memo to Rob Lehman, September 9, 1987.

139. Stremlau, letter to Lehman, September 11, 1987.

140. Philip Stewart, memo to Rob Lehman, September 9, 1987. The other sources used for this description of the Moscow meeting are Stremlau, letter to Lehman, September 11, 1987; and Stanger, *Dartmouth Conference Task Force on Regional Conflicts, New Thinking on Southern Africa, September 1–3, 1987: Stenographic Record.*

141. Gouttierre's presentation is found in Thomas E. Gouttierre, "Transcripts from the Dartmouth Conference, Moscow, 1988, from the Notes of Thomas E.

Gouttierre," n.d. The account of the meeting is based on Brendan Kiernan, *The Dartmouth Conference, Task Force on Regional Conflict Prevention and Settlement (Eleventh Session), Stenographic Record, National Reconciliation and Regional Conflicts, Moscow, USSR, February 15–17, 1988* (Dayton, Ohio: Charles F. Kettering Foundation, 1988).

142. Summaries of these meetings, and a transcript of the meeting with Vorontsov, were distributed to the American embassy in Moscow. They were collected in Gouttierre, "Transcripts from the Dartmouth Conference, Moscow, 1988."

143. Kiernan, *The Dartmouth Conference, Task Force on Regional Conflict Prevention and Settlement (Eleventh Session), Stenographic Record,* 129.

144. Ibid., 113.

145. Anders Aslund, *Gorbachev's Struggle for Economic Reform,* updated and expanded edition (Ithaca, N.Y.: Cornell University Press, 1991), 73, 137. For more on Shmelev, see Stephen Cohen's 1989 interview, "The Rebirth of Common Sense," in *Voices of Glasnost: Interviews with Gorbachev's Reformers,* ed. Stephen F. Cohen and Katrina Vanden Heuvel (New York: W. W. Norton, 1989), 140–156.

146. See, for example, Nikolai Shmelev, *Spektakl' v chest' gospodina pervoro ministra* (Moscow: Sovetskii Pisatel', 1988).

147. This account of the discussions is based on Alan Holiman, "The Dartmouth Conference, Task Force on Political Relations, Whither the Course of Economic and Political Change? Moscow, USSR, February 18–19, 1988, Transcript," Charles F. Kettering Foundation, Dayton, Ohio, n.d.; and Alan Holiman, "The Dartmouth Conference, Task Force on Political Relations, Whither the Course of Economic and Political Change? Executive Summary, Moscow, USSR, February 18–19, 1988," Charles F. Kettering Foundation, Dayton, Ohio, n.d. The suggestion that Shmelev gave the economic report is based on internal evidence.

5. The Peak of Glasnost and Collapse

1. Rob Lehman, memo to David Mathews, July 7, 1987.

2. A. S. Cherniaev, *Shest' let c Gorbachevym: Po dnyevnikovym zapisyam* (Moscow: Izdatelskaya Gruppa "Progress"—Kultura," 1993), 208. For an account of the Politburo meeting, see Yegor Ligachev, *Inside Gorbachev's Kremlin: The Memoirs of Yegor Ligachev* (New York: Pantheon Books, 1993), 304–308. The date of the meeting is taken from Raymond L. Garthoff, *The Great Transition: American-Soviet Relations and the End of the Cold War* (Washington, D.C.: Brookings Institution, 1994), 349. Shishlin, speaking to Stewart, described the meeting as lasting three days, beginning on April 2. The important matter here is that it took place just a few weeks before the Austin meeting.

3. Hugh P. Callahan, Jr., *Dartmouth Conference XVI, Stenographic Record of a New Basis for the U.S.-Soviet Relationship, Austin, Texas, April 25–29, 1988, Lyndon Baines Johnson Memorial Library* (Dayton, Ohio: Charles F. Kettering Foundation, 1988), 96.

However, a few minutes later another Soviet speaker, probably Boris Grushin, said: "There is no discussion. This is not discussion. This is the traditional condemnation of the other side" (p. 102).

4. R. Daley, memo to K, May 5, 1988. The text in the memo would have appeared in the "Letter from Home," sent to Kettering staff and associates sometime shortly after.

5. Callahan, *Dartmouth Conference XVI: Stenographic Record of a New Basis for the U.S.-Soviet Relationship,* 92.

6. Chris Carlson, memo to Rob Lehman, Suzanne Morse, Hal Saunders, Randa Slim, and Phil Stewart, June 2, 1988.

7. *Dartmouth Conference XVI: A Soviet-American Dialogue, April 24–May 7, 1988* (Dayton, Ohio: Charles F. Kettering Foundation, 1988), 23.

8. Norman Cousins, "A New Design for Soviet Society: Dartmouth Conferees Probe the Realities of *Perestroika* and *Glasnost,*" *Christian Science Monitor,* June 5, 1988; Carlson, "Observations of Dartmouth Plenary Sessions"; and Callahan, *Dartmouth Conference XVI,* 92–94.

9. Callahan, *Dartmouth Conference XVI,* "Plenary Sessions: Observations," 122–123. The author of the latter document is not given. He was present at both the plenary sessions and the sessions of the Regional Conflicts Task Force, which suggests that it may have been John Stremlau.

10. Ibid. The text of their responses, with the speakers unnamed, is found in Callahan, *Dartmouth Conference XVI,* 124–129.

11. Ibid., 129–130.

12. Ibid., 135–163. The description of the session is taken from that text, "Plenary Sessions: Observations"; and Carlson, "Observations of Dartmouth Plenary Sessions."

13. Steve Strickland, "Report from the Meetings of the Political Relations Task Force," May 10, 1988.

14. David Mathews, memo to Rob Lehman et al., May 11, 1988.

15. Callahan, *Dartmouth Conference XVI,* 247.

16. This account of events after the conference in Austin is based on Kettering Foundation, *Dartmouth Conference XVI: A Soviet-American Dialogue, April 24–May 7, 1988,* 30–36.

17. Bob Kingston, memo to David Mathews and Rob Lehman, March 23, 1988.

18. It was entitled *Perestroika Papers—an Exercise in Supplemental Diplomacy.*

19. *Orange County Register,* May 3, 1988.

20. The publicity efforts for Dartmouth XVI are described in a memo from Rob Lehman to David Mathews, September 12, 1988.

21. *Los Angeles Times,* May 1, 1988; *Orange County Register,* May 1, 1988.

22. For a summary of the content and the implications of the speech, see Garthoff, *The Great Transition,* 365–367.

23. "Dartmouth Conference Task Force on Arms Control: Prospectus 1989–1991." The name of the author is not given, but it was probably Stewart, who had written similar memoranda before.

24. Evangelista notes the relationship between Aspin and Kokoshin, both present at the January 1989 meeting, and argues that these contacts helped both Kokoshin and Aspin counter the "enemy image" in their countries. Kokoshin appeared before Aspin's committee in March 1989, two months after they saw each other in Moscow. See Matthew Evangelista, *Unarmed Forces: The Transnational Movement to End the Cold War* (Ithaca, N.Y.: Cornell University Press, 1999), chap. 13.

25. For details on Burt and his involvement on arms control issues, see Strobe Talbott, *Deadly Gambits: The Reagan Administration and the Stalemate in Arms Control* (New York: Alfred A. Knopf, 1984).

26. For the development of this expertise through the 1980s, see Jeffrey T. Checkel, "Organizational Behavior, Social Scientists, and Soviet Foreign Policymaking" (Ph.D. diss., Massachusetts Institute of Technology, 1991), chaps. 8–10.

27. Dale R. Herspring, *The Soviet High Command, 1967–1989: Personalities and Politics* (Princeton, N.J.: Princeton University Press, 1990), 265.

28. The list of Soviet participants in the Kettering archives is far longer and includes such prominent figures as Karen Brutents, Akhromeev, and Primakov. But the copy in my possession has either an "x" or a question mark by their names. I have taken that to mean that the list was preliminary and the people so marked came only briefly or not at all.

29. This account of the meeting is based on Allison Stanger, *The Dartmouth Conference, Task Force on Political Relations, Moscow, January 19–21, 1989* (Dayton, Ohio: Charles F. Kettering Foundation, n.d.).

30. Interestingly, in the preceding meeting of the Arms Control Task Force, a Soviet speaker had said that the Cold War was already over.

31. This description of the meeting comes largely from Hugh P. Callahan, Jr., *Dartmouth Conference, Task Force on Regional Conflicts, Prospects for U.S.-Soviet Collaboration in Regional Conflicts, New York, NY, December 5–8, 1988, Stenographic Record* (Dayton, Ohio: Charles F. Kettering Foundation, n.d.).

32. Randa M. Slim, *Dartmouth Conference, Task Force on Regional Conflict Settlement and Prevention: New Soviet and U.S. Political Thinking Applied to Regional Conflicts, Moscow, USSR, May 9–12, 1989, Stenographic Record* (Dayton, Ohio: Charles F. Kettering Foundation, n.d.), 119.

33. Harold Saunders, "Opening Presentation: Dartmouth Conference Regional Conflicts Task Force, Moscow, May 10, 1989."

34. One group that the author joined at a meeting two years later met in a hotel room. The two analysts in the group talked about their region at length seated comfortably in stuffed armchairs. They knew each other well and discussed the issues as if carrying out another part of an extended conversation.

35. For a summary of Soviet policy in the region and the changes evident by 1989, see Garthoff, *The Great Transition,* 671–674, 745–746.

36. Alan Romberg, memo, "Subject: Dartmouth Conference Task Force on Regional Conflict, May 10–11, 1989—Southeast Asia"; and "Southeast Asia—Areas of Agreement," n.d., faxed September 6, 1989.

37. Thomas Gouttierre, "Dartmouth Regional Conflicts Task Force, Afghanistan," faxed August 15, 1989.

38. Slim, *Dartmouth Conference, Task Force on Regional Conflict Settlement and Prevention,* 37.

39. David Ottaway of the *Washington Post* asked: "'Old thinking' prevails in those regions [of the Third World] on all sides? Why?" Saunders cited this to the task force. See J. Scott Lauby, *Dartmouth Conference, Task Force on Regional Conflict Settlement and Prevention: U.S.-Soviet Relations in a Rapidly Changing World: Prospects for New Thinking in Regional Conflicts, Washington, D.C., November 26–December 1, 1989, Stenographic Record* (Dayton, Ohio: Charles F. Kettering Foundation, n.d.), 14–15.

40. Lauby, *Dartmouth Conference, Task Force on Regional Conflict Settlement and Prevention, Washington, D.C., November 26–December 1, 1989,* 21, 35.

41. Ibid., 67.

42. Ibid., 59, 73. The speaker on Eastern Europe surmised that the new parliament had a lot to do with this influence.

43. Harold H. Saunders, memo with Phil Stewart's thoughts to David Mathews, December 7, 1989.

44. J. Scott Lauby, *Dartmouth Conference, Task Force on Regional Conflict Settlement and Prevention, Toward a New Soviet-American Dialogue on Regional*

Conflicts, Leningrad, USSR, June 11–15, 1990, Stenographic Record (Dayton, Ohio: Charles F. Kettering Foundation, n.d.).

45. Paul Doty, "Doty's Notes from Dartmouth Task Force on Arms Control, April 20–22, 1990, L'Enfant Plaza Hotel, Washington, D.C."

46. Ibid.

47. Ibid.

48. George Bush and Brent Scowcroft, *A World Transformed* (New York: Alfred A. Knopf, 1998), 45.

49. Doty, "Doty's Notes, April 20–22, 1990."

50. This account of the discussions comes from J. Scott Lauby, *Dartmouth Conference Task Force on Arms Control and Security, U.S.-Soviet Relations in a Changing World: Toward New Structures for Security, Washington, D.C., April 20–22, 1990* (Dayton, Ohio: Charles F. Kettering Foundation, n.d.); and Doty, "Doty's Notes, April 20–22, 1990."

51. Lauby, *Dartmouth Conference Task Force on Arms Control and Security, April 20–22, 1990,* 59.

52. Ibid., 24.

53. A paper made available at the meeting, which outlines a similar set of ideas and even uses some of the same language, makes it seem likely that this was Malashenko. See "A Promise of Disharmony (Optional: From Russia, with Love)," April 22, 1990. In the paper, he wrote: "Those parts of the empire that were never integrated into Russia and which are gravitating toward the West or, let us say, the Moslem world, will eventually go, but the rest of the country will hardly suffer a mortal blow. Actually, the opposite may be true."

54. For the Soviet debate on the issue, see William E. Odom, *The Collapse of the Soviet Military* (New Haven, Conn.: Yale University Press, 1998), 187–193. The leadership did agree to experiment with contract soldiers, an experiment mentioned at the task force meeting.

55. Susan Eisenhower, *Breaking Free: A Memoir of Love and Revolution* (New York: Farrar, Straus, and Giroux, 1995), 251.

56. Philip Stewart, note, November 1999. This discussion with Arbatov took place in 1996 or 1997.

57. Kozyrev's name was added by hand to Paul Doty's list of Soviet participants.

58. He is listed as Valentin Larion in Kettering Foundation, *Dartmouth Conference VII: A Soviet-American Dialogue July 22–27, 1990, Leningrad, USSR* (Dayton, Ohio: Charles F. Kettering Foundation, 1991). For more on his writing, see Odom, *The Collapse of the Soviet Military;* and Raymond L. Garthoff,

Deterrence and Revolution in Soviet Military Doctrine (Washington, D.C.: Brookings Institution, 1990).

59. Edwin Dorn, letter to William Raspberry, August 10, 1990. Dorn calls her "Natalya Eliseyevna."

60. The absence of women and non-Russians was nothing new, of course. The same complaint could have been made of most American delegations; the number of women in the American delegation in Leningrad was unusually high. But the absence of women from the Soviet delegation was noted in comments on Dartmouth XVII by Dorn (letter to Raspberry). The absence of non-Russians must be regarded as particularly striking at a time when ethnic conflict was beginning to rend the Soviet Union.

61. This summary of the discussions comes mostly from Kettering Foundation, *Dartmouth Conference XVII: A Soviet-American Dialogue.*

62. Dorn, letter to Raspberry.

63. For more on this link, see Jane I. Dawson, *Eco-Nationalism: Antinuclear Activism and National Identity in Russia, Lithuania, and Ukraine* (Durham, N.C.: Duke University Press, 1996).

64. Paul Doty, "Notes on Dartmouth Conference (XVII) Leningrad— July 23–25," n.p., n.d. Many thanks to Paul Doty for providing a copy of this document.

65. Anatoli Sobchak, Office of the Mayor of Leningrad, transcript of a meeting on July 27, 1990.

66. Rob Nelson, "Plenary, Leningrad, 7/25/90," audiotape.

67. Rob Nelson, "Norman Cousins, 7/24/90," audiotape.

68. Bob Kingston, memo to David Mathews, Hal Saunders, and Phil Stewart, July 24–25, 1990 (handwritten).

69. Antonia Handler Chayes, letter to David Mathews, August 23, 1990.

70. Stewart formally left Dartmouth at the end of the Leningrad meeting and the faculty of Ohio State University two months later to help the Kellogg Company create new business in the former Soviet Union.

71. Anatoli Glinkin and Susan Purcell, "Latin America," December 5, 1990.

72. Apollon Davidson and Helen Kitchen, "Future Possibilities for U.S.-Soviet Cooperation in Africa," December 5, 1990.

73. Thomas Gouttierre, "South Asia: Role of Regional Conflicts in the Soviet-U.S. Relationship in the Future," December 6, 1990; and Thomas E. Gouttierre, "Regional Conflicts Task Force Working Paper: Afghanistan," faxed December 3, 1990.

74. Bush and Scowcroft, *A World Transformed,* 510–517. The main issues were arms control and aid for Soviet economic reform. The main subject discussed seems to have been the turmoil in the Soviet Union. An exception was Cuba, with the Americans pressing for a reduction in Soviet support of Castro.

75. J. Scott Lauby, *Dartmouth Conference, Task Force on Regional Conflict Prevention and Resolution: Assessing the Lessons and Prospects for Cooperation in a Post-Soviet World, December 4–8, 1991, Washington, D.C., Stenographic Record* (Dayton, Ohio: Charles F. Kettering Foundation, n.d.), 94.

76. Paul Doty, "Moscow Impressions, October 1991," October 26, 1991.

77. Paul Doty, "Report on Conversations with Sergei Rogov on Post-START and Post-CFE Arms Reduction on October 24 and 25, 1991," October 26, 1991.

78. This account is from Doty, "Report on Conversations with Sergei Rogov."

79. Hal Saunders, memo to David Mathews, March 26, 1992; Paul Doty, memo to Hal Saunders, May 13, 1992. Doty was less circumspect about the influence of Rogov's ideas on Bush's proposal and Yeltsin's response than indicated here.

80. The American proposals and Yeltsin's response are described in Amy F. Woolf and Mark M. Lowenthal, *START II: Central Limits and Force Structure Limitations,* CRS Report for Congress 93-35 (Washington, D.C.: Congressional Research Service, 1993); and Amy F. Woolf, *START and Nuclear Arms Control: Chronology of Major Events, 1982–1992,* Report for Congress 92-535, updated June 26, 1992 (Washington, D.C.: Congressional Research Service, 1992). For a brief account of the START II negotiations, see Steven A. Hildreth and Amy F. Woolf, *Nuclear Arms Control after START,* CRS Issue Brief IB91148, updated June 29, 1994 (Washington, D.C.: Congressional Research Service, 1994).

81. The account of the meeting is based on Lauby, *Dartmouth Conference, Task Force on Regional Conflict Prevention and Resolution, December 8, 1991*; and Voorhees, notes, Dartmouth Conference Regional Conflicts Task Force, December 8, 1991.

82. Hal Saunders, memo to members of the Dartmouth Regional Conflicts Task Force, May 6, 1992.

6. New Approaches from a Rich Tradition

1. Mikhail Gorbachev, "Address to the Forty-third Session of the United Nations General Assembly," issued by TASS, New York, December 7, 1988.

2. Hugh P. Callahan, *Dartmouth Conference Task Force on Cooperation in Security, Defining the Russian-American Security Relationship, March 17–20, 1992, Moscow, Russia, Stenographic Record* (Dayton, Ohio: Charles F. Kettering Foundation, n.d.), 19–21. The subsequent account of the meeting draws on this report.

3. Ibid., 58–59.

4. Harold Saunders, Maxine Thomas (Kettering Foundation), and Harry Boyte (Humphrey Institute, University of Minnesota), memo to David Mathews, March 26, 1992.

5. J. Scott Lauby, *Dartmouth Conference Task Force on Regional Conflict Prevention and Resolution: Toward a New Russian-American Dialogue on Regional and Societal Conflict, May 24–29, 1992, Moscow, Russia, Stenographic Record* (Dayton, Ohio: Charles F. Kettering Foundation, n.d.), 18–19.

6. Ibid., 14.

7. Ibid., 15–17.

8. Ibid., 13.

9. Gennadi I. Chufrin and Harold H. Saunders, "In Practice: A Public Peace Process," *Negotiation Journal* 9 (April 1993): 155–177.

10. Ibid., 177.

11. The new direction was outlined by Harold Saunders in a memo to members of the Dartmouth Regional Conflicts Task Force, May 6, 1992.

12. J. Scott Lauby, *Dartmouth Conference Task Force on Regional Conflict Prevention and Resolution: The Dartmouth Process, Ethnic Conflict, and Tajikistan: Toward a New Phase of Russian-American Interaction, December 6–10, 1992, Washington, D.C., Stenographic Record* (Dayton, Ohio: Charles F. Kettering Foundation, n.d.), 6, 7, 15.

13. Ibid., 8–9.

14. The full story of the Inter-Tajik Dialogue is told in Harold H. Saunders, *A Public Peace Process: Sustained Dialogue to Transform Racial and Ethnic Conflicts* (New York: St. Martin's Press, 1999; Palgrave paperback, 2001), chap. 7.

15. Harold Saunders and Randa Slim, "Managing Conflict in Divided Societies: Lessons from Tajikistan," *Negotiation Journal* 12 (January 1996): 31–46.

16. Ibid., 7.

17. "USG Attendees at the 9/29/95 Discussion on the Impact of Ethnic Conflicts in Russia's Near Abroad on US-Russian Relations." Participant list in Kettering Foundation files.

18. J. Scott Lauby, *Dartmouth Conference Task Force on Regional Conflict Prevention and Resolution: Russian-American Relations, Regional Conflicts, and the Application of the Dartmouth Process, May 30–June 4, 1993, Moscow, Russia, Stenographic Record* (Dayton, Ohio: Charles F. Kettering Foundation, n.d.), 5, 7.

19. Gennadi I. Chufrin and Harold H. Saunders, "The Politics of Conflict Prevention in Russia and the Near Abroad," *Washington Quarterly* 20 (fall 1997): 35.

20. The six meetings took place in June 1996, December 1996, October 1997, October 1998, March 1999, and February 2001. The records of these meetings are in the notebooks of Harold H. Saunders.

21. These meetings took place in June and December 1996. The records are in Saunders' notebooks.

22. Saunders, *A Public Peace Process.*

23. David Mathews and Harold H. Saunders, letter to David Hamburg and Cyrus Vance, cochairs of the Carnegie Commission on Preventing Deadly Conflict, January 4, 1996. The idea of two interrelated strategies—the five-stage process of sustained dialogue and a civil society strategy—had been more fully developed in Randa M. Slim and Harold H. Saunders, "Managing Conflict in Divided Societies: Lessons from Tajikistan," *Negotiation Journal* 12 (January 1996): 31–46.

24. The first nine joint memoranda would be published jointly by the Russian Center for Strategic and International Studies to mark the fifth anniversary and twentieth meeting of the dialogue as *Memoranda and Appeals of the Inter-Tajik Dialogue within the Framework of the Dartmouth Conference (1993–1997).* This publication and subsequent unpublished joint memoranda are available from the Kettering Foundation. Saunders wrote an analytical memorandum after each meeting. A rapporteur provided by the Russian Center created a complete record.

25. This relationship between the UN-mediated negotiations and the nonofficial Inter-Tajik Dialogue is the subject of Harold H. Saunders, "The Multilevel Peace Process in Tajikistan," in *Herding Cats: Multiparty Mediation in a Complex World,* ed. Chester A. Crocker, Fen Osler Hampson, and Pamela Aall (Washington, D.C.: United States Institute of Peace Press, 1999), chap. 8.

26. The journal *Accord* in London has published an account of the peace process in Tajikistan, including an article by Randa M. Slim and Harold H. Saunders, "Inter-Tajik Dialogue Process: From Civil War towards Civil Society" (2001).

27. Stanislav Kondrashov, "Between the Past and the Future: The Dartmouth System of Early Warning," *Vremya* [Time], October 3, 2000.

7. The Influence of the Dartmouth Conference on Policymakers and Policy

1. W. Phillips Davison, "Notes on a Conversation with Professor Philip E. Mosely, Director, European Institute, Columbia University, June 29, 1970." This copy of Davison's notes was corrected by Mosely.

2. Margaret Keck and Kathryn Sikkink, *Activists beyond Borders: Advocacy Networks in International Politics* (Ithaca, N.Y.: Cornell University Press, 1998), 16.

3. Norman Cousins, *The Improbable Triumvirate: John F. Kennedy, Pope John, Nikita Khrushchev* (New York: W. W. Norton, 1972), 78–79.

4. Sarah E. Mendelson, *Changing Course: Ideas, Politics, and the Soviet Withdrawal from Afghanistan* (Princeton, N.J.: Princeton University Press, 1998), 84.

5. Sergei Khrushchev, *Khrushchev on Khrushchev: An Inside Account of the Man and His Era,* ed. and trans. William Taubman (Boston: Little, Brown, 1990), 23.

6. James M. Gavin, "Notes on the Meetings with Prime Minister Kosygin in His Office in Moscow on July 16, 1971."

7. The focus of Robert English, *Russia Views the West: Intellectual and Political Origins of Soviet New Thinking* (New York: Columbia University Press, 2000), is precisely how that climate was formed and the contribution the *mezhdunarodniki* at ISKAN and elsewhere made to the ideas that were at the center of perestroika.

8. Roald Z. Sagdeev, *The Making of a Soviet Scientist: My Adventures in Nuclear Fusion and Space from Stalin to Star Wars* (New York: John Wiley and Sons, 1994), 269. The other two were Sagdeev and the eminent scientist Evgeni Velikhov.

9. Jeffrey T. Checkel, *Ideas and International Political Change: Soviet/Russian Behavior and the End of the Cold War* (New Haven, Conn.: Yale University Press, 1997), 91–96.

10. Primakov has said that his convictions about a settlement to the Middle East did not change (Evgeni Primakov, "Answers by Academician Evgeniy Primakov to Questions Posed by Dr. Harold H. Saunders for the Book on the History of the Dartmouth Conferences," trans. Vitali Zhurkin, June 29, 2001).

11. Aleksandr Fursenko and Timothy Naftali, *"One Hell of a Gamble": Khrushchev, Castro, and Kennedy, 1958–1964* (New York: W. W. Norton, 1997), 126–127. Their information comes from the archives of the Foreign Ministry and the Russian Foreign Intelligence Service. This report was sent to Khrushchev on June 1, 1961.

12. Arkadi N. Shevchenko, *Breaking with Moscow* (New York: Alfred A. Knopf, 1985), 45–47.

13. Herbert F. York, *Making Weapons, Talking Peace: A Physicist's Odyssey from Hiroshima to Geneva* (New York: Basic Books, 1987), 277–278.

14. Harold Karan Jacobson and Eric Stein, *Diplomats, Scientists, and Politicians: The United States and the Nuclear Test Ban Negotiations* (Ann Arbor: University of Michigan Press, 1966), 214.

15. There were two exceptions, the meetings of Senators Kennedy and Scott with Brezhnev at the time of Dartmouth VIII in April 1974.

16. Michael R. Beschloss, *The Crisis Years: Kennedy and Khrushchev, 1960–1963* (New York: Edward R. Burlingame Books, 1991), 41. Also see Emanuel

Adler, "The Emergence of Cooperation: National Epistemic Communities and the International Evolution of the Idea of Nuclear Arms Control," *International Organization* 46 (winter 1992): 122.

17. The reader may recall that a misunderstanding of this issue came about partly because of a conversation Fedorov had with Jerome Weisner, made possible by Dartmouth.

18. Philip S. Stewart, "Dartmouth XIII: A Soviet-American Dialogue: Moscow, USSR, November 16–19, 1981," Charles F. Kettering Foundation, Dayton, Ohio, 1982, 8.

19. George Shultz, *Turmoil and Triumph: My Years as Secretary of State* (New York: Alfred A. Knopf, 1994), 510.

20. Harold H. Saunders, telephone conversation with author, April 21, 1997.

21. Harold H. Saunders, "When Citizens Talk," *Kettering Review* (summer 1984): 51–52.

22. Landrum Bolling, e-mail to author, June 8, 2001.

23. Bruce J. Allyn, "Toward a Common Framework: Avoiding Inadvertent War and Crisis," in *Windows of Opportunity: From Cold War to Peaceful Competition in U.S.-Soviet Relations,* ed. Graham T. Allison and William L. Ury with Bruce J. Allyn (Cambridge, Mass.: Ballinger Publishing, 1989), 203.

24. Matthew Evangelista, *Unarmed Forces: The Transnational Movement to End the Cold War* (Ithaca, N.Y.: Cornell University Press, 1999), 193–232.

25. Robert Colby Nelson, interview with Dan Yankelovich, May 4, 1988.

26. Robert Colby Nelson, recording of a working meeting with Rob Lehman, Phil Stewart, and Rob Nelson on Thursday, May 6, 1988.

27. Robert Colby Nelson, interview with Harold Saunders, May 5, 1988.

28. Shulman made the statement in testimony before the Senate Foreign Relations Committee, cited in Adler, "The Emergence of Cooperation," 133.

29. Emanuel Adler, "The OSCE's Security-Community-Building Model," in *Security Communities,* ed. Emanuel Adler and Michael Barnett (Cambridge: Cambridge University Press, 1998), 138–142. Adler defines seminar diplomacy as "all types of multilateral diplomacy (meetings of diplomats, practitioners, civil servants, and academic experts, the use of experts in diplomatic missions) aimed at promoting political dialogue and international cooperation (political, social, economic) and preventing or managing conflict by means of consensual technical or normative knowledge."

30. Adler, "The OSCE's Security-Community-Building Model," 139.

31. See Evangelista, *Unarmed Forces;* English, *Russia and the Idea of the West;* and Checkel, *Ideas and International Political Change.* They argue that these groups helped establish the set of ideas that made the "new political thinking" of Gorbachev and Shevardnadze possible and helped create several specific steps in security policy. These included the imposition of a comprehensive ban on Soviet nuclear testing, the asymmetrical response to the Strategic Defense Initiative, and the troop reduction announced in Gorbachev's 1988 speech to the United Nations.

32. For an evaluation of that influence on national security policy in the two countries, see Evangelista, *Unarmed Forces.*

33. Bobrysheva's disappointment that Korneichuk's remarks in Moscow on his return from Dartmouth I were propagandistic is one example of the limitations of trust based solely on these contacts. But such examples only suggest that such contacts were not sufficient for building trust between the participants. The author would argue, however, that they were necessary.

34. Barnett and Adler, "Studying Security Communities in Theory, Comparison, and History," in *Security Communities,* 414.

35. Landrum Bolling, e-mail to author, July 10, 2001.

36. Landrum Bolling, e-mail to author, June 8, 2001.

37. Robert Colby Nelson, interview with Robert Lundeen, May 4, 1988.

38. Daniel Yankelovich tells a story that took place at one of the meetings of the Political Relations Task Force in the 1980s. He responded to a Soviet official's recitation of what Yankelovich regarded as nonsense in an undiplomatic manner. But, he continued: "[The official] was taken aback initially, but then we became acquainted and I talked to him in subsequent days. He said it was a real experience for him, that it was his first meeting and he had gone in on the assumption that we were just going to give set speeches at each other, and that what impressed him was that we were really serious. That we were working and that we were listening, we were listening and we were trying to, you know, we weren't making prejudgments." Robert Colby Nelson, interview with Daniel Yankelovich, May 4, 1988.

39. Several American scholars noticed that significant arguments had long been breaking out among Soviet academics, but allowing these arguments to come out in front of Americans was a somewhat different thing. See Elizabeth Kridl Valkenier, *The Soviet Union and the Third World: An Economic Bind* (New York: Praeger Special Studies, 1983); and Jerry F. Hough, *The Struggle for the Third World: Soviet Debates and American Options* (Washington, D.C.: Brookings Institution, 1986).

40. Evgeni Primakov, "Answers by Academician Evgeniy Primakov to Questions Posed by Dr. Harold H. Saunders for the Book on the History of the Dartmouth Conferences."

8. The Conduct of Sustained Dialogue

1. In addition to the coauthors of this chapter, those who have contributed reflections in one form or another include Aleksei Arbatov, Landrum Bolling, Antonia Chayes, Gennadi Chufrin, Apollon Davidson, Paul Doty, Thomas Gouttierre, Arnold Horelick, David Jones, Robert Kaiser, Aleksandr Kislov, Stanislav Kondrashov, Andrei Kortunov, Viktor Kremenyuk, Vladimir Lukin, Allen Lynch, David Mathews, Vitali Naumkin, Evgeni Primakov, Susan Kaufman Purcell, Sergei Rogov, Phillips Ruopp, Nikolai Shmelev, Randa Slim, Phil Stewart, John Stremlau, Yuli Vorontsov, Wallace Warfield, and Irina Zviagelskaya.

2. Evgeni Fedorov, "Valuable Contacts," *Pravda,* November 12, 1962.

3. Gennadi I. Chufrin and Harold H. Saunders, "The Politics of Conflict Resolution in Russia and the Near Abroad," *Washington Quarterly* 20, no. 4 (fall 1997): 37.

4. Gennadi I. Chufrin and Harold H. Saunders, "A Public Peace Process," *Negotiation Journal* 9, no. 2 (April 1993); and Harold H. Saunders, *A Public Peace Process: Sustained Dialogue to Transform Racial and Ethnic Conflicts* (New York: St. Martin's Press, 1999; Palgrave paperback, 2001).

5. The origins of the name "public peace process" and the evolution of the five-stage process are described in detail in Saunders, *A Public Peace Process,* xxi, 10–12, 306 n. 3. Saunders first used the phrase in titling a document that came out of an Israeli-Palestinian dialogue in 1991, "Framework for a Public Peace Process: Toward an Israeli-Palestinian Peace." The five-stage process as a conceptualization of a dialogue over time was first suggested in print in Harold H. Saunders, "Four Phases of Non-Official Diplomacy," *Mind and Human Interaction* 3, no. 1 (July 1991): 30. The five-stage process was first presented in Harold H. Saunders, "Thinking in Stages: A Framework for Public Intercommunal Problem-Solving from Experience in the Dartmouth Conference Regional Conflicts Task Force, 1982–1992" (paper prepared for the annual meeting of the International Society of Political Psychology, San Francisco, July 5, 1992).

6. TASS release, October 18, 1960.

Index

Abarenkov, Valery, 232
ABM treaty. *See* antiballistic missile (ABM) treaty
access
    gaining, 13
    importance of, 12–13
ACDA. *See* Arms Control and Disarmament Agency (ACDA)
Adamishin, Anatoli, 17
Adelman, Kenneth, 199
advocacy networks, 8, 334–335
Afghanistan
    discussed at Dartmouth Conference, 186, 187–188, 191–193, 207, 212–213, 224–225, 243, 244, 246, 247, 249, 264, 265, 305–306
    Soviet involvement in, 17, 132, 134, 136, 145, 146, 154–155, 169, 192, 193–194, 212, 225, 239
    U.S. arms supplied to, 183
Africa
    regional conflicts discussed at Dartmouth Conference, 121, 124, 129–130, 186, 187, 188, 238–239

See also Southern Africa Task Force
Africa Institute, 208
African National Congress (ANC), 207, 239
Agnew, Harold, 115
Agreement on Basic Principles of U.S.-Soviet Relations (1972), 151–152, 157
Akhromeev, Marshal Sergei, 196, 232, 257, 260
Albright, Madeleine, 234–235
Alkhimov, Vladimir, 130, 145, 147
Allison, General Royal (Ret.), 127, 128, 162
American Communist Party, 26
Amin, Hafizullah, 132
ANC. *See* African National Congress (ANC)
Anderson, Marian, 36, 41, 43
Andreeva, Nina, 220–221
Andropov, Yuri, 17, 71, 136, 153, 157, 162, 341
Angola, 107, 121, 129, 145, 151, 183, 187, 208, 248–249, 264
    Lusaka Agreement, 209

About the Authors

James Voorhees has been an associate of the Kettering Foundation for more than a decade. He earned his Ph.D. at the Johns Hopkins University Nitze School of Advanced International Studies. He was a member of the board of the Forum for U.S.-Soviet Dialogue. Recognized by the Congressional Research Service for his work during the Gulf War, Voorhees also worked on the staff of the Frost Task Force, which provided support to the emerging parliaments of Eastern Europe and the former Soviet Union. Later he worked for IREX and is currently a senior systems analyst with INDUS Corporation. He has published numerous articles and reports on Russian and East European politics.

Harold H. Saunders is director of international affairs at the Kettering Foundation. He served for twenty years on the National Security Council staff and in the State Department, last as assistant secretary of state for Near Eastern and South Asian affairs. Saunders flew on the Kissinger shuttles and helped draft the Camp David accords and the Egyptian-Israeli peace treaty. He is author of *The Other Walls: The Arab Israeli Peace Process in a Global Perspective* and *A Public Peace Process: Sustained Dialogue to Transform Racial and Ethnic Conflicts*. He has cochaired the Dartmouth Conference Regional Conflicts Task Force and the Inter-Tajik Dialogue since their beginnings.

Vitali Zhurkin is director emeritus of the Institute of Europe in the Russian Academy of Sciences, and was its founding director from 1987 to 1999. He is an academician of the Academy. Zhurkin was deputy director of the Institute for the study of the USA and Canada from 1971 to 1987. His participation in the Dartmouth Conference dates from 1971.

Charles F. Kettering Foundation

The Kettering Foundation is an operating foundation rooted in the American tradition of inventive research. Its founder, Charles F. Kettering, holder of more than two hundred patents, is best known for his invention of the automobile self-starter. He was interested, above all, in seeking practical answers to "the problems behind the problems."

Established in 1927, the foundation today continues in that tradition. The objective of the research now is to learn what it takes to make democracy work as it should.

DIALOGUE SUSTAINED

This book is set in American Garamond; the display type is Garamond Bold. The Creative Shop designed the book's cover; Mike Chase made up the pages. David Sweet copyedited the text, which was proofread by Karen Stough. The index was prepared by Sonsie Conroy. The book's editor was Nigel Quinney.